Market
à la Mode

T0326833

FASHION,

COMMODITY,

AND GENDER

IN

The Tatler

AND

The Spectator

Market à la Mode

ERIN MACKIE

THE JOHNS HOPKINS UNIVERSITY PRESS

BALTIMORE AND LONDON

FOR MY GRANDMOTHER, NANNY J.

The Johns Hopkins University Press
2715 North Charles Street
Baltimore, Maryland 21218-4319
The Johns Hopkins Press Ltd., London

Library of Congress
Cataloging-in-Publication Data
will be found at the
end of this book.

A catalog record
for this book
is available from
the British Library.

ISBN 0-8018-5588-8

Contents

Contents

Figures

Figures

Preface

This study grew out of a fascination with the ways that fashion and style serve as avenues of social and psychological regulation. More specifically, it originates in a sometimes bewildering personal confrontation with middle-class Anglo-American cultural norms that reflect a disdain for fashion and appearances—what really counts is on the "inside"—even as they continue to evince, indeed to depend on, the society's most visceral reactions to those external stylistic differences that mark race, ethnicity, class, generational loyalty, region, educational background, gender, and sexual preference. Bourgeois taste seems affronted by stylistic reminders of differences that threaten its ideal of equality, an equality dependent on a promise of access to the dominant culture that is actually a demand for assimilation into that culture. In this form, the directive for human equality calls as well for cultural homogeneity. If all people are going to be equal, then they all need to be inculcated—through education and "individual initiative"—into those norms of speech, dress, and manner "common" to the nation as a whole. Ideas of "standard English," "decent behavior," and "appropriate dress" are crucial to the encoding and dissemination of these norms. In my own experience in the United States, these norms have been first of all racial, though irreducibly complicated by factors of class, gender, region, and educational background.

Of course there is often some, often touristy, celebration of colorful ethnic styles, even in middle-class Anglo-America. But these differences usually have been allowed only under the proviso that they exist alongside a grateful appreciation of and a willing adoption of white bourgeois standards of language, dress, and behavior. Otherwise they are seen as the stigmata of the underclass, of those "disadvantaged" by their lack of education, employment, and sociopolitical power. And insofar as these norms are demanded by the available venues of education, employment, and empowerment these disadvantages are real enough.

But as recent debates surrounding multiculturalism and the politics of identity have brought to public attention, what goes unquestioned in the older, liberal notion of access is exactly whose culture is being privileged as the site of empowerment. The answer is fairly consistent: the masculinist, heterosexist culture of the white middle and upper-middle classes. This culture comprises its own stylistic norms of language, taste, dress, and manner, norms that may no longer be understood as universal and natural nor even truly "common" in any meaningful sense. The norms of the bourgeois public sphere are as historical, exclusive, particular, and, from perspectives other than their own, as marked as any other indexes of sociocultural difference. Perhaps I first felt the full force of this truth growing up in urban Baltimore, where one learns quickly that "whiteness," far from some natural, invisible condition, is a set of peculiar speech habits, sartorial choices, musical preferences, attitudes, and gestures, all highly marked and imitable.

One argument that drives my analysis is that these bourgeois norms never were as common and natural as they present themselves. They emerged and are maintained only through ongoing interaction — appropriative, exclusive, reformative — with other standards of identification, other regimes of taste and value, like fashion. The designation of bourgeois ideology and its cultural forms as unmarked is a fetishistic mystification of value and one that obscures their history. This history is my topic in this book. I focus on the relatively early period of *The Tatler* and *The Spectator* because by looking at bourgeois ideology and its typical forms of representation in transition and under construction we may most clearly see the traces of their history and the marks of their constructedness. In historical context, looking at these norms before they were the norm, we see, then, what is marked and peculiar about them. Perhaps the most salient mark of the ideology of the bourgeois public sphere is the cloak it throws over its own constructedness and particularity.

THE FORCE OF FASHION

Since the early eighteenth century, with industrialization and the development of mass markets and mass publics, the influence of fashion and consumerism has deepened and broadened, bringing under its sway, some fear, arenas established as alternatives to it. Fashion is usually more than merely the name for stylistic changes in apparel. It is often conceived as an autonomous, or semiautonomous, force, or as a discrete arena of experience and identification, as in "the world of fashion." From the early modern period to this day, fashion has been understood to be in competition with other, more worthy domains of identification. So, twentieth-century fashion reporter Kennedy Fraser laments that fashion's influence is "no longer" confined to lifestyle trends and material pursuits, but has "started to seep down into the realm of those profundities, verities, and values which used to be called moral and spiritual."[1] That is, fashion has successfully competed with the arena of ethical social discourse for not only the bodies but the very souls of the public.

In a recent jeremiad against fashion, feminist cultural critic Joanne Finkelstein warns of our imminent loss of authentic humanity in terms that recall the norms of authentic self-representation advocated within the early public sphere, if in more puritanical, fashion-alarmist tones:

What does it say of our understanding of identity or human character that we have fused together the capacity for conspicuous consumption with the presentation of personality? What does it say of us that we readily accept appearance and habits of conduct as revelations of the private self? What does it say of our social relations that we frequently employ a fashioned self-image and a style of acting in order to create a certain impression through which we hope to influence the opinions others have of us or how they will act toward us?[2]

What indeed? Antifashion alarmism, a puritanical disowning of consumption and its pleasures, is a ground, like that of antipornography censorship, on which the late-twentieth-century left and right often meet. Finkelstein's rhetoric exemplifies how, as a category of cultural criticism, fashion often serves as the demon that must be exorcised from the soul of the social body. Thus, as a *feminine* concern, fashion has been denigrated as trivial and unauthentic, even as it is feared as a dangerous realm of female power; while as a *feminist* concern, fashion has been seen as an instrument of sexual subjugation, or, at best, a tragic waste of time, money, and energy. To its harsher feminist critics, like Finkelstein, fashion becomes a name for consumerist diseases caused by the toxins of patriarchy and capitalism.

Finkelstein's warnings about the sexist, capitalist, corporate dictation of self-image and social relations, however, merit attention. What is questionable is her identification of these forces with fashion. For fashion no longer, if it ever did, works from the top down. Since the 1960s all fashions have been found, if not in the gutter, then at least on the street. And even in the eighteenth century there is ample evidence for the adoption of fashions from the lower to the higher rungs of the social ladder.[3] The notion of mass populations being uniformly imposed upon by ruthless profiteers simply does not hold up under all the evidence for a fashion market ever more fragmented, specialized, and derivative from subcultures.

For fashion may be used to imagine alternatives as well as to manufacture consent. Fashion and consumption, to call on Michael Warner's phrase, are "counterutopias" that offer kinds of pleasure and empowerment not available in the rational public sphere, to groups of people not adequately recognized within that sphere.[4] These groups, historically, have included women, gay men, youth, and ethnic and economic underclasses—those people, in other words, whose identities are not fully recognizable within the purview of the bourgeois public sphere. Here it is worth noting the importance of not treating *fashion* as a stable, unified category, but as a term whose valuative connotations and content shifts historically and locally. *Fashion*, as it takes shape as a critical term in the eighteenth century, most often has negative connotations and becomes a category within which what is socially and ethically suspect about the domestic effects of early modern commerce can be gathered and disowned. Not surprisingly, then, fashion becomes associated with types of people who threaten the integrity of the bourgeois social order. Shut out from social, economic, and political enfranchisement, these groups of people often look to fashion as an arena of distinction and identification that is open to them. So from this point of view, the term *fashion* may bear quite different, positive and liberatory, meanings. Accordingly, such a mode of positive identification cannot be fully recognized as such within bourgeois ideology, but must be trivialized and disowned.

This logic of fashion, as we will see, goes through dialectical twists and turns; for the bourgeois public sphere is deeply invested in the commercial marketplace and its standards of fashion, but veils that investment so that it can claim a status outside the market and its trivial, ephemeral values. This ambivalence produces that stylistic paradox that marks the cultural aesthetic of bourgeois ideology: the fashion for antifashion, the taste for a style that looks like no style at all. This fashion for antifashion continues strong to this day. It may take baldly radical forms, as in the retro-seventies pink, cropped tee shirt bearing the slogan "Fuck Fashion" that I recently saw in a club-kids' boutique—though, these days, such "radical" (anti)fashion statements seem deflated and naive.

The product of corporate and media enterprise, fashion plugs the body into consumer culture, announcing acceptance, challenge, or revision of the limits that culture offers. People produce fashion through selective consumption; the contemporary fashion industry produces its designs by selectively consuming street-style. No clear line between the production and consumption of fashion exists. The fashion system offers no easily formalizable schema of meanings and power relations; its effects may be readable only in local and momentary contexts.

Although it has been conceived as such and therefore often granted an autonomy in cultural discourse, fashion, I think, is no self-enclosed, self-generating system. Instead, as Georg Simmel asserts, fashion is the "product of social demands." Its nature is revealed in the way that "not the slightest reason can be found for the creations of fashion from the standpoint of an objective, aesthetic, or other expediency."[5] Indeed, the aesthetic criterion of "beauty," as Jean Baudrillard points out, is only fashion's "alibi."[6] The study of fashion, while including an account of this aesthetic alibi, must anchor itself elsewhere.

Most important to this study is how fashion becomes a way to talk about historical change, for "the fashion system serves as one of the conduits for capture and movement of this category of highly innovative meaning."[7] Temporally, fashion is located at the intersection of the present with the future and may serve as a place from which each historical moment forecasts its own tomorrow. Fashion then becomes a way of thinking about social reform, a way of expressing progressive desires for a better future. Of course the problem with the transformations offered by fashion is that, as things stand, they are often in the direction not of difference and change but of normative repetition and conformity. Fashionable change may appear, as any historical change may appear to skeptics, as only an illusion, a hypermobility emptied of transformation.

But even though fashion is most widely distributed as a form of standardized novelty that serves the interests of capitalism by creating a deathly immortality of demand, its form, if not its content, is utopian. Though its promise may be arrested in the interests of the status quo, fashion is structured as transfiguration. And it is possible to wrest the transformative potentials of fashion away from conformist ends. So fashion may be read, as Roland Barthes reads it, as just an infinite reflection of itself. But another, alternative vision, one fully respecting the ambivalent dialectic of production and consumption contained within the fashion commodity, can recognize "the lavish waste" and conformist imperatives of the fashion system, even as it also sees in fashion's promise, as Jane Gaines puts it, "a premonition of what revolution might 'feel like.'"[8]

"THE TATLER" AND "THE SPECTATOR"

Here I present a local, historical reading of fashion's operations in early-eighteenth-century England. My inquiry is organized around, though by no means limited to, the evidence presented in the early popular periodicals *The Tatler* and *The Spectator* because, as is well recognized, there is no more complete documentation of life in early-eighteenth-century England and no more exemplary instances of the discursive institution of the bourgeois public sphere. The eight volumes of these periodicals present a veritable encyclopedia of social history and do so from the middle-of-the-road view point that, as is also conventionally recognized, determines dominate ideological formations for the subsequent three hundred years.

Pioneering and exemplary organs of the bourgeois public sphere, *The Tatler* and *The Spectator* register, if sometimes inadvertently, a consciousness of the deep ambiguities, the threats and potentials, of fashion and consumption. These forces seem to colonize the lives and psyches of their contemporaries in dangerous ways, yet at the same time seem open to appropriation for principled change. We find here a central paradox of modern cultural criticism. That is, in order to be effective within commercial society, to appropriate the forces of fashion for their own ends, the papers must enter into the market and establish themselves as a kind of fashion, which indeed they do quite effectively. Yet they must also maintain a critical stance outside the market and the fashionable beau monde in order to legitimate their authority as somehow outside these, and so not subject to the corruptions of ephemerality, superficiality, and vanity that drive the fashion market.

Addison struggles with this paradox in *Spectator* 435. Anxious to equivocate the complicity of his papers with the fashion market even as he confesses it, he distinguishes between the "fixt and immutable" content of "most of the Papers" he writes and "another sort of Speculations," which he considers as "Occasional Papers" and which have as their themes "the Folly, extravagance, and Caprice. . . . every absurd Fashion, ridiculous Custom, or affected Form of Speech that makes its Appearance in the World." Failing to have maintained throughout his project a stance utterly removed from the superficiality and novelty he seeks to reform, Addison fears that the content of the occasional papers compromises their moral and historical value. He acknowledges the status of *The Spectator* as a fashionable commodity in its own right, but this brings with it a concern that the papers, "which were in no little Vogue at the time they were written," will not be accessible to future generations of readers who "will be apt to think that the Fashions and Customs I attacked, were some Fantastick Conceits of my own."

Connected to this anxiety of obsolescence is the fear that these voguish papers are compromised by their reliance on the same ephemeral standards of fashion as their contents: "For this Reason, when I think on the Figure my several Volumes of Speculations will make about a Hundred Years hence, I consider them as so many Pieces of old Plate, where the Weight will be regarded, but the Fashion lost."9 Addison supposes that his voguish papers will survive only by virtue of what in them is *not fashion*. But as this closing metaphor suggests, the initial division of the papers into Addison's two categories — occasional or permanent, fashionable or profound — cannot be maintained. The papers referred to as "old Plate" participate at once in both fashion and value, the weighty and the superficial. This metaphor simultaneously undercuts the opening distinction between occasional and permanent essays and salvages those voguish papers from complete obsolescence and oblivion: their pattern may go out of style but they will always be worth their weight in silver.

About three hundred years thence, looking back at the *Spectator* and *Tatler* papers, I want to recover their fashion. Just as the papers for which Addison claims "fixt and immutable" relevance are in fact implicated in a culture market where fashions in taste are heavily operative, the modish papers he considers "Occasional" by virtue of their open complicity with fashion throw down an anchor into the future that fixes their value for "Posterity." To revise Addison's terms, by regarding their fashion we may redeem the weight of these "Pieces of old Plate."

Acknowledgments

Throughout the writing of this book I have enjoyed the support of friends and family and profited from the assistance of those who read, listened to, and commented on various drafts. I am grateful to the Graduate School at Princeton University and to the English Department at Washington University for the generous support that made it possible for me to present much of this work at conferences. Portions of this text have appeared in *College Literature* and *Architecture: In Fashion* (Princeton Architectural Press, 1994). I thank all the editors for their help.

Through his encouragement, direction, and the example of his own resourceful critical work, Andrew Ross has been a continual motivating force. For his helpful commentary and bibliographic clues, thanks to Eduardo Cadava, the earliest reader of the paper on the hoop-petticoat that initiated this project. Special thanks to the members of WAW, the marxist-feminist reading group, for sharing with me their innovative perspectives, fabulous work, and critical savvy. I am indebted to Janet Gray for her shrewd readings of history, gender, and the commodity, and to Dianne Salfas, whose hard thinking always makes my own more honest.

My revisions were inspired and guided by Laura Brown, who read the manuscript for the Johns Hopkins University Press. Her painstaking and supportive remarks have been an invaluable help. During the last stages of editing, I profited from the scrupulous reading Ethan Bumas gave to the text. My research assistant Lisa Eck has my gratitude for her help in tracking down the illustrations, as does Isaac Green for his work proofreading the text.

Thanks to Celeste Fraser-Delgado for her heartening enthusiasm and to Lynn Weiss for her support and confidence. Much respect to my dance teacher Theodore Jamison and his drummer Monduel Banessia. The discipline, pleasure, energy, and knowledge I found in Theo's classes have sustained my life in St. Louis.

I close by acknowledging my debt of gratitude to Michael McKeon, for the precious gifts of his time, attention, and labor.

Market
à la Mode

Cultural Criticism and the
Tatler *and the* Spectator *Papers*

❧ ☞

He is a genuine
prophet of what we now
describe as culture.

LESLIE STEPHEN,
OF JOSEPH ADDISON
(1904)

THE SWEEP OF FASHION

Between 1709 and 1714, Joseph Addison and Richard Steele published a series of reformative and influential papers in the fictional
personae of Isaac Bickerstaff (*The Tatler*) and Mr. Spectator (*The
Spectator*).[1] Richard Steele edited and largely wrote the earlier paper,
The Tatler, though *The Tatler* contains contributions from other authors, most notably Addison, and correspondence from readers. *The
Tatler* came out three times a week and stated as its explicit purpose
the reformation of manners and morals: "The general Purpose of
this Paper, is to expose the false Arts of Life, to pull off the Disguises
of Cunning, Vanity, and Affectation, and to recommend a general
Simplicity in our Dress, our Discourse, and our Behaviour" (*T*, Dedication to Maynwaring). So while, especially in its earlier numbers,
The Tatler also includes more conventional news coverage, the ethical
and social focus of the paper is prominent from the start.

Two months after the last *Tatler*, the first number of *The Spectator*
appeared, on March 1, 1711; more than *The Tatler, The Spectator* was
a collaborative production of both Steele and Addison. The first

series appeared daily, except for Sundays, until December 1712 (nos. 1-555). Addison, with Eustace Budgell and Thomas Tickell, then put out a second series that ran three times a week from June to December 1714 (nos. 556-635).

Both papers take as their subject matter a broad range of topics crucial to everyday life in eighteenth-century England: dressing and dueling; visiting and conversing; reading and writing; love, courtship, and marriage; education and religion; commerce and finance; business and pleasure. They address a primarily, though by no means exclusively, urban audience made up largely, but not solely, of people in those mid-level economic and social positions we now group under the rubric "the middle class." Taking as their subject the polite conduct of life in all its arenas, public and private, domestic and professional, social and familial, these periodicals were crucial agents in the definition of the cultural ideals of that class. *The Tatler* and *The Spectator* approach their project in an explicitly practical spirit: they do not merely comment critically on social conditions but enter into those conditions in order to change them. Emerging, in part, from the tradition of conduct books, *The Tatler* and *The Spectator* are early, and quite modish, "lifestyle" magazines. Selling new and improved ways of living, they want to refashion the textures of daily life.

In *Spectator* 64, Steele announces: "The most improper things we commit in the Conduct of our Lives, we are led into by the Force of Fashion." This study examines this force of fashion, more specifically the attempts made by these papers to regulate and exploit it. In *The Tatler* and *The Spectator*, the arbitration of fashion, consumption, taste, and manners is fundamental to the project of cultural improvement. Taking on the figurative and literal guises as censor and judge, Addison and Steele write up opinions on the broader principles of proper fashion practice and give precise rulings on specific articles of clothing. *The Tatler* and *The Spectator* speak of fashions not only in clothes but also in religious observance, speech and writing, manners, food, combat, sexual mores, employment, leisure pursuits, and human social types. The prescription of fashion and taste serves not simply to regulate costume but to institute modes of social relations as well, not simply to arbitrate elegance but also to institute specific ideas about nature, law, and humanity. By championing "natural" fashions against the hoop-petticoat; domesticated woman against the sophisticated woman of the world; the polite and aestheticized imagination against the illusions of fancy and enthusiasm; and the decency of bourgeois taste against the depravity of aristocratic taste, these papers advance modern standards of middle-class culture.

My approach in this study is inspired in part by work on the anthropology of consumption, such as that of Mary Douglas and Baron Isherwood, who argue for an understanding of consumption that recognizes more fully its role in the constitution and revision of culture. The consumer takes part in social production: "The kind of statements [the consumer] makes are about the kind of universe he [*sic*] is in, affirmatory or defiant, perhaps competitive, but not necessarily so. . . . Consumption is an active process in which all the social categories are being continually redefined."[2] Fashion and consumption are social practices and so are enlisted in early-eighteenth-century culture as avenues of sociocultural production and identification.

Examining the uses of fashion in these papers in relation to the financial, commercial, and sociopolitical transformations under way at the turn of the century, I map out fashion's place in the culture of early-eighteenth-century Britain. The end of the seventeenth century saw several related revolutions—sociopolitical, financial, commercial, and literary-cultural. I use *fashion* as a central category of analysis because it colored all these movements and helps to articulate, through its analogues, the nature of the relations between them. Fashion is set in analogous relation to a number of topics of pressing concern in the early eighteenth century: paper credit, exchange value, the legitimation of consumption, gender identity, female hysteria, imaginative irrationality, arbitrary and legitimate authority. Embodying the commodification, novelty, and imperative to change that mark the emergence of modern society, fashion provides a fertile ground for the contestation of culture itself.

Fashion's place, then, is not confined, in either the early eighteenth century or the present, to the narrowly circumscribed realm of stylistic selection in apparel. Rather, with the intensification of capitalism, fashion becomes a category of choice — a standard of selection — that shapes the production of attitudes and beliefs as well as that of hats, shoes, coiffures, and dresses. Moreover, as amply exemplified in *The Tatler* and *The Spectator* papers, because of its popular function as a standard of discrimination fashion operates as an important term in cultural criticism, both in the criticism of taste and in broader examinations of the effects of particular modes of production and exchange on cultural life. Defined by novelty, acceleration, and apparently arbitrary and thus unpredictable outcomes, fashion, perceived as a certain kind of (usually faulty) criterion of selection, serves as a magnet for criticism of the play of these forces in cultural, economic, political, and social life. Therefore, as a category of choice, of discrimination, fashion often is stood in competitive relation to other, more motivated and rational, regimes of value and distinction, notably that of the bourgeois public sphere.

I am concerned here with an expansive range of fashion's functions and manifestations. As I build my argument about the role of fashion in cultural criticism I move back and forth among a wide sweep of the registers of fashion's significance. Perhaps most crucially, I am concerned with the *discourse* of fashion as it takes shape around the turn of the eighteenth century. The broad range of fashion's significance makes sense when one looks at fashion not so much as a fixed category denoting this or that type of object but as a term whose meanings and applications develop within and against a larger field of cultural discourse. This field includes the discourses of the aesthetic and of the bourgeois public sphere, to name two arenas of especial interest in this study. To my mind, then, it seems important not to reify the category of fashion. Such an approach may threaten a certain slipperiness in the working of the term *fashion*; yet, I believe this approach is best suited to isolating the historical emergence of fashion, not solely as a modern social practice but also, and inseparable from this, as a modern discursive category. Fashion is no more a fixed term than those other categories like race/ethnicity, sex/gender, class/status, in relation to which it is itself articulated.[3]

My study suggests a continuity between the emerging modern, if preindustrial, fashion market and fashion discourses of the early eighteenth century and those of the present. Continuity, of course, is different from identity. Between the early eighteenth and the late twentieth centuries I do not find in fashion discourse an unwavering line of full correspondence. What I do find is that the paradigm that determines the limits, contradictions, and possibilities of fashion's modern operation is fairly well in place by the early eighteenth century. This does not mean that all these limits, contradictions, and possibilities are realized in the early eighteenth century—indeed, fuller realization will come with the growth of mass markets in the nineteenth century and the revolutions in advertising and mass media in the twentieth. It does suggest that the logic informing later manifestations of the category *fashion* is often apparent in earlier instances.[4]

In the early eighteenth century, fashion performs functions that continue to mark its operation in social practices and cultural discourse. I strive throughout to modulate my discussion through the multiple rhetorical and conceptual registers of fashion and its analogues in ways that show the resonances among them while preserving their particularity. Rhetorically and conceptually, "fashion" may work as a metaphor or a metonymic figure; as a set of apparently autonomous, irresistible, and even insatiable forces—commercial and psychosocial—driving production and consumption; as a kind of master category through which multiple arenas of life and experience can be brought and thought together. And of course fashion may be differently valued, as either a good or evil in itself. Furthermore, what counts as fashion may be variously identified. For example, Bickerstaff and Mr. Spectator often follow a tendency to identify other people's (faulty) stylistic and consumption practices as "fashions" while presenting their own as manifestations of good taste and good sense that ostensibly transcend the fashion system and its irrational arbitrariness. Yet still they vigorously campaign for the popular adoption of *their* stylistic modes and so seem to want to establish them as fashions in their own right. Quite simply, *The Tatler* and *The Spectator* register a deep ambivalence about fashion, especially their own fashionability as modish lifestyle magazines. In them we find the logic of antifashion fashion: what is really stylistically desirable is defined against what is merely "fashionable." This fashion of what is purportedly "antifashion" has proved one of the most enduring modes of modernity. In it we can see one motive force that drives the wheels of stylistic change: in order to maintain its nonpareil prestige, style must continually reject what is (already) established as fashionable.

Change may be undertaken within a number of rationales. One that Addison and Steele routinely reject is the pursuit of change in a kind of ceaseless striving for novelty as a good in itself; this, then, is identified with (bad) fashion. Another rationale, one typical of the reforms proposed in *The Tatler* and *The Spectator*, looks toward stylistic change as a way to escape the tyranny of (established, conventional) fashion. This latter logic, of course, proposes its changes as stabilizing reforms: once they adopt "natural" styles, conforming to "true" principles of taste, men and women may rest easy, no longer buffeted about by the ebb and flow of fashion's ceaseless waves. Even though it does so in an effort to counter (arbitrary) fashionable change, nonetheless this reforming impulse itself introduces alterations in stylistic trends and so, historically, plays a significant part in fashionable change. For, when such reforms successfully take popular hold, they become a mode in their own right. And the cycle of change never rests; as ideological and social imperatives shift, so, then, does the determination of what constitutes "true" and "natural" style.

But I do not want to suggest that fashionable change is wholly determined by the sort of principled, antifashion prescriptions we find in *The Tatler* and *The Spectator*. (And even antifashion stylistic tenets may be unmoored from principle and become aestheticized as purely formal reactions against prevailing modes; in this case antifashion fashion approximates, almost to the point of identity, the conventional notion of fashion as stylistic innovation for its own sake.) Rather, I understand style and fashion as arenas of production and identification where a considerable tug-of-war between socioeconomic and ideological forces takes place. We can see this in the very way that the papers, striving for their own cultural ascendancy, counter "arbitrary" and "tyrannical" fashion with their own "natural" and "sensible" stylistic dictates. I do argue that the reforms in taste and style advocated by *The Tatler* and *The Spectator* are early heralds of a new regime of taste in England. Furthermore, intimately allied as they were with broader social changes, such reforms not only reflect those changes but also serve as ways to manage their effects on the bodies, minds, and institutions of Addison's and Steele's contemporaries.

But exactly what is so wrong with fashion that Addison and Steele must advocate their own stylistic and behavioral codes as not-fashion? "Fashion" often carries in these papers that still damning connotation of the (merely) "fashionable." Being "fashionable" in this sense means being without substance, referent, content, and "true" value. The value of fashion is often shown as purely self-generated and self-sustaining: an illusion fashion perpetrates by duping the victims of consumerism. Perhaps fashion's most dangerous capacity is this tautological ability to function as its own end, the sole justification for its own existence. In this formulation, fashion appears as the tyrant, an arbitrary, absolutist ruler of the kind by this time well discredited in England. *The Tatler* and *The Spectator* counter fashion's absolutist claims to our allegiance. Antifashion discourse thus often serves as part of the larger antiabsolutist discourse formed within the emergent bourgeois public sphere.

Representations that scandalize fashion for its self-perpetuating, tautological relation to itself allow us to glimpse ways in which fashion may be read as a homology, not only of absolute rule but also of capitalism itself. Antifashion discourse, then, draws on both residual (that of absolute rule) and emergent (that of bourgeois capitalism) ideological paradigms, criticizing both. Fashion's reflection of the tautological structure of capitalism can be understood through Marx's summary of the path of capitalist monetary circulation: money into commodity back into money. The cycle "M–C–M . . . appears to lack any content, because it is tautological."[5] The complex countering, accommodation, and management of fashion that takes place in *The Tatler* and *The Spectator* may, then, often be understood as well as an accommodating critique of the institutions and ideologies of capitalism. Fashion talk then serves as a way to isolate and criticize certain consumption patterns and social practices that accompany the intensification of capitalism in England.

Additionally, fashion may be one prominent manifestation of the potentially tautological, self-reflexive forms not only of economic circulation but also of aesthetic-cultural representation that characterize modernity. Viewed, as many from Addison and Steele to Roland Barthes and Anne Hollander have, as a self-contained, self-perpetuated system governed by its own laws, motivated finally simply by a drive toward self-perpetuation, fashion (so the logic goes) "reacts most vividly only to itself, like many other modern arts."[6] But where Hollander celebrates this reflexive, self-absorption of fashion as the mark of its status as "modern art," Addison and Steele are suspicious, seeing in these qualities a sort of empty, unconnected asociality, a kind of referenceless meaninglessness. If fashion is only about fashion then it can't be about much at all. This view of fashion as a self-contained, autonomous system is developed in *The Tatler* and *The Spectator* as a negative critique of these tendencies and so stands as a critique of modes of representation characteristic of modernity. In this the papers recall the more scathingly unqualified criticism of modernity's narcissistic self-reflexivity levied by Jonathan Swift in his *The Tale of a Tub*. So while on the whole Addison and Steele, unlike Swift, champion social, political, and aesthetic cultural changes as harbingers of a progressive modernity, their advocacy is tempered with reservations, but most of all with the impulse to manage and direct these changes. This impulse is nowhere more engaged than in their antifashion discourse.

So, to limit a discussion of "fashion" to apparel, or even to material objects and social manners, would confine the scope of this examination to a narrower compass than fashion has occupied in the colloquial and critical vocabularies of the last three hundred years. When Richard Steels announces in *Spectator* 64 that "the most improper things we commit in the Conduct of our Lives, we are led into by the Force of Fashion," he is talking not about clothes per se but about fashions in mourning observances. What has happened is that going into mourning for any and every petty foreign princeling has become fashionable in London. That most ritualistic mode of dressing and conduct — mourning — one which seems safely removed from fashion's reach by its rigidly prescribed fixity in tradition, nonetheless has been appropriated by fashion.

In Colley Cibber's melodrama of manners, the female fop, Narcissa, announces that "'tis the Fashion now to be the Town talk; and you know, one had as good be out of the World, as out of the Fashion."[7] "The World" is the beau monde, whose complicity with fashion, while obvious, is nonetheless perpetually conjured as a point of reproach. Yet, this circuit of identifications extends beyond fashion and the "World" to include the "Town talk" through which both circulate and are defined. In this sentence fashion occupies a closer relation to the town talk than it does to the world: it *is* the fashion *to be* the town talk. This lets us know that fashion is the talk of the town, but also and more importantly, that to be the talk of the town is to be the fashion. Personal currency and the talk through which it is established and maintained, then, are also manifestations of fashion. In them we can see the blueprint for the celebrity system that will skyrocket in the twentieth century propelled by the mass-media circulation of society and entertainment "news."

As it is taken over from traditional, inherited status hierarchies by the more dynamic social forces of fashionable town talk, social prestige is modernized. On the one hand, this (always only partial) extraction of social prestige from its aristocratic enclave is the work of the rational, bourgeois public sphere which served to realign cultural values toward at once more egalitarian and increasingly aesthetic standards. No longer viewed as a necessary effect of noble birth, taste and the prestige it confers eventually become "purely aesthetic" categories "presumably freed from social prerequisites."[8] However — and this is a fear *The Tatler* and *The Spectator* often register — when taste and prestige are unmoored from their anchoring in the courtly value system they are left open not only to the aestheticizing appropriation of the rational public sphere (an appropriation the papers advocate) but also to appropriation by other social arenas that are not fully identified with the bourgeois public sphere. Some of these, the female-directed beau monde, for example, are understood as piloted by the arbitrary, ethically blind forces of fashion.

For their part, these forces of fashion are represented as operating within a kind of social system modeled after economic, rather than ethical, paradigms of value and as working within an often ruthless and senseless "marketplace" of opinion. The picture becomes more complex when we realize that *The Tatler* and *The Spectator* themselves operate within a commercial marketplace of public opinion and indeed are vying there for the position of leading cultural arbiters. This situation constitutes one of the most generative paradoxes of the papers, and indeed of the public sphere itself.

So fashion's relevance for an understanding of early modernity in England, as I have suggested, may extend broadly into the social institutions, ideologies, representational forms, and even the structural logic of capitalism itself. Such connections are, I think, valuable, indeed inescapable. But I hope to avoid positioning fashion's homology with capitalism as a final, monolithic horizon of analysis, as the point at which the contradictions and "problem" of fashion's discourses may finally be resolved and dismissed. For, whereas examining the analogies among fashion and aspects of early modern capitalism allows us to appreciate the world-historical scope of fashion, it runs the risk of reducing fashion's richly utopian potentials. Perhaps fashion does not necessarily and unidirectionally develop toward some monolithically oppressive and ubiquitous capitalism. Indeed, capitalism itself seems to operate in shiftier, more ambiguous ways, opening up one set of possibilities even as it closes down another. And of course to speak in terms of being "inside" and "outside" of "capitalism" is far too simplistic to do justice to the multiple interrelated spheres of identification and discourse that emerge in early modern England. The most prominent of these arenas are: the public and the private; the state; the bourgeois public sphere; the domestic; the "World" of fashionable society (the beau monde); the realm of the aesthetic imagination; the marketplace (commerce, finance, and industry); the town, court, and country, and relatedly, the urban and the pastoral.

In the early eighteenth century, and today, stylistic practices understood as "fashion" offer avenues of representation and identification that may serve as alternatives to more hegemonic norms and limits, including both those of a reifying and alienating marketplace and those of the bourgeois public sphere. While, for example, Addison and Steele seek to institute styles that elude the pressures of a marketplace dominated by greed, vanity, and self-interest, the women whose fashions they want to regulate are engaged in their own stylistic efforts to claim an autonomy at odds with the paternalistic domestic norms advocated by the papers.

FASHION AND MODERNITY

As I have suggested, the broad concept of fashion I take on here is perhaps even more familiar to us today than it was to those men and women of the early eighteenth century who formed Addison's and Steele's audience. Kennedy Fraser, long-time fashion journalist for *The New Yorker*, speaks of the late-twentieth-century "fashionable mind" which sees every aspect of life through the looking glass of fashion. No longer, Fraser laments, is fashion confined to lifestyle trends and material pursuits but has "started to seep down into the realm of those profundities, verities, and values which used to be called moral and spiritual."[9]

At what historical moment Fraser locates the Golden Age before the fall into fashion is not clear. Already at the turn of the twentieth century, sociologist Georg Simmel notes how fashion has "overstepped the bounds of its original domain, which comprised only personal externals, and has acquired an increasing influence over taste, over theoretical convictions and even over the moral foundations of life."[10] Examination of *The Tatler* and *The Spectator* shows that the broad and deep saturation of fashion into social, aesthetic, ethical, political, and intellectual life was well under way centuries before Simmel cites its presence in the early, and Fraser in the late, twentieth century. For example, Kennedy's figure of a "fashionable" mind distinctly resonates with Addison's pictures of the snuff- and ribbon-crammed brain of the modish beau and the heart of the coquette, with its flame-colored hood at the core, dissected in *Spectators* 275 and 281. Addison's satiric conceits fully anticipate Kennedy's late-twentieth-century anxiety about the saturation of fashion into the most intimate loci of our moral, cognitive, and affective lives.

The grip of fashion on the mental and material lives of men and women follows the saturation of commerce and capital into the culture of the West. Fashion starts to lay broader and deeper holds on our world because of the ways that life is increasingly reified within the commercialized conditions of modern Western society. It begins to be possible to treat attitudes, manners, and ethics as "things" sensitive to the same forces of novelty and obsolescence as hats, shoes, patches, wigs, and hoops. In his history of civilization and capitalism, Fernand Braudel emphasizes that fashion is by no means limited to changes in styles of clothes or even in material culture: "Fashion does not only govern clothing. . . . It governs ideas as much as costume, the current phrase as much as the coquettish gesture, the manner of receiving at table, the care taken in sealing a letter."[11] The culture of fashion and the fashioning of culture are intertwined. So in the late twentieth century, the professional fashion watcher Kennedy Fraser dons the cap of the cultural critic; and in the early eighteenth century, self-styled cultural critics Joseph Addison and Richard Steele become watchdogs of fashion. And while they, like Fraser, lament the deep and broad saturation of fashion into the lives and psyches of their contemporaries, nonetheless it is by virtue of the well-nigh ubiquitous net that fashion casts that it serves them, and Fraser, so well as an instrument of cultural criticism.

Fashion serves this function because it is not simply a kind of thing but a cultural category (in the anthropological sense) through which things — including reified attitudes and behavior — are monitored. The emergence of fashion as a dominant cultural category is a historical event that marks modern Western cultures and marks them as anomalies relative to other cultures.[12] Early-eighteenth-century critics —Mandeville, Addison, Steele, Swift, Pope, Defoe— were highly conscious of what they characterize as a vastly accelerating saturation of fashion-driven consumption in their worlds. Moreover, the objectification and fetishization that characterize the commodity form are themselves instrumental in the institution of the modern aesthetic realm and its accompanying forms of critical analysis.

Twentieth-century theorists have formulated useful ways of thinking about the formative role of fashion in modern cultures. Arjun Appadurai sees the institution of the category "fashion" as the means by which modern Western societies regulate the consumption of luxury goods. The management of consumption through fashion is essential to these societies because goods identified as "luxury items" are particularly important in the symbolic exchange that articulates their culture: they are "goods whose principle use is *rhetorical* and *social*, goods that are simply *incarnated signs*. The necessity to which *they* respond is fundamentally political."[13]

In a similar identification of fashion with the societies of the modern West, Grant McCracken associates the advent of commercial culture with a shift in the very standard of value that directed consumption: goods become valuable not for their patina, their link to the past, but for their novelty, for their *fashionability*, their link to an urgent moment poised between the present and future.[14] Like McCracken, Neil McKendrick, historian of the new consumer society in eighteenth-century England, notes that at this time goods become valued for different qualities than they had been previously: "Where once material possessions were prized for their durability, they were now increasingly prized for their fashionability."[15] Braudel likewise distinguishes the turn of the eighteenth century as a fashion watershed: "One cannot really talk of fashion becoming all-powerful before about 1700. . . . From then on fashion in the modern sense began to influence everything."[16] And Chandra Mukerji associates the rise of fashion with the emergence of what she calls the materialistic culture of the modern West.[17] Like McKendrick and McCracken, Mukerji records as a central event in the history of this culture the shift from traditional to fashionable values: "For the first time, people faced choices in their purchases and had to develop some norms to limit and guide accumulation. . . . Fashion rather than tradition began to be used to regulate pattern of dress."[18]

This shift comes hand-in-glove with the advent of class claims on status. Evaluating worth according to more individualistic and quantitative economic criteria, these claims challenged the traditional, aristocratic status hierarchy which aligned worth with the extra-individual and qualitative criteria of birth. The new standard of novelty —that is, fashion—makes this challenge by turning class into status: "Now an individual could turn income into status immediately and with no need of a long, expensive, and perilous wait over five generations."[19] Emblem of socioeconomic change, fashion becomes a category of cultural criticism, "the key used by many commentators to explain the forces of social imitation, social emulation, class competition and emulative spending."[20] Fashion serves both to embody the new encroachment of class-based, economic pretensions to status and a way to talk about these pretensions and the sociopolitical changes associated with them. In addition to chastening the *nouveau riche*, antifashion discourse often castigates the aristocratic elite, and of course these two functions are linked, even simultaneous. Antifashion talk, among other things, is antidisplay talk and usually directed against the overt performance of status and power. Aristocratic regimes of power historically have been consolidated by such ostentatious performances of power and status; upstarts dressing "above their station" did so in emulation of this aristocratic mode.

But in the newly aestheticized taste critique advanced in *The Tatler* and *The Spectator*, it is not so much status counterfeiting that is criminal as it is bad taste itself. Importantly, Addison and Steele do not criticize the upstart for falsely emulating his or her "betters," but instead call to account *all* overt personal displays, both those of the aristocratic elite and those of the merely genteel. Any extravagant gestures of ostentation are viewed as senseless pretensions. This standard of taste that refuses display intimates a depreciation of aristocratic status by implying that even authentic status is incapable of authorizing ostentatious display.

By directing their energies against lavish show and self-display, Addison and Steele advise that the bourgeois consolidation of power and prestige operate within a very different taste and power regime. The stylistic standards they champion are part of a larger shift from an absolutist into a hegemonic mode of governance that takes place in England throughout the second part of the seventeenth century. In this stylistic regime, legitimacy and strength reside on the "inside" as opposed to the (merely superficial) "outside" and are signified through a stylistic reticence ("modesty") that speaks most powerfully through understatement. Clinging with particular tenacity in the corridors of corporate and bureaucratic power, this regime of style persists to the present. Perhaps it is worth noting that dominance is no less unmistakably proclaimed in the discrete accents of the twentieth-century business suit than it had been in those louder tones of beribboned pantaloons, red-heels, and laced sleeves of the seventeenth-century aristocrat.

Fashion is a historically constituted category of commodity production and consumption, as well as of cultural criticism. As a category of both consumption and criticism, fashion covers a whole cultural network—what Braudel speaks of as "those strange collections of commodities, symbols, illusions, phantasms, and intellectual schemas that we call civilization."[21] Accordingly, through its examination of fashion this study engages issues that stand center stage in eighteenth-century debates about the state of its own civilization: the place of commerce and commodity in culture; the value of novelty; the formulation of modern notions of history; the quarrel between the ancients and the moderns; the representation of revised models of subjectivity and gender; the definition of standards of taste and the institution of the aesthetic. *The Tatler* and *The Spectator* are part of a highly conscious and resourceful criticism that follows in the wake of British commercial expansion and the establishment of the institutions of modern culture. This criticism goes far indeed to articulate the content and functions of these institutions (like fashion) and is itself an ongoing discursive institution within that culture.

The ways that critical standards of cultural legitimacy have worked in relation to the (academic) institutional status of *The Tatler* and *The Spectator* papers are historically reflexive in the extreme. For, these standards, the very object of this study, are themselves traceable to precepts promoted by *The Tatler* and *The Spectator*; yet, though they persist (in more and less direct forms) in the contemporary academy, these standards do not always serve to promote within its walls much critical interest in the papers. Indeed, *The Tatler* and *The Spectator* seem to occupy a kind of subliterary position in the academic canon, a status they share with popular periodicals as a genre.[22] And while I have no interest in staking a claim for the papers in some "higher" realm of canonicity, it does seem worthwhile to make good some of the losses that such a limited and hierarchical notion of legitimacy has incurred.

The "exclusion" at work here is of a peculiar sort. It is certainly not the conventional exclusion of the racially, economically, or sexually marginalized. Indeed, *The Tatler* and *The Spectator* institutionalize what are still fairly centrist cultural standards. The very centrality of the norms articulated in the papers seems to have contributed to their neglect. This is Samuel Johnson's point when he castigates those who too facilely dismiss Addison's contributions to modern criticism: "It is not uncommon for those who have grown wise by the labour of others, to add a little of their own, and overlook their masters. Addison is now despised by some who perhaps would never have seen his defects, but by the lights he afforded them."[23] The ideology of the papers, even if disowned, may seem so transparently obvious as to require little comment. The standards of common sense and common language formulated in *The Tatler* and *The Spectator* have remained so (apparently) self-evident throughout the twentieth century that they have attracted little analytical interest. Belletristic, easy, full of superficially transparent comments that seem to call for little heavy theory and few hard words, they lack the surface complexity and overt ambiguity that attract the attention of one breed of academic.[24] Ephemeral, quotidian, diffuse, fragmented, of multiple and sometimes shadowy authorship, the papers also lack the unified monumental integrity that signal substantial literary status to another kind of academic. And it is not only that *The Tatler* and *The Spectator* are not complex enough for the tastes of conventional literary critics; they are not exclusively literary enough. So much of what they say addresses extratextual social practices that the papers cannot be fully accounted for within the conventional domains of literary studies or intellectual history. Rather, *The Tatler* and *The Spectator* insist upon a broader cultural framework even for their most overtly literary and aesthetic discussions.

So an additional source of neglect stems from the prevalence in the papers of those subjects I concentrate on here — fashion, style, consumption — all trivialized and feminized arenas of activity. The lack of critical attention to these spheres of activity bears witness to the continued operation of a standard that the papers themselves helped establish: that hierarchical line drawn between, on the one hand, trivial, mundane, usually feminine arenas of inquiry and, on the other, the more serious, profound realms of literature, culture, aesthetics, and philosophy. Ironically, *The Tatler* and *The Spectator* devote so much space to the very ephemera and trivia they denounce (though also depend upon) that they put a good deal of their own content outside the domain of exclusively literary and aesthetic analysis. Where *The Tatler* and *The Spectator* are granted a place of importance, as in discussions the bourgeois public sphere, they earn this position only by virtue of their connection to "serious" discourse of Habermasian social theory. To my knowledge, there are *no* critical discussions of the sphinx-shaped fashion repository, the trial of the hoop-petticoat, the lace and snuff-crammed brain of the beau, the hooliganish, fashionable lady shoppers that are central to my own analysis. As areas of interest and expertise identified with girls, queers, youth, and ethnic underclasses, fashion and style have until recently been much neglected, especially in historically oriented studies. But this hierarchy of distinctions is being dismantled in some spheres of critical discourse, primarily those gathered under the rubric "cultural studies." By emphasizing the ways these higher and lower realms of, respectively, criticism and aesthetics, and fashion and consumption are mutually constitutive, I hope that this study may contribute to this critique.

HEGEMONY OF TASTE: FASHION AND THE BOURGEOIS PUBLIC SPHERE

As formulated by Jürgen Habermas, the bourgeois public sphere is an ideally open forum of rational discussion first emerging out of the coffeehouses, clubs, and newspapers in early-eighteenth-century England. It performed social, cultural, and political functions: it served as an arena of social identification for individuals; it provided standards for interaction and public discussion; it established rationales for ever more secularized and commercialized modes of cultural production; it stood as a place outside official state power whence criticism against the state could be launched; and although emerging from and dependent on the marketplace, it served as an arena of alternative social, ethical, and aesthetic-cultural norms.[25]

Some critics have given a respectful nod to the importance of style and taste regulation to the institutionalization of these norms; but few have pursued concrete critical descriptions of eighteenth-century style and taste regulation, especially as it applies to extra-textual cultural production. An account of the specific distinctions, appropriations, and transformations that go into the formation of those standards of taste and style can, however, reveal the means through which bourgeois hegemony began to assert itself.[26]

Through the networks of the press and institutions like the coffee-house, there arose a new notion of a "public" composed of private individuals who came together to debate and negotiate matters of public concern, to formulate "public opinion." Represented to itself through the press, this new "public of the now emerging *public sphere of civil society*" becomes aware of itself as a source of authority and validation separate from, and even opposed to, state authority, previously the only "public" authority. The public sphere serves first and foremost as a *critical* arena where individuals take part in a debate about the principles, interests, and standards that ought to govern their lives. "In the age of Enlightenment," writes Peter Uwe Hohendahl, "the concept of criticism cannot be separated from the institution of the public sphere. Every judgment is designed to be directed toward a public; communication with the reader is an integral part of the system."[27] And as Terry Eagleton emphasizes, at this stage in the development of criticism neither its content nor its functions are limited to the literary: "Criticism here is not yet 'literary' but 'cultural': the examination of literary texts is one relatively marginal moment of a broader enterprise which explores attitudes to servants and the rules of gallantry, the status of women and familial affections, the purity of the English language, the character of conjugal love, the psychology of the sentiments and the laws of the toilet."[28] Largely through publications like *The Tatler* and *The Spectator*, the public sphere becomes the place where an encompassing set of cultural and social norms are formulated for polite modernity.

Focusing on how *The Tatler* and *The Spectator* take charge of behavior, attitude, and belief through their manipulation of standards of taste and conduct, this study isolates and foregrounds operations of power characteristic of the bourgeois public sphere, operations that Habermas's account leaves largely unexplored.[29] In this aestheticized, discursive arena, power hides from its own representation. Here even political discourse becomes transformed by an "antiparty," or de-politicized, rhetoric.[30] Rather than making a spectacle of itself, power embeds itself in those apparently nonpolitical and nonideological are-nas of everyday life that it represents as unexceptional, even trivial. Manners, taste, and style, not despite of but by virtue of their status as mundane, even trivial arenas of activity become all-important av-enues of control. Their significance in the papers springs from nei-ther a simple refusal nor a full acknowledgment of their importance but from a more complex kind of simultaneous acknowledgment and denial. On the one hand, these arenas of activity are useful av-enues for regulation precisely because they are understood as nonideo-logical and nonpolitical, and so not complicit with the coercive and obnoxious forces of absolutism. They elicit, then, less resistance. But on the other hand, *The Tatler* and *The Spectator* do self-consciously acknowledge the importance of extralegislative, apparently non-ideological and apolitical arenas to the operations of their own regu-lative control. It is precisely because "the greatest Evils in Human So-ciety are such that no Law can come at [them]" that Addison and Steele take on the roles as social censors and cultural arbiters (*T* 61).

Nancy Fraser notes the importance of "protocols of style and decorum" to the operation of power in the bourgeois public sphere. Consensus and hence control is achieved through "powerful informal pressures."[31] These informal pressures work through the discourse of "free" and "independent" choice exercised rationally by each indi-vidual. Within the bourgeois public sphere, this discourse presents itself as nonexclusive, as open to all rational individuals, whose ra-tionality and autonomy, to a good extent, is witnessed by their vol-untary identification with the ideals of the public sphere.

The nonexclusivity of the stylistic regime promoted by the papers wraps their ideology of taste in an envelop of paradox. For *all* cate-gories of cultural distinction, as Pierre Bourdieu emphasizes, revolve around some structural exclusion: "Tastes (i.e. manifested prefer-ences) are the practical affirmation of an inevitable difference. . . . In

matters of taste, more than anywhere else, all determination is negation" (56). Wherever taste, then, is a dominant standard of value (and
where is it not?) there will be a considerable degree of negation and
exclusion. The curious paradox of the kind of bourgeois taste promoted by *The Tatler* and *The Spectator* is that it is nonelitist and inclusive, but as such it in turn excludes other "more exclusive" modes of
taste. What is important here is that exclusivity itself becomes a negative value, one which can be leveled at those who need to be excluded. Fraser points out this irony in reference to Habermas's bourgeois public sphere: "There is a remarkable irony here, one that
Habermas's account of the rise of the public sphere fails to fully appreciate. A discourse of publicity touting public accessibility, rationality, and the suspension of status hierarchies is itself deployed as a
strategy of distinction."[32] Even this ostensibly inclusive and egalitarian arena then can exercise "informal pressures" that do exclude and
silence groups unwilling or unable to conform to what, after all, is
only one among a number of competing public spheres.[33]

As Hohendahl points out, the discourse of taste has a history
long predating its permutation into eighteenth-century aesthetics.
Throughout the seventeenth century, "Good taste . . . distinguished
the life style of the aristocracy and the social groups attached to the
aristocracy from the life style of other levels of society; superior taste
was the basis of their claim to cultural leadership."[34] The articulation
of bourgeois, class-based claims to cultural leadership similarly involved the appeal to superior taste and, predictably, were often developed in distinction to aristocratic tastes deemed degenerate and
regressive. From the bourgeois point of view, which is that of *The
Tatler* and *The Spectator*, good taste emphasizes modesty, restraint,
practicality, and decorum in distinction to bad (aristocratic) taste cor-
rupted by ideologically retrogressive qualities of personal ostentation,
irrational excess, arbitrary election, and libertine abandon.

Yet the reform of taste and manners undertaken by *The Tatler* and
The Spectator is perhaps not best understood as a simple supplanting
of the aristocratic codes of taste by some already in place, fully
formed mode of bourgeois taste. Rather, the very objects of reform
are those dominant standards of taste and conduct that, though more

fully dispersed across status hierarchies and class lines, are traceable to those set by the Restoration court. Importantly, these new standards for genteel society serve as a way to consolidate a polite public inclusive of reasonable, decent people of middling *and* upper classes. Ideally, the standards of culture and conduct the papers promote are "universal," appropriate for all virtuous, genteel, tasteful society. Eagleton emphasizes the work of consolidation achieved by public sphere institutions, chief among them *The Tatler* and *The Spectator*. Here, the "major impulse is one of class-consolidation, a codifying of the norms and regulating of the practices whereby the English bourgeoisie may negotiate an historic alliance with its social superiors."[35] However, that this alliance happened on the ground of *class* rather than *status* itself announces the dominance of certain terms within sets of sociocultural categories: class rather than status; hegemony rather than absolutism; persuasion rather than coercion; taste rather than rules.

Both in its overt content and in its operational logic, the bourgeois discourse of taste is characteristic of the large historic shift from absolutist to hegemonic modes of sociopolitical control. Hegemonic power governs through the individual internalization of normative standards which are increasingly embodied not so much in formal legislation but in modes of style, taste, manners, sentiments, and affections—those "protocols of style and decorum" referred to above.[36] Most important, these modes and attitudes are instituted not through coercion but through persuasion; they are understood to be freely adopted or declined by each individual. People revise their behavior and lifestyles not under the duress of sumptuary laws or formal edict—religious or secular—but propelled by desires felt as individual and personal, truly one's own. Such wants and satisfactions go far to constitute the deepest sense of self. Successful incorporation into the bourgeois social order involves not a person's subjugation of his own will to that of the "law" but the absence of any distance between that will and the "law": "To dissolve the law to custom, to sheer unthinking habit, is to identify it with the person's own pleasurable well-being, so that to transgress that law would signify a deep self-violation."[37] As conduits to the intimately subjective realms of self, the operations of taste, style, affection, and habit become crucial circuits of control. Ultimately, the logic of persuasion and identification that characterizes operations of power in the bourgeois public sphere achieves one awesome apotheosis in twentieth-century advertising.

The absence of formal modes of social regulation makes the job of self-styled cultural watchdogs like Addison and Steele all the more decisive. As Steele puts it: "In a Nation of Liberty, there is hardly a Person in the whole Mass of the People more absolutely necessary than a Censor" (*T* 144). The regulation of taste and consumption practices through more informal means is crucial at this time when there is an explosion of goods on the market and yet no sumptuary legislation on the books and little active taboo to regulate their consumption.[38] The secularization and liberalization of society opens it up to cultural contestation. In reference to consumption, the very liberality of the market calls for its regulative restriction, achieved in *The Tatler* and *The Spectator* through an arbitration of taste that manages consumption through rationally directed selection. Appadurai points out how this direction of taste performs functions similar to taboo and sumptuary legislation. The prescription of taste is "no less effective in limiting social mobility, marking social rank and discrimination, and placing consumers in a game whose ever-shifting rules are determined by 'taste makers' and their affiliated experts."[39]

As noted, fashion itself may work as a principle of selective regulation, attributing value and desirability and so directing our purchase and consumption of goods. But if understood (as Addison and Steele frequently do when they are attacking rather than appropriating it) as an autonomous agent responsive only to the senseless forces of novelty, vanity, and self-promotion, fashion, like the women, fops, and fools who are its victims, is not fit to manage itself. Conventionally, fashion often figures as a tyrant, imposing its whims on the weak with all the abandon of arbitrary authority. As such, argues Simmel, fashion fills a vacuum left in modern society by the absence of absolute authority in political life: "For man requires an ephemeral tyrant the moment he has rid himself of the absolute and permanent one. The frequent change of fashion represents a tremendous subjugation of the individual and in that respect forms one of the essential complements of the increased social and political freedom."[40] But far from ceding it to fashion, this space left by the retreat of absolute authority is one that Bickerstaff, as self-appointed Censor of Britain, himself seeks to fill. It is fully accepted that taste and morality cannot be legislated; but this is by no means an acceptance of their deregulation or of their regulation by the iron whims of fashion.

Within the context of public sphere discourse, one way to look at fashion, then, is as a public arena of identification and value that may at some moments stand in competition for social dominance with the specifically bourgeois public sphere. As revisionists have noted, Habermas's narrative does not account for this constellation of often competing and conflicting arenas of identification. Fraser discusses Habermas's "failure to notice other non-bourgeois public spheres" and points to the existence of "a host of competing counterpublics, including nationalist publics, popular peasant publics, elite women's publics, and working-class publics" (7). Geoff Eley concurs, emphasizing the important existence of publics that compete with that of the bourgeois public sphere "not just later in the nineteenth century, when Habermas sees a fragmentation of the classical liberal model of *Offentlichkeit*, but at every stage in the history of the public sphere."[41]

Discussing the relation between the bourgeois public sphere and the arena of mass consumption, Michael Warner characterizes consumption as a "counterutopia" that exists in a kind of complementary relationship with the public sphere, offering an arena for the representation of just those particularities and differences jettisoned by the bourgeois public sphere's ideology of the subject: "Even from the early eighteenth century, before the triumph of a liberal metalanguage for consumption, commodities were being used — especially by women — as a kind of access to publicness that would nevertheless link up with the specificity of difference." In an essay on the consumer economy in the eighteenth century, Timothy Breen points out that "the consumer market may have been a source of female empowerment. . . . The acquisition of goods by women in this economy was an assertive act, a declaration of agency."[42]

In ways that support such revisions, I find that evidence in *The Tatler* and *The Spectator* complicates the scene of the public sphere's early evolution and contradicts the rather uniform, conflict-free picture Habermas draws of it. Rather, we find the papers engaged in an ongoing struggle to define and maintain a discursive arena of social regulation, an attempt that must always be renewed and reaffirmed in the face of competing arenas of cultural value and social identification. The constitution of the bourgeois public sphere arises from dialectical confrontations with a number of other, often alienated, spheres of experience and understanding. For example the rhetoric employed by the papers, while ultimately confirming a standard of rationality, only does so through a kind of transformative appropriation of the irrational rhetoric of the fancy. And while this tactic serves in an important sense to discipline the potentially unruly forces of fancy and the imagination, it also imports those forces, if under constraint, into its own discourse. What we now call rational public sphere discourse does regulate fancy and the imagination, but it can only do so by itself becoming significantly aestheticized. Analogous relations exist between the early formative public sphere and the arenas of fashion, social prestige, commerce, and consumption, all of which public sphere discourse often seems simultaneously to disown and inhabit in ways that not only regulate consumption and its related social practices but also significantly determine the affiliations and investments of the public sphere itself. Because it is such a central target for *The Tatler*'s and *The Spectator*'s attacks on faulty consumption practices, illusory values, and insubstantial standards of taste and personal identification, fashion exposes a wide range of exactly those conflicts with competing public arenas that are glossed over in Habermas's account of the public sphere.

Thus we come to see that the rational bourgeois public sphere is itself a utopian realm of social identification and cultural ideals; it is not the only one. I want to suggest that the very formation of the rational bourgeois public sphere generates counter-models even as it creates itself. By incorporating, though always ambivalently and under a veil of mystification, certain aspects of fashion and commodification while simultaneously distancing themselves from the "evils" of fashion by assigning them to women, fops, fools, the French, and the West Indians, the papers consolidate other spheres of identification understood as competitive with their own. The contradiction that makes it possible for the papers to escape reification by embracing it also makes possible other "escapes," other utopian sites. So, the very kinds of fashion practices that are so condemned may themselves constitute another alternative, both to reification pure and simple and to incorporation within the limited and normative purview of the public sphere. Naturally, these other utopian outlets are not recognized as such by the discourse of the public sphere but must be envisioned through the reactions against them enacted within that discourse. I suggest that fashion can be used in ways that not only counter the reductive and reifying forces associated with commodification but also counter the hold of the bourgeois public sphere.

COMMERCE AND CULTURAL CRITICISM

From the perspective I have adopted here, we can see *The Tatler* and *The Spectator* embroiled with a force of fashion conceived of as arbitrary and autonomous in a contest over the direction of style, consumption, and manners. But victory in this contest may threaten the papers' hold on the very ground they stake out. For when a style is widely adopted it becomes a fashion, and so the more successfully the periodicals supersede (arbitrary, commercial) fashion in the direction of style, taste, and manners, the closer they come to emulating fashion itself. Fashion, then, works as both a threat against the reasoned, progressive reforms advocated by *The Tatler* and *The Spectator* and, in a revised configuration, as one avenue for this reform. So the critique of fashion and commodification in *The Tatler* and *The Spectator* operates not to simply stymie these forces but to set up a dialectic between commerce and criticism that proves positively generative for both.

Habermas and those who follow on his heels with revisions and applications of this notion of the public sphere all stress the commercial roots and ongoing commercial context of this ostensibly disinterested, rational arena of public discussion. Looking for the origins of the public sphere, Habermas finds them in the links between the acceleration of commerce and the development of the press: "With the expansion of trade, merchants' market-oriented calculations required more frequent and more exact information about distant events. . . . The great trade cities became at the same time centers for the traffic in news. . . . Almost simultaneously with the origin of stock markets, postal services and the press institutionalized regular contacts and regular communications."[43] The relationship Habermas articulates between the marketplace and the public sphere is causal: "The social precondition for this 'developed' bourgeois public sphere was a market that . . . made affairs in the sphere of social reproduction as much as possible a matter of private people left to themselves and so finally completed the privatization of civil society."[44] Similarly, Eley discusses the ways that the emergence of the bourgeois public sphere depends on social and commercial economic transformations that predate its emergence in the eighteenth century: "The category of the public was the unintended consequence of long-run socioeconomic change eventually precipitated by the aspirations of a successful and self-conscious bourgeoisie whose economic functions and social standing implied a cumulative agenda of desirable innovation."[45]

So while the bourgeois public sphere understood itself as distinct from both the marketplace and the state, taking each as its critical object, I emphasize this dialectical interchange between commerce and criticism, not in order to collapse the distinction between them but in order to understand how they are mutually constitutive. This interrelation establishes itself as processes of commodification lead to an abstraction of cultural production from its function of social representation and so to the perceived autonomy of the cultural artifact and its arena of operation. Thus, even as cultural production becomes ever more indebted to commerce, it simultaneously *appears* ever more autonomous. Likewise, the critical discourse that arises around this secularization of the aesthetic claims independence and autonomy from political and commercial arenas; analogously the model of modern bourgeois subjectivity foregrounds autonomy, independence, and self-regulation as its defining characteristics. Conditions of abstraction and autonomy characterize all these spheres of life, providing analogies that connect what bourgeois ideology has worked so strenuously to divide.[46]

The rationalizing projects of social management undertaken within the bourgeois public sphere *need* the more unruly realms of fashion and consumption. Unstable, and irrational, fashion becomes an object for the containment and rationalization of bad, often "feminine" forces present both in the marketplace and on the domestic scene. As themselves fashionable and innovative papers competing on the opinion market for the role of principal cultural arbiter, *The Tatler* and *The Spectator* do not so much repress or expel the objects of their criticism as inhabit, appropriate, and transform them.

By emphasizing the periodicals' own status as fashionable commodities, I pull at the tensions that evolve from their simultaneous involvement in, and disavowal of, commodity culture. Their strategy works well but involves the papers in a contradiction: they owe much of their success to their status as a voguish commodity, but they cannot fully admit that status. In "Cultural Criticism and Society," Theodor Adorno discusses such a contradiction. He points out how the cultural critic both participates in and refuses the object of his criticism — his own culture — thereby adopting a difficult position outside the context of which he must necessarily be part. "The cultural critic is not happy with civilization, to which alone he owes his discontent. He speaks as if he represented either unadulterated nature or a higher historical stage. Yet he is necessarily of the same essence as that to which he fancies himself superior."[47] But this contradiction is generative, if in a slightly paradoxical manner. It allows for the production of cultural ideals that both contribute to the further reification of culture and provide the standards according to which this reification may be criticized: "By making culture his object, he objectifies it once more. Its very meaning, however, is the suspension of reification."[48]

So although fashion may be condemned and apparently disowned by *The Tatler* and *The Spectator*, to a great extent the control, even the dismissal, of fashion is exerted there not simply by retreating to a realm that transcends the superficial ephemera of the mode but by entering — if in a mystified way — the mode, the fashion market itself. This ambivalence of involvement in, and distance from, the contemporary social scene is self-consciously assumed by the Spectator persona, who has mastered the discipline of "living both in the World, and out of it" (*S* 27). The forces of commodification, commercialization, and fashion that shape the ways of the world become *both* grist for the mills of Addison's and Steele's critique of modern life *and* the conditions of their success. So while, as in *Spectator* 64, the papers assert the principles of "Nature, Law, and Common Sense" against the senseless sway of fashion, their own success depends on their effective marketing of these principles that gesture to sites of value outside the market. Nature, law, and common sense, then, compete not merely *against* fashion, but also, in a sense, *as* fashions. These principles are promoted on a market neither completely demonized nor completely naturalized, one where real value is neither forfeited in advance simply by its complicity with commercial exchange nor guaranteed success merely by virtue of its "natural," inherent rightness.

Behind the projects for the regulation of fashion in *The Tatler* and *The Spectator* stand a secure secularism and a tacit acceptance of the basic principle of consumption: that human desires are valid. Joyce Appleby emphasizes how seventeenth-century economists validated "the pursuit of unlimited profit" as a "socially acceptable goal," and so delegated to the market the "pervasive influence [subsequently] attributed to it."[49] And it is from within a society understood to be saturated with market forces that Addison and Steele launch their campaigns of rational interference. For the papers work to counter what are perceived as the dangerous consequences of these transformed relations between the market and society. They write to modify the powerful seventeenth-century notion of an economic order that, even as it permeates society, is nonetheless "impervious to social engineering."[50] It is against the threat of a society driven by the sometimes ruthless, sometimes senseless, unpredictable whims of a market economy beyond rational social management that Addison and Steele advance their reforms.

Yet while the papers are concerned with the social and ethical effects of the market, they usually cheer along the expansion of commerce and trade. At a period when the earlier, seventeenth-century trend of what we would call free-trade economics was being legisla-

tively revised under pressure from (especially) domestic textile man-
ufacturers, *The Tatler* and *The Spectator* are engaged in formulating a
set of more generally social responses to both the threats and potentials of a newly expanding, free-wheeling marketplace.[51] On the one
hand, the very project of social reform of the passions of mankind
that Addison announces in *Spectator* 16 accepts the continued expression of these passions, just as the projects for sartorial reform accept
a basic materialism and allow for consumption, involvement in the
market, and even the cultivation of a degree of luxury.[52] Yet, on the
other, there is a drive toward regulation, toward channeling these
passions for consumption into avenues mapped out on ethical and
social coordinates, rather than on the valueless grid of profit and loss.

ONE

Fashion, the Fetish, and the Rise of Credit

⊰⊱

If we will be
useful to the World,
we must take it
as we find it.

SPECTATOR *179*

AGRICULTURE, LABOR, CREDIT: THE CAPITALIZED WORLD

The world in which Addison and Steele found themselves was one increasingly saturated by capital and commerce, one generated ever more by the forces of novelty and change. Often figured in ways that hyperbolically embody these impulses, fashion serves as a kind of magnet for anxieties about the intensified commercialization, indeed the capitalization, of the world. Because of fashion's high profile in capitalist society, its critical negotiation can tell us a lot about various stages in, and strategies for, the naturalization of the market and the rationalization of capitalism. At the end of the seventeenth century the institutions of early modern capitalism were flourishing in England: "Every index of economic growth showed an advance: agricultural output, capital investment, imports from the Indies and the New World, the range and quantity of home manufacturing."[1] Assertions of considerable consequence have been made about this explosion of production, finance, and commerce. While varying widely in their focus and ideological allegiances, historians of the period consistently are concerned with the proliferation of strategies—financial, sociopolitical, cultural, industrial, commercial, and symbolic—generated in response to an English world centered on the booming markets it increasingly dominated and was increasingly dominated by.

Looking beyond the industrial revolution for the institution of modern capitalized forms of finance, wage labor, commerce, and consumption, historians give sightings of a number of early modern "revolutions"—a "financial revolution," a "commercial revolution," a "consumer revolution"; often these are understood to lay the groundwork for the later eighteenth-century industrial revolution. So P.G.M. Dickson claims that the financial revolution initiated in the 1690s established the basis for the industrial revolution.[2] Similarly emphasizing the radical changes that precede industrialization, Christopher Hill notes how the commercial revolution of the late seventeenth century had economic, political, and social effects comparable to those of the eighteenth-century industrial revolution. This commercial revolution instituted "a new type of economy" that tied home manufacture to international trade and colonization.[3] Emphasizing the centrality of domestic manufacture and home markets, Joan Thirsk gives an account of the manufacturing and agricultural projects already under way in the sixteenth century. In the seventeenth century, these transformed the economic structure of England, redistributing wealth on a broad scale and involving a geographically and socially broad spectrum of the population in the market, as both producers and consumers. "These industrial employments," argues Thirsk, "heralded the development of a consumer society that embraced not only the nobility and gentry and the substantial English yeomen, but included humble peasants, labourers, and servants as well."[4] Looking at the later, and more glamorous, stages in the evolution of this consumer society, McKendrick, together with J. H. Plumb and John Brewer in *The Birth of a Consumer Society*, proposes that eighteenth-century England witnessed a "consumer revolution" that laid the groundwork for the ensuing industrial revolution.[5]

However, the new economy and the new sociopolitical forms that these historians document are not merely products of intensified exchange (i.e., of purely *commercial* activity), but as Hill, Thirsk, and Appleby emphasize more than McKendrick, they result as well from shifts in property relations and the production framework.[6] These consumer-market oriented "revolutions" must themselves be accounted for, and this is best accomplished by seeing them within the framework of a more foundational shift: the long transition from feudalism to capitalism. Eighteenth-century consumer society with its more and more complete orientation around market values — private property, individual enterprise, efficiency, economic rather than moral and social obligations — is rooted in agrarian capitalism. An examination of the series of changes contributing to the structuring of English society as a capitalist society needs to look beyond the spheres of exchange and merchant capital (though these are important) toward that agricultural sector of production where capitalism gained its first foothold and which dominated the English economy until the nineteenth century.[7]

So it is that Marx's search for the roots of the capitalism takes him back centuries before the advent of nineteenth-century industrialism and outside early modern mercantilism to England's transition from feudalism to agrarian capitalism.[8] In the "primitive accumulation" of large landholders and their "expropriation" of agricultural producers, Marx locates the "classic model" for humankind's fall into capitalism, alienated labor, and commodified social relations. And as one economic historian notes, Marx's account of primitive accumulation defines a problem that has come to dominate debate, both marxian and nonmarxian, on the origins of modernity in the West: the historical emergence of capitalism, understood not simply as an economic structure but as a more broadly integrative historical formation that itself makes the discretely economic (i.e., as distinct from the social, political, religious) even thinkable.[9] This separation out of the economic, accomplished through the emergent discipline of political economy, is a key step in broader modern divisions within the field of knowledge. For this period sees the emergence of those increasingly discrete categories of knowledge that largely define the map of the "human sciences" for the ensuing three hundred years:

not only political economy but also, for example, the cultural aesthetic with its critical discourses, psychology, sociology, modern historiography, and ethnography.[10]

For my purposes here, the historical–social changes that require emphasis are: first, the way that the market in land institutionalizes the purchase of status, that process of turning money into prestige; second, the contributions that the land and labor market make toward the constitution of what C. B. Macpherson has called a "market society" and what Thirsk and McKendrick call a "consumer society," since it is here that fashion flourishes; and finally, the effects that the commodification of land and labor have on social relations, and so on what it means to be human.[11] For the commodification of human energy and potential provides both a conceptual and sociomaterial context for what is often cited as one of fashion's own most dire depredations: the degradation of the human into the merely material and the subsequent alienation and loss of autonomy.

In early modern England, the intensified commodification of land and labor brings with it an accelerated social and geographical mobility and feeds into a new view of human value and social relations. Throughout the seventeenth and eighteenth centuries, England's economy was dominated by the agricultural sector; likewise, the social hierarchy was centered on land ownership, as it had been since time immemorial. However, the continued primacy of land, its products and producers, in the socioeconomic structure does not attest to some simple persistence of traditional economies and social relations; for the terms of ownership, modes of production, and so the very meaning of land and the very substance of the social hierarchy it supported all shifted. Land, then, looks less like a clear and even ground of continuity than a shifting foundation whose very constitution is altered under the pressure of economic and sociopolitical change. Around the turn of the seventeenth century, the rapid and extensive transfer of land is the vehicle for a huge wave of social mobility among the gentry and aristocracy, some families climbing up the socioeconomic scale, others sliding down.[12] And while this buying and selling of land did not dismantle the hierarchical scaffold—after all, one thing that made land desirable was its ability to underwrite social status—it did shift the ground on which it stands. When status can be bought, the social hierarchy shifts from its previous foundation in inherited honors onto its more modern ground of class and available capital. As Michael McKeon points out, "it was through the wholesale adoption of 'antiaristocratic' elements that the aristocracy persisted in early modern England."[13]

Of course, the enormous transfers of land that Lawrence Stone documents as an index of his famed "crisis of the aristocracy" were undertaken not simply to buy prestige but to turn a more strictly economic profit. The period of the late sixteenth and early seventeenth century was one of population growth, high prices for agricultural produce, and an expanding European, as well as domestic, market for agricultural products. The irresistible allure of profit motivated the rationalization of land management and the development of innovations in agricultural techniques.[14] This period saw innovations not merely in land ownership but also in techniques of agricultural organization and production.[15] Having bought land as an investment at prices dictated by the market, the landholder needed to get back his capital in profits. One way to do this was to modify leaseholds and raise rents.[16] More than simply a new financial burden on the tenant, the renegotiation of short-term leases and raising of rents was in itself a sharp departure from traditional customs that ordained long-term, multigenerational leaseholds at fixed rents. As profit replaced custom, the traditional moral and social obligations that had governed relations between landlord and tenant were supplanted by a mode of relations more systematically economic.[17] In addition to renegotiating their leases and racking up their rents, landowners began enclosing land for agricultural (rather than, as in the sixteenth century, pastoral) production, thereby privatizing and rationalizing farming. Seventeenth-century enclosure, reflects Appleby, stands as an emblematic "microcosm" of the "macrocosmic restructuring of English society" which promoted the individual over the group, the economic over the social, the private over the communal, and efficiency over moral obligation.[18]

These developments in land ownership and agricultural production changed the socioeconomic status of agricultural produce in the seventeenth century. Whereas in the Tudor period and earlier, processes linked to the production of food — from farming through marketing and milling to baking — were seen as "principally social rather than economic activities," in the seventeenth century, "food lost its special character and became a commodity like all others."[19] Although, as E. P. Thompson reminds us, even after the actual model of food production had changed and with it the legal constraints on production and distribution, the residual socially focused model persisted throughout the eighteenth century as part of the "moral economy" within which the poor asserted their rights and protested rising prices.[20]

The commercialization of agriculture, then, brought on foundational changes in the structuring of the English economy and the social relations emergent from it. By the Restoration these changes were largely complete and legally institutionalized in a number of provisions, many initiated during the Interregnum, that promoted the autonomy of landowners and of the labor market: the abolition of feudal tenure; government deregulation of wages; the successful bid of landlords against the property rights of copy holders; the defeat of restrictions on enclosure; and in 1685 the dissolution of apprenticeship regulations for all but servants hired by the year.[21] "This is the century," writes Thompson of the eighteenth, "which sees the erosion of half-free forms of labor, the decline of living-in, the final extinction of labor services and the advance of free, mobile, wage labor."[22] Macpherson sees the commodification of labor as the most crucial criterion of "the possessive market society": "It is to emphasize this characteristic of the fully market society that I have called it the *possessive* market society. Possessive market *society* also implies that where labour has become a market commodity, market relations so shape or permeate all social relations that it may properly be called a market society, not merely a market economy."[23] The commodification of labor establishes an economic, rather than more purely social, relation not only between one person and another but also between that person and his or her self. The enlightenment doctrine of rights is based on the protection of absolute property rights. Human rights, then, consist of the person's property in one's own self, in one's own labor. This property is absolute and alienable; it can be bought and sold.[24] More generalized, intellectual concepts of personhood (like those of Hobbes and Locke, for example) incorporate the alienation and reification that attend the establishment the institution of wage labor. And alienation and reification come at human identity from both directions — production and consumption. As producers, people engage with a marketplace where they are, in an important sense, bought and sold; so as consumers they enter the market to buy those commodities ever more crucial to the enunciation of their selves. With its extreme proximity to the body and its capacity to represent gender, social class, ethnicity, nationality, political affiliation, sensibility, and character, the fashion commodity intimately associates the personal with the commercial and so invites reflection on the commodification of the human.

Fashion enjoys an intimate proximity, then, with both the personal body and commerce itself. Fashion, as Elizabeth Wilson puts it, is "the child of capitalism."[25] In a market that depends more and more on acceleration and novelty to increase profit — to open markets to new commodities and to prevent glut in their distribution — fashion may easily become the privileged standard of production, distribution, and consumption, embodying as it does a structure of accelerated production of seemingly infinitely renewable novelty. As Nicholas Barbon writes in his *Discourse of Trade* (1690):

> Those Expences that most Promote *Trade*, are in Cloaths. . . . Fashion or the alteration of Dress, is a great promoter of *Trade*, because it occasions the Expence of Cloaths, before the Old ones are worn out: It is the Spirit and Life of *Trade*; It makes a Circulation, and gives a Value by Turns, to all sorts of Commodities; keeps the great Body of *Trade* in motion; it is an Invention to dress a Man, as if he Lived in a perpetual Spring; he never sees the Autumn of his Cloaths.[26]

Likewise, though with less exhilaration and more apprehension, a contributor to *Spectator* 478 observes how "the Variableness of Fashion turns the Stream of Business, which flows from it now into one Channel, and anon into another; so that different Sets of People sink or flourish in their Turns by it." Fashion is both creature and creator of accelerated capitalized production. Trying to provoke his audience into an admission of the complicity between vanity, greed, and prosperity, in "The Grumbling Hive" Bernard Mandeville pinpoints the pivotal place of fashionable change, "fickleness," to the growth of England's industry and wealth:

> Envy itself, and vanity,
> Were ministers of industry;
> Their darling folly, fickleness,
> In diet, furniture, and dress,
> That strange ridic'lous vice, was made
> The very wheel that turn'd the trade. (182–87)[27]

The world that Mr. Spectator lives both in and out of is the world of the mode, which is also the world of the capitalized, commercial, and materialist West. Confronted with the transformations that brought this world into being, he engages in programs for their accommodation. One key socioeconomic event attended to in the cultural criticism not only of Addison and Steele but also, for example, of Defoe, Swift, and, later, David Hume, is the institution of the credit economy in 1694 with the establishment of the Bank of England and the National Debt.[28] These institutions entailed a stock market that dealt in government funds and a banking system that now handled loans, advances, and share portfolios. William Pietz describes these financial institutions as "the most visible, and at the same time, the most mysterious" manifestation of capitalist society; he follows Marx's own account: "It is in *interest-bearing capital* . . . that capitals finds its most objectified form, its pure fetish form. . . . Capital — as an entity — appears here as an independent source of value; as something that creates value in the same way as land rent, and labor wages. . . . The transubstantiation of the fetish is complete.[29]

In England this "transubstantiation" was complete by the seventeenth century, when there was already in place an international money market controlled by credit and discounting and, from 1663 on, a futures commodity market, like the markets in government funds and joint-stock companies, open to speculation by the notori-

"A Perspective View of the Bank of England," from William Maitland, *The History and Survey of London from Its Foundation to the Present Time*, 3rd ed. (London: T. Osborne, 1760), vol. 2, facing page 846.

ous "stock-jobbers."[30] These transformations in the world of finance and the further identification they brought between private profit and national interests changed modes of sociopolitical relations and social consciousness itself, both of which became based on commerce and the exchange of mobile property, rather than on the holding of real property.[31] The abolition of feudal tenures, the commodification of labor, and the commercialization and rapid transfer of land unsettled faith in the solidity of real estate and its social relations. J.G.A. Pocock analyzes the intellectual and psychological effects of the complicity between government and capital that was viewed by many contemporaries as a threat to property-based conventions of political and social relations:

> The danger lay with the owner of capital, great or small, who invested it in systems of public credit and so transformed the relations between government and citizens, and by implication those between all citizens and all subjects, into relations between debtors and creditors. It was not the market, but the stock market, which precipitated an English awareness, about 1700, that political relations were on the verge of becoming capitalist relations.[32]

In this account of the effects of credit capitalism, Pocock notes that credit is gendered as feminine (Defoe's "Lady Credit") and those men engaged in speculation are in danger of losing their reason and themselves to the passionate seduction of this fickle femme fatale. Predictably, the financial market underwritten by credit also was figured as feminine, with all the connotations of fantasy, instability, and danger that attend that assignation. Property, as Pocock says, "has ceased to be real and has become not merely mobile but imaginary."[33] Resituated in the realm of a chimerical future, property and its circulation are unmoored from the stability and comprehensibility of the present and even the material, and transformed in accordance with the imagination and its mercurial laws of desire. Feminine, unstable, seductive, fed on fantasy and desire, fashion, of course, is the commodity mode that most concretely embodies this restructuring of property. In tandem with the rise of commercial capitalism in the early eighteenth century, fashion begins to take the shape it has retained for the past three hundred years — the accelerated production and distribution of socially prestigious goods under the coercion of apparently arbitrary change and perpetual novelty.

In the case of Lady Credit we see one significant instance of the key role played by the symbolic feminine in the critical representation of capitalism and its institutions. The prominent place that women and all that is symbolically feminine, including fashion, take in the critical discourse of early-eighteenth-century British society is bound up with all that seems socially, politically, and ethically dubious about early modern capitalism. This cultural-symbolic role of the feminine as inherently unstable, as lacking self-identity and the ability to regulate itself, provides the logic that allows what seems irrational about capitalism at once to be rendered recognizable and laid open to rational regulation. If women cannot control their own consumption habits then all the more reason for masculine intervention and management. If Lady Credit falls into a swoon with every turn of the financial and political tide, then all the more call for men to administer her cure by putting the nation on an even keel, politically and financially. The feminine figures the potential excesses, instabilities, and irrationalities of the market that modern economic man sought to rationalize, contain, and manage.

COMMERCIAL IMPERIALISM AND THE CASE OF CALICOES

Overseas trade is important for the study of fashion, both because the introduction of exotic goods fostered a taste for the novel and because fashion in England was usually identified with imported goods and styles. The eighteenth-century beau monde sustained itself on Chinese tea and porcelain, first Levantine then Caribbean coffee, North American tobacco, and West Indian sugar (and therefore on African American slaves), East Indian calicoes, French and Italian silks, French manners and French tailoring. Fashion historian Anne Buck states: "The finest silks worn by men and women of fashion during the first half of the century were imported from France and Italy."[34] Embargoes levied on French silks and Indian calicoes in the early eighteenth century, far from checking, indeed enhanced their

desirability by heightening their exclusivity and expense: "The prohibition of imported goods had the effect of making them fashionably desirable, for supplies were available through a flourishing smug-
gling trade."[35] Importantly for the social acceptance of fashionable
change, the idea of consumption as a productive force was formulated in defense of the importation of fashionable Indian calicoes.[36]
And the fashion for these fabrics led to innovations in English industry seeking its share in a fashion market dominated by imports.[37]

"The single Dress of a Woman of Quality is often the Product of
an hundred Climates," writes Addison in *Spectator* 69. Of course,
dress consists of much more than fabric, and in the early eighteenth
century the modish woman carried a "Muff and Fan . . . from different Ends of the Earth [probably from, respectively, Canada, or perhaps Russia, and then China or Japan]." She wore a scarf "sent from
the Torrid Zone" and a tippet "from beneath the Pole." But simply
going to the ends of the earth was not enough. Stylish dress required
precious metals and gems delved from its depths: the silver of the
brocade petticoat "rises out of the Mines of *Peru*, and the Diamond
Necklace out of the Bowels of *Indostan*" (*S* 69). Addison celebrates
this sartorial extravagance; mapping out the stylish woman, he creates
a glorious emblem of the beneficial, harmonizing effects of England's international commerce.

Here, then, is another example — more positive than that of Lady
Credit — of the way that the feminine serves the accommodation of
capitalism to national interests. As Laura Brown has shown, fashionable female consumption serves not only as an object of attack in the
criticism of the domestic luxury fed by commercial imperialism but
also as an alibi for that same commercial imperialism. The excesses of
capitalism and imperialism thus can be understood as generated in
response to women's seemingly insatiable desires for luxurious commodities: "In the discourse of early eighteenth-century mercantile
capitalism this [the adorned female figure] is the most common trope
of all, by which the agency of the acquisitive subject and the urgency
of accumulation are concealed and deflected through the fantasy of
a universal collaboration in the dressing of the female body."[38] This
trope occurs as well in *Tatler* 116, which I discuss at more length in

"The Royal Exchange," from Maitland, vol. 2, facing page 898.

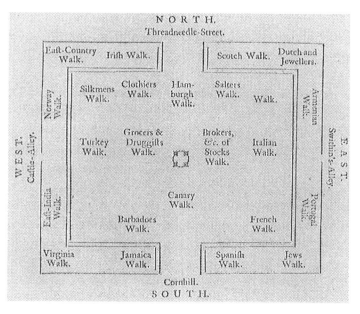

"Plan of Exchange," from Maitland, vol. 2, page 901.

the third chapter. Here Bickerstaff considers the proper adornment of woman in what amounts to a celebration of mercantile commercialism:

> I consider Woman as a beautiful Romantick Animal, that may be adorned with Furs and Feathers, Pearls and Diamonds, ores and Silks. The Lynx shall cast its skin at her Feet to make her a Tippet; the Peacock, Parrot, and Swan, shall pay Contributions to her Muff; the Sea shall be searched for Shells, and the Rocks for Gems; and every Part of Nature furnish out its share towards the Embellishment of a Creature that is the most consummate Work of it.

It is on the bodies of women that the guilt of empire is displaced and then transformatively aestheticized.[39] In both papers Addison's aestheticized female figure functions as just such a transformative alibi. Her outfitting stands as the summation of Britain's pursuit of commercial, military, and cultural dominance. But the figure does even more ideological work. As a stylized, harmonious composite of imperial booty, the fashionable woman depicted here approaches a type of Britannia figure, an allegory of harmonious empire.

Addison's picture, of course, is a nationalist utopian fantasy. Revealing the conflict and exploitation conspicuously absent from Addison's emblem of international harmony through trade, Hill drafts a blueprint of English commercial growth that reveals its aggressively military and colonialist roots. Hill shows how commerce was itself exploited by politics in ways that centralized and coordinated colonial, military, mercantile, and economic interests for the pursuit of colonization, corporate profit, and national identity.[40] In the seventeenth century England's access to world markets intensified; between 1700 and 1780 foreign trade almost doubled.[41] Much of this trade was with its trans-Atlantic colonies and its outposts in the east; by 1702 about a quarter of London's and perhaps a fifth of all national imports came, not from other European markets, but from India and the colonies.[42] This expansion depended on an identification of corporate and national interests that meshed in a web where the discrete strands of national, military, and commercial interests are all but indistinguishable.

England's imperial policy was established by the Navigation Act, instituted in 1651 and renewed in a modified form in 1660. It put all colonies, chartered and proprietary, under parliamentary control and ensured for English shipping a monopoly on trade in those colonies.[43] Another object of these Navigation Acts was the establishment of a huge fleet of commercial ships that functioned as a naval reserve. Through three wars with its Dutch rivals, England seized power over the slave and Far East trades. This expansion had consequences that reached far into the political as well as the commercial future: "the nucleus of all later settlements in India had been won before 1670."[44] The old, and then the new, East India Companies, monopolies protected first by Cromwell and then by Parliament, were largely responsible for the importation of calicoes, silks, coffee, and tea. These monopolies established English control in Indian territory, laying the foundations for the British empire. In 1655 Jamaica was captured and the hugely profitable slave trade was established from that base. With the Restoration came Catherine of Braganza, more direct slave trade in Portuguese West Africa, and the sugar and gold trade with Brazil. The negotiations that ended the War of the Spanish Succession brought England the monopoly on slave supply to the Spanish American Empire and secured her the upper hand over the French in control of the world's seas and markets.[45]

The 1688 revolution brought a turnaround in English trade policies: monopoly protection was eroded and free trade officially established by parliamentary legislation. The East India Company, under pressure from home textile manufacture, was rechartered under terms that demanded greater exportation of English commodities.[46] Yet while this restructuring seems to have opened up trade by putting strictures on monopolies, it was spurred by basically protectionist and mercantilist pressures from the home textile industry reacting against the saturation of Indian calicoes into domestic markets. That is, what from one perspective looks like a move toward free trade also, from a slightly different angle, reveals principles of regulation and protectionism.[47] Appleby analyzes these events, showing how clothiers calling for a strictly regulative trade policy recycled the balance-of-trade theory originally put forth as a paradigm of the free market as "the self-sustaining interaction of international commerce." In contrast, the protectionist clothiers use the theory not to show how international economy is a self-sustaining, self-balancing entity but to argue for legislation that would *produce* a balance in an economy that does not regulate itself.[48] In its inability to regulate itself, in its tendency to erratic fluctuations, the market, like the credit that sustained it, needs rational management. In this it, again, is analogous to woman herself, who, as mentioned, often is represented as the chief consumer, especially of luxury import goods. Understood thus as both the most likely abuser and primary beneficiary of the commercial imperialism that supplies those goods, woman becomes identified on some levels with the market economy. This identification puts both woman as consumer and the economy as provider in analogous positions of objects subject to rational, male regulation.

The mercantilist crisis over the importation of East Indian calicoes is a shining example of the interaction of commerce, economics, industry, and fashion. Appleby's account shows fashion concretely intertwined with the socioeconomic validation of consumption. The defense of the East India Company against the balance-of-trade mercantilists generated arguments that redefined wealth and, related to this, the very nature of consumption: "East India Company spokesmen . . . acknowledged that half their volume was consumed at home. This admission required a defense of domestic consumption which of necessity undermined the whole structure of ideas associated with the balance of trade, because it challenged the idea that wealth was specie that could only be secured from the settling of favorable accounts. A new definition of wealth was in order."[49] This new definition of the wealth of the nation rests on the novel idea that consumption is itself a wealth-producing activity. Consumption, it is discovered, produces demand, now conceived as elastic and manipulatable: "consumption was analyzed as a constructive activity . . . a self-sustained momentum for economic growth, which did not rely on favorable balances." "The maverick spirit of fashion" revealed in the craze for calicoes hovers like a guiding genius over this rethinking of wealth, consumption, and demand.[50] The boom in fashion for Indian calicoes brought to light the messiah of elastic demand and so

opened a new age of economic opportunity: markets could be created. So fashion contributes to the formation of modern, demand-
producing commerce, forcing the rethinking of consumption in
ways that further integrate it into the life of the nation.

Concerned more with innovations in manufacture than, like Appleby, in economic thought, Mukerji tracks the tale of calicoes in
great detail, narrating their progress from foreign imports to domestic products. She argues forcibly for the role of demand in the creation of new capitalist production, but her approach puts more emphasis than Appleby's on how this demand was itself produced by
forces of commercial capitalism and imperialism. Mukerji, like Appleby, notes that the fashion for calicoes rekindled the trade balance
debate and generated the counterassertions that established the irrel-
evance of that debate. But the more materially grounded story Mukerji tells is full of conflict: the balance-of-trade disputes were not
confined to an intellectual arena; they were acted out on the streets
and finally resolved in the factories of England. Outraged at the
swatch snipped from their market by Indian imports, the English textile industry lobbied successfully for a ban on the importation of
these fabrics. Black markets arose; the rich continued to flaunt their
fine calicoes but lost them when militant workers rampaged the
streets ripping the cotton off women's backs. Mukerji's analysis shows
the fashion for calicoes generating not merely economic theoretical
problems that were then resolved by conceptual innovations but an
embodied and material contest between the competing interests of
domestic production and foreign imports that was resolved only by
innovations in capitalist production.[51]

The case of the calicoes is one instance of how England's imperialist commercialization took place through an interchange between
the foreign and domestic worlds that restructured both, revising the
constitution and identity of the English world — a change signaled
by the title of empire, Great Britain. And while the function of *The
Tatler* and *The Spectator* in the production of a bourgeois culture is a
commonplace, they are no less part of the creation of a specifically
British culture, nationalistic and imperialistic. This is the context

within which Mr. Spectator defines his project: "As the great and only End of these my Speculations is to banish Vice and Ignorance out of the Territories of *Great Britain*, I shall endeavour as much as possible to establish among us a Taste of polite Writing" (*S* 58). "Us" here refers not simply to the English but also to the Irish, Welsh, Scottish, and the colonialists — who are all ideally to be united not merely by territorial appropriation, commercial colonization, and parliamentary act but also by a shared identity formed in accordance to cultural values held in common.

CONSUMPTION, THE FETISH, AND THE MODERN INDIVIDUAL

As part of their production of modern British culture, *The Tatler* and *The Spectator* advocate specific ideals of modern British character, ideals that take into critical account the effects of commercialization and consumption on human identity. As consumers, as well as producers, of the wealth of the nation, men and women in eighteenth-century Britain embodied new social roles and took on new identities. The eighteenth century witnessed the elaboration — through formulations of cognition and psychology and through the development of modes of representation (e.g., the novel) — of a revised model of subjectivity, that of an autonomous, biologically gendered individual whose value lay in interior resources of integrity and value.

The modern individual is the modern consumer: "This connection between consumption and individualism, largely wrought in the eighteenth century," writes McCracken, "is one of the great cultural fusions of the modern world."[52] Of course this fusion is not without its contradictions. The person's very individuality is at once confirmed and threatened by consumption. Defining his or her sexual, social, and ethical identity through the selection and use of goods, the modern consumer risks a kind of psychic colonization by the commodity, a process often represented as the loss of identity.[53] In her study of Alexander Pope's *Rape of the Lock* and *Windsor Forest*, Brown shows how the spoils of mercantile expansion commodify both human and national identity at once:

47

Belinda's self-generating aesthetic derives from her tendency to merge with the commodity, and it produces a consequent problem of identity . . . which is Belinda and which is the goddess of the commodity? In the same way, *Windsor's* ideology derives from the absorption of the products of trade into the English landscape. Which is the nation and which is the commodity? The poem's greatest insight is its failure to distinguish.[54]

The Tatler and *The Spectator* are filled with accounts of fashion victims who, like Pope's Belinda, merge with the commodity and seem to lose their very selves. These cases dramatize, in remarkably literal ways, processes of libidinal investment in capitalism and its objects of desire. Women are most vulnerable to this sort of psychic colonization by the commodity: "Were the Minds of the [female] Sex laid open, we should find the chief Idea in one to be a Tippet, in another a Muff, in a third a Fan, and in a fourth a Fardingal" (*T* 151). Here again we can see the intimacy between the feminine and the capitalized market, especially those aspects perceived as perilous. The ambivalent logic of feminine "nature" allows it to at once pose a threat to rational social control and to provide the very possibility for the implementation of that control. Quite simply, the same innate instability that renders women the peculiar dupes of fashion leaves them open as well to the rational direction of such paternalistic managers as Addison and Steele.

Although women are most susceptible to the seductions and corruptions of the fashion commodity, because they share the essentially feminine preoccupation with the mode, certain types of fancy men, like the fop and the beau, are also at risk. The contents of the beau's head dissected and inventoried in *Spectator* 275 provides a catalog of modish paraphernalia that vies with Belinda's dressing table: "We observed a large *Antrum* or Cavity in the *Sinciput*, that was filled with Ribbons, Lace and Embroidery. . . . Another . . . was stuffed with invisible Billet-Doux, Love-Letters, pricked Dances. . . . The several other Cells were stored with Commodities of the same kind" (*S* 275). The critical exposure of these fancy men becomes a way in *The Tatler* and *The Spectator* to disparage a set of masculine types associated variously with a set of compromising milieus, all feminized in their representation: the politically regressive, dissolute Restoration francophile court culture; connected to this, the largely female-oriented and directed beau monde, especially in relation to its courtship rituals; and, in more mediated and shadowy ways, the emergent homosexual subculture of Molly clubs. As I show in the fourth chapter, these types of badly feminized men serve as foils for a new sort of masculine ideal, domestic but not effeminate, worldly but not corrupt, a man of public culture who finds his final self-affirmation in the private, familial realm. The production of this new male ideal depends, as does that of his female counterpart, on disciplining "bad" feminine forces both as they produce negative female types — the jilt, the coquette, the idol — and negative male types — the fop, the beau, the pretty fellow, the smart fellow. Such "bad" femininity often shows itself in the excessive devotion to fashion and, more generally, in the ostentatious personal displays indulged in by all these types, male and female.

As we read about anatomies of brains and hearts that reveal bodies colonized by red hoods, ribbons, laces, and embroideries (*S* 275, 281); about a shopkeeper taken to task by Bickerstaff for salaciously displaying to public view a pair of lady's slippers in his Pall-Mall shop (*T* 143); about Mrs. Margery Bickerstaff, whose family, in order to keep her fortune, prevents her from marrying by supplying her with a steady supply of fashionable clothes onto which she displaces her libidinal energies (*T* 151); about girls at risk of losing their hearts to a sword-knot or a pair of fringed gloves (*T* 151), we enter a world where people quite simply worship fashion. In this world, shopping becomes a ritual of urban life, a ritual that provides voyeuristic pleasures, as well as materials for the internal and external fashioning of the self (*S* 336). Associated with the outside of the body, fashion is exterior and material; yet libidinally invested and so absorbed into psyche, the fashion commodity is interiorized and dematerialized, becoming part of an intangible realm of fantasy. In twentieth-century critical thought, these symbolic, fantastic capacities of the commodity are accounted for through various conceptualizations of fetishization — ethnographic, marxian, psychoanalytic, sociological.[55]

There is a correspondence between Addison's and Steele's critique of fashion and the notion of fetishization, both as it was emerging in the seventeenth and eighteenth centuries in discussions of the fetish religions of African societies and as it develops in the nineteenth and twentieth centuries, especially in psychoanalytic and marxian thought.[56] The primitive fetish is a ritual object with important apotropaic and occult properties. It is endowed with powers that, to those that do not share the fetish, seem incommensurate with its value. Further, "primitive" people who practice fetish religions share with eighteenth-century women their loose hold on rationality and its logic of causality. The primitive is a feminized type, and the woman, with her atavistic "Pictish" war-paint, her childish attraction to gay surfaces and sparkling gewgaws, is a primitive type.[57] And just as primitive peoples are shown as devoted, beyond all reason, to their fetishes, so women are depicted as peculiarly prone to the seductions of what we call commodity fetishization.

Unfolding the "problem of the fetish," Pietz catalogs four themes that uniformly mark the notion of the fetish throughout its history:

> (1) the untranscended materiality of the fetish: "matter," or the material object, is viewed as the locus of religious activity or psychic investment; (2) the radical historicality of the fetish's origin: arising in a singular event fixing together otherwise heterogeneous elements, the identity and power of the fetish consists in its enduring capacity to repeat this singular process of fixation, along with the resultant effect; (3) the dependence of the fetish for its meaning and value in a particular order of social relations . . . and (4) the active relation of the fetish object to the living body of an individual: a kind of external controlling organ directed by powers outside the affected person's will, the fetish represents a subversion of the ideal of the autonomously determined self.[58]

Although never named as such, the fashion commodity as represented in *The Tatler* and *The Spectator* shows all these features of the fetish. Likewise, the criticism launched against it appeals to the same enlightenment concepts that support the European discourse about "primitive" African fetish worship: the autonomous self; a rational-political rather than sacral-psychological social order; a technological, empirical mastery of natural laws that discredits the superstitious misapprehensions of causality that attribute to the fetish its false value; and secular commercial regimes of value that segregate "personal" psychic and sacred values from material objects whose worth should be perceived as purely "instrumental and commercial."[59]

Both the discourse of the fetish and that of fashion are *critical* discourses concerned with exposing the false values of an alien, and misguided, culture. Addison's and Steele's account of fashion, like the early accounts of fetish worship, registers itself as a demystification of an illusory set of values and thus as an articulation of "real" value. The objects of Addison's and Steele's critique are certain spheres within their own culture — spheres, like those of fashion and consumption, that they seek in a sense to regulate and so annex to their own more rational arena of social control. These competing realms of value are represented as alien and misguided; so the periodical personae must assume a considerable distance from them in order to validate their own critical authority. And, just as the discourse of rationalized consumption in *The Tatler* and *The Spectator* is always running the risk of losing that distance and so dissolving into a kind of fashionable discourse in its own right, so, Marx will claim, does the rational, secular discourse of political economy slip into the very fetishization of value that it sees itself as superseding.[60]

This fetishization of capital should be seen in relation to the process of secularization. On the one hand, the ascendancy of capital depends upon the conceptual and ethical premises of rational secularism for its own dominance. Yet, on the other hand, capitalism may appear to violate the premises of rational secularization insofar as its ideology is understood, as it is by Marx, to perpetuate its own mystical, fetishistic misrepresentations of value. The development of capital in the West comes hand-in-glove with the process of the secularization, a process that one historian suggests is complete in England by 1700.[61] Understood not as the erosion of religion per se but rather as its separation from other spheres of life, secularization removes life from its structuring foundation in religion. No longer is existence uniformly mapped out according the temporal and spatial coordinates of Christianity; there arise separate, more or less autonomous provinces of life — the religious alongside rather than foundational to the social, political, intellectual, and economic.[62] In terms of socioeconomic life, when land, labor, and capital are removed from the governance of custom and religious precept, they come under the dominion of secular systems of political economy. Political economy then develops claims for the autonomy of markets and for the inevitable validity of their jurisdiction of value.

Using fetishism as a term "to characterize the capitalist process *as a whole*," Marx defamiliarizes and demystifies capitalism, its regime of value and its modes of social integration. From this perspective outside capitalist ideology, the political economy through which capitalism justifies itself appears as "an atheological 'religion of everyday life.'"[63] More locally and superficially, capitalism fetishizes by endowing material objects with values that revise the nature of both people and things through a chiasmic structure that inverts the animate and the inanimate, producing those reified social relations and personified material relations that Marx discusses in the first chapter of *Capital*. Luce Irigaray's discussion of Marx's analysis of the commodity fetish leads her to exclaim in italics: "*This phenomenon has no analogy except in the religious world*."[64] She only echoes Marx himself, who writes that in order to understand capitalist fetishization we must work through analogy with "the misty realm of religion."[65]

From the perspective of the commercial, technological West, fetish societies are inadequately secularized; they continue to confuse the sacred with other spheres of value. Likewise, from an alien perspective, capitalist society seems to perpetuate its own fetishistic misapprehension of value, locating it not in the exploitation of surplus labor value but in the autonomous operations of the market and especially in capital's own capacity to reproduce itself. To the enlightened, commercialized, secular West, the discourse of fetishism does not simply represent some generic "other" but provides a way to articulate the very basic problem of "the nature and origin of the social value of material objects."[66] And so the fetish, in its turn, serves Marx as an instrument with which to probe the nature and origin of capitalist social values.

There are links, then, between the processes of fetishization in modern capitalist cultures and forms of fetish practice in the "primitive" societies from which the term is borrowed. One idea that feeds into my formulation of the early modern commodity is that, as our culture is increasingly capitalized, the status of the commodity becomes increasingly sacralized, charged with immaterial, "magical" properties.[67] Significantly, social critics like Addison, Steele, Pope, and Swift (for example) register a high degree of consciousness about the perils and possibilities that such a shift in the status of the commodity offered their contemporaries and the institutions through which they led their lives.[68] And while Addison's and Steele's antifashion discourse, operating in much the same way as the (anti)fetish discourse outlined by Pietz, by no means launches an attack on capitalism *tout court*, it does selectively isolate certain of capital's commercial and financial effects on the basis of the false values they produce.

Recent critical accounts of the modern shift into a ritualized sacralization of commodity culture differ in their time frames, just as claims for the birth of an institutionalized fashion system vary in their dates. Much attention has been paid to the intensive commodity cultures of nineteenth-century Europe with its monumentally conspicuous Bon Marche, Harrods, Crystal Palace, and other industrial-commercial exhibitions. Rosalind Williams identifies the genesis of "dream world of the consumer" at the turn of the nineteenth century and cites the Paris Exhibition of 1900 as exemplary:

> The 1900 exposition incarnates this new and decisive conjunction between imaginative desires and material ones, between dreams and commerce, between events of collective consciousness and of economic fact. . . . Consumer goods, rather than other facets of culture, became focal points for desire. The seemingly contrary activities of hard-headed accounting and dreamy-eyed fantasizing merged as business appealed to consumers by inviting them into a fabulous world of pleasure, comfort, and amusement.[69]

But an examination of the early-eighteenth-century commodity and the venues of its exchange and consumption show that such links between commerce and fantasy, pleasure, and amusement were forged well before the nineteenth century. Indeed, in its reliance on the financial institutions of credit and the speculative venture, the entrenchment of capitalism in the seventeenth and eighteenth centuries was itself founded in the "seemingly contrary" conjunction between commercial and fantasy life.[70] One implicit thesis of this study is that these same conjunctions between "imaginative desires and material ones" so often claimed for the nineteenth century are fully present in the early eighteenth century. The institutions that fostered such conjunctions, not only retail shops but also museums and scientific repositories, and the effects of this conflation of fantasy, desire, and material objects are the subjects to which we turn to next.

TWO

In the Very Sphinx of Fashion: The Fantastic Fashion Commodity

⊲⊳

THE LOOK OF THINGS: COMMODITIES, THE GAZE, AND THE IMAGINATION

Much of the satire in *The Tatler* and *The Spectator* documents the plights of the victims caught by retail ruses, and it advances projects for their salvation through a regulation of consumption. Listing the contents of contemporary commodified hearts and minds, publishing the plans for a sphinx-shaped fashion museum, indicting a hoop-petticoat in the fashion court, the *Tatler* and the *Spectator* papers reflect a preoccupation with a set of problems summed up in the question: What should we do with all these things? This question is inflected on a number of levels — economic and sociopolitical, cognitive, aesthetic, pedagogic, and ethical. By looking at the place of things in *The Tatler* and *The Spectator* we get an idea of some principal ways this issue was thought out during Britain's early and crucial period of financial and commercial expansion.

The worlds of *The Tatler* and *The Spectator* are peopled by things. In *Tatler* 151, Steele remarks on an elderly lady who, since she lost her mind to fashion, is not so much a person as a shop: "The Memory of an old Visiting Lady is so filled with Gloves, Silks, and Ribands, that I can look upon it as nothing else but a Toy-shop." Eighteenth-century "toy-shops" were for adults, not children, and sold fashionable accessories and knickknacks. Clearly, the "old Visiting Lady" spent ample time browsing through these venues of gimcracks and gewgaws. And she pays dearly for it, losing nothing less than her mind. The lesson of *Tatler* 151 is that these gloves, silks, and ribbons have gotten into psychic spaces where they do not belong. What belongs in a shop has somehow colonized a mind. How this happens and what, if any, good may come of it are two issues addressed by this chapter.

The place of things in our lives is central to cultural formation, and in early-eighteenth-century London, things were taking up more and more places — mental and material — in public and private life. In their history of eighteenth-century English retail, Lorna and Hoh-Cheung Mui pinpoint the period 1709-1711 as the dawn of innovations that flower into the full-blown modern retail trade by mid-century. Expanding at an unprecedented rate, retail trade almost doubles by the end of the century.[1] From the turn of the century on, shops develop ever more sophisticated strategies for enticing the customer; likewise, the cabinet collections of curiosities evolve into forms close to those of the modern museum, becoming institutionalized and public like the repositories of the Royal Society and the East India Company. Fruits of science, industry, commerce, and colonization, more and more things were being offered up to the hungry gaze of the consumer. The search for pleasure, status, identity, knowledge, and meaning through consumption was accompanied by a growing consciousness of the seductions of advertising and the perils of reification. "Every sign or shop," remarks Fanny Hill on her first stroll through the streets of London, "was a gazing-trap."[2] To catalogs of the perils of the London street — open sewers, congested traffic, pickpockets, con artists, hooligans, pimps, and punks — we can add the snares laid by retailers newly conscious of the profitable arts of advertising and display.

It makes sense that empiricism and its theories of cognition and perception — especially of *visual* perception — were formulated (by Newton and Locke) and popularized (by Addison, for one) at a time when there was a great influx of things to look at, as well as increasingly sophisticated and accessible institutions for their display. The newfangled retail trade and its consumer devotees have points of analogy with the new empirical science and its aficionados. Both the new science and the burgeoning retail trade are materialist and visually oriented institutions; both involve collection/consumption and display; historically, both develop through advances in technology and profit heavily from the ever-quickening stream of goods flowing into English markets from commercial ventures abroad. These analogies between the new science and the new market are apparent in contemporary criticism of the excesses of the consumer and of the scientific virtuoso. Just as luxury consumption intensified under fire from social critics, so the pursuit of the new science advanced in the face of an ongoing critique of the empirical materialism, acquisitive obsessions, and delusional schemes of the virtuosi and scientific projectors.[3] The devotee of the mode, with his or her collection of fashionable accessories, and the dedicated man of science, with his collections of butterflies, bones, and beetles, are both criticized for what we would call their fetishization of objects. So Alexander Pope ridicules the virtuosi who collect around the throne of Dullness in the fourth book of his *Dunciad*:

> Then thick as Locusts black'ning all the ground,
> A tribe, with weeds and shells fantastic crown'd,
> Each with some wond'rous gift approach'd the Pow'r,
> A Nest, a Toad, a Fungus, or a Flow'r. (397–400)

Just as Addison's and Steele's consumer victims, like the old visiting lady with her toy-shop mind, are figured in ways to suggest that they *become* the objects they consume/collect, so here Pope identifies these virtuosi with the objects — insects — they devotedly study: they approach "thick as Locusts." This simile suggests that, forsaking objects of higher contemplation and confining themselves to the narrow sphere of earthly materialism, these men have become more insect than angel, invested in and identified more with locusts and flies than with their Creator. The Goddess commends them on the insignificance of their studies:

"O! would the Sons of Men once think their Eyes
And Reason giv'n them but to study *Flies!*
See Nature in some partial narrow shape,
And let the Author of the Whole escape:
Learn but to trifle. . . . " (453-57)

In these passages, Pope presents the misguided devotion of these empiricists to small, low life-forms in explicit comparison to the proper religious devotion of those who turn their attention toward the heavens and their Creator. He implies here that the collecting mania of the new empiricists can be understood as a species of misdirected religious enthusiasm. By thus coloring his scientific collectors with the shades of false idolatry, Pope suggests that (to recall Marx's characterization of the commodity fetish) in order to find analogies for the value virtuosi (erroneously) attach to their specimen objects "we must take flight into the misty realm of religion."[4]

The dominance of the visual scene cuts across many spheres of life—commercial, scientific and intellectual, psychological, and, connected to this, aesthetic. Since processes of vision are so central in the eighteenth century's constitution of these spheres, their proper regulation becomes crucial. Both the virtuoso and the shopper are seduced into their obsessions through their eyes; the gazing traps laid by the retailer and the empiricism of the new science both depend on the visual. And to a great extent through new scientific methods there emerges the modern hierarchy of the spectator as the controlling subject, and the spectacle, that which is looked at, as the passive object. Satires on both the shopper and the collector probe this hierarchy, showing how objects can take over and consume the subjects, the spectators. Pointing this out in disapproving ways serves to police boundaries between subject and object, consumer and consumed, spectator and spectacle.

It is a commonplace that the eighteenth century is an age dominated by the sense of sight: "Our Sight," writes Addison in *Spectator* 411, "is the most perfect and most delightful of all our Senses." It is important to note at the outset the great degree to which *looking* is understood as a form of *getting,* of visual, imaginative acquisition.

Further, as is apparent especially in the collections of the scientific repository and the museum, having things is identified with knowing things. *Things* become cognitive, and affective, objects through the gaze. It is in this sense that we consume and acquire the objects we look at, incorporating them into our mental and emotional landscapes. And because looking operates as a mode of acquisition, the discourse of the gaze overlaps with the discourse of consumption. Both looking and getting feed into and are driven by the imagination and its sometimes fantastic desires; both, then, often involve processes of reification and fetishization.

The very act of perception endows things with immaterial, imaginative properties. Speculating on the pleasures of imaginative perception, Addison remarks : "Things would make but a poor Appearance to the Eye if we saw them only in their proper Figures and Motions" (*S* 413). Pursuing its visual and imaginative pleasures, the mind supplements objects with "imaginary Glories" and "pleasing Delusion[s]" of its own invention (*S* 413). While these fantastic embellishments are celebrated as a kind of surplus value created by the aesthetic imagination, they, or something very like them, become suspect in relation to fashionable objects. For, as represented in these papers, the problem with fashion commodities is that they are so often mistakenly glorified and peculiarly conducive to undesirable delusions. What, we must ask, distinguishes the pleasing delusions of the healthy imagination from the delusive fancies of the fashion-fed psyche? Similarly, the novelty at the core of the fashionable object is vital as well to the most highly valued aesthetic objects: "Every thing that is *new* or *uncommon* raises a Pleasure in the Imagination, because it fills the Soul with an agreeable Surprise, gratifies its Curiosity, and gives it an Idea of which it was not before possest" (*S* 412). As these parallels suggest, there are points of intersection between the realm of the aesthetic and the realm of fashion. For both the commodity fetish and the proper aesthetic object have their most important effects on the imagination, but these effects are clearly different. Disciplining the imagination depends on the ability to recognize these differences; it is from such distinctions that the realm of the cultural aesthetic emerges.

As part of this job of disciplining the imagination, distinctions are made between good and bad kinds of looking. Himself an eponymous embodiment of the visual faculty, the Spectator's reform is overtly centered on the uses and abuses of that faculty. This reform depends on establishing distinctions between various modes of good and bad consumption and vision. Even as, for example, Addison celebrates the visual acquisition of imaginative objects as one of life's great and most genteel pleasures, other kinds of looking, especially other modes of visual, imaginative consumption come under attack in the papers. So while the polite connoisseur is esteemed for his mental stockpile of images, the old visiting lady, the anatomized beau, and dissected coquette, for example, are satirized for their accumulation of fashionable mental and affective objects. While Mr. Spectator bases his own critical authority on his apparently tireless gaze trained on the play of all the world surrounding him, the way that modish women are consumed by the scenes of *their* world is criticized as a weakness, a vulnerability to the delusive spectacles of mere shows and outsides.[5]

Such seeming contradictions, or at least ambiguities, call forth two lines of treatment. On the one hand, we need to tease out the implications of the overlap between these "good" and "bad" sorts of looking and acquiring, especially between the good and bad sorts of what I call "imaginative consumption," a term which may refer both to window shopping and the working of the polite imagination. On the other hand, attention is due to exactly how the boundaries between good and bad visual accumulation, good and bad seeing and imagining, are established and maintained. For one central job of *The Tatler* and *The Spectator* is this policing of the gaze and the modes of consumption, imagining, and desiring it feeds.

Conceit, metaphor, and allegory are powerful allies in projects of improvement; they bring a certain latitude to representation and charm their audience into a fancy for reform. Addison is highly conscious of the persuasive power of "Similitudes, Metaphors, and Allegories" (*S* 421). Exemplifying the sorts of informal pressures associated with hegemonic, rather than absolutist and coercive, social control, the essays depend on persuasion, on convincing their audience not that they *must*, and not only that they *should*, but that they *want to* change their ways. The very nature of the ideology, and so of the rhetoric, of *The Tatler* and *The Spectator* leads them to exploit those discursive strategies that afford greatest access to the inner hearts and minds, and so to the desires of their audience. Written in the codes of the imagination, fanciful rhetoric grants such access to the psyche. Mastery of the discourse of fantasy is mastery of the mind: "how great a Power . . . may we suppose lodged in him, who knows all the ways of affecting the Imagination" (*S* 421). One so skilled can infuse in his readers any ideas he pleases. This use of the imaginative capacities of language characterizes the rhetorical strategies of those "Polite Masters of Morality" among whom we may count Addison himself (*S* 421).

Yet, something unsettling happens when these rhetorical weapons are trained against the fancies of fashion: they generate a destabilizing resemblance between the object of criticism — the vain, illusive fetishes of fashion and commodity — and the very forms this criticism takes — speculation, imaginary conceits, dream visions, allegories. The magical allure of things depends on their fetishistic charms, on the intangible, illusive powers and meanings they acquire in human culture and the human psyche. The persuasive power of the *Tatler* and *Spectator* papers written against these delusions often depends as well on these same symbolically charged charms of the imagination.

Part of an urban literature geared toward the accommodation of social, economic, and material changes, *The Tatler* and *The Spectator* produce, in Michael Ketcham's phrase, an "imaginative order" to make sense of the realm of exchange.[6] The tension arises from the fact that this "imaginative order" is exactly that — imaginative, a product of the fancy, a speculative project.[7] Throughout *The Spectator*, the papers refer to themselves as "Speculations," and so hint at an affinity between themselves and those flighty, feminine phantoms of credit, the market, and the imagination that they would manage and order. Fantastic, insubstantial, vivid, appealing, modish — many of the essays on fashionable foibles and seductions take on qualities, both formal and substantial, that they identify at the heart of fashion's errors.

Spectator 460 exposes the emptiness of those "thousand unaccountable Conceits, gay Inventions, and extravagant Actions," by producing a countering conceit, an allegorical dream vision of the Palace of Vanity. The allegory constructs a specifically modern, modish pandemonium where affectation, flattery, gallantry, and narcissism are the demons, and cosmetics, feathers, fans, and mirrors their diabolic emblems. Here Fashion sits at Vanity's feet along with two other "false Graces," Flattery and Affectation. With the metaphors of financial jargon, Vanity's futility is architecturally bodied forth in her palace, figured as an speculative scheme about to burst: "The Foundation hardly seem'd a Foundation . . . and the Top of the Building being rounded, bore . . . the Resemblance of a Bubble." The Palace of Vanity, the beau's head chock full of fashionable paraphernalia, the coquette's heart stashed with flame-colored hoods, the lady's toy-shop mind stocked with ribbons and gloves, the sphinx-shaped fashion museum, the hoop-petticoat on trial — these critical conceits, I argue, are deeply invested in the economies of goods and desires they satirize.

In the *Tatler* paper where Bickerstaff proclaims himself "Censor of these Nations [of Great Britain]" he also refers to that office as a "fantastical Dignity" (*T* 144). Can the Censor claim a position of advantage if his projects for reform are as fantastic as those they disparage? He can, because this strategy generates not contradictions that collapse into nonsense but revised notions of the proper objects and functions of fantasy and desire. Appropriating the objects and formal strategies of their criticism — fashionability, fancy, and the fantastic conceits of their rhetorical configuration — these projects counter conceit with conceit, fight fire with fire. Yet *The Tatler* and *The Spectator* occupy the arena of fancy in order to govern it, in a sense, to liberate it from the arbitrary, alienating, destructive, delusional regime of fashionable emulation. Addison's and Steele's strategies, then, do not disown but preserve these forces of fancy in ways that they can understand as compatible with reason, social and personal progress, and national well-being.

I view this strategy as an exemplary instance of one way that bourgeois ideology rationalizes what is troubling about capitalism —

its production of fetishization, reificaton, social and personal alienation. Unable to condone these "bad" effects of capitalism and equally unable to disown the capitalist commercial project *tout court*, bourgeois social thought begins to draw its own characteristic distinctions between good and bad consumption, proper and improper investment in material goods. Because of the fetishistic intimacy between the commodity and the fancy, these distinctions, in part, are grounded in the distinction between the healthy and the disordered imagination.

ANATOMY OF THE CONSUMER

Were the Minds of the [female] Sex laid open,
we should find the chief Idea in one to be a Tippet,
in another a Muff, in a third a Fan,
and in a fourth a Fardingal.

TATLER *151*

The Tatler and *The Spectator* determine what are legitimate and illegitimate concessions to the world, good and bad fashions, uses and abuses of the imagination. The indulgence of distorted fancy, or the unrestrained capitulation to the nonsensical customs, and costumes, of the world are not merely symptoms but also causes of individual and social decay. They are as well avenues of reform and progress. *The Tatler* and *The Spectator* are concerned with the influence of consumption and the fantasies that accompany it on the individual human heart and mind, for these are the motors of social and ethical reform. They react against what they perceive as their contemporaries's dangerous imaginative and libidinal overinvestment in things and seek to discipline the fancy — the hearts and minds — of their readers as well as their modes and manners.

Noting the degradation that men and women fall into when they embody too perfectly the externals of their culture — the fashions and fripperies of daily life — Addison and Steele exploit, even as they deplore, the deep penetration of the commodity into the psyches of their subjects. These things are heavily fetishized; they stand in for human relations, even the subject's relation with her self. *The Tatler* and *The Spectator* show how human desire and potential are absorbed into the lifeless object, displacing psychic and erotic energy onto the dead end of the terminally dehumanizing commodity. Whether or not this sort of investment in consumption is necessarily a displacement of desires from their "true" objects, as the papers assume, is a question I keep open, if only to appreciate the extent to which answers to it are ideologically charged and historically informed. For my concern here is with the historical and ideological features of the responses *The Tatler* and *The Spectator* give to the commodity fetishism of their society.

In keeping with their custodial stance, the *Tatler* and the *Spectator* papers are concerned with the pitfalls of consumption. Addison's and Steele's reactive responses against consuming passions reflect a world where people were placing hopes, dreams, and desires in commodities, where human creativity and potentials for transformation were being attached to things. Fashionable articles hold this sway over the modern consumer because they are highly prized tokens in the economies that produce social, sexual, and cultural values. Anxious to exercise the taste that signals cultural competence, men and women become avid consumers. Shopping is not mere consumption; the selection and use of things *produces* meaning, identity, and social relationships. Likewise the textual public sphere represented by *The Tatler* and *The Spectator* is not merely a site for the construction and dissemination of discursive opinion; it is as well an arena "for the formation and enactment of social identities."[8] In an important sense, then, what takes place in the confrontation between these papers and the ever more dominant arena of fashionable consumption is a kind of competition for the social identities and psychic investments of the public.

Predictably, Addison and Steele are more attentive to the perils than to the productive pleasures of fashionable consumption, and they emphasize the fatalities and limitations of the desires it both feeds on and produces. Fashion fetishes, they demonstrate, induce a fragmented metonymic of desire. Susceptibility to this disorder is represented as a peculiarly feminine trait and the metonymic desire it produces supports the conventional charge of woman's inconstancy, the flight of her affection from one object to another. Female desire attaches to detachable, changeable objects; women fall for the fashion rather than the man: "Many a Lady has fetched a Sigh at the Toss of a Wig, and been ruin'd by the Tapping of a Snuff-Box. It is impossible to describe all the Execution that was done by the Shoulder-Knot while that Fashion prevailed, or to reckon up all the Virgins that have fallen sacrifice to a Pair of Fringed Gloves" (*T* 151). In *Spectator* 15, Addison echoes this "unaccountable Humour in Woman-kind" and links it to "the numberless Evils that befall the Sex," who, until their education is reformed, will lie prey to "every Embroidered Coat" that comes their way. This passionate investment in the show of fashion represents an erroneous expenditure in the economy of desire. When all attention is given to the outer man, not much is left for the inner, the "real" man: "A sincere Heart has not made half so many Conquests as an open Wastcoat; and I should be glad to see an able Head make so good a Figure in a Woman's Company as a Pair of Red Heels" (*T* 151). Women conduct their more generally social, as well as their erotic, lives through an economy of fashion. They define value and character according to patterns of consumption: "Talk of a new-married Couple, and you immediately hear whether they keep their Coach and six, or eat in Plate: Mention the Name of an absent Lady, and it is ten to one but you learn something of her Gown and Petticoat" (*S* 15).

Fetishization of fashion can lead to disasters more complete than bad object choice or a trivial social life: it threatens to cancel human relations and social institutions. In *Tatler* 151, Bickerstaff completes his disquisition on women's consuming passions with the example of his great aunt, Mrs. Margery Bickerstaff. Eager to keep her thousand-pound portion among themselves, the family exploited Mrs. Margery's weakness for fashion to prevent her marriage. "The Method they took," explains Bickerstaff, "was, in any Time of Danger to throw a new Gown or Petticoat in her Way." So the first time marriage seems imminent, her father "dressed her up in a Suit of flowered Sattin." Replaced by a narcissistic fancy for her newly outfitted self, fancy for the suitor dissolves: "she set so immoderate a Value upon her self, that the Lover was contemned and discarded."

The pattern is repeated throughout Mrs. Margery's long life. A final flare-up of desire, at the age of sixty, is extinguished in the nick of time by a set of "Cherry-colour'd Ribands."[9]

In general, according to Addison and Steele, the problem with investing too greatly in consumption is that it implicates both men and women in sexual, social, and cultural networks that produce superficial relationships, debased lives, and vacant thoughts. As they internalize the objects of their consuming passions, people are at risk not only of falsifying their desires and their values but also of losing their identities. Locating meaning in things, people strive to become them. As they satirize the ways that things came to replace human identity, Addison and Steele then define what is human in opposition to these things and to the very fashion of accumulating them. So Steele exposes the lady in *Tatler* 151 who has lost her mind to gloves, silks, and ribbons; she is no longer human but mercantile, a "toyshop." The contents of the beau's head dissected and inventoried in *Spectator* 275 provides a similar storehouse of modish paraphernalia:

> The *Pineal Gland* . . . smelt very strong of Essence of Orange-Flower Water. . . . We observed a large *Antrum* or Cavity in the *Sinciput*, that was filled with Ribbons, Lace and Embroidery. . . . Another . . . was stuffed with invisible Billet-Doux, Love-Letters, pricked Dances . . . In another we found a kind of Powder, which set the whole Company a Sneezing, and by the Scent discovered it self to be right *Spanish*. The several other Cells were stored with Commodities of the same kind, of which it would be tedious to give the Reader an exact Inventory. (*S* 275)

This list bears a telling likeness to the inventory of another beau's apartment cataloged in *Tatler* 113: "Four pounds of scented snuff . . . a Quart of Orange-Flower-Water . . . Two embroidered Suits . . . a Dozen Pair Red-heeled Shoes, Three Pair of Red Silk Stockings . . . Five Billet-doux . . . Lessons for the Flute" (*T* 113). One brain, anonymous. One apartment, quantified. A pair of indiscriminate stereotypes. Equivalency, lack of individuation, fragmentation, and objectification characterize the beau's commodified identity. These features mark as well the discourses of the inventory and the anatomy

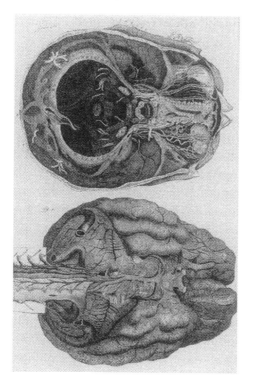

"Anatomie" (Dissected Head), from *Encyclopédie, Recuiel de Planches* (Paris: Briasson, David, Le Breton, Durand, 1762-77).

used to expose and scandalize his dehumanization. The representation of the anatomized, objectified mind suggests a subjectivity with neither integrity or depth: the "inside" is consumed by the "outside," the psyche displaced by the wares of the vendor. A beau's brain, like his apartment, is a mere compendium of fashionable *things*. Because of his failure to maintain adequate barriers, either cerebral or architectural, against the trivia and detritus of the world, both the beau's mind and his lodgings are the final resting places for the rubbish of the beau monde. The cause of death? Paralysis by fashion. Not only the head but also the heart can be lost to fashion. In *Spectator* 281 Addison reports on the dissection of a coquette's heart, its uppermost chamber encasing "a Flame-coloured Hood." While this pair of examples may seem to suggest that devotion to fashionable consumption indiscriminately affects both men and women, there is an implicit gendering at play. In the case of the beau the corruption is of the brain, the mind, the seat of rationality. In the case of the coquette, on the other hand, what is lost is not the mind but the heart, the seat of the affections. This difference, then, is gendered in the conventional way that links masculinity with the mind and rationality, and femininity with the heart and emotions. If, as I argue, these satiric anatomies expose the loss of what is vitally human to the deathly commodity, then it is implied here as well that what is distinctly human about women is different—anatomically, biologically different—than what is human about men. So, among other things, at work here is an assumption, graphically figured forth, of biological sexual difference.[10]

The coquette's desires are inscribed on her heart; at its core lies a miniature portrait of "a little Figure . . . dressed in a very Fantastick manner." This "little Idol" is the "Deceased Beau," the same whose brain is anatomized in *Spectator* 275 a week before. Both flamboyant images—that of the "Flame-coloured Hood" and that of the fantastically got-up beau—are equally *objects* of the coquette's heartfelt affection. All image and no substance, an exceedingly little figure notable mostly for his dress, the beau is more mannequin than man. Above all, the beau, both as he figures himself and as he is figured on the coquette's heart, is a *visual* object: flamboyant, fragmented, superficial, and reified, the perfect object of desires fed on fashion.

The inventories of the beau's brain and of the coquette's heart draw on both the discourses of anatomy and of commercial inventory. The shared rhetorical features of these discourses and their mutual application here are indexes of a broader parallel development in early-eighteenth-century England between new scientific and commercial formations. Scientific repositories (such as the one where the beau's head and the coquette's heart are stored), like commercial shops, were important stages for the organization, display, and distribution of things. The two taxonomic loci intersect. Having purchased his repertory of fashionable accessories from London's shops, the beau becomes an object suitable for the virtuoso's (as well as the coquette's) collection, fashioning himself as a prized specimen. Too heavy investment in fashion drains the beau of his humanity and so his life. Under the scalpel of empirical science, his cadaver is as lifeless, indeed as deathly, as the snuff, ribbons, and toilet water that embalm his brain.

To understand this conflation of mercantile and scientific languages it helps to look at the framing device of the paper. Both inventories are part of "a very wild Extravagant Dream" Addison has after spending a day at an "Assembly of Virtuoso's [sic]." As *dream visions* both these dissections are fantastic allegories. Framed as illusions — it's only a dream — these papers expose the fantasies that inhabit the hearts and minds of their contemporaries. These allegories of commodified hearts and minds mimic exactly the reification they satirize. The "objects" discovered through these "dissections" are, on one level, allegorical signs not of the actual objects themselves but of desires for and obsessions with these objects. But because of the nature of the deformed relation between the commodity and the human that is under scrutiny in these papers, their allegory is best read as no allegory at all. The satire strikes deepest when the allegory is dissolved and the representation is taken literally. The flame-colored hood, the snuff and toilet water, the ribbons and fans, then, are not mere signs of desires, meanings, obsessions that are in any way distinct from themselves. Taken literally, the desires, meanings, and obsessions are identical to, and inseparable from, their objects — the hood, snuff, toilet water, ribbons, and fans. And that is exactly the problem. What the anatomies of the beau and the coquette expose is a fusion of humanity and commodity.

It is, I think, this collapse of the difference between hearts and hoods, brains and snuff, people and things, inside and outside, that *The Tatler* and *The Spectator* are most concerned to scandalize and reform. What makes the allegory, then, formally and tonally peculiar is its denial of its own allegorical status. Yet finally, because this collapse of the difference between inside and outside, between desire and its object, between vehicle and tenor, is exactly what is under attack here, the papers are also making a plea for the reestablishment of distinctions that make not only allegory but, it is suggested, humanity itself possible. Through this "legitimate" use of the fancy, Addison exploits his fantastic conceit in order to reclaim sites of humanity he fears are being lost to the empire of goods.

Clearly the habits of the frivolous and fashionable are under assault here, but to what extent are the practices and language of the scientific virtuosi also being satirized? And related to this, to what extent are the Spectator's "dissections" complicit with the very reification and fragmentation they satirize? If this were Swift, we could be sure that the new science, as much as the new mode, was under assault as a modern agent of corruption. But Addison quickly shifts attention from the virtuosic origins of the dissection's catalog to the degraded humanity it describes. And while the perfect match between the beau's brain and the discourse of scientific investigation reflects somewhat satirically on both, I think questions of agency and representation remain. That is, where do we locate this corruption of humanity into bits and pieces — in the consumption practices this anatomy seeks to expose, or in the discursive practices of the anatomy itself? Perhaps in both, and that is why the medical anatomy so inevitably melts into the commercial inventory. Representation, after all, is a mode of exchange and just as capable as shopping of producing fragmented, reified human beings.

As we see in these dissection fantasies and, as well, in the "penalties" imposed, for example, on fashion "criminals," coffeehouse hecklers, and gamblers, Bickerstaff and the Spectator are at risk of reproducing the logic of fetishism even as they satirize it. In *Tatler* 162, Bickerstaff, self-appointed "Censor," relates his strategies for enforcing his mandates. One method is simply to deprive the fashionable offender of the instruments that support his affectation. So the Censor seizes the canes "of many Criminals of Figure." More imaginatively, he may also change men into things emblematic of their offenses: "I have degraded one Species of Men into Bombs, Squibs, and Crackers, and another into Drums, Bass-Viols, and Bagpipes."[11] On one level, the Censor is only establishing a congruency between what these men really are and how they appear. Enforcing a congruency between inside and out, between signifier and signified, Bickerstaff is not deforming but reforming the order of things by his "degradation." Like the roving packs of gamblers Bickerstaff has

"shut up in Kennels," these men have already forfeited their humanity by their conduct (*T* 162).[12] Yet, there is a tension here. From one
perspective, this "penalty" merely marks the "actual" corruption of
the internal subject who has *already* given himself over to an identification with bad manners, fashion, or vice. But as he degrades men
to dogs, musical instruments, shoddy lampoons, and small explosives,
Bickerstaff's correction seems to participate in and reinforce the same
reification that it punishes. Of course, his use of these forms and figures is highly self-conscious and so asserts a distance from and control over the reification he morally chastises and rhetorically exploits.

WHAT YOU FANCY: SHOPPING, FETISHIZATION, AND THE PLEASURES OF THE IMAGINATION

Things get inside a person's head and heart through the eyes: imaginative consumption is inseparable from visual consumption. Heads
may become a toy-shops as much by simply looking at things as by
owning and using them. Fancy—for things as well as people—is
engendered through the eyes, begot and nourished by the fascinated
gaze: "We cannot indeed have a single Image in the Fancy that did
not make its first Entrance through the Sight" (*S* 411). Because the
gaze furnishes men and women with materials for the transformation
of their physical and mental selves, it is a powerful avenue for both
abuse and reform. In what follows, I look at the representation of this
gaze and its objects first in accounts of shops and shopping trips, and
finally in the Spectator's plan for the cultivation of the polite imagination. The pleasures of both shopping and the imagination enlist
the gaze, and through this, the mind, and through this, the body.
Both follow a model of psychosomatic interdependence that informs, as well, contemporary accounts of hysteria (the vapors).
There is constant commerce between the eyes, the imagination, and
the body.

The indulgence of consuming passions may mean enslavement to
the market: "every shop was a gazing-trap." Exceeding the prudence
of a sober mercantilism, there is something feminized, erotically
meretricious about these displays of things set out to snare the
passerby. The suggestive analogies between the desire for women laid

bare before the gaze and for things spread out under the eyes of shoppers are quite alive in the descriptions, many of them critical, of contemporary retail and shopping practices. Strolling through the stalls of the Royal Exchange, Edward Ward's London Spy lays out this association with customary baldness: "We went up, where women sat in their pinfolds begging of custom with such amorous looks, and after so affable a manner, that I could not but fancy they had as much mind to dispose of themselves as the commodities they dealt in."[13] The intimacy of women and goods, of spectacle and eroticism, of sexual and commodity fetish, is vividly enacted to this day in red-light districts where prostitutes exhibit themselves in storefront windows.

The shop offers special challenges to social critics in the eighteenth century who want to manage the cluster of social practices that make up what we call "shopping." The proper codes of behavior for both shopkeeper and shopper, the proper modes of display and ornamentation of the shop, exactly what constituted a legitimate shop and legitimate shopping become topics of considerable attention. Discussions of shops and shopping reveal a heavily gendered — indeed sexualized — blueprint of social space where, especially early in the century, the fashionable retail shop seems to hold no very respectable position.

In the *Tatler* for Thursday, March 9, 1710, there appears an "AD-VERTISEMENT," presumably placed by the "Censor," Isaac Bickerstaff himself:

> The Censor having observed, That there are fine wrought Ladies Shoes and Slippers put out to View at a great Shoemaker's Shop towards St. *James's* End of *Pall-Mall*, which create irregular Thoughts and Desires in the Youth of this Nation; The said Shopkeeper is required to take in those Eye-sores, or show Cause the next Court-Day why he continues to expose the same; and he is required to be prepared particularly to answer to the Slippers with green Lace and blue Heels. (*T* 143, italics reversed)

This shopkeeper, so the Censor protests, is selling sex — creating "irregular desires" — at the same time he is selling style "the Slippers with green Lace and blue Heels." He does this by staging the commodity on the street theater of the display window. One way the newly emergent art of advertising works is through what might be called a theatricalization of retail trade. Here, the commodity "put out to View" is a feminine fetish (a woman's shoe) and, presumedly, is consumed by the gaze of the adolescent male passerby ("the Youth of this Nation"), becoming part of a masturbatory fantasy (creating "irregular Desires"). The commodity display, then, according to the charge leveled here, verges on the pornographic. Here the commodity fetish and the sexual fetish are one.

The function of clothing, and of shoes especially, in sexual fetishization is a commonplace and, if we can count the evidence of this *Tatler* paper, had been so for some time before it was named and theorized by Sigmund Freud. According to Freud's account, the fetish — here the lady's shoe — is erotically stimulating not because of its connection with the woman's body but because of its symbolic identity as supplement for the absent phallus. Freud remarks, with ironic approval, on the efficient operation of the fetish as an object of desire. "[The fetish] is easily accessible," he says. "What other men have to woo and make exertions for can be had by the fetishist with no trouble at all."[14] Or, as in *The Tatler*, for the small trouble of strolling down Pall Mall past the shoe shop. Addison is more censorious; the blue-heeled, green lace slippers are too accessible. He wants to block the opportunity for such easy indulgence of "irregular" desires. His strategy is simple enough, for his representation of the fetish differs from Freud's in the causality it assumes. The object, the shoe, actually *creates* the irregular desires in the passerby; remove it and you remove the perversion. Aside from a kind of protobehaviorism in its logic, this "advertisement" graphically underscores the link between the management of fashion and the management of desire.

Thirty years after the publication of *Tatler* 143, Samuel Richardson writes a letter of self-justification to his physician George Cheyne, pinpointing this "Advertisement" and its logic of fetishization as the same sort of perversity that fuels misreadings of his own *Pamela*. He cannot be held responsible for this sort of twisted misconstrual of his text: "To be sure there is no Writing on these Sub-

"Woman's Shoe," England circa 1720. Multicolored silk brocade. Los Angeles County Museum of Art, M.67.8.133.

"Woman's Shoe," England circa 1770–75. Black silk satin: embroidered with yellow flowers. Los Angeles County Museum of Art, CR.268.63–66a,b.

"Woman's Shoe," France 1715–40. Pale green silk satin, silver lace, sequins. Los Angeles County Museum of Art, M.64.85.7.

jects to please such a Gentleman as that in the Tatler, who cou'd find Sex in a *lac'd shoe*, when there was none in the Foot."[15] So Richardson distances himself from, even denies, the alleged prurience of passages in his own novel. But Richardson's ingenuous disavowal of sexual provocation is unconvincing, both as it relates to *Pamela* and to the fetishistic gaze of the strolling window-shopper.

Along with the artful, seductive display of the commodity comes the promise that pleasure, comfort, and entertainment are available for the looking. As more and increasingly luxurious shops spring up in London, window-shopping becomes an pleasant pastime for the leisured classes, though, as we will see, those who *worked* in retail were often not amused. Display counters and windows were put in shops, and window-shopping evolved, full of cheap, voyeuristic thrills for the shopper, full of frustration for the shopkeeper. In this period, these "superfluous" and pleasure-oriented features of shopping are not yet wholly developed, fully exploited, nor indeed generally condoned, even by retailers. There is a debate over shopping that makes it a topic especially useful for an exploration of contemporary views on commodities and consumption.

Contests over what constitutes legitimate shopping take their place beside and in similar terms as disputes over standards of taste and fashion. While fashionable ladies and gentlemen whiled away their time on excursions to swank stores, upright tradesmen like Daniel Defoe lamented the transformation of the plain, functional shop into the mirrored, gilded, frenchified, modish resort of "women . . . fops and fools."[16] His rhetoric against spectacular retail display as feminized and irrational is a close ally of that levied in *The Tatler* and *The Spectator* against ostentatious display of all sorts, but particularly against the sensational personal exhibitions of foolish women and fops. Defoe sees no use for these high-overhead retail shops with their bow windows, mirrors, plate, crystal, and other extravagant trappings. Worse than merely expensive, this flamboyant paraphernalia is just so much frippery sure to drive away substantial patrons and attract only those worthless customers "most taken with shows and outsides."[17] Here again, as in *The Tatler* and *The Spectator*, is that commonplace assumption that susceptibility to "shows and outsides" signals mental and ethical weakness and that these flaws are constitutionally native to women and effeminate men. Only those who lack adequate resources of rationality, and, it is implied, financial resources as well, will be so taken in by the fancy shop.

Nonetheless, laments Defoe, some shopkeepers, especially those with little stock to sustain them, still try to trade on appearances. Defoe associates this sort of spurious marketing with the French, who "are eminent for making a fine outside, when perhaps within they want necessaries." "Indeed," he remarks, "a gay shop and a mean stock is something like a Frenchman with his laced ruffles, without a shirt." The English, especially, should steer clear of the French mode since they tend to "over-do the French themselves." Finally, Defoe argues, the point is moot; these retail tactics are doomed to failure and will inevitably bankrupt the modish shop.[18]

Predictably, the sober Defoe has as little patience with modish lifestyles as he does with fancy shops, and he devotes a chapter of his *Complete English Tradesman* to reviling "Extravagant and Expensive Living."[19] Defoe urges a strict distinction between the life of fashion and the life of trade:

> Trade is not a ball, where people appear in masque, and act a part to make sport; where they strive to seem what they really are not, and to think themselves best dressed when they are least known: but it is a plain visible scene of honest life, shown best in its native appearance, without disguis [*sic*] . . . A tradesman dressed up fine, with his long wig and sword [is] . . . like a piece of counterfeit money, he is brass washed over with silver, and no tradesman will take him for current.[20]

Of course, trade is becoming all of these things. Taking on the spectacular and transformative functions associated with theater and the masquerade, shops become places of pleasure as well as business. At this period when entertainment—most conspicuously the opera and the masquerade— was becoming commercialized, commerce, in turn, was becoming recreational. Defoe's attempts to segregate business from pleasure, disclosure from disguise, the legitimate from the counterfeit, trade from fashion itself speaks of the blurring of these spheres in actual practice. Mrs. Crackenthorpe, the persona of *The Female Tatler* and "a Lady that knows Everything," provides a more celebratory picture of the retail theater, one composed from the same features of display, pleasure mixed with business, fanciness and fops, but given a more complex shading of both appreciation and derision. Her narrative dramatizes how the modish shop, figured as a theater, and its foppish clerks, drawn as opera singers, take on the aura of suspect sexuality that surrounded the masquerade as well as the stage and its players.[21]

Mrs. Crackenthorpe relates her shopping trip in the *Female Tatler* for Monday, July 25, 1709.[22] Like her male counterpart, Isaac Bickerstaff, Mrs. Crackenthorpe is an acknowledged arbiter of elegance. When a group of ladies with a high "Opinion of [her] *Fancy in Cloaths*" ask her to go shopping with them at Ludgate Hill, she is happy to oblige. Mrs. Crackenthorpe sees shopping as a form of leisured entertainment, "as agreeable an *Amusement* as a Lady can pass away three or four Hours in." She appreciates the luxury Defoe condemns. It is inseparable from the fabulous delights that shopping offers: "the *Shops* are perfect *gilded Theatres*." The staging of the commodity takes place in a realm of fantasy separate from the mundane world and transforms those who participate in its pageant. Mrs. Crackenthorpe becomes queen for the day.

But exactly who or what stands center stage in these theaters — here specifically operatic theaters — is unclear. Is it the shopkeepers themselves, whom Mrs. Crackenthorpe calls "the Performers in the *Opera*. . . . the sweetest, fairest, nicest dish'd out Creatures"? The customer? Or the goods on display — the silks, brocades, velvets, satains, mohair (she calls off twenty-six types of cloth in a litany of luxurious abundance)? The reliance of opera on set design, special effects, and showy costume — that is, opera's nature as an essentially spectacular rather than dramatic form of representation — was recognized, usually critically, as soon as it was introduced from Italy in the first decade of the eighteenth century.[23] Both performer and set, both mercer and his wares, contribute to the spectacle that is the show of shopping.

A commercialized and intensely popular, indeed explicitly *fashionable* entertainment, the theater (dramatic and operatic) was a venue for display both on and off stage. In the theater two shows go on, sometimes the most compelling one in the audience (*S* 168). In the "gilded Theatre" of the fancy shop the staging of the commodity takes place in a realm of fantasy whose border with the outside world is architecturally, materially permeable. One does not only look onto but actually walks onto the boards of the shop. The line that separates the performer from his role also seems blurred here, for the mercers—"you wou'd guess 'em to be *Italians*"—live in their everyday, modish life the parts they perform in the theaters of their shop, pursuing in both arenas that masquerade of fashion that Defoe laments. Indeed, just as Defoe's criticism implies, the status of the Ludgate shops emanates in good part from the mercers' own reputations as high-stylers: "These Fellows are positively the greatest Fops in the Kingdom, they have their *Toilets*, and their *fine Night-Gowns*; their *Chocalate* in a Morning, and their *Green-tea* two hours after. *Turkey Polts* for their Dinner, and then *Perfumes, Washes,* and *clean Linen* equip 'em for the Parade." As we see in this litany of their day, the mercers' performance of prestige rests heavily on the props of fashionable consumption.

In that they are figured as Italian opera performers, egregious fops, and as neuter "Creatures," the sexual status of these shopkeepers is being questioned in serious ways. The Italian castrati were the object of much contemporary fascination and ridicule, and the association of Italy and sodomy was conventional. Bringing together the character of the fop and that of the Italian opera singer, Mrs. Crackenthorpe makes plain the emerging association between the fop and the sodomite. The Ludgate tradesman—who is anything but the stalwart, complete English tradesman of Defoe's treatise, who is in fact Defoe's worst nightmare—stands as an early instance of an emergent modern type of effeminate exclusively homosexual man, marking what Randolph Trumbach calls "the transformation of the fop into the molly." Always a character associated with women and the domestic scene, but not previously an assumedly homosexual character, the fop's effeminacy "in real life and on the stage, came to be identified with the effeminacy of the then emerging role of the exclusive adult sodomite."[24]

Here where real life and staged life blur in and out of each other across the permeable surface of the display window, where foppish mercer and Italian opera performer merge, the fashionable shop is gendered queer. The emerging modern association between effeminacy, fashion, theater, spectacle, and male homosexuality provides the context for this gendering. One basic term of this association is that hierarchy of spectator and spectacle mentioned earlier. As spectacular bodies, performers on the stage are objects of the gaze and as such feminized and sexualized bodies. Examining the eighteenth-century politics of the gaze and its attendant sexual ideology, Kristina Straub points out that "the gendering of the spectator as male and the spectacle as female seems to emerge . . . in the eighteenth century." Whereas in the Renaissance and earlier, power lay with the spectacle rather than with the spectator, this power differential begins to shift and the spectacle begins to take on its modern conventional associations as feminized, sexualized, objectified, that over which power (of the spectator) exerts itself.[25] These operatic foppish mercers, then, with their staginess and obsession with personal display are sexually and socially stigmatized by their roles in the theater of commerce. At the same time of course, retail trade itself is so stigmatized by such theatrical analogies.

So while Mrs. Crackenthorpe's depiction of the fashionable manner of the retailers makes it clear that this is an integral part of the *"gilded Theater"* she appreciates, she, like Defoe, also mocks them for it. "No Composition," she writes, "can be more ridiculous, than a Creature made up of *Beau* and *Business*." The confusion in the mercers' professional identity between the *"Beau* and *Business"* carries with it an analogue of, and perhaps a euphemism for, the ambivalence in their sexual identity, comprising both the masculine (businessman) and the effeminate (beau). As her shopping expedition shades into satire against the tradesmen for failing to maintain the distinction between fashion's "conceited Niceties" and "the Sphere of Industry," Mrs. Crackenthorpe tries to reassert a separation of commerce and fantasy. Following the gender connotations of this opposition — fanciness and fashion as feminine, business and industry as masculine — we can see here as well an attempt to sort out the sexual terms rendered ambiguous in the mercers' "ridiculous" "Composition."

Yet business and fashion are conflated not only in the "Beau of Business" and his modish shop but also in Mrs. Crackenthorpe's own shopping pleasure, though she cannot fully admit the nature of that pleasure. After she has had her fun, Mrs. Crackenthorpe restores the prudent distinction between fancy and fashion, on the one hand, and business and industry on the other. Mrs. Crackenthorpe's account of the shopping trip is strung uneasily between the quite tangible pleasure she takes in this scene of operatic, sensational, effeminate frivolity and the need to register her self-conscious disavowal of its "low" and "ludicrous" sources.

A letter to *Spectator* 336 narrates a shopping trip from a quite different perspective—not of the shopper but of a shopkeeper who signs herself "Rebecca, *the distress'd.*" Like Mrs. Crackenthorpe, Rebecca relates a speculative shopping trip—window-shopping, but her letter paints this activity in quite different colors. She complains of "female rakes" who loiter in her china and tea shop, treating it like a "Club," pulling out everything but buying nothing. They trivialize her trade and waste her time. In her distress, Rebecca asks the Spectator to publish her complaint to teach these "idle Ladies of Fashion" that shopkeepers have better things to do "than to cure Folks of the Vapours *gratis.*"

Rebecca is a victim of fashion, or at least a victim of the fashion victims who invade her shop, haul out her stock, and then leave without spending a shilling. The bothersome patrons are specifically *fashionable* women, in a bad way. They divert themselves with a kind of shopping hooliganism, "tumbling over [her] ware," stirring up a great "Racket and Clatter," and disordering "the whole agreeable Architecture" of her displays. They participate in the old aristocratic style of arrogant and destructive conduct: "These Rakes are your Idle Ladies of Fashion" (*S* 336). By calling them "rakes" the shopkeeper at once compromises the femininity and characters of these ladies; rakes are male aristocrats who misbehave in stylish ways. These female rakes may not be roistering through town breaking the windows of "Cits," but their shopping style inflicts its own cost on the city retailer. Participants in a highly conventionalized style of male conduct, these female rakes stir up gender trouble: in their masculine self-assertion they trespass the limits of feminine decency.

Rakish behavior is reprehensible along class lines as well. Not only male but also specifically aristocratic, the rake embodies codes of (mis)behavior based on assumptions of status-linked cultural privileges that the *Tatler* and the *Spectator* papers denounce as they snatch the standards of cultural and social value away from a "degenerate" aristocracy and plant them in their own ethically normative, bourgeois camp. Airing her indignation in the letter to *Spectator* 336, "Rebecca, *the distress'd*" participates in an ongoing campaign for bourgeois standards of conduct and consumption.

Fashion and class-privilege are apparent even in the ailments of the rakish ladies. Alternatively called the spleen and the vapors, this is a chic disease, associated with a leisured and refined lifestyle and part of a popular cult of sensibility. In *Spectator* 216 the vapors is referred to as "this fashionable reigning Distemper." Rebecca's letter cites this modish distemper as the proximate cause of these ladies' visit to her shop. They seek diversion from their somaticized ennui: "under pretence of . . . diverting the Spleen," they shop. The commodity cures. Much to the shopkeeper's annoyance, the healing properties of shopping are independent of any actual purchase:

> These Rakes are your Idle Ladies of Fashion, who having nothing to do, employ themselves in tumbling over my Ware. One of these No-Customers (for by the way they seldom or never buy any thing) calls for a Set of Tea Dishes, another for a Bason, a third for my best Green Tea . . . this is too dear, that is their Aversion, another thing is charming but not wanted: The Ladies are cur'd of the Spleen, but I am not a Shilling better for it: Lord! (*S* 336)

Not only the cure, but also the cause of the vapors is linked to the commodity: just as the voyeuristic shopping trip may soothe the ladies's commodity cravings and cure the vapors, so unfulfilled cravings for things may bring them on. Generated by an overstimulation of the fancy that disorders the "spirits," hysteria connects through the imagination to the commodity fetish. The "case studies" of hysteria (the vapors, the spleen) offered by "Sir John Midriff, Knt M.D." show the noxious effects that the desire for modish things — diamond rings, white damask gowns, petticoats, new china, silver spoons — had on a number of petit bourgeois wives.[26] Or rather, these cases document the effects brought on by the *disappointment* of that desire: the vapors, fainting fits, in a word hysteria. First, their husbands' promises of windfall profits elevate the ladies into ecstasies of expectation; then, when stocks fall and their hopes shatter, they sink into depression, fits, vapors, the spleen.

Sir John attributes these ladies' vapors to their sheer disappointment.[27] Though embodied and quite real, this disappointment is grounded on a fantasy, on an imaginative projection of consuming pleasures to come. They are not hysterical over the loss of anything they ever actually possessed, but over the loss of their dreams of possession. In that the possession and loss they experience are fantasies, this cause of the vapors related by Sir John Midriff, like the cure of the vapors narrated by Rebecca in *Spectator* 336, depends on the *imaginative* consumption of the commodity.

The cure, as well as the cause, of these ladies' spleen and vapors depends on the way that the commodities are fetishized. Fetishization has to do with all the nonmaterial qualities and uses of the object — mystical, fantastic, and psychosexual. As Marx puts it, fetishization involves the "metaphysical subtleties and theological niceties" of the commodity, the capacities it has to transcend its sensuous, material body.[28] In their work on economic anthropology, Mary Douglas and Baron Isherwood formulate consumption as "a ritual process" that works to order our experience in the world. As Rebecca's letter to *Spectator* 336 shows, shopping is ritualized, and like the shaman's chants, the priest's prayers, and the witch's spell, it can dispel bad spirits. The vapors, according to contemporary aetiology, was caused by a disordering of the spirits, of the passions.[29] Its symptoms of disorientation, bodily and emotional instability, and fainting are alleviated in the china and tea shop by rituals of consumption that apparently restore harmony and order to the constitution. But like everything "sacred," the rite of shopping is double-edged; its valuation as white or black magic depends on which side of the counter one stands. For the shopkeeper, rather than exorcising bad spirits, the shopping ritual of these fashionable female rakes is itself a kind of demonic possession: "I can compare 'em to nothing but to the Night-Goblins" (*S* 336).

Speculative consumption depends on the exercise of the imaginative faculties and through them has an effect on both body and spirit. Likewise the plan for the cultivation of aesthetic pleasures involves the imaginative appropriation of visually acquired objects; and like window-shopping and other forms of commodity fantasy, this aesthetic acquisition is a tonic for body and soul. In the initial essay of the series, Addison touts his pleasures of the imagination as a boon to health: "the Pleasures of the Fancy are more conducive to Health, than those of the Understanding. . . . Delightful Scenes, whether in Nature, Painting, or Poetry, have a kindly Influence on the Body as well as the Mind." Specifically, this exercise of the fancy, just like shopping, dispels the vapors by dispersing "Grief and Melancholly" and setting "the Animal Spirits in pleasing and agreeable Motions" (*S* 411).

By pointing out these correspondences, I hope to make explicit the connection between Addison's ideas of visual, imaginative possession and the models of commodity fetishism they replicate: both are ways that things get into people's heads. That Addison presents the acquisition of imaginative objects in counterdistinction to the acquisition of property speaks of the ways that the aesthetic faculties are conceived in opposition to the material and economic realms whose operations they actually mirror. Addison's plan for cultivation of the imagination is also a scheme for the acquisition and expenditure of aesthetic capital. Stocking the poet's, or the gentleman's, head with a fund of images and metaphors involves processes of objectification and imaginary consumption operative as well in the furnishing the imagination of commodity abusers—the old visiting lady, the coquette, the beau, and the female rakes. The gaze of the polite connoisseur and the modish shopping enthusiast both feed on images of things—ribbons, snuff, china, landscapes, statues, paintings, poems.

It is hardly surprising, therefore, that Addison's inquiry into the machinery of looking is inseparable from the discourse of scientific empiricism. Both the retail shop and the public repository are designed for the display of information that is predominantly visual: looking is a means for possession as well as knowledge. It is the visual faculty, after all, that "furnishes the Imagination with its Ideas" (*S* 411). In so doing, however, it also co-opts the faculty of touch, acquiring very nearly a palpable solidity. "Our Sight . . . may be considered as a more delicate and diffusive Kind of Touch," theorizes Addison, "that spreads it self over an infinite Multitude of Bodies" (*S* 411). The pleasures of the imagination are enjoyed as the pleasures of property. The "man of Polite Imagination," Addison proposes, "often feels a greater Satisfaction in the Prospect of Fields and Meadows, than another does in the Possession. It gives him, indeed, a kind of Property in every thing he sees" (*S* 411). What begins as a polemical distinction between material possession and visual meditation ends as the figurative transformation of the latter into the former, of visual and imaginative consumption into a sort of grasping imperialism. Free of temporal or spatial restrictions, the imagination roams, bringing "into our reach some of the most remote Parts of the Universe" (*S* 411). The English desire for economic mastery — taking in, mapping out, and divvying up its colonial territories — becomes its aesthetic.

The model of the productive and healthy imagination that Addison draws up is itself a kind of epitome of "good" accumulation and consumption. "Good" because purely visual and imaginative consumption is dislodged from, even as it discursively mirrors, the processes of materialist, indeed imperialist, accumulation which it stands as an alternative to. As pure spectacle the objects of the imagination are understood to transcend the contingencies of the economy itself, allowing each spectator "a kind of Property in every thing he sees" (*S* 411). In this way the polite spectator ideally acquires full control over the objects of his desire; and so the threat of a disruption in the hierarchy between the spectator and his object, between the consumer and the thing consumed, is circumvented. For Addison's project guarantees the mind's appropriation *of* objects, rather than (as is the case with the beau, the coquette, and the old woman) the mind's colonization *by* objects. The distinction, a dialectical one, depends on perceptual self-mastery. In Addison's view, control comes about through reshaping objects that have been assigned their qualities via human cognition and then subjecting these objects to rational criteria. Endowed with properties and tied to purposes beyond themselves, objects are refashioned in ways that make them seem less autonomous, all the more one's own. Addison advocates the careful containment of visual objects, the rationalist domination of imaginative pleasure, within a space that is disembodied and aestheticized. His purely mental venue stands as an alternative to both the shop and the museum collection.

THE FANTASTIC FASHION REPOSITORY

As a final exhibition of imaginative consumption, let us consider in some detail the plan for the sphinx-shaped fashion repository proposed in a letter to *Spectator* 478. In ways that are significantly analogous to, as well as crucially distinguished from, the Spectator's own projects for the proper functions of vision, imagination, commodity, and consumption, this plan suggests how commodity culture and the objectification of the imagination it entails may provide the enabling conditions for, as well as the objects of, a progressive consumption critique. Commodities, along with the processes of visual consumption and imaginative objectification they generate, are both the objects of criticism and the medium in which this criticism is conducted.

Shopping produces fantasies, but in *Spectator* 478 commodity-induced fancies are not so much disorders of the imagination as directions for the management of the things that nourish it. Here in the sphinx of fashion, fashions are incorporated into and contained by an architectural project that disciplines them. A purely speculative project, yet one with features of the fashion emporium and the museum — both quite real institutions — this plan occupies a somewhat contradictory space contiguous to Addison's imaginative realm of pleasure, the early museum, and the fashionable retail shop.

Established in the interests not only of personal adornment but also of national identity and science, the repository is connected to modern Britain's self-conscious desire to study and know itself. In order to do this, domestic as well as exotic cultures, the present and the future as well as the past are reified as objects of knowledge. The fashion repository is a place where eighteenth-century polite projectors are historicizing their own age through its commodities, its fashions.

The Shopping Trip

One day in early September 1712 two gentlemen go out shopping: one has a number of purchases to make, and the other, his friend, goes along for company. This friend, a certain "A. B." writes a letter to *The Spectator* and it is published as no. 478 on Monday, September 8.[30] A. B. gives only two sentences to the actual shopping expedition. What happens on this trip takes place more in the imagination than in the shops. A. B. tells not of purchases but of projects; what is acquired is the imaginative material for a fantastic repository of fashion.

A. B. takes little pleasure in shopping. His letter begins with a description of his embarrassment at his friend's shopping habits: "He was very nice in his Way, and fond of having every thing shewn, which at first made me very uneasy." A. B. never says exactly why this niceness makes him uncomfortable. Is he uneasy because he thinks his friend is being a pesky customer, putting the shopkeepers to all sorts of unnecessary trouble? If so, he is an anomaly; other contemporary accounts of shopping, in *The Spectator* and elsewhere, show no similar reservations about making demands on salesclerks. Perhaps A. B.'s anxiety is traceable to some sense not of his own but of his friend's shopping anxiety, in that the demanding "niceness" may be the mark of uncertainty as well as discernment.

In either case, the problem is one of making choices. The work of discrimination, the exercise of that niceness that A. B.'s friend displays, became more and more demanding with shifts in the practices and symbolic nature of consumption. The transition between the seventeenth and eighteenth centuries brought with it a major redefinition of the commodity: one historian formulates this shift as a replacement of the older standard of "patina" value by the new standard of fashion.[31] Things come to be esteemed not so much for their continuity with the past but for their novelty, for their reference to change rather than to tradition. The advance into the future starts to look like progress and the backward glance toward the past like regression. Shopping in the early eighteenth century begins to manifest its modern character as a labor-intensive activity for the harried consumer who now requires a steady supply of information (all too quickly made obsolescent) in order to decipher what messages are being transmitted by which purchases.[32]

The redefinition of value around qualities of novelty and change — that is, the installation of fashion as the dominate standard in the production and use of commodities — did not go unchallenged. There is a continual contest over what ground can be taken by fashion. Even those who, like Addison and Steele, were critical of this new standard of fashion often waged this contest through modish commodities (including the fashionable *Tatler* and *Spectator* papers). Commodities carry the information and meanings from which culture is produced; the rites of consumption help to order and make sense of life.[33] Yet this stabilizing aspect of the rituals of everyday life is only one side of the picture. Through alterations in the material practices that construct cultural meaning those meanings themselves are reformulated. The very materiality of culture is what opens it to historical change: consumption is a process that continually produces and redefines social categories.[34] Constructing their own inner and outer, physical and spiritual, worlds of value and meaning, men and women shopping in the eighteenth century were making choices in processes of consumption that are part fantasy and part material reality.

In A. B.'s letter we find a dramatized recognition of the economic, social, and even political work that fashion can do. Some, subterranean perhaps, awareness of the gravity of the task of shopping may be read in the anxiety A. B. admits as he accompanies his friend. His initial discomfort is soon replaced, however, by a kind of rapt fascination: "He was very nice in his Way, and fond of having every thing shewn, which at first made me very uneasy; but as his Humour still continu'd, the things which I had been staring at along with him began to fill my Head, and led me into a Set of amusing Thoughts concerning them" (*S* 478). As he is led into a "Set of Thoughts" about the things displayed before him, A. B. moves hurriedly from the objects themselves to the ideas they generate. Sliding precipitously from the narrative of a shopping trip to a speculative fantasy , A. B.'s account contains precious little information about the actual shops and their stock. The wealth of lovely, palpable things that the *Female Tatler's* Mrs. Crackenthorpe delights in on her shopping trip—the "Garden-Silks . . . Italian Silks, Brocades, Tissues, Cloth of Silver, or Cloth of Gold . . . Mantua Silks . . . *Geneva* Velvet, *English* Velvet, Velvets Emboss'd"—are absent from A. B.'s story. He never says exactly what his friend is shopping for or what exactly they looked at. From the conversations and speculations A. B. reports, we assume that his friend is shopping for fashionable things; but not a single *thing* is named nor a single shop identified. Whereas Mrs. Crackenthorpe's fancy seems generated directly *by* the material profusion of the shop counters, A. B.'s speculations seem to *supplant* the overlooked material goods.

That is, it appears that A. B. seeks to ease his shopping anxiety with his intellectual speculations and so to rationalize the experience of being in the market. His transition from shopper to speculative projector takes place through the field of vision: "The things which I had been staring at . . . began to fill my Head." As a "projector," or promoter of projects for sociocultural improvement, A. B. depends on the same visual acquisition of goods as does the window-shopper.[35] Things in the shops become a display not just for the potential purchaser but also for the gentleman philosopher, the middling kind of polite projector within whose ranks we also number Mr. Spectator himself. One thing A. B.'s trip to the stores shows is how the consumption of the commodity is as conceptual and imaginative as it is economic and material. Fixing his gaze on the commodity, man is consumed not simply by a desire to purchase but also by a desire to speculate and expound.

A. B. begins his thoughts with musings on the political economy of fashion. Noting the destabilizing, if generative, effect fashion has on the economy, A. B. remarks to himself "how far the Vanity of Mankind has laid it self out in Dress, what a prodigious Number of people it maintains, and what a Circulation of Money it occasions." A. B. winds up this thread of thought with a characterization of the workings of fashion on the labor market: "The Variableness of Fashion turns the Stream of Business, which flows from it now into one Channel, and anon into another; so that different Sets of People sink or flourish in their Turns by it." The quite conventional terms in which the bad economy of fashion is clothed here are powerfully charged: vanity is a sin, folly comes close, and variableness is a feminine trait that forestalls all value.

Even as he distracts himself by turning his attention inward and away from the anxiety-provoking scene before him, A. B. gives a clue to at least one source of his uneasiness: he is not entirely comfortable in the fashion market. This is a common complaint but one which he cannot make to his companion. A. B. fears that his "moral Reflections . . . might have pass'd for a Reproof" of his friend, absorbed as he is in his shopping trip. A. B. keeps these thoughts to himself and decides to "fall in with [his friend] and let the Discourse run upon the use of Fashions." The discussion that follows first looks at the way fashion works in social relations. Here it produces the same "Variableness" that mark its presence in the economic arena. This instability shows up in the social sphere as the ambivalence of fashion's status-defining capacities: because fashion marks social hierarchies it may also subvert them.

We should not underestimate the anxiety that this potential for status instability provoked in early-eighteenth-century London, where, because of recent immigrations, it was becoming more difficult to know for certain much of anything about one's fellow residents. The capitalization of agriculture and of industry, the emergence of the wage-labor market, the escalation of commercial opportunities, and the burgeoning improvement of transportation: all fed into a newly constituted urban metropolis. In more and more situations, people "knew" one another only by appearance and thus had to evaluate status and character largely on the basis of dress, manner, and accent, all of them counterfeitable.[36] Connected to this social context, distinctions between legitimate and illegitimate fashion often rest on notions of the counterfeit and the genuine, monetary terms that put in considerable time as epistemological and moral categories. The problem of money, like the problem of clothes, is one of reference: what underwrites the banknote or the suit of clothes becomes crucial to the functioning of both financial and social economies.

Richard Sennett emphasizes the provisional and theatrical nature of urban fashion practices. The purpose of street clothes, he argues, "was to make it possible for other people to act as if they knew who you were." The point was not "to be sure of whom you were dealing with, but to be able to behave as if you were sure."[37] Anonymity provides the blank site on which one might erect an identity — spurious or honest — with all the handy materials of fashion. So served by fashion's flair for dressing up, anonymity came part and parcel with social mobility in the eighteenth-century city. And although this contingent, slippery side of fashion may have been accepted and even advocated by some (Sennett cites the notoriously worldly Lord Chesterfield), the anonymity and charlatanism of the urban social scene vexed those who sought a ground for authentic identity and stable social knowledge.

The transgressive potential of fashion feeds on human vanity and folly. Clothes may counterfeit identity because people are easily taken in by false signs. They fall for appearances: "how much Man is gov-ern'd by his Senses, how lively he is struck by the Objects which ap-pear to him in an agreeable Manner." Like credit, like women, clothes too readily generate empty and perilously attractive signs se-ducing men into all sorts of regrettable responses. Taken in by a fool in fine clothes, one may pay him more attention and respect than to the "Man of Sense appearing with a Dress of Negligence."

But this evidence that clothes may deceive is offered not so much to undermine the judgments based on them as to reinforce our sense of the social and psychological gravity of fashion. While they distrust fashion's instrumentality in social and ethical misrepresentation, A. B. and his friend also conceive of a correct practice of fashion, a way of matching true value with its exterior signs and so closing the subver-sive gap between the sign and the referent. They urge even the most sober citizen to enter into a cautious transaction with fashion in or-der to live candidly in the world. The "Man of Sense" has an oblig-ation to attach to himself the sartorial insignia of his value, "that all proper Duty or Respect might attend [his] Appearance": for "a Man of Sense appearing with a Dress of Negligence, shall be but coldly received." This emphasis on the obligation of dressing up to one's character and status suggests that A. B. addresses an audience of solid, serious, middle-aged men who, out of their (admirable) lack of preoccupation with the mode, are more likely to under- than to over-dress.

The Sphinx of Fashion

Having established these fashion precepts, A. B. and his friend start to talk about the repository: "At last the Subject [of fashion] seem'd so considerable, that it was propos'd to have a Repository builded [*sic*] for Fashions, as there are Chambers for Medals and other Rarities." The building is to take the form of that ancient feminine enigma the sphinx. The sphinx serves as an emblem of fashion itself: like the sphinx, fashion threatens to devour and destroy. She is ambiguous: inconstant and prolific, speculative and material, hazardous and life-enhancing, at once irrational and open to regulation. Monstrous, hybrid, and feminine, fashion is the sphinx whose riddles must be solved by the citizens of the marketplace.

But decorated in bas-relief with curling locks, ribbons, lace, looking-glasses, powder puffs, patches, combs, and sword-knots, the sphinx's facade is updated and domesticated with the familiar signs of contemporary eighteenth-century fashion. Here, in this imaginary design for a fashion museum, as in the practices of fashion itself, the familiar and mundane are grafted onto the exotic and fantastic. Not only is the sphinx-museum an emblem of fashion but she is also herself *fashionable*, outfitted with all the paraphernalia of erotic modernity. The design for the museum replicates the body-as-fashion that we have seen on display in the anatomies of the beau, the coquette, and the old visiting lady. And as are the psyches of those fashion victims, this corporeal monument to fashion's mastery (both as the mastery of and the mastery over fashion) is packed with things. Like the painted and patched faces of fashionable ladies, the sphinx's face/facade is inscribed with cosmetic artificiality. Only the face of the sphinx is human and here that face/facade is rendered as fashion itself. We recognize, then, our own human relation to the sphinx in the glass of fashion.

The plan for this museum remains sketchy at best. There is much that we will never know. Was the museum supposed to realize the sphinx's entire body or only the facade? Where would it have been built? One wonders how such a design would alter the London cityscape. What would it look like to eighteenth-century spectators? To us it seems high kitsch; and, saturated with the flat parodies of postmodernism, we undoubtedly arrogate to ourselves a kind of superiority of irony over A. B. and his friend. But given the playful, if purposeful, tone of the proposal and the high degree of self-consciousness with which fashion is being monumentalized, we must question whether our knowing amusement is really so far removed from the responses of its architects and their early modern audience?

Contemporary fashions serve as both the contents and the package for this house of style; the outside of the building is but a decorative stencil of the interior stocked with specimens.[38] At this time, new styles for women were brought from France on fashion dolls — mannequins. In the repository, specimens of every known style are to be arrayed on fashion dolls and then labeled, boxed, and shelved "as regularly as Books in a Library." The currency of the collection is guaranteed by rule: "every one who invents a Fashion shall bring in his Box." The "inventors" will be encouraged to advertise by decorating their boxes "with some amorous or gay Device" in order to "the sooner draw the Eyes of the Beholders." Organized for easy reference, all of fashion may be called up to serve the specific purposes chartered by this project. This repository is the fruit of a discussion of the *use* of fashion. The epigraph Steele choose for the paper is the well-worn tag from Horace's *Ars Poetica* (71–72): "Usus/Quem penes Arbitrium est, & Jus & Norma" (To use belongs the judgment and law and rule.) Use, practice — what is worn — determines fashion as surely as it does language. Just as the Académie Française and, to some extent, the Royal Society sought to regulate the use of language and thus control the medium central to the conduct of life, so the fashion repository would establish its control over sociocultural life by regulating the use of fashion.

In order to "gain the Approbation of the Publick," whose interests are central to the project, A. B. and his friend provide a list of objectives. The first has as its aim the cosmetic uses of fashion. The repository is a treasure-house of style; here people may consult the holdings to find out which fashions suit them best:

> First, That every one who is considerable enough to be a Mode, and has any Imperfection of Nature or Chance, which it is possible to hide by Advantage of Cloaths, may, by coming to this Repository, be furnish'd her self . . . with the most agreeable Manner of concealing it; and . . . every one who has any Beauty in Face or Shape, may also be furnish'd with the most agreeable Manner of shewing it. (*S* 478)

While this use of fashion to flatter appearance may seem unremarkable, it is by no means a given in fashion practice. People often sacrifice their appearances to the pursuit of the mode, and much fashion journalism presents itself as a philanthropic project for the salvation of these fashion victims. To the present, liberation from slavery to fashions that are not flattering is a frequent promise of the traffic agents of style: in screaming orange letters a cover of *Glamour* (August 1992) proclaims a "NO LIES GUIDE" telling "WHEN TO BUCK THE BEAUTY TRENDS."

Serving a purpose analogous to *Glamour*'s guide, a "gentleman qualify'd with a competent Knowledge in Cloaths" would be employed at the repository to direct visitors to the styles appropriate for each. As a distributor of information about fashion, the repository takes on some of the functions of both the shopping trip and the social visit. Since neither fashion magazines nor fashion plates were yet produced in England, people depended heavily on fashion news gathered by visiting shops and each other. They could see the latest in textiles at the mercer's shop; but for the cut of clothes, the style, they relied heavily on looking at and hearing about what other people were wearing. The other major source of intelligence about the latest feminine styles was the (invariably French) fashion doll. Yet at this time, while England was at war with France, French dolls became a rare luxury, forbidden by embargo. In January 1712 at least one contraband effort was successful: "'I was almost in Despair of ever more seeing a Model from that Country,'" writes an ecstatic female correspondent to *Spectator* 277, "when last *Sunday* I overheard

. . . [that in] *King-street Covent-garden* there was a *Mademoiselle* completely dressed just come from *Paris*."

Stocked with dolls dressed in specimens of every style, the fashion repository would provide public access to scores of them. The domestic production would liberate the English from their reliance on French fashion, an ongoing campaign waged by *The Tatler* and *The Spectator*. Mr. Spectator dreads as much as he desires the end of the War of the Spanish Succession because it would mean the lifting of embargoes against French fashions: "What an Inundation of Ribbons and Brocades will break in upon us? What Peals of Laughter and Impertinence shall we be exposed to? For the Prevention of these great Evils, I could heartily wish that there was an Act of Parliament for Prohibiting the Importation of *French* Fopperies" (*S* 45).[39] And the second objective of the repository centers on the nationalistic goal of promoting English fashion. Noting how "the Ballance of fashion in *Europe* . . . now leans upon the side of *France*," A. B. and his friend propose to change this. Standing in the center of the universe of style, their repository would set all standards for fashion and so give to England the ascendancy in her ongoing fashion war with France. It would then "become as common with *Frenchmen* to come to *England* for their finishing stroke of Breeding, as it has been for *Englishmen* to go to *France* for it" (*S* 478). This proposal suggests that it is as much in England's interest to regulate the balance of fashion as it is to regulate the balance of trade. The two are intertwined, and "balance" in the mouth of the Englishman usually means not equity with France but dominance over her.

It is artificial to isolate English objections to French fashions from more global antagonism to the French — their government, their religion, their commercial and colonial ambitions. These prejudices may have actually guided English taste, especially in men's clothes. On a broad register of style, (prerevolutionary) eighteenth-century French costume held closely to the stiff formality of court dress, while English fashion moved toward a more relaxed, comfortable, and "natural" costume of the leisured country life.[40] This new style of relaxed informality influenced manners as well as clothes. *The Spectator* approves of this new trend in terms that, if not explicitly anti-French, are unmistakably anti-Papist: "Conversation, like the *Romish* Religion, was so encumbered with Show and Ceremony that it stood in need of a Reformation. . . . The Fashionable World is grown free and easie . . . Nothing is so modish as an agreeable Negligence" (*S* 119). Again and again, (bad) fashion is the (French/Papist) tyrant whose hold is broken by the restoration of reformed English taste.[41]

The ascendancy of French style dates to Louis XIV's fabulous tyranny of consumption. As one historian puts it, "Louis XIV transformed consumption into a method of rule."[42] His was a tyranny of fashion in the most complete sense. Full of artificial light and reflective surfaces, Versailles's Hall of Mirrors set the pattern for all that was most exquisite, luxurious, and sensational in contemporary design. In utter contrast, the private apartments where the aristocrats lived at court kept the style of the dark ages—dim, dank, dirty, and cramped. Life at Versailles reflects on a large scale the same overinvestment in exterior show at the expense of personal comfort (and personal hygiene) that marks Defoe's stereotypical Frenchman who flaunts "his laced ruffles" though he goes "without a shirt."[43] Addison describes the allegorical figure of artistic Vanity as "dressed like a *Frenchman*" and the figures from his paintbrush as all "*Petit Maîtres, and . . . Coquets*": "The Drapery of his Figures was extreamly well suited to his Faces, and was made up of all the glaring Colours that could be mixt together; every part of the Dress was in a Flutter, and endeavoured to distinguish it self above the rest" (*S* 83). In England, zealous pursuit of fashion was identifiably a "French" characteristic and could imply complicity with all that was wrong with the French, including the absolutist ideology of the ancien régime.

Pursuing its simultaneously nationalistic and scientific aspirations, the fashion repository mimics institutions like the Académie Française and the Royal Society. Accordingly, the third proposal is for the repository's specifically academic, even scientific, function. Here would be material data for future generations of scholars who would no longer have to depend on texts for their understanding of fashion history. As a site for empirical verification of fashions, this institute would advance the study of costume. As things stand in

1712, historians still depend on outdated scholastic methods: A. B. notes how "several great Scholars, who might have been otherwise useful to the World, have spent their time in studying to describe the Dresses of the Ancients from dark Hints." These dark, textual hints are worse than a waste of time; they are positively misleading. A purely textual approach leads to a reliance on the most fallacious sort of etymological analysis and could "perswade the Age to come, that the Farthingal was worn for cheapness, or the Furbeloe for warmth."[44] As a progressive institution, one of the aims of the repository is to insure that modernity will be better preserved than antiquity. The fashion repository represents, however fancifully and even satirically, a use of progressive institutions and scientific technologies to advance knowledge about modernity itself.

Fashion can speak for itself and clear up the inaccuracies generated by both text and prejudice. As it ages and sours, each generation considers the next as unprecedented in its degenerate capitulation to luxury. By providing material evidence that the past generation pursued fashion just as extravagantly as the present, that "it might have been as expensive in Queen *Elizabeth's* Time only to wash and quill a Ruff, as it is now to buy Cravats or Neckhandkerchiefs [*sic*]," the repository would hush the complaints of the old against the profligacy of the young. Again, this fourth benefit of the repository, like the third, is to the advantage of youth and modernity over age and antiquity.

As we see in the plans for its design and function, one model for the repository is a library. Its plan draws as well on cabinets of curiosities, or as they are called here, "Chambers for Medals and other Rarities." The repository shares with these early museums, and with the retail shop, this function of housing, arranging, and displaying things. Indeed, the term *repository* was in the eighteenth century a "euphemism" for *shop*, especially for a store dealing in "fancy draperies, haberdasheries, or other special articles."[45] This last usage of *repository* extends the semantic field of the term in ways particularly suitable to *The Spectator's* repository of fashion, where people may "window-shop" to their hearts' content.

There are broad and deep connections between these new resorts of retail and the cabinet collections of fine and curious objects. Both gather together things from all over the world, and indeed both are historically products of the expansion of trade and development of technologies throughout the sixteenth and seventeenth centuries.[46] Both are resorts of visual entertainment. Appropriately, the East India Company had its own repository of curiosities in London and, along with the Royal African Company, was a corporate sponsor of the Royal Society repository.[47] The Royal Society's collection of specimens of natural history, art, ethnography, and technology is probably the closest model for A. B.'s fashion museum. Housed at Gresham College from the 1660s until 1712, it was one of the earliest institutional collections.[48] The Royal Society repository would have been prominent in the public eye at this time because a new gallery for the collection had been completed only four or five months before. This building was designed by Christopher Wren and may be his last.[49]

The influx of exotica, curiosity, and luxury did more than enrich material life; it simultaneously expanded geographic and conceptual horizons, changing ideas about what the world is made of. More specifically, it changed England's notion of itself. In *Spectator* 69 Addison emphasizes how things imported to England are incorporated into the natural, urban, and domestic landscape and alter the face of the nation. All wants supplied through perfectly equitable redistribution in a world of uniform abundance, England enjoys in good conscience the world of commodities washed up on her shores: "Our rooms are filled with Pyramids of *China*, and adorned with the Workmanship of *Japan*. . . . [We] repose our selves under *Indian* canopies. . . . Our Eyes are refreshed with the green Fields of *Britain*, at the same time that our Palates are feasted with Fruits that rise between the Tropicks" (*S* 69). The commodified domestic and pastoral English landscape described here could seem hybrid and unnatural were the connotative values shifted slightly. The domestication of the foreign and exotic can easily flip-flop into a denaturalization and alienation of the familiar and domestic.[50]

Changing the face of the nation, these things change as well the face and figure of the individual Englishman. At this time English fashion is peculiarly foreign. Although most cloth worn by the English was domestically produced, almost all fashionable textiles were imported: "The single Dress of a Woman of Quality is often the Product of an hundred Climates" (*S* 69).[51] Of course, dress consists of much more than fabric, and in the early eighteenth century the modish woman carried a "Muff and Fan . . . from different Ends of the Earth [probably respectively from Canada, or perhaps Russia, and then China or perhaps Japan]." She wore a scarf "sent from the Torrid Zone" and a tippet "from beneath the Pole." Going to the ends of the earth was not enough; stylish dress required as well precious metals and gems delved from its depths: the silver of the brocade petticoat "rises out of the Mines of *Peru*, and the Diamond Necklace out of the Bowels of *Industan*" (*S* 69). Addison celebrates this sartorial extravagance; mapping out the stylish woman, he creates a glorious emblem of the beneficial, harmonizing effects of England's international commerce. Ordered, indeed stylized—the loot of empire is aestheticized. The harmony of the woman's costume mirrors the utopia of perfectly balanced trade that Addison represents in *Spectator* 69. Like the repositories housing the spoils of the new worlds, the fashionable woman exhibited England's commercial prowess in a carefully arranged presentation of luxury goods. The erection of the museum, like the outfitting of the fashionable lady, ties into the rise of Britain's commercial and cultural imperialism; fashion becomes a mode for the expression of nationalistic, as well as personal, identity.

But the early modern museum was by no means exclusively concerned with the remote or even the rare. There was as well a passion for collecting one's own world. This interest probably had several sources. The discovery of new worlds changed the western European concept of itself; it relativized it to a certain extent and generated the beginnings of comparative cultural studies. So exploration led to new interest in things at home and to collections of local natural history, of artifacts from one's own history and of contemporary technological advances—such as optic glasses and microscopes.[52] Another, more medieval impulse fed into this collecting passion. Early collections often showed an encyclopedic bent; some seemed to have as their object a sort of concretely embodied universal history of the world.[53] By having everything, man could know everything.

Something like this reasoning motivates Thomas Sprat's thoughts on the Royal Society's collection. The aim of the Society was the advancement of knowledge; Sprat thought this would best be served by an encyclopedic collection of things. He describes how the fellows "have already drawn together into one Room, the greatest part of all the several kinds of things, that are scatter'd throughout the *Universe*."[54] So Sprat's conception of the repository operates on the same logic as Addison's visual faculty, bringing together within (at least visual) grasp "the remote parts of the Universe" (*S* 411). In order to fulfill its dream of utter comprehension, such a collection would gather within its compass the not-so-remote parts of the universe as well. In a collection of everything, the mundane, familiar, and domestic necessarily have a place. Referring to Sprat's vision (and it remained just that) for the Royal Society Repository, Michael Hunter discusses this early modern scientific aspiration "to construct a universal taxonomy which would accurately mirror the order of nature" and points to its relation to that other impossible dream pursued by a Royal Society fellow—John Wilkins's project for a universal language.[55]

A. B. and his companion share with Sprat and Wilkins their universal, encyclopedic desires; they want their repository to mirror the universal order of fashion by collecting and preserving specimens of *every* style. The whole cosmos of style could be encompassed within the interior of the sphinx and there organized, cataloged, contained. Through collection comes possession comes knowledge comes power. In true Foucauldian manner, the repository controls fashion by establishing itself as the clearinghouse for information about fashion: this information determines what fashion *is*. As Douglas Crimp notes in an essay on museums and modernism, along with the asylum, the clinic, and the prison, the museum is an institution that disciplines and confines.[56] On the one hand, the architectural identification of the repository with the sphinx alludes to the dark enigma and threat of fashion. Yet, on the other hand, the repository's institutional, rationalizing aspirations speak of the scientific confidence that these same dangers can be managed. In the sphinx, fashion is possessed and *known*—its riddles solved and rationalized.

Tensions, however, remain. Even as it contains the sphinxlike mystery and danger of fashion, the museum is also contained in and by the sphinx. The systematic ordering of fashion takes place within a feminine, monstrous body. The production of knowledge remains inextricably wrapped up in the riddle that, finally, is its inexplicable origin.[57] The attempt to reduce the fashion system to the linear and progressive system of the historical museum produces contradictions that may complicate our understanding of both fashion and the museum.

As institutions devoted to preservation, historicization, and stability, museums would seem to be diametrically opposed to fashion, focused as fashion is on fleeting novelty, the present, and change. But, as Richard Altick documents, early modern collections depended just as fashion did on the charms of novelty.[58] People were attracted to these assemblages of things, as they were attracted to other fashionable resorts and commodities, because they offered marvelous novelties. Indeed, in the eighteenth century, museums themselves were novel institutions frequented by the leisured and curious in much the same manner as they visited the theater, pleasure gardens, or the newly outfitted retail shops. Furthermore, as a regulator of taste, the sphinx-shaped museum itself becomes fashionable and indeed circular in its functions. Potentially, the fashion museum would have a hand in the design, and so the production, of the very objects that it is established to document. The museum collection is invested in fashion and fashionability in ways that suggest that the production of the object is inextricable from the production of knowledge about that object.

Does the museum capture fashion in its system or is it captured by fashion's system? Are the two institutions related in ways that are mutually informative? Just as the museum's investment in fashion threatens to disrupt its rationale, so its historicizing, stabilizing order seems to alter the nature of its contents. Buried in the museum, anything that is collected would seem to immediately lose its status as fashion;

yet, outside the walls of the museum (as within), styles also quickly lose their fashionability. Internment in the dustbins of an ever-accelerating history or internment on the dusty shelves of the museum— both wrench style from the instant between the present and the future that is the twinkling of fashion. But the idea of fashion as a theoretical machine being driven relentlessly forward by the intermeshing gears of obsolescence and novelty is misleading. Fashion's apparent logic is only a cover for what is more often a repetitive cycle of recirculation. In recalling its own past, fashion becomes itself its own museum of style.[59]

THE FASHION REPOSITORY PROJECT IN CONTEXT

I see in A. B.'s letter to *Spectator* 478 a program for the containment and regulation of one particularly high-profile set of things—the fashion commodity. As such, it seems in line with the Spectator's own projects for rational and normative reform of fashion practices. Because the repository is generated by the commodities on display before the gaze of the polite projector A. B., it is all wrapped up in the same the fantastic, fetishized commodity it would contain and regulate. And this ambivalence is also something A. B.'s project shares with the *Spectator* and the *Tatler* papers. But what is Steele's reading, as Mr. Spectator, of the project he publishes in no. 478? Specifically, does he recognize in it aims affiliated to his own?

Most of the aims of the fashion repository are in line with the subordination of fashion to uses beyond itself, a line toed by Addison and Steele. But how seriously are these uses of fashion taken, by the projector A. B. and by Mr. Spectator? Of course A. B.'s project is presented as a fanciful conceit, a playful project. In his editorial response to A. B.'s letter, Steele plays along by proposing with parodic gravity that a corporate board be established to oversee the administration of this eminent institution. But the satiric cartoon Steele sketches of those eligible for appointment to the board exposes his low estimation of the project itself. He laments that those best suited for this office, the "Old Beaus" are almost extinct, and so selection must descend to the pool of modern fops. Here we have the satiric convention of entropic decline: even men of fashion aren't what they used to be. These modern fops spend their lives in passive and pointless compliance to fashions they do not necessarily even like. Presumably, the old beaus cultivated distinctive styles, signatures of themselves, in counterdistinction to the new generation of fops who are mere "Time-Servers" of fashion. Responsive only to their own terror of being out of fashion, modern men of fashion exhibit the same spineless fluctuation in both their dress and their ethics. Their nearly vicious fickleness qualifies them for a lifetime of service to fashion:

> Such, also, who from Facility of Temper, and too much Obse-quiousness, are vitious against their Will, and follow Leaders whom they do not approve, for Want of Courage to go their own Way, are capable Persons for this Superintendency. Those who are loth to grow old, or would do any thing contrary to the Course and Order of Things out of Fondness to be in Fashion, are proper Candidates. (S 478)

So Steele countenances the project only as an "ingenious Method" for quarantining these fashion casualties off from the rest of society. Steele represents the repository as a kind of prison for the criminally fashionable. The board of directors are also the inmates. Steele would collect together in the repository not only fashion but also the fashionable, and not because they are valuable but because they are worthless. Anyone who knows enough about fashion to qualify for a job at this institution is presumed to be its victim.

Dismissing it as a flight of ridiculous, if amusing, fancy, Steele reads the proposal as satire and so shuts down the museum of fashion. He mocks the modishness the institution, yet never addresses its po-tentials as a historical institution that could reclaim fashion for other, laudable ends. Steele's mocking response may simply be in line with his reading of the letter as a satire on the very project it proposes, a familiar game and one best known from Swift's *Modest Proposal*. Still, even if it is framed as a satire on itself, the repository nonetheless builds fashion up and unfolds its potentials in a fascinating amalgam of institutional aims and architectural styles.

The parodic context of the project which Steele's response affirms is linked to its complicity with fashion: saturated with fashion, the project can only be a joke. A. B. can only be playing with those big ideas of historical and national interest: the joke lies precisely in the incongruity between fashion and the museum. As if anyone would ever think fashion worthy of museum preservation! So while the nationalistic, pedagogical, and in every sense reformative and progressive aims of the project have much in common with Mr. Spectator's own programs, because they are quite literally institutionalized in and through fashion in a way that, to Steele's mind, ridiculously exalts fashion, the project cannot be read as anything but a satire on fashion.

THREE

Lady Credit and the Strange Case of the Hoop-Petticoat

⊲⊳

THE STRANGE HOOP-PETTICOAT

O Garment, heavenly wide! thy spacious Round
Does my astonish'd Thoughts almost confound.

THE HOOP-PETTICOAT *(1736)*

Mr. Spectator, I must needs tell you there are several of your Papers
I do not much like. You are often so Nice there is no enduring you,
and so Learned there is no understanding you. What have you to do
with our Petticoats? Your Humble Servant, *Parthenope.*

SPECTATOR *140*

Protesting the public display of green and blue slippers, anatomizing the beau's lace- and snuff-crammed brain, publishing the plan for A. B.'s fashion repository—*The Tatler* and *The Spectator* again and again take on the fantastic fashion commodity (*T* 143; *S* 275; *S* 478). Patches, powdered wigs, tricorn hats, buckled shoes, and hoop-skirts, these are the sartorial signs of the eighteenth century. In the twentieth-century imagination, a definitive image of this culture is that of Marie Antoinette, patched, powdered, and hooped, in big hair and bigger skirts.[1] In a 1938 MGM film, costume designer Andre decked out Norma Shearer as the doomed, hooped queen and unveiled her to a hungry, depression-racked America that could feast on the spectacle of luxury and on the spectacle of its ruin.[2]

In America, images of the eighteenth century have been produced not only by Hollywood but also in large part by the historical theme park at Williamsburg, Virginia. Memories of childhood vacations there are stocked with a deftly displayed material culture. In Williamsburg the retailing of the eighteenth century banks on what may be the strongest bond between early and late modernity—a life ever more dominated by the markets that sustain it. Yet this ground of sameness serves as an usually invisible support for an entertaining spectacle of difference. Reproducing the things of the age in all their irrefutable materiality, Williamsburg produces a fabulous and tactile eighteenth century, at once mesmerizing in its exoticism and insistent in its authenticity. The attraction of the *really* different is strong. Consumption opens the gate to a kind of time travel; commodification is the magic carpet. Unfolding this tangible fantastic world of our past in ways that enhance rather than diminish the fantasy, guides and guidebooks, shops re-created and mansions restored play on our temporal parochialism. Williamsburg rematerializes the past, beaming it down onto a twentieth-century landscape quite prepared to take it on in the spirit of enlightening enterprise. Our attraction to the novelty of the antique and, complementing this, to the familiarity of the commodity make the trip into the eighteenth century a smooth one. Whether we travel on the thoroughfares of popular entertainment, on the byways of antiquarianism and connoisseurship, or along the shaded lanes of the academy, the eighteenth centuries we reach are mutually recognizable. Whether celebrated as the realization of truly civilized life or deplored as the poison fruit of barbarous exploitation, the external, material forms of eighteenth-century life have an equal hold on the tourist, the collector, and the historian. Manners of Byzantine complexity, preternaturally white powdered heads, excruciatingly small waists, and preposterously proportioned hoops—all

"Movie Costume for Norma Shearer in MGM Production of *Marie Antoinette*," by Gilbert Adrian. Gray chiffon, silver lamé, silver passementerie, silver sequins, silver bugle beads, and transparent paste stones. Los Angeles County Museum of Art, M.86.237a,b.

paint a picture of a culture governed by standards of artifice and formality that we see as almost irretrievably distant from our own. Our eighteenth century becomes a place of aestheticized formality and commonplace extravagance, life there a kind of Zen of decorum whose excess of order becomes part of the general surplus of style.[3]

Within this construction, the hoop becomes a rich icon of eighteenth-century life and, most importantly, of the distance between that life and our own. Huge, complex, expensive, immuring the body, the hoop seems a kind of cage that traps women. Navigating the contraption—through doors, into chairs and coaches, up stairs, and down narrow streets—demanded considerable skill and work. Clearly the hoop got in the way. Yet the fashion lasted for almost a hundred years, waxing and waning through permutations of breadth and dimension. Epitomizing the quixotic tenacity of fashion itself— neither convenient, comfortable, economical, nor by many accounts even attractive—the hoop held on in the face of practical difficulty and outright attack to become a sartorial symbol central to the iconography of the eighteenth century. Why the hoop? becomes a core question in the study of eighteenth-century culture.

Why the hoop? is a question eighteenth-century cultural critics asked. Though to us it may serve as a perfectly integral emblem for the high artifice of the ancien régime, the hoop was never naturalized, never completely acculturated. A stranger in its own land, from its first appearance in England around 1708 the hoop was decried by some, including Addison, as a perverse interloper. Or perhaps it was acculturated in a way, but only as a sign of the alien. Identified with the feminine, most specifically with illicit female reproduction, with the excessive and the fantastic, with the most uncurbed onslaught of fashion's flood, the hoop is often represented as a kind of exoticism in the midst of eighteenth-century life. "O Garment, heavenly wide! thy spacious Round / Does my astonish'd Thoughts almost confound," exclaims an anonymous poet in 1736 with a bewilderment as stylized as the fashion to which it is a response.

One finds the hoop in a place as strange as paradise. Off in the South Pacific, on tropical islands far from the hue and cry of fashion, Captain Cook and his crew stop in Tahiti on their third voyage. At their departure they are presented with gifts. Wrapped in yards and yards of bark-cloth, a young Tahitian woman, a walking bolt of fabric, comes to the ships in this traditional gift-giving costume.[4] A remarkable sight to Western eyes, yet they had all seen something like it before. Cook's journalist gives readers back home a good idea of this exotic costume by comparing it to the familiar "circular hoop-peticoat [sic]."[5] The 1790 edition of the *Voyages* supplies an engraving that confirms the likeness. Its hooplike form reaching high up above the waist, the Tahitian outfit bears a close resemblance to the last phases of the hoop in English court dress at the turn of the nineteenth century. Here the high waist of the new, classically allusive *empire* fashion was awkwardly combined with the formal hoop.[6] Constructed by a great quantity of cloth wrapped and folded around the woman, the Tahitian gift-costume is actually hoopless; yet it is hooplike. The hoop is evoked to clarify the image of the exotic native in the minds of the British reader. Precisely because it was an alien in their midst, the hoop is useful to the writer as he tries to establish a connection between home and the unknown, between Europeans in hoops and Tahitians in bark-cloth.

The exoticism of the hoop does not so much measure our distance from the eighteenth century as confirm our relation to it. This relation is based not on any empathetic understanding of the hoop we may cultivate but on that very lack of sympathy for and understanding of the hoop that we share with its contemporaries. Any distance that the hoop measures between the eighteenth century and the present is also a gap that estranged eighteenth-century culture from itself. Far from obscuring the eighteenth-century's perception of itself, these distances of estrangement are critical distances that foster specifically modern forms of self-consciousness and cultural self-awareness.

In the early eighteenth century the appearance of the hoop-petticoat gave rise to a good deal of speculation, often satiric, always fascinated. Although the hoop's similarity to the older farthingale is often noted, it is also clear that there is no organic, continuous evolution between the one and the other. The hoop sprung forth in England around 1708; the farthingale hadn't been worn there for four generations.[7] This discontinuity supported representations of the hoop as something sui generis, a prodigy, even a monster of sorts. With no rational history, the hoop gave rise to myths, like the story in the 1748 "Heroi-comical" poem *The Hoop-Petticoat*, which narrates the tale of Venus's gift of the hoop to a jilted coquette. The hoop was but one (though particularly emblematic) element in a sar-

"A Young Woman of Otaheite bringing a Present," from *A Collection of Voyages round the World performed by Royal Authority. Containing a complete Historical Account of Captain Cook's First, Second, Third and Last Voyages*, 5 vols. (London, 1790), vol. 5, facing page 1552.

torial life whose artifice, discomfort, and formality were fully appreciated by contemporaries. Modern fashion, rhymes an anonymous poet in 1733, is a sadistic dictator:

> O're yon poor Nymph, how Tyrant like you [Fashion] reign!
> From the free use of her own Limbs restrain;

> And every Part with unseen Fetters chain.
> Her Hands are Shackl'd and her Legs are ty'd;
> Close pinion'd down her Arms on either Side.[8]

Fashion's imperatives impose an artificiality shown here as positively crippling: style is contortion. There is a strong streak of prurience in this passage: the fetishized female becomes the object of an implicitly s/m gaze. This single image of a woman in fashion's bondage supports a contradiction prevalent in the sentimentalized and rationalized erotic discourse of the eighteenth century: softly sentimental representations of benevolent sympathy are all tied up with images of the tortured bodies and anguished psyches that elicit them. It is not clear that the pleasures of pity are separable from the darker delights of pain. The passage here reproduces this contradictory duplicity between benevolent sympathy and sadism: as it projects an image of the narrator as a rational, sympathetic man who can recognize and so liberate women from the shackles of fashion, it simultaneously fuels a sadistic desire that lingers over the images of bondage and torture that motivate the principled rejection of fashion. Dissociated from male desire, the darker side of this eroticism is displaced onto fashion. Such tactics are conventional; fashion becomes a scapegoat for masculine anxieties about femininity and sexuality.

And, as the petticoat mythographer shows, the hoop was a real fashion natural, perfectly adaptable to the extreme styling of the fine ladies of the eighteenth century. As such it becomes the particular target of masculine antifashion satire, which is also usually misogynist satire against autonomous female desire. So Lucinda, the heroine of the 1748 "Heroi-comical" poem, puts on her hoop-petticoat and sallies forth in full effect:

> And practices a Thousand killing Airs;
> Each look, each gesture she refines with Toil,
> And learns with Art to force the studied Smile.
> Encompass'd now within her sev'n fold Shield
> The Female Warrior issues to the Field.[9]

Armed with her attitude and her petticoat, Lucinda is presented as an Amazon, and she is on a love campaign. She's got the power and she gets her beau, rocking along in her hoop, breaking hearts and china: "And Chairs and tables in her Haste o'erthrew; / Huge China Vessels issu'd on the Ground, / Here Jars and Tea-Cups mingl'd with the Slain."[10] Women in hoops are pushy and shamelessly conspicuous—"Ten thousand Eyes were fixt on her alone."[11] Puffing her up with irresistible powers of sexual attraction, the hoop gives Lucinda the advantage in the battle between the sexes. She comes out on top, exultant over the defenseless Lysander.

Such female erotic power lies at the core of masculine anxiety about and disapproval of the hoop. The hoop is the instrument of Venus, but of an illegitimate Venus. Through it women get some control over their own sexuality not simply because, as in the poem, it guarantees successful seduction but also because the hoop can serve as a shield to hide illicit pregnancy: "What wonders dost thou show? What Wonders hide? / Within the Shelter of thy useful Shade, / The pregnant *Flora* passes for a Maid."[12] In these ways, the hoop is dangerous because it allows women to control the expression and effects of their own sexual desire.

The hoop passed on to its progeny, the crinoline, its always baffling, irrational, and usually disreputable character. Inspired by the sheer weirdness of the crinoline, in his *Chats on Costume* early-twentieth-century fashion raconteur Rhead Woolliscroft tries to recapture the magic in a lineup of jarring similes:

> It has been said that Milton was a man from his birth. The crinoline, like Milton, is an exception to every law of development. It had, like Milton, neither infancy nor adolescence, but sprang full armed, like "Athene from the train of Zeus," or perhaps, like Topsy in "Uncle Tom's Cabin," it was never born, but just "growed"—and it grew—like a mushroom . . . in a night.[13]

Like Milton, like Athene, like Topsy, and like a mushroom: Woolliscroft hops in despair from one figure to another. He seems unsure how to talk about the crinoline. Yet this inexplicability seems part of the nature he is trying to portray. Certainly his simile sampling follows a common groove: there is no explaining the crinoline. Colored and contrary, the crinoline, if not an outlaw, is outside the law.

But early psychologist of clothes J. C. Flugel understands the deeper laws that drive women into crinolines, laws of desire for feminine dignity, presence, and power. "Indeed," Flugel notes, "the crinoline has been looked upon as a symbol of female domination."[14] Provocative of masculine anxiety and aggression, fashions that serve female desires for autonomy and power historically have been condemned as irrational and dismissed or suppressed. It is precisely as an agent of these desires, as an instrument of woman's resistance to patriarchal imperatives, that the hoop is condemned at Bickerstaff's bar in *Tatler* 116. And in these terms, the hoop may be read as a kind of emblem of the wide field of consumption itself. For consumption, especially fashionable consumption, offered to women an arena of empowerment that accommodated in a positive way what Michael Warner calls their "specificity of difference."[15] As such, female consumption, like female sexuality, becomes an object of masculine dread and repression. In their hoops women, it is feared, evade the rationalizing, paternal regulation that Addison and Steele (for example) seek to institute through their papers.

Thus we see that the discussion and final "trial" of the hoop-skirt staged in *The Tatler* works to appropriate and direct the practice of female fashion in ways consistent with the domestic female roles prescribed by bourgeois gender ideology. In the threat of the hoop we see one instance of how fashionable consumption and display may empower women, here specifically by affording them greater sexual autonomy and larger claims on social space. Addison's trial of the hoop is staged as a redemptive return of woman to her natural form, her natural self, a salvation of woman from the distorting and alienating fancies of the tyrant fashion. It is crucial not to fall into what may be seen as the modern analogue to this sort of redemptive logic: that is, to view women in hoops as passive victims of capitalism's injunction to consume fashionable commodities. Women, as we can see in satires against the hoop, profit from the armor and potential for concealment afforded by the fashionable hoop. And, as we will see, it is not as consumers per se that Addison objects to women in hoops, but as consumers whose choices encourage female autonomy and power.

This is not to deny the connections between femininity, fashion, and capitalism actively at work in antihoop satire. Indeed, the hoop serves as a symbolic analogue of exactly those (inevitably feminized) forces of caprice and, especially, ungovernable *reproduction* that men fear in their economy. Overdetermined as an object of masculine anxiety by its explicit associations with both sexuality and fashionable consumption, the hoop, like the sphinx, is a symbol of the monstrous, grotesque female, an aspect of that "grotesque consuming body" which the emergent institutions of bourgeois culture seek not to banish but to incorporate through their civilizing discipline.[16]

FEMALE TROUBLE: WOMEN, FASHION, CREDIT, AND DOMESTIC STABILITY

In *Tatler* 116 Addison as Bickerstaff, Censor of Britain, adjudicates woman's property—her hoop, a commodity on the fashion market—and through this legislates woman herself, a commodity on the marriage market. This scene of fashion on trial establishes broad connections between woman and fashion: both are unstable and irrational, and so in need of masculine, rational direction. The characteristics that connect fashion and women are ones that both share with contemporary allegorical representations of Lady Credit. Fashion, women, and credit are embedded in a shared symbolic matrix: thinking about and representing them involves a good deal of analogy and sheer overlap. One common trait that contributes to the representation and regulation of all three is their hysterical instability. As we will see in Addison's depiction in *Spectator* 3, like so many of her contemporaries in the beau monde, Credit is a hysteric, and her devotees, the market speculators, are victims of the vapors—itself a peculiarly *fashionable* complaint. All suffer from an overactive fancy and disordered imagination. The natures of woman and fashion are marked by the whimsical caprice, arbitrary change, and addictive involvement that characterize credit. And Credit is a woman on the verge of a nervous breakdown. Coming to the rescue in their rhetorical guises of physician, censor, and judge, Addison and Steele draw up directions for natural women, sensible fashions, and stable credit—all important instruments for the reproduction and representation of bourgeois ascendancy.

We find in Bickerstaff's "court" a masculine regulation that works through his refashioning of the modish, fantastic, hooped female body. Stripping her of this "unnatural" encumbrance, Bickerstaff returns woman to "nature" by replacing her hoop with a rational mode of dress. He cuts her down to size and brings her back to her senses. Liberated from slavish submission to the tyrant fashion, the woman is free — free to go home. Crucial to modern alignments between the public, external, and artificial on the one hand, and, on the other, the private, internal, and natural, the female body becomes the focal point for a reorganization of the domestic, and with it the public, sphere. More than mere fashion is on trial in Bickerstaff's court. In order to get some sense of the stakes of this confrontation between the sober judge and the insolent hoop, it is useful to look briefly at the revision of and revaluation of the domestic sphere under way at the turn of the century. Women were central to this cultural shift and their nature, female nature, underwent considerable reconstruction in its course. Popular periodicals were active sites of these cultural formulations, especially those like *The Tatler* and *The Spectator* that targeted women as a dominant segment of their audience.

Commodities on the marriage and prostitution markets, consumers on the commodity markets, denied full enfranchisement yet full of potent reproductive powers, women occupy a peculiar place in Western culture as both subjects and objects in networks of exchange. The relation of women to *The Tatler* and *The Spectator* mirrors this doubled character. The papers are oriented toward women in every sense: women are objects they scrutinize and produce and subjects who read and consume them. Women are named as the most direct target of Addison and Steele's reformative projects: "there are none to whom this Paper will be more useful, than to the female World" (*S* 10). And in their reliance on and exploitation of women these papers are typical. Kathryn Shevelow shows how many early periodicals depended on women both as cultural signs with which to write their reformative schemes and as audiences to whom to sell them.[17] Women were central to the ideologies of these projects that both promoted and contained women's involvement with print culture.[18] So valuable was access to a female sensibility and audience that Thomas Baker, offering a female counterpart to the Bickerstaff persona, masquerades as a "Mrs. Crackenthorpe, *a Lady that knows every thing*" when he writes his *Female Tatler* (1709).[19] In a bid for authenticity that calls to mind the Betty Crocker ad campaign of the mid-twentieth century, Baker even commissions an engraved portrait of the fictional lady, and this is soon printed in the heading of each paper.

Just as Baker uses "Mrs. Crackenthorpe" to put a pretty face on his own masculine supervision, female involvement in the papers was often manipulated in ways that dodge, rather than foster, female autonomy. As the periodicals developed, an earlier openness to woman's participation — largely through letters — evolves into an ever-sharpening focus, not so much on the publication of women's own desires and perspectives as on their prescription.[20] Access, as Shevelow insists, does not mean enfranchisement; the process of women's inclusion in public and popular discourse was inseparable from their restriction within the limits of its conventions. Though the papers absorbed and published much writing by and for women, they were inevitably edited and published by men and served paternalistic, if not severely patriarchal, ends.

The Tatler and *The Spectator* are major players in the bourgeois ideological projects that Shevelow traces in the popular print culture of turn-of-the-century England. The development from *The Tatler* to *The Spectator* shows a growing concern with the direction of private, rather than the investigation of public, life. Especially in its early days, *The Tatler* caters to a broad range of interests and includes much political news as well as musings on more personal and domestic issues (*T* 1). But a shift is apparent as *The Spectator* takes up where *The Tatler* leaves off. From the first number, *The Spectator* is presented as a series of single-issue essays with an almost purely moral, speculative, and pedagogical focus.[21] Whereas *The Tatler*, at least partially, maintains its public, masculine orientation around the coffeehouse, *The Spectator* presents itself as an eminently domestic commodity, produced in the private apartment of Mr. Spectator and consumed by genteel families with their toast and tea (*S* 10).

In their position at the head of the tea table and the heart of the

newly valued domestic sphere, women are important to the periodical, as to the culture at large, as "conveyors of a new middle-class
ideology in the making."[22] The new ideology prescribes that women
stay at home and gear every effort of self-creation to *purely* domestic,
familial roles: "The utmost of a Woman's Character is contained in
Domestick Life; she is Blameable or Praise-worthy according as her
carriage affects the House of her Father or her Husband" (S 342).
The ideal genteel woman has almost no contact with the worlds of
industry and commerce, politics, or science. She produces, consumes,
administers, and learns within household walls for familial ends. The
retired is the natural life for woman; forays into the larger world of
urban society are undertaken only to remind her of the superior attractions of domesticity (S 15).

One problem with keeping women on their native domestic ter-
rain is that female nature is naturally perverse and innately vulnerable
to the seductions of the world's senseless vanity, artifice, and caprice.
In *Spectator* 15 Addison reflects on "this unaccountable Humour in
Woman-kind, of being smitten with every thing that is showy and
superficial." Their "light, fantastical Disposition," is a "Natural Weakness" and exposes women to fashion-related risks: "A Girl . . . is in
danger of every Embroidered Coat that comes in her Way. A Pair of
fringed Gloves may be her Ruin." To escape the snares of "Lace and
Ribbons" and worse, women must be trained to do what comes naturally.[23] So in *Spectator* 15 Addison sermonizes on the solid rewards of
domestic retirement from the world of fashion and fops, and in *Spectator* 104 Steele drafts "a short Rule for Behaviour" for women that
can guide at once their "Dress, Words, and Actions." The precept is
simple: all any woman need do is "recommend her self as a Sister,
Daughter, or Wife" in everything she wears, says, and does.

Sisters, daughters, and wives must wear skirts, if only to ensure
that men wear the pants in the family. The creation of public and
private spheres of life involves the maintenance of sartorially marked
gender distinctions and prerogatives. The main feature of *Spectator*
104, where Steele gives his short rule, is a letter from a "correspondent" complaining of women in "Amazonian" riding costume.[24]
The fashion for riding habits had been recently set by the Dauphine,

"Riding Habit," Venice, Italy, circa 1780. Watered silk, linen, silver. Los Angeles County Museum of Art, M.82.162a-c.

Marie Adelaide, who tired of changing her clothes and started wearing riding costume all the time as a kind of antifashion uniform.[25] It is a hybrid outfit: male on top with coat, hat, and vest, and female on bottom with a petticoat skirt. As such it confounds the conventional sartorial signs of gender.

But the masculine riding habit is censured not simply because it in itself formally transgresses gender boundaries but also because it facilitates more material transgressions. It is the dress for women out of the house, women at large, women going places. Resonating with the commonplaces of the day, a conduct book warns: "Too immoderate Exercise is immodest for young Women; and so is gadding Abroad."[26] In their riding habits women announce their intention of "gadding Abroad"; in his letter, a correspondent to *Spectator* 104 announces his intention of keeping them at home. By telling women what to wear, men would confine them within well-defined gender and spatial boundaries.

After almost mistaking a young woman in riding habit for a very pretty boy, the correspondent to *Spectator* 104 censures equestrian cross-dressing as a violation of "that propriety and Distinction of Appearance in which the Beauty of different Characters is preserv'd." Euphemistic and aestheticized, this complaint begins by couching fears of gender treachery in terms of contemporary taste theory: it is a matter not of sex and masculine privilege but of propriety, beauty, the preservation of decorum. But soon enough, the gentleman voices the real threat: "If the *Amazons* should think fit to go on in this Plunder of our Sex's Ornaments, they ought to add to their Spoils and compleat their Triumph over us by wearing the Breeches" (*S* 104). Where will it end? Launching a counteroffensive against these "Amazons," the correspondent recommends his own short rule for female sartorial behavior: "All that needs to be desir'd of them is, that they wou'd *be themselves*, that is, what Nature design'd them" (*S* 104). Steele, Addison, and this planted "correspondent" are loyal campaigners for traditional family values. As always, the fabrication of these values asserts their preexistence in the natural order. The sheer fiction of natural authenticity that this ideology depends on is its source of strength. In this fabricated natural order, women become a medium for the consolidation of a feminized, intimate domestic sphere where the virtues and values of decent families can be reproduced and nourished.

These papers participate in an ongoing definition of the legitimate sphere for female activity. Specifically, they are at work on the construction of a private world of naturalized, feminized domesticity, a sane asylum from the fraudulent public world with its commercial ethics and its consuming passions. The alignment women/nature/home makes it possible to think about an Edenic domestic sphere that precedes (nature before culture) the fall into the world, the corruptions of the marketplace. In its pure ideological formulation, the domestic sphere, the family nest, is immune from contamination by the toxins of commodification, interest, and instability that

pollute the worldly world. Women must stay at home in order to fulfill their "natural" function and so ensure the value and stability of
the home. Just as crucially, the home ensures the cultivation of the
right kind of women and the right sort of femininity—complacent,
retiring, oriented entirely around the family.

Of course, there is nothing new in this command for women to
stay home; the domestic propaganda of the early eighteenth century
rests on a long tradition. What is remarkable is the need to rearticu-
late and reinforce this command. The creation of the bourgeois private sphere is an ongoing, centuries-old project that reformulates its
responses in the face of shifting pressures and goals. One set of pressures is economic; this was intensified around the turn of the eighteenth century by the sheer growth—intensive and extensive—of
commercial and economic expansion. Not completely at ease with
new commercial and financial conditions, men demonize the sources
of their anxieties as threateningly feminine and both symbolically
and literally sequester them out of harm's way. Both the need to banish, or at least stabilize, the "bad" feminine forces at work in the
world and the need for a private, domestic sphere immune from the
perils of that world and vitalized by "good" feminine forces bear
witness to anxieties about control and dominance. The consolidation
of a naturalized, emphatically bourgeois domestic culture achieves
not merely control over the hazards of the capitalized world but even
dominance within that world, largely through an ongoing, highly
adaptive manipulation of those bodies, concepts, and practices marked
as feminine.

The management of troubling feminine forces is part of an attempt to conceive both of a rational capitalist market and a natural
domestic sphere and participates in a masculine fantasy of complete
triumph over feminine forces of disorder. The horrific vision in *Spectator* 104 of women gaining "compleat . . . Triumph" over men "by
wearing the Breeches" is the nightmare double of this same dream of
domination. The kind of control prevalent in Addison's and Steele's
papers aims to prevent at least two things: any evasion of the masculine constraints that confine women to the home and any too-stark
exposure of the constraining force itself. It is during this period that

masculine domination is revised away from the patriarchal and severe toward the paternal and benevolent. In Addison's and Steele's periodicals the admonitions are gentle, even indulgent; the satiric touch is light; the reins that lead women onto the straight and narrow paths of domesticity are silken. By offsetting any intimidating, high-minded sternness, the nearly ironic self-consciousness of the censorship of women and fashion only strengthens its appeal to the softer sex. Severity is dissembled. Sometimes the very agents of right opinion, such as the correspondent to *Spectator* 104, are themselves ruffled by a gentle parody that smooths away any rough, authoritarian edges. More than a spoonful of sugar goes down with the moral medicine prescribed by these periodicals, but the spirit of masculine will is alive and well within this kinder, gentler rhetoric. This is patriarchy with a human face.

While the tone of the papers — self-conscious, modulated, even velvet — is significant as more than a mask, it is also that. Even as the domestic and private sphere is defined as outside the marketplace and immune from its callous commercial ethics, it depends as always on the marketing of women. What is different is the felt need to mask the commodification of women and to give the forms of "nature" to their fetishization. This is a central feature of eighteenth-century domestic womanhood and results at least partially from the development of affective family bonds and the famed companionate marriage.[27] Although women still functioned as commodities, their connection to exchange, to the marriage market, was obscured to a great extent by the "sentimental" bonds of marriage and even further by their actual confinement to a domestic sphere being defined along with them as extra-commercial. Consequently, sentiment, affect itself, opens up as an avenue for the structuring not simply of familial and social systems but also of each individual's desires. As Nancy Armstrong and Leonard Tennenhouse show, "the new domestic ideal . . . provided a form of power exercised through constant supervision and the regulation of desire, thus preparing the cultural ground in which capitalism could rapidly flourish."[28]

The financial instrument crucial to this consolidation of capitalism and generative of much desire in the seventeenth and eighteenth centuries is credit, private and public. While the productive virtues of credit were readily apparent, it was also clear to many, including Addison and Defoe, that the very qualities that made credit so generative of value and solvency also posed threats to the security of that solvency and the stability of that value. One problem with credit, like the problems with fashion and the female character, is that it depends on superficial signs which all too easily, and all too often, may be empty. This emptiness, the lack of stable distinctive features that secure identity, makes these signs easy to mirror and counterfeit. Credit thrives on empty talk, on signifiers unmoored from signifieds: debts floating on floating signs strung along into an always-deferred future. The conditions of credit's immateriality, its "unrealness," were the conditions of its success. When debts were called in, when people tried to *realize* their credit, disaster struck, value fell, men and enterprise were ruined. Credit's instability, of course, is generated by its erratic, unpredictable *reproductive* capacities. The struggle is always, in both the human sociosexual and the financial arenas, to bring reproduction under control, to know who the father is and to know what the value is so that financial and social continuity may be managed and predicted.

As Addison and Steele counter the excesses of fashion, women, credit, and imagination, they do more than simply denounce, they create. Pitting their rationalized fashion against the hoop, their natural domesticated woman (a prototypical house angel) against the sinfully sophisticated woman of the world, they participate in the engineering of tamed and house-broken species of woman, fashion, imagination, and desire. And as they construct these reformed ideals, Addison and Steele often do not so much eradicate as exploit the foibles they reproach. For example, feminine irrationality is the object of much censure, yet there is no suggestion that it may ever be corrected through an entirely successful reform. On the contrary, it persists as the justification for its own reform and so provides the rationale that supports Addison's and Steele's projects.[29] Since inconstancy, irrationality, and superficiality are natural to women, are women's *nature*, these qualities cannot be perfectly eliminated. The ideology of the natural that these periodicals draw on for the justification of their project happily prevents that project from ever being completed and rendered obsolete.

FASHION ON TRIAL

In a Nation of Liberty, there is hardly a Person
in the whole Mass of the People
more absolutely necessary than a Censor.

TATLER *144*

There runs a Story in the Family, that when
my Mother was gone with Child of me about three Months,
she dreamt she was brought to Bed of a Judge.

SPECTATOR *1*

The effectiveness of their crusade for domesticity, nature, and reason largely depends on how well Addison and Steele dramatize, allegorize, and ironize their way into their audience's affections and trust. The engaging conceits of dream visions and fashion courts do not only charm the reader, they also legitimize the papers by ensconcing them within reputable social and discursive institutions. Taking on the mantle of the law, Mr. Spectator and Isaac Bickerstaff become judges of morals and manners, arbiters of elegance, and legislators of decorum. They legislate what people should wear and how they should act. Reaching down into the minutiae of everyday life, they want to institute their ideology on the level of quotidian social practice. In their papers Steele and Addison write up opinions on the general principles of sartorial and social conduct, but they also give precise rulings on specific commodities — red-heeled shoes, canes, snuff boxes, coaches, and of course, hoop-petticoats.

The hoop is first mentioned at the end of *Tatler* 110. The paper opens on the scene of Bickerstaff's "court"; the judge is ruling on a case involving the abuse of reason perpetrated by the fashionable lovemaking of a coquette and a beau. This paper establishes the satiric legal conceit — fashion on trial — that forms the context of Addison's case against the hoop-petticoat in *Tatler* 116. This "court" serves as a tribunal for the interrogation of fashionable people and things. Filling the void left by the abolition of sumptuary laws, the court advocates the order of reason in contemporary life: Bickerstaff defines the purpose of his fashion court: " As other Courts were often called to demand the Execution of Persons dead in Law, so this was held to give the last Orders relating to those who were dead in Reason" (*T* 110).[30] The first suspect brought forth this session is a "Mrs. Rebecca Pindust," who has "put to Death several young Men in the Parish." Her weapons are the slings and arrows of outrageous fashion: "a Looking-glass, and . . . certain Attire," the "evil Art and magical Force" of her killing looks. But the judge finds fault not so much with Mrs. Pindust as with the beaux who encourage this romantic hyperbole. Bickerstaff lays the guilt and the sentence at the door not of the lady but of the man "who in any Letter, Billet, or Discourse, should tell a Woman he died for her."

Yet while men are held liable for their perpetuation of these senseless courtship rituals, the motivations that drive men to participate in these rituals, and indeed the practices themselves, are traceable to women. Men act badly when they make love because they are playing to the ladies. As "Tim Switch," correspondent to *Tatler* 29, sees it, men are seduced by feminine wiles into fashionable extremes in attire and conduct: "Dress and Chivalry have always been encourag'd by the Ladies, as the Two principal Branches of Gallantry." Only his desire to conform to these female standards leads "a wise, experienc'd, and polite Man" to comply "with the Dress commonly receiv'd, and . . . to violate his Reason and Principles" by participating in duels (*T* 29, italics reversed). Bickerstaff concurs with Switch's analysis of the "true Source of this Evil [dueling and foppery]." He comments on how women impose their "Tyranny in Love" through a hyperbolic, irrational drama of courtship that scripts not merely duel, but the more rhetorical gestures of "killing looks" and the inflated, heavily stylized discourse of fatal attraction and lethal insult that people like Mrs. Pindust and her admirers indulge in. So, although they may be taken into various degrees of complicity with these ultimately feminine customs of social and erotic competition, at base men are the more rational creatures and so more responsible for the maintenance of good sense in courtship. Led astray by erotic desire or simply the desire to get on in the world, men may capitulate to the world's nonsensical modes. Yet although they may take leave of, men may as well return to, their senses. Women, on the contrary, have little to lose and not much to come back to.

The penalty Bickerstaff would have men pay for their erotic hyperbole is harsh and, like much satiric punishment, involves a literalization of the offensive figures. A man who claims to have died for a lady "should, if [the woman] be pleased, be obliged to live with her, or be immediately interr'd, upon such their own Confession, without Bail or Mainprize" (*T* 110). This sentence meets some resistance from one of Mrs. Pindust's admirers, who steps forward to defend himself. Fashionable, impertinent, full of himself and curses, the fellow comes before the bar. This box-tapping, pox-hurling gentleman is an established stereotype, a cartoon of himself. Tapping, blustering, swearing, he shares a fetish and mode of address with Pope's "Sir Plume of snuff-box justly vain," who speaks so persuasively on Belinda's behalf in canto 4 of *The Rape of the Lock*:

> He first the snuff-box open'd, then the case,
> And thus broke out—"My Lord, why, what the devil?
> Z———ds! damn the lock! 'fore Gad, you must be civil!
> Plague on't! 'tis past a jest—nay prithee, pox!
> Give her the hair"—he spoke, and rapp'd his box. (126-30)[31]

With comparable aplomb, Mrs. Pindust's admirer challenges Bickerstaff's authority, addressing him as "old Stiffrump": "Who gave thee Power of Life and Death? What-a-Pox hast thou to do with Ladies and Lovers?" Railing on against Bickerstaff, the beau fidgets and gestures with his box, tapping out snuff in emphatic tattoos that punctuate his tirade. Predictably, Bickerstaff is annoyed; he interrupts the beau "in the midst of his Eloquence" and snatches the snuffbox away from him. Rendered "immediately speechless," the young man is "carried off stone-dead" from the court.[32] Without his snuffbox to support his élan and his oratory, the beau collapses speechless. It is the box as much as the law that has the power of life and death over the beau. Punishing, indeed paralyzing, the young man by taking away his box, Bickerstaff, as much as his opponent, depends on the stylish trinket for the assertion of his authority and will. Here in the fashion court, the snuffbox is transformed from an accessory in foppish designs against reason into an instrument for the execution of the law.

Hooped Ladies

The beau vanquished, Bickerstaff adjourns the court and on his way out is presented with a letter informing him that "all those of the fair sex" were beginning "to appear pregnant . . . as was manifest by a particular Swelling in the Petticoats." While he discounts rumors that all the hooped ladies in London are pregnant, Bickerstaff nevertheless emphasizes his dislike of this "new and unaccountable Fashion." Since the court is out for the day, he postpones any definitive judgment for the time being. He will give it due consideration and bring it to the bar at a later date. *Tatler* 110 closes with Bickerstaff's admonition that women "abstain from [making] all Dresses" with hoop-petticoats until he has delivered his judgment on that mode. As we see here in *Tatler* 110 and will see again and again, the threat of the hoop is inseparable from female reproductive and more generally sexual powers. The hoop, like the farthingale before it and the crinoline after it, is associated with, usually illegitimate, pregnancy. For three centuries what strikes men most about these elaborate structures is that they provide a means of female sexual autonomy.[33]

Another related aspect of the hoop that makes it a clear candidate for Bickerstaff's prosecution is that it, like the equipages of the rich, takes up a lot of space, public as well as domestic.[34] It demands accommodation, but whether it has any right to this accommodation is a matter for the courts to decide. To make way for the hoop, wider staircases were put in houses; coaches were redesigned so that hooped ladies might ride in them (*T* 113).[35] In *Tatler* 113, the hoop comes up in the petition of one "William Jingle, Coachmaker and Chairmaker of the Liberty of Westminster," who solicits Bickerstaff to hear his case for the hoop. Since it produces a market for all sorts of new commodities, the hoop, Jingle argues, should not be banned but championed. The ingenious Jingle has blueprints for two new kinds of coaches; one requires that the lady be lowered into and raised from the coach by a pulley. The balance of Jingle's career hangs on Bickerstaff's decision; he is understandably anxious to hear the verdict. And Jingle isn't the only one calling for Bickerstaff's quick decision on the hoop. In the same post that brings Jingle's plea comes "a Female Petition, signed by several Thousands" begging for Bickerstaff's verdict on the hoop. These ladies are eager to get on with their dressmaking. Bickerstaff's procrastination is holding up commercial and domestic industry in many quarters. Finally, a little more than a week later, on January 4, 1709, Bickerstaff keeps his promise and gives his decision.

In *Tatler* 116, Bickerstaff as judge, both arbiter of elegance and adjudicator of property, hears the case of a woman and her hoop-petticoat. Condemned as irrational and unnatural, the petticoat is executed by dismemberment. The woman — just another fashion victim — is stripped of her hoop, pardoned and released; the avuncular Bickerstaff "always give[s] great Allowances to the Fair Sex upon account of the Fashion." He appropriates the hoop frame and incorporates it into the architecture of his "court" as a kind of canopy tent over his judicial bench. Bickerstaff does not simply discard the fashions he condemns but takes them up and uses them for his own ends. The hoop-frame becomes a dramatic decorative accent that enshrines his pontifical position in its resemblance to "the Cupolo of St. *Paul's*." The quilted petticoat that covers the hoop is cut up and redistributed according to orders which include, in addition to some charitable projects, designs for Bickerstaff's own "Stomachers, Caps, Facings of [his] Wastcoat-Sleeves, and other Garnitures suitable to [his] Age and Quality." The hoop, commodity on the irrational, unstable, and arbitrary fashion market, is thus reduced and rationalized in this directed redistribution of its body. The woman's body, in turn, is diminished, deprived of its "unnatural" extension, and returned to its "natural" form. Thus Addison dramatically legislates woman's body in conformity with the observation from Ovid's *Remedia Amoris* that serves as epigraph to this paper: "pars minima est ipsa puella sui" (a woman is the least part of herself).[36]

Within its modest frame, this "trial" brings together strands that can be traced out to a larger network of financial and social issues.

And in all of these issues, as in the trial itself, the feminine is a dominant figure in patterns of conceptualization and representation. What constitutes "female nature," and so what features of social, domestic, and economic life can be portioned off to the female — all these issues, more and less directly, are implicated in Addison's disputation with the hoop-petticoat.

Lady Credit

The construction of femininity that supports the condemnation of the hoop is graphically represented in contemporary allegories of credit as well. Looking at some of these representations advances our understanding of the anxieties that motivate the conviction of the hoop-petticoat. The hoop and credit participate in a discursive proximity; representations of both draw on and feed back into a heavily gendered symbolic structures that form the basis of early-eighteenth-century British culture.

As we have seen, in the early eighteenth century, credit is explicitly female and commonly allegorized as Lady Credit.[37] The nationalization of the credit economy through the establishment of the Bank of England and the Public Debt in the 1690s drew to credit considerable attention from those concerned about its sociocultural, as well as its more discretely economic, effects.[38] This nationalization of credit, however, is only one aspect of an entirely credit-saturated economy where, due in part to the specie shortage that was aggravated by the 1696 decision to keep the silver standard, the bulk of business was transacted through complex networks of debt.[39] Everyone worth anything was in debt. The financial instruments so crucial to the proliferation of capitalism in the seventeenth and eighteenth centuries carved out a market based on the intangible, fertile, profitable, and potentially empty phantom of credit.

A whalebone-and-hemp-supported bubble raised on the baseless foundation of woman, the hoop itself can stand as a sartorial allegory of credit-based speculation, of the Project. In a single quatrain of his "Upon the South Sea Project" (1721), Swift draws together images of inflated hoops, speculative bubbles, and the perverse femininity of lady gamblers, warriors, and witches:

> Undone at play, the female troops
> Come here their losses to retrieve;
> Ride o'er the waves in spacious hoops,
> Like Lapland witches in a sieve. (97-100)[40]

Kept afloat on the hollow orbs of their hoops, these Amazonian mermaids ("the female troops") are icons of the South Sea Bubble itself: empty, illegitimate, hazardous, and feminine. And although Addison does not explicitly construct an allegory between hoops and credit, a comparison of the representation of the hoop and the representation of credit calls up homology after homology. Both are desire-enslaving, fashion-driven and fashion-driving, empty, jerry-built structures supported only by all-too-manipulable markets where rumor, taste, and opinion are retailed along with stocks, bonds, and petticoats.

Of course representations of credit vary in accordance with their authors' views on political economy. Swift relentlessly refuses to acknowledge credit's virtues while Addison's picture of credit is more ambivalent. He sees credit as a necessary and desirable, yet nonetheless a hazardous, and innately unstable, financial instrument. In *Spectator* 3, Addison paints Lady Credit as a virtuous but infirm woman:

> She was . . . a greater Valetudinarian than any I had ever met with, even in her own Sex, and subject to such Momentary Consumptions, that in the twinkling of an Eye, she would fall away from the most florid Complexion, and the most healthful State of Body, and wither into a Skeleton. Her Recoveries were often as sudden as her Decays. (*S* 3)

So while Addison's Lady Credit is undeniably amiable and virtuous, she is also a hysteric, a passive victim of a specifically female malady.

The contradictions and instability of feminine nature that trouble fashion, credit, and woman herself are diagnosed in the pathology of this modish eighteenth-century ailment — hysteria (also known as the vapors and the spleen). A look at her medical profile shows that Lady Credit is not just any woman, but a very sick one. Her portrait, as painted by Addison and Defoe, draws not merely, as J.G.A. Pocock describes it, first on the allegory of *Fortuna* and then of

Virtue in Distress. Rather, in both these representations, Credit is the very picture of a *hysterical* woman.[41] Representing his own ambivalence about the instability and malleability of credit, Addison diagnoses, as much as he describes, his Lady Credit. Because she is hysterical, she is always at risk; though seeming to thrive, she may collapse in the blink of an eye "and wither into a Skeleton." Defoe comes across a similarly infirm Credit in the *Review* for Thursday, February 1, 1711: "I Hardly knew her, she was so lean, so pale; look'd so sickly, so faint" (*Review* 7:134). Rather than the strumpet Lady Luck, fickle dominatrix of men's fortunes, these pictures of Lady Credit show a submissive invalid awaiting doctor's orders.

As Bernard Mandeville, physician and satirist, explains in a medical treatise of 1711, hysteria results from a deficiency of spirits that brings on both bodily and mental distress.[42] One thing that hysteria dramatizes is the tangle of psychosomatic interdependence. The psychic elements involved in hysteria are the passions and the imagination, the capacities of fantasy and desire. The sensitive mind and the fertile, reactive imagination are most vulnerable; weaker, frailer constitutions are less able to resist hysteria's disruption. Light-headed and delicate by nature, women, especially genteel ladies, were especially predisposed.[43] Finally, hysteria is only a (patho)logical extension of innate frailties defined as essentially feminine. Woman being imbalanced at her very core, her condition is chronic; her only hope lies in submission to the doctor's orders.

Associated with the cultivated refinements of a leisured, upper-class life, the symptoms of hysteria — headache, heart palpitations, faintness, depression, anxiety, teariness — become the signs of a new style of virtue.[44] As John Mullan explains, hysteria and hypochondria were central to the development of revised notions of sentimental, domesticated virtue in the eighteenth century. The affective and ethical mix dubbed "sensibility" incorporates a whole range of traits: a virtuous soul, a fertile and passionate imagination, and a frail constitution. Finally, morbidity sets in: the virtuous heroine becomes all but indistinguishable from the pathetic hysteric. "Illness," as Mullan puts it, "became the last retreat of the morally pure."[45] Passive, porcelain, wasted, dead — Samuel Richardson's heroic victim Clarissa is a paragon of feminine sensibility. Thirty years earlier, Addison's depiction of a sweet, weak, hysterical Lady Credit already assumes this same alignment of vapors and virtue.

Credit is both a hysterical woman and the cause — through the speculative ventures she underwrites — of hysteria in others. The pseudonymous Sir John Midriff documents an epidemic of credit-induced hysteria in his volume of "case-studies."[46] Taking medical stock of the human wreckage left in the wake of the South Sea fiasco, the satiric doctor exposes the ludicrous extent of people's emotional, as well as material, investments in fantastic schemes and ridicules the greed, delusion, and materialism that motivate it. In a popular and colloquial form, these investment-induced cases of hysteria and hypochondria dramatize an identity between credit and the bodies of the investor. But this is not just any body; what Sir Midriff's patients and Addison's Lady Credit share is the body of the hysterical woman. This body is dangerously vulnerable to influence. The forces Addison's Lady Credit is prey to are political: she waxes under Whig power and wanes under Tory. In the case of Sir Midriff's patients, the influence is more directly financial — the stock market — and it works through an imagination overwrought by investment. One of his first patients, Lady Arabella Blackham, suffers, sheerly from her losses on the market, many of the same symptoms as Mandeville's patient and Addison's Credit. Marked by fainting fits, inexplicable outbursts of tears and laughter, hysteria manifests as bodily and emotional vacillations that mimic the fluctuations of the stock market. Through this process of empathic simulation, credit possesses those invested in her, body and soul. Mirroring the market, the minds and bodies of the speculator lose their autonomous identity. It is not enough to say that Lady Blackham's health is affected by the fluctuations on the market; Lady Blackham's health becomes the fluctuations on that market. She "had never been well since the Fall of the Stocks."[47]

While Addison's portrait of Lady Credit softens her features into those of a victim, nonetheless in her translation from Fortune to Virtue, Credit maintains her essentially unstable nature. The form this instability takes does change a reprehensible fickleness to a pathetic infirmity. The virtue of a hysteric is constitutionally unstable; she is perpetually at the mercy of exterior management in order to maintain some slight semblance of equilibrium. Like Pope's ladies "with no characters at all," Lady Credit's mercurial nothingness leads to irrational, anarchic behavior, yet it also leaves her open to calculated masculine control.[48]

Emphasizing even more strongly than Addison Credit's equivocal instability, Defoe graphically evokes her intense femininity, fertility, instability, and danger—"this Mother of Great designs," "the great Mystery of this Age," this "phantom," "this invisible *je ne scay quoi*, this non-natural, this emblem of something, though in itself nothing" (*Review* 3:5; 6:32; 6:31). Like woman, credit, "in itself nothing," can only be the least part of herself; the very contradictions that construct her foreclose her purchase on any stable identity.[49] Credit exalts individuals and nations to profit zeniths and plunges them into the hells of debt. The emblem of an unrealizable future where all will pay off and be repaid, credit is the fantasy on which men erect their projects: honest, fraudulent, or simply preposterous; and woman is the fantasy on which Addison erects his project: paternalistic, transformative, and sanguinely rational.

The "feminine" instability of credit, fashion, and women, their unaccountable humors, make them at once threatening sites of anarchic menace and fertile fields of possibility, undefined and so susceptible to regulative demarcation. This ambivalence is clear in the difficulty Defoe has describing and evaluating credit and the projects she engenders. Credit may be the nonpareil of financial innovation, the gear that drives the wheels of commerce; yet it is easily violated, perilously open to abuse. Defoe laments the emergence of phenomenally preposterous ventures, flimsily backed by a conjectural credit. These "have rais'd the Fancies of Credulous People to such height, that meerly on the shadow of Expectation, they have form'd Companies, chose Committees, appointed Officers, Shares, and Books, rais'd great Stocks, and cri'd up an empty Notion to that degree, that people have been betray'd to part with their Money for Shares in a *NEW-NOTHING*" (*Projects*, 12). Credit may be "Nothing" but this nothing proves to be both a quite real threat and an actual promise.

For as Defoe also emphasizes in this *Essay upon Projects*, credit backs
trading ventures, technological advancements, manufacturing expansion, and land improvements that he considers "without question as
great benefit as any Discoveries made in the Works of Nature by all
the *Academies* and *Royal Societies* in the World" (15). Women, fashion,
and credit share a paradoxical nature: they can become anything and
everything because they are in themselves nothing. This disturbing
potential for emptiness — in female nature, in the signs of credit, in
fashion — threatens domestic, financial, and social stability.[50]

The problem Defoe has pinning credit down, and the profuseness
of speculation generated around her, is echoed in the account of the
hoop-petticoat offered by a "correspondent" in *Spectator* 127.[51] Posing
the question, "Why the hoop?" and finding himself "wonderfully at a
loss" about the use, origins, and moral implications of the hoop, the
correspondent relates the conjectures that have grown up around it:

> There are Men of Superstitious Tempers, who look upon the
> Hoop-Petticoat as a kind of Prodigy. Some will have it that it por-
> tends the Downfall of the *French* King, and observe that the Far-
> thingale appeared in *England* a little before the Ruin of the *Span-
> ish* Monarchy. Others are of Opinion that it foretells Battel and
> Bloodshed, and believe it of the same Prognostication as the Tail
> of a Blazing Star. (*S* 127)

Like credit, the hoop is hard to construe; like credit, its significance
rests in the future, on an outcome about which one can only speculate.[52] But these prophetic speculations are soon dismissed, and the final figuration of the hoop in this letter recalls both Defoe's depiction
of the fantastic castles raised on ethereal credit in his *Essay on Projects*
and the epigraph to *Tatler* 116 — a woman is the least part of herself:

> When I survey this new-fashioned *Rotunda* [the hoop] in all its
> Parts, I cannot but think of the old Philosopher, who after having
> entered into an *Egyptian* Temple, and looked about for the Idol of
> the Place, at length discovered a little Black Monkey enshrined in
> the midst of it, upon which he could not forbear crying out . . .
> What a magnificent Palace is here for such a Ridiculous Inhabi-
> tant! (*S* 127)

The "little Black Monkey" inside the structure of the hoop/rotunda is woman herself, humanoid but not quite human, mischievous and troublesome, the *"zoon philokosmon, an Animal that delights in Finery"* as Addison puts it in *Spectator* 265. Defoe often registers dismay at the outcome of his analyses of credit and projects, acknowledging without quite resolving the perplexities he encounters in this new financial market that seems impervious to conventional ethical categorization. Addison is more positive, confidently submitting fashion to moral judgment and steady regulation at the hands of satire and the laws of reason and nature. The ideology of moderation followed in *The Tatler* and *The Spectator* does not require an abandonment of credit, of women, the financial market, or even of fashionable clothes, but a pursuit of these objects directed by rational criteria.

Satire versus Fashion

As he attempts to establish the rule of reason over fashion, Bickerstaff's case against the hoop-petticoat dramatizes two related fissures within the social system. First, there is a rift between the practice of fashion, here embodied in the hoop, and the practice of reason, manifest in the "law" practiced by Addison at this "trial."[53] This conflict then unfolds as one between fashion and nature. That fashion is irrational is an obvious and perennial complaint. The form its correction takes here is specifically satiric and ties into contemporary trends to keep women at home and so out of public places of resort and debate. Fashion, as Addison's anxiety about the voluminous hoop emphatically shows, can be used like satire to secure space in the social domain. Satire is, among other things, a strategy to stake out discursive territory in ideological conflicts. Fashion in the early eighteenth century, as now, shared many of the positioning, dissenting, and aligning functions of satiric discourse. Like satire, fashion can be practiced aggressively. So although textual disputes over social issues were not generally open to them, women could and did claim ideological positions and political alliances through an explicit semantic of fashion. The wearing of "party patches" to announce loyalty to either the Whigs or the Tories is well known (*S* 81). Asserting their political identity through cosmetics, these women are satirized by

Addison as aggressively unfeminine—a "Body of *Amazons*" drawn up in "Battle-Array against one another." Women's public participation in party politics is divisive and unnatural: "It only serves to aggravate the Hatred and Animosities that reign among Men, and in a great measure deprives the Fair Sex of those peculiar Charms with which Nature has endowed them."

Less celebrated but equally politically charged is a new fashion in women's caps noted in *Spectator* 265. These eighteenth-century ladies are wearing colors: "I am informed that this Fashion spreads daily, insomuch that the Whig and Tory Ladies begin already to hang out different Colours, and to shew their Principles in their Head-dress." Addison dismisses this report, as well as his friend Will Honeycomb's speculation that the colored caps signal the ladies' variously colored moods: "For my own part, I impute this diversity of Colours in the Hoods to the diversity of Complection in the Faces of my pretty Country Women." Addison simply refuses to recognize the motivated, rational uses (political or personal) that women have made of their fashionable caps. By formalizing and aestheticizing these signs, he saps them of content—political and psychological. Apparently, if they want to make anything more than a fashion statement, women should leave their colors at home.[54]

Addison's role as judge of fashion supports his right as a satirist and as a man to legislate not simply what women should wear but also what entry women may gain to territory—both ideological and material—in the public sphere. He sets the horizons of meaning and dictates how one may get access to it. Women use fashion to take up public space, symbolically and materially. Inasmuch as this is a confrontation between satire and fashion, Addison is not merely hearing the case of the hoop-petticoat but also defending his own case as a satirist. Satire, not fashion, it is decreed, is to be the legitimate procedure for claiming one's ground; so satire is figuratively legalized in all the trappings of Bickerstaff's "court." This is tantamount to saying men not women are allowed to occupy and allocate social space. A satiric woman is no lady; she forfeits her social standing by the very act of claiming it.

Nature and Reason versus the Hoop

The hoop, the patch, the party-colored caps are tokens that buy women access to public discourse and social territory out of the bounds of the legitimately feminine. The conflict between fashion and reason staged in this trial easily mutates into a conflict between fashion and nature, especially where, as here, that nature is being legally defined and instituted through commodity regulation. In order to serve as an emblem of a natural domestic realm, women must be divested of the emphatically artificial hoop-petticoat. The hoop is at odds with a conception of woman's body as "natural," as unconstructed, and it is hostile to the masculine desire that assumes unchallenged control of this body. Insofar as woman's "natural" function is procreation, her appearance should signal sexual desirability and, related to this, sexual availability — though only within the bounds of decency. Yet, the fashion of the hoop aggressively counters respectable conventions of sexual desirability. It does so in an apparently — but only apparently — contradictory, double-faceted manner.

First and most obviously, the social space claimed by the hoop is an antisexual space: the hoop blocks sexual advances, inconveniencing masculine desire. As the epistolary gentleman of *Spectator* 127 writes: "I find several Speculative Persons are of Opinion that our Sex has of late Years been very Saucy, and that the Hoop-Petticoat is made use of to keep us at a distance." This use of the hoop as body barricade could be positively regarded, from a patriarchal perspective, as a shield that protects women's chastity. This would make the hoop congenial to at least one set of masculine desires — for the preservation of reproductive property and of the legitimacy of the patriline. And this is the argument advanced in *Tatler* 116 by the "Council for the Petticoat," who defends the hoop as a kind of whale-bone and hemp chastity belt "of great Use to preserve the Honour of Families." It is a stock satiric argument. In *The Rape of the Lock* these virtue-preserving qualities are assumed only to be questioned by Pope, who stations "fifty chosen Sylphs" to guard Belinda's petticoat: "Oft have we known that seven-fold fence to fail, / Tho's stiff with hoops, and arm'd with ribs of whale" (2.117-22).[55] Similarly, Pope's *Second Satire of the First Book of Horace* notes the hoop as part of the mediating machinery that stands between a woman's body and her seducer: "Could you directly to her Person go, / Stays will obstruct above, and Hoops below, / And if the Dame says yes, the Dress says no" (130-32).

This argument from chastity is rejected by Bickerstaff. He, like Pope, doubts the invulnerability of even such an Ajaxlike shield; for he fears that women, rather than men, control this body armor. In female hands, the shield would be misused: it would not protect matrimony, but undermine it. Anxious to establish once and for all that the hoop is without excuse, Addison counters the argument from chastity by citing its dangerous, sexually empowering potentials: "the great Temptation it might give to Virgins, of acting in Security like married Women, and by that Means give a Check to Matrimony, an Institution always encouraged by wise Societies." Chaperoned by the hoop, repelling well-intentioned beaux with their brazen self-assurance, even virgins get fresh. The feelings of personal security and sexual self-confidence that hoops provide are grounded in the effects of bodily size and physical force they impart to their wearers. So the "pretty Maid" in *Tatler* 116 says she put on her hoop because "she had a Mind to look as big and burly as other Persons of her Quality."

Further, as the speculation on the origins of the hoop in *Spectator* 127 makes clear, the hoop, far from preserving chastity, may actually encourage promiscuity by allowing women to control the signs of illegitimate maternity. The history of the hoop tells the tale of women's exploitation of fashion for their own bad ends: it is a history of sartorial abuse and sexual autonomy. Female use of the hoop results in a confounding of the conventional signs of sexual status, experience, and availability. This symbolic, as well as practical and material, disorder points to the instability of the function and nature of the hoop-petticoat, and, in fact, the hoop has its mythic origins in just such confusion. Specifically, it perplexes the signs of maternity in an ambivalent dynamic that may both conceal and reveal pregnancy, either by hiding illegitimate pregnancy and so disguising scandal or by making everyone look pregnant. The conjectures about the origins of the hoop in *Spectator* 127 center on this duplicitous dynamic and here the contradictory ambivalence — hiding pregnancy and revealing it — is rationalized in the narrative of a subversive fashion plot: "It is generally thought some crafty Women have thus betrayed their Companions into Hoops, that they might make them accessory to their own Concealments, and by that means escape the Censure of the World." This fashion hoax levels those hierarchies that define women by smoothing "all Distinctions," setting mother and daughter, maid and matron, wife and widow "upon the same bottom."

And this is not just a paranoid satirical fantasy of Addison's. No one seems to have any exact idea of how the hoop came into fashion; the story offered here still appears in histories of dress. This account is not so much an explanation, either in *The Spectator* or elsewhere, as a cover-up for the absence of an explanation. Thus in *The Encyclopedia of World Costume*, the irrecoverable origins of the Spanish farthingale, the hoop's great-great grandmother, is narrated as the tale of a pregnancy hoax: "Nearly all attribute [the introduction of this structure] to different members of the royal houses of Europe who wished to conceal an unwanted, embarrassing pregnancy." As Boucher notes, "the origin of paniers [hoops] is still a subject of controversy."[56] It is difficult to pin down the origins of the hoop, and the hoop makes it hard to determine the social standing of the women who wear it. Like her contemporary credit, who "makes honest Women Whores, and Whores honest women," the hoop conceals the true adulteress and makes "well-shaped Virgins" bloat up and waddle "like big-bellied Women" (*Review* 6:31; *S* 127). So while the representation of the hoop in *Tatler* 116 as an obstacle to (legitimate) sex and in *Spectator* 127 as an incitement to promiscuity at first may seem contradictory, in the logic of patriarchal erotics they are complementary: both evade the jurisdiction of masculine desire that Addison presents as legitimating and benevolent. The feminine control of sexuality and reproduction that the hoop provides women is the psychological analogue to the material barricade it erects around their bodies: both are repulsive to masculine desire.

Like the adulteress whose illegitimate pregnancy violates the patriline, a woman in a hoop is a kind of fraudulent monster, an unsightly imposition on contemporary social space and even, we see in *Spectator* 127, on the future. Here classical precedent is cited to predict posterity's reading of the hoop. Alexander the Great is said to have buried huge suits of armor in India "in order to give Posterity an extraordinary *Idea* of him, and make them believe he had commanded an Army of Giants." Similarly, it is conjectured, if a hoop is preserved "in any Repository of Curiosities, it will lead into the same Error . . . unless we can believe our Posterity will think so disrespectfully of their Great-Grandmothers, that they made themselves Monstrous to appear Amiable."[57]

Seeking to restore woman's body to nature by removing it from the monstrous armor of the hoop, Addison does not abandon a system of social signification and relation based on commodity consumption. Rather, he advocates the use of things in a mode that fabricates from commodities themselves an image of a "natural" order, apparently beyond the reach of the arbitrary, mercurial fluctuations in the fashion market. He does this, appropriately, in a simulation of jurisprudence which, as Pocock says, is "concerned with the administration of things and with human relations conducted through the mediation of things."[58]

We see then how the conflict between fashion and reason staged in this paper mutates into a conflict between fashion and nature, especially where, as here, nature is being legally defined and instituted through commodity regulation. Bickerstaff is of the opinion that the hoop-petticoat is disruptive to human relations, especially relations between the sexes and, connected to this, that it perverts woman's relation to her natural body. Exploiting the power of commodities to transform social relations, he seeks to reform these relations.

First of all, this involves a change of clothes, in fact a change into clothes from the hoop, which is figured not as clothing but as an architectural structure—a thing occupied rather than worn: "My pretty Maid," asks Bickerstaff in *Tatler* 116, "do you own your self to have been the Inhabitant of the Garment before us?" By mistaking the hoop for clothing, Bickerstaff implies, women misuse this particular commodity. This erroneous use of the hoop results from its misidentification, and both are part of the violation of nature assigned to the hoop. The hoop violates the structures of domestic architecture and transgresses the limits of propriety. A woman in a hoop cannot be domesticated, for, quite literally, she cannot get into the court where that domestication is adjudicated. She must "be stripped of her encumbrances, till she [becomes] little enough to enter [Bickerstaff's] house." The woman in the hoop cannot come into the courthouse because she is already "an "Inhabitant" of a kind of "hoop-house" of her own. In the course of the trial, not only does Bickerstaff divest the "pretty Maid" of her hoop, he also appropriates its frame into the architecture of his own house.

Stripping woman of her hoop, Bickerstaff's reduction of the territory of the feminine is couched in the rhetoric of restoration. Tutelary and benevolent, he promises to liberate the lady from this ungracious obstacle . He will rescue women from fashion's tyranny. But, as always, liberation comes with an agenda. While the hoop with its resistance to men suggests that there is something in male desire that merits this resistance, Bickerstaff's liberation of woman from the hoop returns her to the "natural" order of a sexuality that does not elude male control and so does not tinge masculine desire with this suggestion that its dominance may warrant resistance.

In order to accomplish this restoration, Bickerstaff, acting as prosecutor as well as judge, appeals to a nature that has been violated by the arbitrary and irrational tyranny of fashion. That fashion has imposed upon and even replaced nature becomes clear in the woman's defense: "That if she laid [the hoop] aside, People would think that she was not made like other Women" (*T* 116). The shape of the hoop, her plea suggests, has already become naturalized as the shape of woman's body; without her hoop, the "pretty Maid" will appear deformed. So, Addison's satire suggests, fashion turns the world topsy-turvy: the grossly hyperbolic, extended form of the hoop is mistaken for the natural human shape. Social practice has replaced woman as the least part of herself with something bigger and has done this so effectively that the very paltriness of woman (as she appears in Ovid's epigram and in Addison's courthouse) has been effaced by fashion's supplements. The problem with getting back to nature, as becomes clear from the abundant attempts to do so, is that there is no nature before it is fabricated. The apparent contradiction between nature as the determining origin of cultural limits and nature as cultural production is in full play here. In his domestic court, where, as Censor of Britain, he legislates the realm of the public from the legitimizing ground of the private and natural, Addison goes to the bar to contest the unnatural nature asserted by fashion in order to make a claim for nature as defined by law.

Divested of her hoop, woman must masquerade in self-identity; her nature must parade as nature. Addison's attack on the hoop is emphatically not a simple condemnation of luxury and extravagance. Addison does not ban female indulgence in the luxury market supported by England's international commerce.[59] Indeed, he is willing to ornament woman with all the precious gems and textiles carried by British trade from the furthest reaches of the globe. But this adornment is normative; it takes the stylization of female appearance out of the hands of women and submits it to the control of a "nature" that serves as handmaid to paternalism. Expressed as good taste, there is a harmonious identity between the ends of this "nature" and Addison's own desires, and so they share an agenda: "As the Hand of Nature has poured on [women] such a Profusion of Charms and Graces . . . so I would have them bestow on themselves all the additional Beauties that Art can supply them with, provided it does not interfere with, disguise, or pervert, those of Nature." Woman is herself "a beautiful Romantick Animal," and so, as part of the natural, it is only fitting that she

> be adorned with Furs and Feathers, Pearls and Diamonds, Ores and Silks. . . . and every Part of Nature furnish its share towards the embellishment of a Creature that is the most consummate Work of it. All this I shall indulge them in; but as for the Petticoat I have been speaking of, I neither can, nor will allow it. (*T* 116)[60]

Yet, there is a contradiction between this easy admission of expenditure in the luxury market and Bickerstaff's initial rejection of arguments that defend outlay on the hoop as a great boon to the trade and industry that serve this market. From the highly rationalized contradictions embodied in this shifting argument first against, then in favor of, lavish expenditure, the hoop-petticoat rises as the signpost that guides the apparently inconsistent turnaround. Bicker-staff confesses that arguments for the hoop as a booster of trade and industry would be convincing, except for the great expense it imposes on families. Outlay on such luxury, at least on the hoop, is "by no Means to be thought of till some Years after a Peace." Writing about three years before the Treaty of Utrecht in 1713, Bickerstaff calls for wartime austerity. He urges also that encouraging the purchase of hoops "would be a Prejudice to the Ladies themselves, who could never expect to have any Money in the Pocket" (*T* 116). Behind the immediate rationalization of his argument for domestic thrift in uncertain times, we might see an anxiety about the "unnatural" transformations that the commodity is prey to. The hoop becomes here a sign of the wild card in the game of capitalist commodity exchange; but Addison won't play unless he can stack the deck. Importantly, the call for frugality is abandoned as soon as the hoop is rejected: expenditure is excusable after all, as long as it is on commodities whose value and form at least seem more fixed by nature.

The hoop cannot be pinned down. It is blatantly destabilizing; its origins are either scandalous or irrecoverable; and it is quite dramatically displacable, undergoing transfigurations from garment to architectural structure and back again, with interest. Divested of its status as woman's garment, the hoop is exposed as an architectural structure and as such it is appropriated by the court. Finally, severed from its infrastructure, the petticoat is returned to garment form in a rationalized redistribution of the commodity that is both charitable and remunerative: Bickerstaff gives orders to cut up the petticoat into clothes for the deserving poor and for himself. The progress of the hoop exemplifies the way that commodities are prone to unsettling and restabilizing appropriations, subversive and normative transformations that highlight interests and expose contradictions in the social practices through which nature, gender, meaning, and power are negotiated.

Woman and fashion, objects of man's passion, are naturalized in a mode that returns them to masculine sexual access and sociolegal regulation. Insofar as this is a victory over a controlling and irrational fancy, the text of this "trial" and the epigraph offered as a commentary on it are in accord. In *Remedia Amoris* Ovid, like Addison, promotes a program for the mastery of feminine wiles: a man who wants to cure his fancy should take a long hard look at his beloved stripped of all cosmetics and ornaments. Ovid has a plan to dissolve the cathexis of the fetish. When one sees what woman really is—the least part of herself—desire for her will evaporate.[61] In *Remedia Amoris*, woman becomes sexually remote not because she wears a hoop but because man engineers her undesirability.

From this perspective Ovid's purpose is opposed to Addison's. Addison strips the woman of her cumbersome hoop in order to restore her sexual proximity. So although Addison shares in a general way Ovid's goal of regulating desire, he directs this regulation differently. The complete rationalization of desire is, as Ovid demonstrates, its death. What Addison calls for is not an abdication of passion but a rechanneling, a cathexis onto a different set of fetish objects: not hoops but "furs and feathers, pearls and diamonds, ores and silks"— those commodities that signify woman as natural, supplements to the commodity woman that render her transparent and tautological—nature masquerading as nature. In marked contrast with the hooped woman, the natural woman is comfortingly easy to read. The domineering woman in her insolent hoop must be replaced by the natural woman—knowable, governable, divested of social magnitude.

So women do not in this essay remain stripped and reduced to the least parts of themselves; rather they are reconstructed by, and as, "natural" commodities. This refashioning of woman in the mode of the natural protects masculine desire by fixing it on an object that appears innocent of perversion by the market. Claiming mastery over obstacles raised by feminine perversity in both spheres, Addison's project promotes masculine desire as it is directed at both financial and sexual speculation. Of course, this project of naturalization is threatened by the logic of gender which underwrites it. The very meagerness of woman as the least part of herself leaves very little material evidence of woman's essential nature. This nothingness of essential femininity is both the motivational anxiety and the enabling condition of Addison's project. This lack in the feminine other, the space that threatens absence of definition, of stability, of grounded essence is the same manipulatable space that makes the feminine vulnerable to masculine construction and control. It is this perverse logic—I would call it the irreducible logic of the feminine in Western culture—that marks the deeply structured similarities between credit, fashion, and woman herself.

So when we, like the lady "correspondent" in *Spectator* 127, ask "Why the hoop?" not so much in regard to origins that may be irrecoverable but in relation to Addison's fixation on it for his exemplary prosecution, the choice seems richly overdetermined. The hoop is culpable as the most extravagant novelty in a fashion system that encourages novelty as an end in itself. It poses as an article of clothing, but its ruse is blasted when it is exposed as building, a "Rotunda" inhabited and possessed by women. It offends by extending woman's domain into areas legally and socially prohibited to her— access to public space and social discourse, control of the signs of sexual status. Serving as a kind of emblem of all that obscures masculine control of reproduction, it calls up profound sociosexual anxieties. It is damned as a monstrosity that goes against the grain of nature. And, finally, as a disguise for the lack, the absence, the nothing which woman must be if she is to be accessible to masculine management, the hoop-petticoat is guilty of a subversive fashion hoax against the metaphysics of the natural woman.

FOUR

Fashion Plates: Subjectivity, Style, and Gender

⊲⊳

INTRODUCTION: THE BOURGEOIS INDIVIDUAL UNDER CONSTRUCTION

The roles of fashion, style, and taste in the production of character types in *The Tatler* and *The Spectator* offer a key to understanding the early representation of bourgeois subjectivity and its competing models. Throughout the eighteenth century and beyond the papers served as ethical guides; this guidance was in good part given through the promotion of emulative human types. Locating *The Spectator* in the tradition of conduct books beginning with Castiglione's *The Courtier* and Casa's *Galateo*, Samuel Johnson emphasizes Addison's role as an "*Arbiter elegantiarum,* a judge of propriety" in the regulation of everyday life. "To teach the minuter decencies and inferior duties, to regulate the practice of daily conversation, to correct those depravities which are rather ridiculous than criminal, and remove those grievances which, if they produce no lasting calamities, impress hourly vexation": these are primary functions of the papers.[1] Probing deeper into the "commonplace that [the papers] addressed themselves to the reform of manners," C. S. Lewis sketches a line of continuity between the code of civil manners advocated by Addison and Steele and that followed by genteel Anglo society into the twentieth century: "That sober code of manners under which we still live today, in so far as we have any code at all, and which foreigners call hypocrisy, is in some important degree a legacy from the *Tatler* and the *Spectator*."[2] We find this code embedded in the features—ethical, psychosexual, social, physical—of the characters that people the pages of *The Tatler* and *The Spectator*.

In his evaluation of Addison's career with *The Spectator*, Johnson estimates as unparalleled his portrayal of the life and manners of his contemporary scene.[3] The *description* of character and manners is linked to their *prescription*: Addison and Steele are as much mirroring to their audience what they should be as what they are. We begin to see here ideal portraits of specifically modern identities emerge right alongside those of the types they sought to replace, or at least displace from positions of sociocultural prestige.

It must be emphasized that the position the papers occupy in the development of this modern, biologically gendered, bourgeois individual is on a ground of transition. The papers' liminal position has a number of specific effects on their portrayal of character, especially on their redrawing of the representative distinctions between the sexes. Most generally, what it generates is a remarkably visible negotiation between older, residual prestigious types and the newer, revised characters under construction. The papers' transitional position is a boon because it allows us to see the modern bourgeois individual under construction. This constructedness—so apparent in the difficulties the papers have in coming to terms with problems of mediation between the internal and external, between what is authentic and what is merely superficial—is at odds with the very fictions of authentic, naturalized individuality it produces.

One key feature of the ideal subjectivity presented in these essays is its authenticity. The modern subject is perhaps above all else a naturalized, even dehistoricized, essentialized individual. What is natural and essential is the individual's authentic self, conceived as an interior refuge of integrity and value, and serving as a stabilizing psychic ballast in a world where many of the traditional hierarchical models for life were falling away. Above all, this essential authentic self is a sexed self: before all else the modern subject is a man or a woman.[4] The very attempt to differentiate masculine and feminine on the grounds of innate biological difference produces new types of men and women.

Fashion's role in the development of the emerging modern character plays center stage in the gendering of that character. In the late seventeenth and early eighteenth centuries the map of social geography was being redrawn along highly gendered, highly differentiated spheres: public/masculine/commercial and private/feminine/familial. The effective separation of these spheres depended in good part on the formulation of gender as "natural" and incommensurable difference.[5] When masculine and feminine are defined in terms of absolute difference, the social representation of gender takes on more clearly defined forms. Male and female are marked by more heavily distinguished forms of dress and behavior even as they are relegated to increasingly separate arenas of activity. Male dress is not fully distinguished from female dress as purely masculine until the eighteenth century.[6] The bourgeois male of the rational, egalitarian public sphere secures both his sexual and his social identity by eschewing the concern with fashion and the devotion to display that are associated with both femininity and a regressive, aristocratic social order.

Rooted in the same context of shifting gender definitions, the exclusively homosexual, effeminate type emerges at the same time and, providing the necessary foil, reinforces the new strictly masculine style of self-presentation. So the modern shifts in gender categories are matched not only by an increased differentiation between the clothes worn by men and women but also between the clothes worn by real men and mollies.[7] Any departure from the increasingly sober male uniform—whether it be the overt transvestism of some of the mollies or the suspicious frippery of the fops—begins to look like gender treachery. Concerns with dress in the eighteenth century are charged with sexual, even more than class/status, anxiety.

In the essays the arena of identification and value understood as the realm of fashion and its beau monde present direct threats to the ideals of humanity promoted by Addison and Steele and, more generally, by the ideology of the public sphere per se. Fashion and style are often negatively evaluated as at best empty, and at worst deceptive, signs, with no necessary, and often an illusive, relation to ethical referents. Capitulation to fashion threatens one's character and, since character is being conceptualized as an internal and personal subjectivity, it threatens one's very self. At work here, then, is that conventional notion of fashion as a form of collective insanity, working against the interests of the rational individual to reduce her to a mere stereotype, a flat fashion plate.

Fashion itself may usurp the authority of defining desirable and undesirable social types. People may get respect simply by being fashionable; there are trends in types of people as well as in dress. The papers document the blight of fashionable types on the social landscape of the town. Addison and Steele respond to these conventionally fashionable types as to public nuisances: because fashion is irrational, capricious, and unstable it certainly should not, according to them, be entrusted with the direction of human character.

Sensitive only to the hollow standards of the beau monde, the models for people of fashion are often developed unchecked by, and sometimes in direct contradiction to, any reference to the solid virtues advocated by the papers. The dismal possibility that human identity may be enthralled to the arbitrary, meaningless, and alienating forces that drive the fashion market emerges in the commercial context of urban modernity, as does the construct that prevents it: the stable, interior, personal, and unique self that may resist this colonization by external and impersonal forces. So Addison and Steele popularize their "three-dimensional" ideal of the internally defined, authentic, and inimitable individual, to counteract the (perceived) desire people have to become instead two-dimensional stereotypes — fashion plates.

As unreservedly external cultural codes of representation, fashion, style, and beauty culture provide sites of tension where the cultivation of internal value and its (external) representation, on the body or on the page, struggle to produce and limit each other. On the one hand, Addison and Steele's portrayal of locally particular, *individual* identities calls for characterizations heavily marked by codes of dress, cosmetics, gestures, manners, habitation, occupational and leisure activities. On the other, Addison and Steele explicitly work against what they see as trivializing and even dehumanizing tendencies to construct and evaluate human character purely in terms of those superficial, counterfeitable, unstable marks. Above all else, they want to get underneath it all and excavate/erect a model of character that is at once founded on criteria outside of mere fashion, of external sociocultural conventions, and yet also able to be represented and recognized within those conventions and even to serve as a kind of alternative fashion.

Because the traits valued in the papers — modesty, stability, lack of affectation, constancy — tend to run counter to the currents of fashion, the cultivation of their stylized public expression creates a kind of paradoxical (anti)fashion that asserts the primacy of internal and ethical over external and stylistic characteristics — a kind of fashion for moral transparency, a style that looks like no style at all, a style that says no style is needed. In order to become visible and so instituted as an ethical and social standard, the absence of conspicuous stylized display itself becomes stylized and conspicuous, if according to a more "subtle" and "refined" code of representation.[8] To use Pierre Bourdieu's terms, the absence of distinction becomes, in this paradigm of style, its own mode of distinction.[9] So, the curious paradox of the specific standard of bourgeois taste promoted by *The Tatler* and *The Spectator* is that it advances a fairly inclusive and nonelitist standard of taste; yet this of course necessitates the exclusion of other "more exclusive" modes of taste. What is important here is that exclusivity becomes a negative value, one which can be leveled at those who need to be excluded. *The Tatler* and *The Spectator*, then, promote a vogue for fashion statements that disavow the ascendancy of fashion and by doing so assert strength of character. Addison and Steele present the revised mode of natural, unaffected style not merely as a socially and ethically superior one but also as one that preserves the very authenticity and integrity of the self.

It may be useful here to review briefly the construction of human individuals in *The Tatler* and *The Spectator* in relation both to the tradition of character writing and to the discourse of the public sphere into which the papers import that tradition. *The Tatler* and *The Spectator* take up the convention of character writing, directing it toward their own reformative ends, producing attractive, repulsive, or merely ludicrous characters who embody traits to be cultivated or excised by the reader. Lesson after lesson against folly or for good sense is driven home by vividly realized, highly contextualized contemporary types that are to model the readers' own self-improvements.

As J. W. Smeed notes in his study of the Theophrastan character, during the seventeenth century the growing "fashion for writing characters" set authors on quests for novel types not yet treated in the canon of character writing.[10] So, beyond its function as a system of stylistic signs denoting this or that particular character type—red heels marking the "Smart," a cane hanging from the fifth button of the coat, the "Dapper," and so on—fashion plays a role in the generic development and rhetorical practices of character writing itself.[11] Like all fashions, that for character writing was fueled by novelty and innovation. Predictably, contemporary life with its newly evolving professions and shifting social, political, and national identities provided rich fields for commentators scouting out yet-uncataloged human specimens. Following classical models, seventeenth- and eighteenth-century writers continue to adapt persistent ethical types—the vain man, the proud man—to contemporary models. They also give increasing attention to types defined by nationality, occupation, class, taste, and by their roles in the various urban institutions of London—the coffeehouse, the retail shop, the molly club, the Exchange, the Mall, the Royal Society. The bifurcation of characters into, on the one hand, the ethical, and, on the other, the social types eventually blends and merges. In the eighteenth century, as Smeed puts it, "the virtues and vices are exemplified in clearly defined social types and so depicted as to demonstrate their importance, for good or ill, within their particular social sphere."[12]

Drawn with localized historical and social features, the character is modernized. Smeed notes the importance of Addison's and Steele's papers in this development of characters, that, above all else, are secular and social.[13] I would add that the secular and social include the private and subjective, and that the definition and integration of these spheres — social/public/external and subjective/private/internal — proceeds in ways fraught with ideologically generated tensions. These portraits emerge from social landscapes where commercial and technical acceleration, urbanization, and cultural change often seem to threaten the integrity and identity of the very characters they produce. *The Tatler* and *The Spectator* advocate an ideal of subjectivity whose relationship with the sociocultural remains vexed because it is committed above all else to *internal* standards of integrity and authenticity that must, in order to secure their ascendancy, be perceived as finally outside sociocultural confirmation or refutation.

As part and parcel of a fairly optimistic and progressive view of human nature and human history, Addison and Steele provide models and narratives for the "developing" character whose reform hinges on changes effected through the internal motors of the psyche, those personal, autonomous cognitive and affective forces that we call subjectivity. Ostensibly divorced from social and historical particularities, conceived as a personal space ideally independent of the world, a place where true value and understanding reside, the inner man or woman becomes identified with the "real" person, the authentically human. Many of the characters in *The Tatler* and *The Spectator*, then, possess that precious, private space of interiority, of modern subjectivity, that comes to full flower in the midcentury English novel.[14] The character writing in these papers occupies a transitional point in literary history, one that looks back to the ancient Theophrastan character and forward to the modern English novel.

But the fictional portraits of *The Tatler* and *The Spectator* draw on and circulate back into realms of sociocultural practices beyond, though certainly not exclusive of, the literary. And the literary and the social, the textual and the extratextual, inform one another in an exchange foundational to the reform projects of *The Tatler* and *The Spectator* themselves. Both papers assume actively reciprocal relationships among cultural media, daily life, and human development. The ethical faults they redress may be produced by bad textual influences — frivolous romances or racy Restoration plays, for example — as well as by things in "real" life, such as corrupt social milieux, poor education, false ambitions.

The effect of media on social life and the individual is double-edged: it may threaten the individual and society at large with corruption through the consumption of the "wrong" material, or, with the consumption of the "right" stuff, may provide a kind of redemptive channel for positive change. *Spectator* 156 illustrates the negative effects of the media on the fashionable ladies and gentlemen who read romance fictions. Under the influence of these frivolous texts, both male and female readers are infected with "a sort of secret Ambition . . . each-side to be amiable in Imperfection, and arrive at the Characters of the dear Deceiver and the perjured Fair" (*S* 156). Far from resisting stereotypes, people actually aspire to them. Yet on the bright side, precisely because of the eagerness with which people were fashioning themselves on patterns offered by popular print culture, Addison and Steele had considerable, even immediate success propagating their own revised styles of polite characters. For good or ill, the formative influence of media on the human character is unquestioned. What is open to debate is exactly what defines good and bad models and whose authority can institutionalize them.

This debate and the struggle over authority that it comprises takes place in that arena of public discourse and identification that, following Habermas, we know as the bourgeois public sphere. As I have discussed at some length in the introductory chapter, because power in this sphere worked not through coercion but through the more hegemonic modes of persuasion and free choice, the reforms it promotes depend on the revision of internal psychic and affective forces of will, agency, and desire. Furthermore, as an aspect of this hegemonic operation of power, the exercise of power itself is somewhat veiled and dissimulated, working through informal, apparently power-free zones of conduct and influence, what Johnson refers to as "the minuter decencies and inferior duties" of life in contrast to those explicitly power-laden and ideologically charged arenas of religion and politics. In fact, Johnson suggests that *The Tatler* and *The Spectator* were instituted "to divert the attention of the people from publick discontent" by supplying "to minds heated with political contest . . . cooler and more inoffensive reflections."[15] What critics of the public sphere point out is that these purportedly ideologically neutral top-

ics themselves serve ideological, even political, functions. In relation
to the ideological productions of the public sphere, *The Tatler* and *The
Spectator* are notable for their contributions to that model of (supposedly) universal human nature on which communication, consensus, modern civility, and indeed modern imperial civilization depend.

The bourgeois public sphere presented itself as an inclusive arena
of discourse, one where conventional boundaries of wealth and status were bracketed. Ideally, *anyone* could buy, read, and correspond
with a newspaper, enter into a coffeehouse discussion, take part in
the debate over the conduct of both public and private life that took
place in these institutions. An examination of the character types
promoted by institutions of the public sphere like *The Tatler* and *The
Spectator* shows, however, that this anyone could not be, well, just
anyone, but was a quite specific somebody. Analyzing the ideological groundwork of this model of subjectivity, Michael Warner points
out that while "it is supposed" within the public sphere "that all particularities have the same status as mere particularity" and so are all
equally inconsequential, the very "ability to establish that frame of
reference is a feature of some particularities." Predictably, the particularities that bring with them the ability to establish the frame of reference of the public sphere are those of whiteness, maleness, and
middle-classness. These can only be seen as unspecific, as unmarked
within a frame where they are understood as universal and so where
everything else — the feminine, the nonwhite, the under- and even
the elite class — is marked by differences seen as particular and specific. By pointing out that particularities of race, class, and gender
(whiteness, middle-classness, and maleness) cannot be treated as
"merely paratactic or serial difference," we see how these differences
are already coded as marked and unmarked. As is now well recognized, the bourgeois public sphere's ideology of universality and authenticity relies on this encoding of what is male, white, middle-class
as the normal, the unmarked and so invisible, the universalizable.[16]

However, the concrete specification of these "unmarked" features
of normality, the self-conscious stylization of the bourgeois subject
that we find in *The Tatler* and *The Spectator* blows its own cover as
natural, universal, and nonparticular. Because the papers occupy such

a transitional phase in the institutionalization of this mode of internal, self-authenticating subjectivity, they come perilously close to fully disclosing the constructed peculiarity of what they would understand as inalienable, natural, and universal. These papers show a model of bourgeois subjectivity still under construction. And while its generation from a set of quite specifiable and exclusive particularities ultimately limits its claims to access and universality, this ideal of a self-authenticating, autonomous individual, with an abstractly *human* value, is formulated as much as a progressive and liberating alternative as a regulative norm. That, of course, is the source of its great power.

THE GOOD, THE BAD, AND THE UGLY

It has been the Purpose of several of my Speculations
to bring People to an unconcerned Behaviour, with relation to
their Persons, whether Beautiful or Defective.

SPECTATOR *87*

Exclusivity becomes, within the ideology of the papers as within the bourgeois public sphere generally, a negative value but, nonetheless, one that itself can be used as the basis of exclusion and so one that may serve as revised forms of social prestige and elitism. The ambiguities, ironies, and apparent paradoxes of this antiexclusion exclusivity are nowhere better illustrated than in the series of letters narrating Mr. Spectator's negotiations for membership within a prestigious social club, the Ugly Club. This begins with a letter in *Spectator* 17 from one "Alexander Carbuncle" relating the formation at Oxford University of an "Ugly Club," complete with its founding constitution "*The Act of Deformity*." The Ugly Club, Carbuncle tells us, was established as a burlesque on "*the Handsom Club*" according to principles neatly antithetical to the conventional standards of beauty culture enshrined in its rival. But adhering to its own quite exacting standards, the Ugly Club is no less exclusive, and therefore potentially fashionable, than its antitype: the merely plain will not get in the door; all members must be exquisitely ugly.

Emboldened by the club's new mode of antibeauty, Mr. Spectator stops trying to disguise his squat face with a high wig and a long beard in the hope that this flaw, now flaunted, will win him admittance (*S* 17). His wish is granted, but not before serious deliberation of his qualifications. It is not clear that a squat face gives him an adequate claim to ugliness. But he takes his chances and applies, and in *Spectator* 32, a member reports on the club's consideration of his case.

Mr. Spectator's application is complicated by two factors, both related to appearance and both overridden by considerations of internal character traits understood as independent of physical identity, of the cultural coding of the body as ugly, handsome, or merely plain. Ugliness finally has little to do with it. Mr. Spectator is admitted on the strength of his character, not the defects of his person. But before this can happen, the club has to modify its commitment to strict criteria of superficial, external, physical ugliness. Chartered on principles that, while significantly revising the content of social desirability (ugliness rather than beauty) do not go outside the external and superficial criteria of the body for their standards of inclusion. The Ugly Club's reforms, like those of its rival Handsome Club, go only skin deep. Because his case demands that the criterion of appearance be jettisoned altogether, Mr. Spectator's involvement reorients the club's policy: it replaces external, physical standards with internal ones having to do with character and ideology, with ethos rather than body. The society sets aside Mr. Spectator's physical (dis)qualifications and gives weight instead to his ideological identity that mirrors the club's own. The Ugly Club's previous commitment to strict standards of personal appearance are to be understood, then, as a slightly misguided implementation of a basically sound policy: the opposition to the fashion and beauty culture that holds tyrannical sway over polite society.

That no one has ever actually seen Mr. Spectator puts the first wrinkle in his application. The club must take Mr. Spectator's word for his own ugliness. Second, as I have mentioned, it is unclear that Mr. Spectator is ugly enough to gain membership in this society. Fortunately, the club's president advocates Mr. Spectator's candidacy, citing the good press the Spectator gives the club in *Spectator* 17. Unavailable for their personal inspection, members turn to *The Spectator* to see how its creator "look'd in Print" (*S* 32). There they find "the pleasant Image of [their] Proselite" applauding them for daring to be ugly.

Mr. Spectator, then, remains invisible. He is admitted not, as is usual, by virtue of his personal appearance but by virtue of his appearance in print. He gains admittance on the strength of his principles that uphold not so much the standard of ugliness against that of beauty but a standard outside all merely external and superficial criteria, positive or negative. He is admitted sight unseen, on principles he has himself defined. And this solution, by a kind of cancellation of the first problem—Mr. Spectator's invisibility—brings with it the suspension of the second issue—his possible lack of sufficient personal ugliness. If looks don't count, then his own run-of-the-mill homeliness bars no doors.

Mr. Spectator's invisibility is all important, not only here but throughout his periodical enterprise. So while in this single instance his evasion of personal observation may seem merely circumstantial—the club meets at Oxford, he is in London—the Spectator's invisibility is no accident: it is a cultivated aspect of his character, one on which the ethos and perspective of the paper depends. An embodiment of public-sphere nonparticularity, Mr. Spectator cannot be *identified*. Withholding his own identity, he tends, chameleonlike, to take on that of whatever company he finds himself in: "I have been taken for a Merchant upon the *Exchange* for above these ten Years, and sometimes pass for a *Jew* in the Assembly of Stock-Jobbers at *Jonathan's*" (*S* 1).

"In short," he writes, giving his own character in the first *Spectator* paper, "I have acted all the parts of my Life as a Looker-on, which is the Character I intend to preserve in this Paper." A "Spectator of Mankind" rather than "one of the Species," he introduces himself in the first number of the paper by putting himself outside the crowd and above the fray. This supremely critical, and voyeuristic, position from which he may silently, invisibly survey the world establishes the Spectator's authority. Constructing a fantasy of himself as unidentifiable, unconfined by any material circumstance, he may pass, specterlike, through all scenes of life. Distance and immunity from the objects of his speculations are the conditions of his criticism: so advantaged, he "can discern the Errors in the Oeconomy, Business, and Diversion of others, better than those who are engaged in them" (*S* 1).

Quite simply, Mr. Spectator adopts a position of profound privilege in relation to the objects of his gaze and of his critique. The Spectator's invisibility has its counterpart in his ability to render others transparent; because you can't see him, he can see right through you. "The inward Disposition of the Mind" is "made visible" to his veiled surveillance (*S* 86). Often ironic, such critical detachment not only provides him with a "better Perspective" on the world but also protects him from the world. His projects depend on this distance and immunity so completely that his greatest fear is having his cover blown, of becoming visible: "the greatest Pain I can suffer, is the being talked to, and being stared at" (*S* 1). In print, he throws a veil of secrecy around all those identifying features of body, dress, and complexion, and all those indexes of name, age, and address that place him in rather than apart from the world.[17] Once seen, the Spectator would become the object of another's gaze and, potentially, of another's evaluation, another's criticism. His protective shield of skeptical detachment commands its own price: the fear of being recognized as part of and so attached to the world he would elude.

The critical authority supported by the Spectator's invisibility remains intact through the process of his admission to the Ugly Club. What is more, the principles on which that invisible authority rests determine this process in ways that subtly alter the criteria and so the ideology of that club's original charter, "The Act of Deformity." With its echo of the Act of Uniformity, this parodic charter suggests a trivializing secularization of the principles of religious conformity institutionalized by that act and points up the ludicrous righteousness of these clerics of the high church of homeliness. Presented with a highly desirable, if not exquisitely ugly, candidate, the club broadens its application of the constitution in ways more attuned to the spirit than the letter of the law. Mr. Spectator's intervention effects a kind of new dispensation that dematerializes and abstracts the club's creed. Members who had been wedded to regulations of superficial deformity are soon silenced, and alterations to the club's charter are approved. It is easy to see that if the Ugly Club became too tightly bound to standards of personal appearance it would become not a voice of dissent from the conventions of beauty culture but a mere negative reflection of that culture, still mirroring its superficial standards and the form, if not the content, of its fashions. On the primacy of principles over forms, the president and Mr. Spectator strictly concur; *Spectator* 17, where the Spectator praises the club, and *Spectator* 32, where the club praises the Spectator, echo one another in mutual affirmation.

But the devotion to the spirit of the law exhibited by Mr. Spectator and the president is not successfully communicated to all their audience. In *Spectator* 87, one ugly wannabe, Rosalinda, writes in to apply for membership. Her letter reveals a vision of the club from a baldly literal, superficial, and, predictably, fashion-oriented perspective, precisely that which the Spectator and the club's president work to counter. Rosalinda is beautiful; she tells us so herself. Confessing herself "in every respect one of the Handsomest young Girls about Town," Rosalinda admits "how very Defective [she is] in every thing that is Ugly." Her appeal shows how, to the fashion victim, exclusivity and novelty have intrinsic values higher than that of beauty itself. Rather than daring to be ugly, Rosalinda is anxious to get in on a new trend. So while *Spectator* 17 praises the club as a force that counteracts the narcissistic preoccupation with external appearance, Rosalinda's later letter in *Spectator* 87 shows that the club is still being sought out as a modish institution for the expression of personal vanity.

Of course we are to understand that Rosalinda has misunderstood the principles of the club and so to read her letter as a dramatic satire on her own vanity. And as much as this is satire on fashionable, flighty young ladies, it is also a satire on fashion itself, showing its irreverence for all enduring values, even that of personal beauty, the very alibi for its own operations.[18] The observation that fashion lies beyond not only good and evil but even the beautiful and ugly is conventional and one often mistakenly thought to discredit fashion. But this uncanny autonomy even from aesthetic criteria is fashion's strength, both as a savage, alienating, and manipulative force and as a visionary power that, if only for the sake of profit and novelty, pushes beyond chartered horizons of style, redrawing the limits of the permissible.

Rosalinda's confusion of the Ugly Club with a fashion-setting institution may actually be no confusion at all. Held up as the standards of inclusion to a desirable society — the Ugly Club — and advocated in the popular media, even the cultivation of internal, abstract, character traits may constitute a kind of fashion. Moreover, by reorienting what is an explicitly and increasingly modish club toward internal, abstract criteria, Mr. Spectator's involvement can be seen as introducing, or at least intensifying, fashion's saturation into these ethical, subjective realms. For in order to become a member of the fashionable Ugly Club one must not simply *look* a certain way but, more importantly, one must *be* a certain way, adopting the attitudes of the authentically unfashionable. But inclusion is still the key; Mr. Spectator *wants in* no less avidly than Rosalinda. And, as the Spectator's satires on fashion so often reveal, fashion is nothing but what is in. By using popular media and the appeal of exclusivity to promote an "authentic" ethical standard outside of physical appearance, the Spectator wants to make the real thing the in thing.

GOT TO BE REAL: INSIDE/OUTSIDE AUTHENTICITY

The kinds of fashion reforms advocated by Addison and Steele are aimed more at the inner man and woman than the mere externals of behavior and dress; they depend on an ideology of authentic subjectivity. Advocating the internal over the superficial, the real over the merely simulated, this ideology is at odds with its own representation and dissemination. For while the exemplary function of the types offered in these papers necessitates their imitation, the papers also repeatedly criticize facile imitation, or simulation, even of desirable social types. Thus the ridiculous "Pretty Fellow" is defined as a pathetic imitation of the true "Gentleman," and the rake is distinguished by Steele, at loving length, from his sorry imitators (*T* 21; *T* 27). Jack Dimple, the "Pretty Fellow" of *Tatler* 21, and "Nobilis," the rake manqué of *Tatler* 27, are ethically polar types: Dimple is a weak character trying to be better than he is and Nobilis is a virtuous man trying, for fashion's sake, to be worse than he is. Yet they share a common fault: trying to be what they are not. Based merely on the outer signs — the clothes, manners, tastes, and conduct — of the types "gentleman" and "rake," Dimple's and Nobilis's imitations are doomed to failure because they are just that, mere imitations, simulations of external traits without internal supports. They have made themselves not rakes or gentlemen but counterfeits of the rake and the gentleman. The papers insist that true gentility or true rakishness can only come from within, that these characteristics belong to an interior subjectivity not attainable through mere "superficial" simulation. One objection to fashionable stereotypes is that they are stereotypes, and thus accessible through a kind of mechanical mimicry that permits people to cultivate an external equivalency with a desired type at the expense of their own assumedly individual personal character.

But how then are the positive models offered by these papers supposed to work if not through imitation of the same sort disclaimed as shallow simulation or base counterfeit? This problem is structurally analogous and thematically related to the vexed relationship *The Tatler* and *The Spectator* bear to fashion itself: how to exploit the dangerous yet desirably influential cultural medium (fashion, simulation) without becoming enthralled to it? And of course, widespread imitation is a crucial feature of fashionability itself.[19] Just as any significant adoption of stylistic reforms offered to counter fashion produces its own fashion, so any adoption of the good character types advocated by the papers depends on imitation (as emulation); this is the point of producing them.

To address this apparent contradiction is to get at the core of an essentially ideological problem of representation generated by a cultural politics founded on authenticity. We have already seen this contradiction inflected in the Spectator's own "invisible" character. Most broadly the pattern for positive types follows the logic of restoration: a return from affectation to sincerity, from the false values of the world to the true integrity of the personal self, from the superficial to the essential, from the stereotypical to the authentic individual. What differentiates the true gentleman from his base imitator the "Pretty Fellow" is that he is just being himself: the gentleman is a type of man not reducible to typology. The type for the true gentleman can only be articulated by the disavowal of typification and imitation. This logic is analogous to that which informs Addison's and Steele's approach to fashion, style, and beauty culture at large: real beauty appears through a refusal of self-display; the desirable mode is a kind of "natural" style that refers to ethical realities outside the limits of fashion's conventions. Similarly enmeshed in the paradoxes generated by this ideology of authenticity, the proper use of the positive character types in *The Tatler* and *The Spectator* involves a kind of imitation of their refusal of imitation. Basically, Addison and Steele ask readers to imitate their stereotypes in order to be more real.

In order for personal authenticity and integrity to coexist with ethical change and so with reform, any emulation of the examples offered by Addison and Steele requires a "real" assimilation, a true change of heart not a mere change of clothes. The linchpin of Addison's and Steele's engine of reform, this distinction between the superficial and the essential, the affected and the authentic, is held in place by a kind of aggressive inattention to the reciprocity between inside/outside. Because it is so crucial to the model of subjectivity advocated in the papers, it seems appropriate to examine at some length how the barrier between inside/outside is guarded in *Spectator* 16.

Concerned more with elegance than ethics, correspondents write in asking the Spectator "to be very satyrical upon the little Muff that is now in Fashion," to comment on "a Pair of silver Garters buckled below the Knees," or to inveigh against "fringed Gloves" (*S* 16). Explaining why he cannot fulfill these requests, Mr. Spectator defines the nature of his critical project: "I must once for all inform my Readers, that it is not my Intention to sink the Dignity of this my Paper with Reflections upon Red-Heels or Top-Knots, but rather to enter into the Passions of Mankind, and to correct those depraved Sentiments that give Birth to all those little Extravagancies which appear in their outward Dress and Behavior" (*S* 16). Attention to the trivia of fashion is beneath the dignity of the paper. Mr. Spectator has bigger fish to fry. He will leave alone "those little Extravagancies" whose alteration, in any case, could have only the most superficial improving effect. Rather than the symptomatic excrescences of fashion, Mr. Spectator is after roots, origins, first causes: "The Blossoms will fall of themselves, when the Root that nourishes them is destroyed" (*S* 16).

Yet, while putting himself above attention to the ephemeral "blossoms" of fashion, Mr. Spectator does admit it is a job that somebody has got to do: "I must own, that I have Thoughts of creating an Officer under me to be entituled [*sic*] *The Censor of small Wares.*" This officer would serve, in the medical figure Addison adopts, as "Surgeon" under Mr. Spectator as "Physitian." Addison goes on to define a strict division of labor between these two roles that mirrors the distinction he begins with between the merely superficial "symptoms" of folly and their true underlying causes: "The [surgeon] might be employ'd in healing those Blotches and Tumours which break out in the Body, while the [physician] is sweetning the Blood and rectifying the Constitution." As cosmetic and subordinate as his role may be, nonetheless the surgeon's skills are needed for the excision of those "Tumours" of fashion's cancer, the "long Swords or sweeping Trains, bushy Head-dresses or full-bottom'd Perriwigs" that "the young People of both Sexes are so wonderfully apt to shoot out into" (*S* 16).

Admitting the need for a surgical assistant and so for treating mere externals, Mr. Spectator compromises the initial assertion that his only concern will be the internal roots and causes of folly. And the physiological figure Addison adopts here itself tends to confuse "natural" physicality with cultural conventionality and so the personal, internal causes of fashion abuse with their external, physical symptoms. Rhetorically, these levels of fashion's manifestation are further confounded by the shift from a surgical into a botanical metaphor: trendy young people as plants shooting forth overluxuriant fashion foliage. If, as the figure asserts, these are *natural* growths sprouting from *internal* compulsions, then it seems that the line is blurred between the mere "Indications" of folly and the internal seat of those "Passions" that gives rise to them. And indeed it is. Yet, this metaphor also simultaneously supports Addison's rhetoric of the reform of nature itself. Although the assistant surgeon, the censor of fashion, may be of short-term use in controlling the proliferation of external signs through which "those depraved Sentiments" are manifest, any long-term, permanent cure must involve a rectification of the natural, physiological "Constitution." Still the question of the purely superficial, and thus superfluous and trivial, nature of fashion remains open.

Taking up his next point, that as a satirist and reformer his object is not the individual but the species, Mr. Spectator changes hats, shifting his self-representation from physician to sovereign. In a classical allusion of dubious felicity, Mr. Spectator cites antique precedent: "I think it was *Caligula* who wished the whole City of *Rome* had but one Neck, that he might behead them in a Blow. I shall do out of Humanity what that Emperour would have done in the Cruelty of his Temper, and aim every stroak at a collective Body of Offenders" (*S* 16). And this new figure — Caligula executing offenders — recalls that of the surgical assistant: both hack away at the bodies of the transgressor. But here, as a kind of mock evil emperor transvalued, a Caligula slashing his subjects — but for their own good — the Spectator himself wields the knife.

Reading this figure, as I do here the entire paper, more seriously than it is intended, one may take the Caligula allusion up through one more turn. And I think such an excessively serious reading is justified because Addison's own violent, brutally physical figures themselves produce a tonal excess, importing connotations at odds with the civil mockery that shimmers across the satire's surface. What the Caligula figure finally does is translate the Spectator's own concern with the minds of men into the embodied and violent metaphors that earlier enter into the description of his assistant surgeon's corporal duties. This translation involves as well an intensification. More than a surgeon, the Spectator acts as executioner, he gets at the psychic roots of folly not by changing the minds of his subjects but by decapitating them. The whole rhetorical transaction speaks of the mind as body and of the Spectator's frustration at the deep connection between them. By launching his attack on the psyche from the outside through the head, he admits this connection, and his attack again violates the distinction between external and internal, between the "Excrecensies" of fashion and the "Passions of Mankind." The division of labor between the censor of petty wares, involved in the arbitration of external appearances, and the moral censor, engrossed in the deeper, more "real" matters of the human psyche, is not sustained. An interiority immune from contact with its external manifestations proves difficult to maintain.

Both *The Tatler* and *The Spectator* give ample attention to topknots and red heels, to hoop-skirts, patches, and colored caps, to the particularities of fashion. By no means does either paper shy away from legislating gender, morality, and social relations through specific reforms of dress and manner. It proves, finally, difficult to maintain the division between the ethical, internal, and permanent, on the one hand, and the material, external, and transient, on the other. This is not to say that Addison collapses this distinction and renders it inoperative; it is the fulcrum on which hinges the whole ideology of representation and subjectivity within which the papers work.

Legislating fashion, the papers stylize a model of the authentically human and so hypostatize it. Creating rhetorical fictions for the representation of the real, they rely on sociocultural conventions that produce and portray interior realms of ethical and emotional life independent of sociocultural conventions. One thing that differentiates Addison's and Steele's ideal characters from the simulated stereotypes they counter is their greater investment in the fictions of their own integrity, of their own authenticity, and of their own transparent mediation.

It's got to be real. Of course, their commitment to authenticity confers persuasive power, moral fiber, and cultural credibility to Addison's and Steele's visions. So Michael Ketcham concludes his study of *The Spectator* noting its effective production of the "myth of the modern age": a dream of inner authenticity, of a self immune from the affectations and impostures of the World, one that finds its own affirmation in personal, intimate groups, primarily the family.[20] From this space of privileged domesticated interiority, urban man sought to give "imaginative order" to the realm of exchange and so create, sustain, and communicate "a stable and benevolent community."[21] Of course, our critical understanding of this myth must acknowledge the ways that it is as exclusive as it is creative, as repressive as it is communicative, as contradictory as it is stable, and as fictional as it is historic.

GENDER AND SEXUAL DIFFERENCE

Addison and Steele rethink character in terms of gender definitions that are shifting in line with the emergent concept of biologically innate, rather than socially secured, sexual difference.[22] The category of sexual difference challenges the older notion of a hierarchal distinction between the sexes—women as imperfect knockoffs of men. "In the later seventeenth and eighteenth centuries," writes Michael McKeon, "England acquired the modern wisdom that there are not one but two sexes; that they are defined not by behavior, which is variable, but by nature, which is not."[23] *The Tatler* and *The Spectator* contribute their formulations of masculine and feminine to this shift which Thomas Laqueur locates firmly in the eighteenth century: "Sometime in the eighteenth century, sex as we know it was invented."[24] As he explains, this knowledge is historical, originating not in scientific progress but in sociopolitical revolutions that removed women from economic production and other arenas of public life:

> The context for the articulation of two incommensurable sexes was . . . neither a theory of knowledge nor advances in scientific knowledge. The context was politics. There were endless new struggles for power and position in the enormously enlarged public sphere of the eighteenth and particularly the post-revolutionary nineteenth centuries. . . . When, for many reasons, a preexisting transcendental order or time-immemorial custom became a less and less plausible justification for social relations, the battleground of gender roles shifted to nature, to biological sex. Distinct sexual anatomy was adduced to support or deny all manner of claims in a variety of specific social, economic, political, cultural, or erotic contexts.[25]

Sexual difference supports and naturalizes the categorical division of these contexts by gender, and so is part of the separation of spheres that marks modern culture: private is divided from public, the home from the world, consumption from production, feminine from masculine.[26] Clear-cut and incommensurable gender categories, stabilized as part of the very sexual nature of the individual, become the order of the day. Oriented around quickly conventionalized notions of both the natural body and the interior individual self, sexual difference serves to incorporate the individual, body and soul, into the newly written social texts of both the public sphere and the private home.

Kathryn Shevelow discusses print culture's role in institutionalizing these gendered distinctions between the public and private, the world and the home.[27] Working on the popular level to promote "the notion of women as different in kind rather than degree from men," papers such as *The Tatler* and *The Spectator* were instrumental in the regendering of the world.[28] The ideology of sexual difference permeates the papers: "There may . . . be," writes Addison "a kind of Sex in the very Soul" (*S* 128). And in *Tatler* 172 Steele assumes without hesitation such an essential and abstracted sexual distinction: "I am sure, I do not mean it an Injury to Women, when I say there is a Sort of Sex in Souls. . . . That the Soul of a Man and that of a Woman are made very unlike, according to the Employments for which they are designed."

Sexual difference produces new reproductive bodies, displacing the Aristotelian/Galenic isomorphic view of male and female: "Organs that had shared a name — ovaries and testicles — were now linguistically distinguished. Organs that had not been distinguished by a name of their own — vagina, for example — were given one."[29] Rooted in the natural, anatomized body and abstracted as soulful essence, gender distinctions — masculine and feminine — are compounded with sexual difference — male and female.[30] This naturalizes and dehistoricizes gender difference and produces new medical and social categories of the naturally and unnaturally sexed person: for example, on the one hand, the passive bourgeois woman and, on the other, the effeminate and exclusively homosexual male. Such sexualized gender differences, McKeon suggests, come gradually to take categorical dominance over traditional hierarchical status differences as social paradigms shift into heavier reliance on the category of economic *class*.[31] Sexualized gender differences serve as a new, alternative ground of embodied authenticity as the older reliance on inborn status distinctions falls away. When the essential differences among people are understood as those of sex more completely than those of status, the representation of sexual difference — in clothing, for example — becomes a higher priority than that of socioeconomic difference. While other facets of identification — status/class, nationality, ethnicity — are by all means fully present, sexual difference assumes its modern form as perhaps *the* most essential marker of the core self. Thus at this period, the marking of gender differences becomes an object of more primary scrutiny and anxiety than the marking of status difference.

Integral to the gendered modern character, in both normative and transgressive incarnations, sexual difference supports the definition of sets of separate feminine and masculine virtues and so becomes a distinction crucial to the determination of value and personal worth — of character. Discussing the idealized role of wife/mother in the eighteenth century, Lynne Friedli emphasizes how anxiety over clear, discrete sexual categorization fed into the invention of the modern category "woman."[32] The virtuous, modest, domestic woman is a product of sexual difference. Her negative counterpart, the worldly, fashionable, libertine whore lingers on within the residual paradigm of sex as a hierarchical spectrum. Kathryn Norberg discusses the type of the libertine whore, who, although rooted in seventeenth-century discourse, persists well into the eighteenth century as the prostitute heroine of pornography: "She owes little to the new notions of sexual difference. . . . She knows nothing of woman's supposedly inherent modesty and cares little for her role in the family. She is a public woman of a particular sort, who existed in a time when the division between public and private was not yet defined."[33] The distinction between virtuous and vicious women is then played out in terms of relative assimilation to models of sexual difference. Emotionally, socially, and financially independent, taking both active and passive economic and sexual roles, participating in the sociosexual economy as both seller and commodity, the libertine woman corrodes difference sexually and socially.[34] She is not properly feminized. And while Addison's and Steele's faulty women characters are not prostitutes, they do display other traits of Norberg's libertine woman: her disregard of family and the domestic scene; her preoccupation with public display and the sociosexual power it confers; and, in a word, her lack of respect for sexual difference.

The paradigm of sexual difference has equally transformative effects on the male character and ideals of masculinity. Furthermore, these masculine transformations are themselves articulated in reference to the feminine, especially the bad libertine feminine. Randolph Trumbach examines the history of male gender definition in early-eighteenth-century England, giving particular attention to emergent modern notions of exclusive hetero- and homosexuality. Just as with the reformulation of ideal womanhood, that of ideal masculinity works within the paradigm of absolute sexual difference. The demand for absolute sexual difference is met by criteria of sexual object choice:

> There remained one unbreachable difference between men and women: men did not know what it was like to desire males sexually. Only women and sodomites knew that. Therefore, what the nineteenth century called *homosexuality* and *heterosexuality* are not distinctions to be found in universal human nature. They were, instead, products of a gender system that had appeared in the early eighteenth century.[35]

Men are men because they desire women; thus men are men because they are not mollies, because they do not desire other men. Men who do desire other men sexually are not real men. The new code of masculinity redefines the character of the sodomite as a kind of "he-whore" who emerges in the very first decades of the eighteenth century. Identified by his effeminate manner, his dressiness, and often his transvestism, the molly is the new sodomite. Trumbach notes how this self-naming of members of a developing urban homosexual subculture "starts a long tradition . . . whereby the slang terms for prostitutes in one generation subsequently are appropriated for sodomites (e.g., queen, punk, gay, faggot, fairy, and fruit). It makes it clear that the sodomite viewed himself, and was seen by others, no longer as a rake but as a species of outcast woman."[36]

The prostitute and the modern, effeminate male homosexual are linked not only by their street-names, but also by the roles their gender identities play in the economy of sociosexual difference: "The molly, like the prostitute, was an individual entirely defined by his sexual behavior. Together, the prostitute and the sodomite displayed the boundaries of appropriate gender behavior for the majority of people in their societies, where true women were not whores, and real men were not sodomites."[37] And while what we would call homosexual men only appear a few times and fleetingly in *The Tatler* and *The Spectator* papers, this paradigm of sexual difference shows up not only in the illegitimate but also the ideal masculine characters. Just as the feminine virtue of the domestic woman is secured by her distinction from the improperly feminized libertine woman of the world, so the masculine integrity of the new model gentleman depends on his difference not merely from women but also from the invariably overdressed and effeminate fop, beau, and pretty fellow.

Fashion as a cultural code, then, is marked not simply by status (as modes of a corrupt, regressive aristocracy) but even more by gender, as part of a set of essentially feminine foibles. Likewise, the critique of effeminacy in men involves not only the condemnation of social decadence but also of an effeminacy that is starting to signal homosexuality. The nature and extent of men's involvement in fashion, in what Elizabeth Wilson tags "the cultural metaphor for the body," serves to define what the masculine body should and should not be.[38] Men are admonished to keep their distance from this feminized arena of signification; their bodies, it is implied, are emasculated by the marks of the mode. Sexual difference removes bourgeois women more completely from the arenas of production, relegating them more and more to spheres of leisured consumption. At the same time it puts certain kinds of consumption and leisure activities outside the bounds of the properly masculine. So Mrs. Jenny Distaff, with prejudices closely allied with Bickerstaff's own, cites as particularly offensive to ladies those "Men who affect the Entertainments and Manners suitable only to our Sex" (*T* 36).

The construction of these separate spheres of masculine and feminine activity and symbolic dominion is of a dialectical nature. There is considerable spatial/symbolic reciprocity between the gendered separation of spheres, just as there is a good deal of overlap in the masculine and feminine sets of desirable traits. And *The Tatler* and *The Spectator* bear ample witness to a kind of domestication of masculine virtue that emerges with more fanfare later in the century in the fuller expression of sensibility and sentimentality. In a sense, the bourgeois male can afford this intimacy with domesticity as long as his value as a legitimately masculine man is guaranteed by his essential difference from the effeminate homosexual man. This is one instance that reveals how the reformulation of social geography and the fixing of woman in her domestic sphere did not take place without reframing the social sites and ideals of masculinity. It is my impression that *The Tatler* and *The Spectator* evince an anxiety about the masculine character and his spheres of activity that matches, and perhaps exceeds, that surrounding their treatment of the female character. For it is the white, middle-class, *male* individual who must stand — universalized, departicularized, unmarked, and unconstructed — as the central icon of bourgeois subjectivity. He becomes this icon largely through what his identity repels: the bad feminine and, related closely to this, the effeminate, modern homosexual.

CASTING THE FEMALE ROLES: COQUETTES, JILTS, AND WOMEN OF SENSE

That both masculine and feminine ideal characters are defined in negative relation to a type of "bad" femininity embodied by the whore and the effeminate sodomite attests to the pivotal position of the female person and femininity itself in the revisions of gender identity.[39] Defining "the eighteenth-century myth of passive womanhood," Ellen Pollak outlines the formative legal, economic, and sociopolitical roots of the new feminine ideal and looks at its propagation through conduct books and the similarly normative *Tatler* and *Spectator* papers.[40] She shows how as upper- and middle-class women withdrew from economic productivity and came to be identified almost exclusively with a domestic realm of consumption, they became as well "the embodiment of moral value" that defined interior space, both psychic and architectural.[41] Subjective interiority has its analogue in the private familial home, presided over by the domestic woman. The woman as custodian of both places, the domestic nest and the inner life, is a familiar nineteenth-century type — the angel in the house. That angel's great-great grandmother flutters through the pages of *The Tatler* and *Spectator*, beckoning the female reader away from their fashionable and dissolute resorts — shops, carriages, visits, card games, balls, puppet shows, masquerades, routs, ridottos, court-days — to join her in an enlightened and virtuous domesticity.

Even as women are being enlisted as subjects in and symbols of a realm of domestic virtue, affective sincerity, and personal integrity, as part and parcel of the same project, they are criticized for their *innate* frivolity and fashion-mad foolishness. The split between these two sets of traits often shows up clearly dichotomized in *The Tatler*'s and *The Spectator*'s favorable and unfavorable characters of women. And while the reform of women may seem doomed from the start by their inborn fickleness, as I note in the previous chapter, this instability of temperament makes them available objects for manipulation, even for rational ends. Properly managed, whimsical, mercurial femininity becomes a kind of easy malleability, a flexibility that may bend with the right, as well as the wrong, guidance. This is one way of resolving the contradictory formulation, apparent in *The Tatler* and *The Spectator*, of women as naturally flawed in ways that threaten the realization of their natural character. Jane Spencer notes this contradiction and sees in it an exposure of the contradictions in paternal benevolence: "It seems that eighteenth-century women needed a good deal of educating into their 'inborn,' 'natural' feminine qualities."[42]

Addison elaborates the "light fantastical Disposition" of women in *Spectator* 15. I cite this essay at length because it lays out a constellation of issues that control the delineation of female character in these papers: the idea of women's specific, sex-linked nature; this female nature as weakness; the central role of fashion and beauty culture in the manifestation of this weakness; the dangers that women thus pose for themselves; and most importantly, the role of *The Spectator* in saving women from themselves:

The usual Conversation of ordinary Women very much cherishes this Natural Weakness of being taken with Outside and Appearance. . . . A Furbelow of precious Stones, an Hat buttoned with a Diamond, a Brocade Waistcoat or Petticoat, are standing Topicks. In short, they consider only the Drapery of the Species, and never cast away a Thought on those Ornaments of the Mind, that make Persons illustrious in themselves, and Useful to others. When Women are thus perpetually dazzling one another's Imaginations, and filling their Heads with nothing but Colours, it is no Wonder that they are more attentive to the superficial Parts of Life, than the solid and substantial Blessings of it. A girl, who has been trained up in this kind of Conversation, is in danger of every Embroidered Coat that comes in her Way. A Pair of fringed Gloves may be her Ruin. (*S* 15)

This passage throws into high relief women's affinity for unrealness, for artificiality and superficiality. But natural weakness is only partially to blame for this usual and, Addison is saying, pointless way of life. Dupes to their mindless, intuitive fascination with bright, shiny, and highly patterned objects (a fascination they share with children, primitive peoples, Yahoos, and pet birds), women are not well served by conventional female education. Dominant socialization methods foster a race of women who value themselves and others wholly on externals. "The last Sighs of a Handsome Woman," writes a correspondent to *Spectator* 33, "are not so much for the Loss of her Life, as of her Beauty. . . . Woman's strongest Passion is for her own Beauty."

In order to restore women to their senses, their desires must be reformed. Women must be reeducated in a way that takes their minds as well as their bodies, their thoughts as well as their looks, into account (*S* 66). This call for the broader intellectual cultivation of women sounds liberal and progressive, but its goal is only women's more total domestication. One objection to conventional female education is its promotion of worldly status achieved through self-display. Reformed education encourages instead retirement, modesty, and a social reputation based on a conspicuous absence from, rather than presence in, the world. The more liberally educated woman takes her homework to heart and, realizing the vanity of the world, confines herself to the domestic sphere of her own free will.

Home and family provide the sole context for the proper female character. Steele gives a "short Rule for [female] Behavior" in *Spectator* 104: "Every young Lady in her Dress, Words, and Actions [should] recommend her self as a Sister, Daughter, or Wife, and make her self the more esteemed in one of those Characters." A woman, as Steele elaborates in *Spectator* 342, has her identity only in complementary relationship to men: "All she has to do in this World, is contained within the Duties of a Daughter, a Sister, a Wife, and a Mother."[43] Just as her identity is prescribed by patriarchal kinship relations, the domestic woman maintains a carefully circumscribed relation to dress and social distinction: "[Female duties] are likewise consistent," continues Steele in *Spectator* 342, "with a moderate share of Wit, a plain Dress, and a modest Air."

The modest, good, domestic women with their plain dress and demure air have their antitype in the women of fashion, the women of the world. Defined by their pursuit of fashionable distinction, these women are publicly oriented and self-affirming, rather than domestically directed and self-effacing. The specific character types, then, that compete with those familial roles of wife, sister, and daughter are laid out with equal clarity: the coquette, the idol, the jilt, all the tyrannical beauties who aggressively seek conquest (the erotic "slaying") of men. A dichotomy between the retired and the worldly, between the modest and the fashionable woman partitions the gallery of female portraits in *The Tatler* and *The Spectator*. These dualities structure a number of the papers that present female types in pairs of virtuous and vain.[44]

Conscious display of beauty, wit, and charm, the overt presentation of the body through distinctive modes of dress — these are marks of self-assertion that Addison and Steele persistently recode as unattractive. The beautiful Emilia displays not her personal charms but her low opinion of them (*S* 302). Any *apparent* effort a woman makes to attract attention is read as an unsightly mark of flawed character. So the coquette Lydia tosses away her charms with every gesture she makes to exploit them: "Her Attractions would indeed be irresistible, but that she thinks them so, and is always employing them in Stratagems and Conquests" (*T* 126). Beauty on display is not a pretty sight: "a great Deal of Beauty in a very handsome Woman," Steele remarks in *Spectator* 38, may be "turned into Deformity . . . by the meer Force of Affectation." Especially when, as here in *Spectator* 38, affectation performs the dance of erotic play: "Her Fan was to point to somewhat at a Distance, that in the Reach she may discover the Roundness of her Arm; then she is utterly mistaken in what she saw, falls back, smiles at her own Folly, and is so wholly discompos'd, that her Tucker is to be adjusted, her Bosom expos'd, and the whole Woman put into new Airs and Graces" (*S* 38).[45]

Addison and Steele raise the cry of "Affectation" against those fashion practices that women use to construct socially powerful and autonomous personal identities, especially those practices that serve sexual self-determination. In these portraits of "bad" women it becomes clear that the worldly woman of fashion is worse than vain and frivolous: she is sexually threatening.[46] Addison makes explicit the connection between fashion and female sexual aggression in *Spectator* 15, where he concludes the paper by "observing that *Virgil* has very finely touched upon this Female Passion for Dress and Show, in the Character of [the Amazon warrior] *Camilla*." Personal display is physical aggression, closely allied with specifically sexual aggression. Overt expression of female sexuality is branded unfeminine and so unattractive. The aggressive deployment of beauty, the strategic arts of dressing at men and throwing killing glances, are most vividly distilled in the full-blown eighteenth-century fashion diva: the idol. In *Spectator* 73 this type is displayed in all her vain glory. An idol is simply a woman "wholly taken up in the Adorning of her Person." She is not satisfied with the companionship and respect of men but demands their worship. Most emphatically women of the town, "your *Idols* appear in all publick Places and Assemblies, in order to seduce Men to their Worship." Engrossed by misdirected ambition, the idols are paired in contrast with their positive antitypes, those ladies who attain distinction not through personal display but instead "by the Education of their Children, Care of their Families, and Love of their Husbands" (*S* 73).

The forms of the idol are legion, but whether "like *Moloch*" they are worshiped "in Fires and Flames," or "like *Baal*" they "love to see their Votaries cut and slashed," they share a public, aggressive expression of sexuality and an alienation from domesticity that marks them (if "only" figuratively) as a class of as demon-monsters (*S* 73). The idol's love of sexual sway is shared by that other sadistic type, the jilt, who is distinguished from a third type, the coquette, only by the latter's more carefully preserved chastity. "A Coquet," counsels Bickerstaff to a young man who has lost his heart to one, "is a chaste Jilt, and differs only from a common One, as a Soldier, who is perfect in Exercise, does from one that is actually in Service" (*T* 107). A later *Spectator* paper slightly revises this definition, distinguishing the types further by the jilt's greater sadism: "The Coquet is indeed one degree towards the Jilt; but the Heart of the Former is bent upon admiring her self, and giving false Hopes to her Lovers, but the latter is not contented to be extremely Amiable, but she must add to that Advantage a certain Delight in being a Torment to others" (*S* 187).

Along with their heartless — that is, unsentimental — sexual drives, bad female types are guilty of dissimulation; they give "false Hopes" and false impressions. The prominence of this will to dissimulate is so distinct that it marks the true identity of female types that may seem polar opposites, like the prude and the coquette: "The *Prude* appears more virtuous, the *Coquet* more vicious, than she really is"; "They are Sisters of the same Blood and Constitution, only one chooses a grave, the other a light, Dress" (*T* 126). Mistresses of appearances, women exploit dress, cosmetics, and the whole stylized choreography of social interaction to seem what they are not. Their true selves then become opaque — a problem perhaps especially for the Spectator, whose authority, as we have seen, rests on his ability to render others transparent. That idols, coquettes, jilts, prudes are hard to read, threatens Bickerstaff and the Spectator not merely as men but also as critics. In order to assert masculine control and critical authority, female mastery is named deception and dismantled under the banner of revelation and reform. We have seen this process at work in Addison's case against the hoop-petticoat in *Tatler* 116. Women must be rendered natural and transparent in order for men to retain not only sexual but also critical ascendancy over them.

The Spectator commands women to take off their paint and show their real faces. In *Spectator* 41 Steele rebukes the race of female "Picts" who wear makeup so heavy that it obscures their identity and masks their emotions, sealing them off from the penetrating scrutiny of husbands, beaux, and spectators. The case of the Picts shows a deep relation between feminine artifice, actionable misrepresentation, and threatening female aggression. These Picts wear a kind of war paint that gives them, Mr. Spectator and the Pict's unhappy husband think, an unfair advantage in the battle of the sexes

As with Addison's attack on the hoop-petticoat in *Tatler* 116, Steele's censure of heavy makeup in *Spectator* 41 is couched in legal discourse. The critic invokes the authority of the law to give his judgment weight: his word is law. Mr. Spectator acts as advocate for a deceived husband who thinks he has grounds for divorce from his Pict. The legal principle the husband cites "makes one of the Causes of Separation to be *Error personae*, when a Man marries a Woman, and finds her not to be the same Woman whom he intended to marry." As an apology for what may seem his own culpable ignorance of the identity — or at least the appearance — of the woman he married, he asserts "that there are Women who do not let their Husbands see their Faces 'till they are married" (*S* 41).

The gentleman's lament—"when she first wakes in a Morning, she scarce seems young enough to be the Mother of her whom I carried to Bed the Night before"—and his account of the construction of the body through cosmetic art have much in common with Swift's poems—"A Beautiful Young Nymph Going to Bed," "The Progress of Beauty," "A Lady's Dressing Room," "Strephon and Chloe." Like the men in those poems, the correspondent to *Spectator* 41 is actually horrified not by women's paint but by the real, aging, material body beneath. He complains that the illusion isn't real:

> They are some of them so Exquisitely skilful this Way, that give them but a Tolerable Pair of Eyes to set up with, and they will make Bosom, Lips, Cheeks, and Eyebrows by their own Industry. As for my Dear, never Man was so inamour'd as I was of her fair

Forehead, Neck and Arms, as well as the bright Jett of her Hair; but to my great Astonishment, I find they were all the Effect of Art. (*S* 41)

The mercantile and industrial metaphors—"setting up" with the capital stock of "a Tolerable Pair of Eyes" and then producing "by their own Industry" a whole line of attractive (false) features—suggest that the Picts venture into spheres of enterprise and production off-limits to women. As Pollak points out, the ideal domestic woman is a consumer, not a producer; she should not produce even her own appearance, her own identity.[47]

In his supportive response to the letter, Mr. Spectator names this self-fashioning of women as their death. Contrasting the natural and properly British woman with the artificial race of Picts (the ancient race of peoples who inhabited England before the Romans), Steele elaborates a conceit that poses the painted lady as a regressive, primitive type reemerging in a kind of racial atavism. "The *British*," he writes, "have a lively, animated Aspect; The *Picts*, tho' never so beautiful, have dead, uninformed Countenances." Natural vitality makes the British face easy to read: "The Muscles of a real Face sometimes swell with soft Passion, sudden Surprize, and are flushed with agreeable Confusions, according as the Objects before them, or the Ideas presented to them, affect their Imagination." In contrast, the cold death-masks of the painted Picts offer no such window on the soul: "But the *Picts* behold all things with the same Air, whether they are Joyful or Sad; The same fix'd Insensibility appears on all Occasions" (*S* 41).

Like the coquette and the jilt, the Pict is deceptive and opaque, and like them she is a tease: "A *Pict*, tho' she takes all that Pains to invite the Approach of Lovers, is obliged to keep them at a certain Distance," because "a Sigh in a Languishing Lover, if fetched too near her, would dissolve a Feature; and a Kiss snatched by a Forward one, might transfer the Complexion of the Mistress to the Admirer" (*S* 41). Like the coquette, the Pict's artifice makes her hideous.[48]

In confirmation of his argument against paint, the Spectator offers an anecdote he has from his fellow clubman Will Honeycomb. Calling up a set of misogynist, satiric commonplaces, Will tells, in a less repulsive register, the same story as Swift's "A Lady's Dressing Room." In Swift's poem, the suitor's snoop through his Chloe's dressing room ends in a severe case of sexual nausea; he loses desire for the whole sex. Will's reaction is less severe — he loses his attraction to the Pict alone; moreover, this loss is his gain, a liberating "cure" of his sick fancy for a cruel coquette (*S* 41).

Hiding behind the hangings in her dressing room, Will witnesses the elaborate construction of the Pict's face: "She worked a full half Hour before he knew her to be the same Woman." He watches, Spectatorlike, from a privileged position of invisibility: "He stood very conveniently to observe, without being seen." His gaze operates without hindrance; unseen, he can penetrate fully into the mysteries of the lady's dressing room. When Will begins to see the face he recognizes, he emerges from hiding, catching the Pict-coquette, quite literally, red-handed. Caught in the act, the Pict stands amazed, her face split in two: "The *Pict* stood before him in the utmost Confusion, with the prettiest Smirk imaginable on the finish'd side of her Face, pale as Ashes on the other." Contrary to the Spectator's characterization of Pict and Brit, here it is the bare, not the painted, face that looks deathly, "pale as Ashes." Exposed and mortified, the woman suffers more at Will's hands. He takes off with all her makeup, leaving her two-faced (*S* 41). Cut off from her cosmetics, the lady has only one means of self-integration: in order to appear humanly symmetrical, she'll have to take off her face. She must efface her self.

Significantly, Will's attraction to the Pict-coquette does not survive the exposure of her bare face, stripped of its artifice. His lovesickness, in typical Petrarchan fashion, is a symptom of his idealized fetishization of the woman's appearance and is cured not so much by the exposure of her "real" face as by the exposure of the material and labor on which her appearance depends. For what is revealed when the Pict puts on her face is the "unreality" of the object of Will's own, conventionally masculine desire.

Will's anecdotal scene presents an abbreviated allegory of the Spectator's own operations of surveillance, exposure, and reform. The humiliated, half-painted Pict stands an emblem of the object of the Spectator's scandalizing gaze. Stripping women of their hoops and their paint, again and again, the narratives in *The Tatler* and *The Spectator* demand the abandonment of feminine arts and threaten ruin and despair to those who persist in them. The essays chronicle the dark, ineluctable fate of the fashionable as one menacing incentive for reform. *Spectator* 33 tells the story of a pair of daughters: the beautiful Laetitia and her plain sister Daphne. Laetitia loses her suitor to her sister when he grows "heartily tired with [Laetitia's] haughty Impertinence." The beautiful fashion plate Honoria in *Spectator* 302 is harassed all her life by "Fear of Wrinkles and old Age." In *Tatler* 107 Bickerstaff tells the story of his own adventures with a heartless coquette, convicted by her own cruelty to a life of despair. Spurning Bickerstaff and marrying another, she pays for her disdain through a kind of instant karma. She is neglected by her husband and "often says to her woman, 'This is a just revenge for my falsehood to my first love: what a wretch am I, that might have been married to the famous Mr. *Bickerstaff*'" (*T* 107). *Spectator* 15 represents the fashionable Fulvia's life as one of constant agitation and anxiety as she rushes to keep up with the rat-race of fashion. Fulvia suffers humiliations she does not even know: "What a Mortification would it be to *Fulvia*, if she knew that her setting her-self to View is but exposing her self, and that she grows Contemptible by being Conspicuous." And fashionable women court worse than contempt. Dangling its lures of "Lace, Ribbons, Silver and Gold," fashion seduces women into unions with empty, dead shells of commodity fetishes, an "Embroidered Coat," or a "Pair of Fringed Gloves" (*S* 15).

The unhappy tale of Brunetta and Phillis in *Spectator* 80 exposes the dangers women face when they strive in the competitive arena of fashion. A pair matched by identity rather than contrast, both women are engaged in a vain contest for distinction through display; both are flawed characters.[49] They are both types of the ludicrously trendy city girl, lampooned by Edward Ward in his verses on "a modish lady":

The only daughter of some trading fop,
Trained half in school, and t'other half in shop
Who nothing by her parents is denied
T'improve her charms or gratify her pride,
Spoiled by her father's fondness and his pounds
Till her wild fancy knows at last no bounds.[50]

The girlhood chums Brunetta and Phillis become bitter rivals as they grow up and into sexual maturity. Wasting their youth in a ceaseless struggle for personal glory, they stage a series of stylistic combats that enlist all their energies and the fortunes of their families: "Their Mothers, as it is usual, engaged in the Quarrel, and supported the several Pretensions of the daughters with all that ill-chosen sort of Expence which is common with people of Plentiful Fortunes and mean Taste. The Girls preceded their Parents like Queens of *May*, in all the gaudy Colours imaginable, on every *Sunday* to Church." This bad, mean-spirited taste is assigned to a specific grid on the social map of London — Cheapside — and so linked to the class of rich, yet uncultivated, commercial families.

Phillis's defective character and taste shows up in her object choice. Her head filled with nothing but colors, she is smitten by a "*West-Indian. . . .* in a Summer-Island Suit . . . too shining and too gay to be resisted." Brunetta, predictably, also develops a fancy for this Creole, and is mortified when he marries Phillis and takes her off to live on a rich plantation in Barbados. With the desperate mimicry of the envious, Brunetta "employed all her Arts and Charms in laying Baits for any of Condition of the same Island." Eventually, she succeeds and goes to live on an estate next to her rival's.

At Barbados, Phillis commandeers an incoming merchant ship, gets first pick of the fabric it stows, and so snatches an unscrupulous advantage in her style wars with Brunetta. After Phillis appears triumphant in a "Brocade more gorgeous and costly than had ever before appeared in that Latitude," Brunetta gets her hands on a remnant and gets her revenge. At the next public ball, she appears in a plain black mantua, attended by a black servant-girl "in a Petticoat of the same Brocade" that had given Phillis the last fashion triumph (*S* 80).

Brunetta achieves her victory not from being more beautiful than Phillis but by turning Phillis's own fashion practices against her and undermining her status by stylistically identifying Phillis with a black slave. Brunetta's ploy literally undoes the semantics of Phillis's display by reversing it: Brunetta styles brocade not as the sign of white colonial power but of black subjugation.

Fashion competition here is charged with the powerful energies of colonialism and racism. A white Creole, Phillis's gentleman in his gaudy suit has adopted the aesthetic of the tropics. The West Indian embodies the connection between hyperbolic personal stylization and the otherness of a "hot" Caribbean exoticism, foreign to the good taste of more purely English sensibilities.[51] Like these city girls, the West Indian cannot distinguish between being fine and being tawdry, and so, like them, dresses in "all the gaudy Colours imaginable." Creole men, as is noted by English commentators throughout the century, "are amazing fond of costly, tinsel frippery; abroad they appear ridiculously gay."[52] Although the garish and flamboyant style of the tropics may be adopted by white Creoles, like the gentleman in this paper, there is little question where all the "color" comes from. As J. B. Moreton laments, unless transformed into Englishmen by benefit of an early education in the metropolis, Creoles remain irredeemably "negrofied."[53] So, this incident curiously anticipates what eventually becomes a conventional and racially charged distinction between the unostentatious yet conspicuously "tasteful" dress of the white European and the colorfully gaudy and "tasteless" dress of the African American. An allegory of the deportation of bad taste from the metropolitan center onto the colonial periphery, the paper condemns such taste by identifying it not only with faulty feminine bodies but also and at the same time with both white Creole and African-Caribbean bodies. English girls gone bad, Phillis and Brunetta, with their faulty, fashion-fed desires, are shown to be libidinally connected to this foreign, tropical style, and, appropriately, their fashion dueling is transported to the West Indies, far from the temperate shores of England.

Under the rules of the kind of style contest engaged in by Brunetta and Phillis, true privilege is marked by not having to com-

"Oeconomie Rustique," Sucrerie, West Indian Sugar Plantation, from *Encyclopédie, Recuiel de Planches.*

pete at all in the arena of mere appearance. Brunetta's retreat into black suggests that she is above the fray; it implies strengths and powers all the more potent for being undisclosed, more substantial for being irreducible to a mere fashion statement. So while the paper condemns the kind of display-oriented status competition engaged in by both Brunetta and Phillis, it does so in a way that exploits the contest to give the upper hand to its own antidisplay ideology. The final "victory" (such as it is) goes to Brunetta for her antifashion style coup. In this way the aesthetic of "understated elegance" is approved by the paper, as it is by *The Tatler* and *The Spectator* generally, though that approval is somewhat displaced and perhaps withheld here, where this aesthetic serves unsightly forms of female ambition. Most importantly, this scene reveals the dissimulation inherent in all class and race motivated styles of underdressing: the refusal of display is the most arrogant and imperious display of all.

In response to Brunetta's fashion coup, Phillis first falls unconscious; then, completely undone, she boards a ship back to England "and is now landed in inconsolable Despair at *Plymouth*" (*S* 80). As for Brunetta, one wonders if she can even enjoy a victory that deprives her of her sole rival. The game is up and, we are to understand, its outcome only bitterness and vainglory.

To avoid the dismal ends of Phillis, Brunetta, Honoria, Laetitia, and the whole race of Picts, idols, and coquettes, women, the papers urge, better get with the program. At the close of *Spectator* 41, Steele lays down the guidelines for proper female cultivation. Offering a kind of ethical culture as an alternative to conventional beauty culture, he insists on the internal springs of true charm and calls for an abandonment of external, cosmetic arts: "As a Pattern for improving their Charms, let the Sex study the agreeable *Statira*. Her features are enlivened with the Chearfulness of her Mind, and good Humour gives an Alacrity to her Eyes. She is Graceful without Affecting an Air, and Unconcerned without appearing Careless. Her having no manner of Art in her Mind, makes her want none in her Person" (*S* 41).

We have seen how Addison and Steele aim their reforms at an interior, ethical realm seen as the source of agency and desire. It is not enough that women wipe the makeup off their faces; they must expunge all art from their minds. Addison and Steele want no mere nominalist converts to their cult of true charm. In *Spectator* 33 a male correspondent offers a program for female ethical-cum-beauty reform that echoes Steele's advice in *Spectator* 41. Like all the programs for reform offered in these papers, this one seeks not to extinguish female desire but to redirect it onto a worthier set of objects. Honoring as a "laudable Motive" women's "Desire of Pleasing," the gentleman in *Spectator* 33 discloses "the true Secret and Art of improving Beauty." Rather than disclaiming women's pursuit of charm and beauty as in itself objectionable, the correspondent offers an alternative method and does so in the conventional language of beauty culture. Against the false claims of cosmetics, he offers the true method for the improvement of beauty. His policy, outlined in five maxims, quite ingenuously names as artful that very cultivation of artlessness pursued by the natural, virtuous woman: "No Woman can be Handsome by the Force of Features alone. . . . Pride destroys all Symmetry and Grace, and Affectation is a more terrible Enemy to fine Faces than the Small-Pox.. . . No Woman is capable of being Beautiful, who's not incapable of being False. And . . . what wou'd be Odious in a Friend, is Deformity in a Mistress" (*S* 33).

These guidelines for the production of true beauty demand not a mere beauty regimen but a disciplined stylization of soul and psyche. The standard "beauty" is redefined; the cultivation of internal, ethical qualities is itself named as a secret art and advocated as an improvement to appearance. The question remains: Is beauty here internalized and "elevated" beyond the accidents of mere appearance, or is virtue "degraded" by being marketed as a cosmetic?

MIRROR, MIRROR: NARCISSISM AND THE REFORM OF DESIRE

Investment in ornament and stylized self-display suggests a conception of the self as a visual object, a mere two-dimensional, stereotyped fashion plate, composed according to superficial criteria for the, often sexual, pleasures of others. So the recipe for real beauty spelled out in *Spectator* 33 ends with a remarkable aside that links women's narcissistic obsession with their physical appearance to their status as mere objects of the male gaze: "It is, methinks, a low and degrading Idea of that Sex, which was created to refine the Joys, and soften the Cares of Humanity, by the most agreeable Participation, to consider them meerly as Objects of Sight. This is abridging them of their natural Extent of Power, to put them upon a Level with their Pictures at *Kneller's*" (*S* 33). Echoing similar sentiments, a correspondent to *Spectator* 53 identifies the origins of female vanity in women's desire to please men who are foolishly "dazl'd by false Charms and unreal Beauty." Accordingly, in order to reform vain female desires, it is necessary as well to reform male desire: "In order to embellish the Mistress [with the true charms of "*Virtue, Modesty, and Discretion*"] you shou'd give a new Education to the Lover" (*S* 53).

The reorientation of desire away from visual exteriors entails a reform of the gaze. As discussed in relation to the visual, imaginative consumption of the commodity in chapter 2, the faulty values of fashion and beauty are confirmed through looking. The narcissistic gaze passionately consumes an image of the self as the object of an other's desire. Narcissism and fashion are closely affiliated in the rhetoric of the paper; narcissistic characters are egregiously fashion entranced and the duplication of identities allegedly produced by fashion's dictates is drawn by the same magnetic pole of homogeneity that attracts like to like.

Directed toward the reform of both masculine and feminine desire, the papers are full of scenes of looking, staring, peeping, gazing, and mirroring. "There is no end," writes Steele in *Spectator* 79, "of Affection taken in at the Eyes only." And while all sorts of reifying, prurient looking are taken to task, perhaps the most reprehensible is the mirror-gaze, the entranced enchantment with the same. In *The Tatler* and *The Spectator*, mirror-gazing is replete with associations of narcissism, a solipsism that bespeaks a misdirection of the eyes and the fancies they feed. Moreover, the fascination with the same, the search for an erotic object that mirrors one's own identity, violates the standards of sexual difference underpinning the gender ideology that dominates the papers. Mirroring connects as well with the logic of the fashion market, where, as the conventional objection runs, men and women strive not to realize their "true" selves but instead to become stereotyped copies of one another. Fashion may be criticized as an arena of blind imitation where clone follows clone lemminglike into the depthless sea of homogenized identity. Finally, economic exchange, like the mirrors of fashion, works through the creation of equivalencies, a leveling and homogenizing of value productive of interchangeable, rather than individual and incommensurate, identities.[54]

Because it touches so closely on central issues of appearance, identity, and desire, this discussion of the gaze, and especially the mirror-gaze, leads into a consideration of the relation of masculine types to fashion, gender, and sexual object choice. Perhaps because the revealing gaze is so central to his own critical project, Mr. Spectator devotes considerable attention to the policing of its abuses as an instrument of "impudence," of vain and superficial desires. A bachelor and asexual being, Mr. Spectator seems especially sensitive to the use of the gaze as an accessory to sexual desire.[55] In *Spectator* 20, the "Correction of Impudence" (i.e., aggressive desire), so near to the Spectator's heart, addresses the "Offence committed by the Eyes." The portrait of the starer offered here shows a man whose ways of looking mirror the Spectator's own, reflecting them by a kind of strict reversal. Rather than conducting his surveillance from behind a set of hangings, as does Will Honeycomb when he spies on the Pict, or behind the shield of a preciously guarded anonymity, as the Spectator does, the starer shows his impudence by cheerfully making a spectacle of himself even as he pursues his own spectatorship of others. A letter from a female correspondent complains of one such fellow who, though already a "Head taller" than everyone else in church, imposes himself even more fully on the attention of the congregation by standing up on a hassock (*S* 20).

There is a positive correlation between the object of the gaze and the mode of viewing. The starer looks at outsides. He wants to see and be seen; his concern is with spectacle, with the play of externally manifested meaning and power. He wants to be seen looking because his proprietary gaze not only reveals others to him but shows his power to others as well. He is a conceited coxcomb; he is up-front. Mr. Spectator, on the other hand, is more subtle and more underhanded. Using his gaze to expose the "inward Disposition of the Mind," he wants to see into, to penetrate appearances (*S* 86). His power to render others transparent, as we have seen, depends on his own invisibility. He is always the looker, never the looked at, always the subject and never the object of the gaze.

Mr. Spectator's mode of surveillance is all the more powerful for going unnoticed. The mode of looking he practices participates in a dissimulation parallel to that of the benevolent paternalism it serves. The kinder, gentler patriarchy may be all the more effective because it wields power obliquely "through the mask of sentiment and liberal benevolism."[56] This is the mode of hegemonic power that accompanied the dissolution of coercive, absolutist forms of rule and characterized the operations of the eighteenth-century bourgeois public sphere.[57] In *The Tatler* and *The Spectator*, major institutions of that public sphere, the exercise of "outdated" forms of display are compromised by their pretensions to a kind of pseudo-aristocratic haughtiness that renders them, in Mr. Spectator's eye, ridiculous. The starer is invested in forms of power that the Spectator, even as he works so hard to discredit them, implies are already passé. Starers, like Picts, are socially regressive.[58]

The faults of the starer lie as much in his own narcissism and exhibitionism as they do in his impudence: he wants to *be* a spectacle as much as to look at one. His female counterpart, the "peeper" displays the same will to make a spectacle of herself (*S* 53). And while the correspondent to *Spectator* 33 laments the way men look at women as "mere Objects of Sight," the gentleman, a "reformed Starer," who writes of the peeper in *Spectator* 53, defends men as victims of feminine wiles: "If [the ladies] do every thing that it is possible to attract our Eyes, are we more culpable than they for looking at Them?" In keeping with the habit of her sex, the peeper doesn't stand up to be noticed; rather, she kneels down and flutters and sighs and hides behind her fan.

Fans are the standard-issue artillery of coquetry, "weapons" for female sexual "assaults" that are won or lost through the lady's dexterity at the fluttering drill—what Swift calls "the whole military Management of the Fan."[59] Withholding and disclosing at the flip of a wrist, fans are perfectly suited to the double standard that governs female sexuality, at once modestly veiling and seductively advertising the blushing, sexually agitated face. Sister of the mask and the veil, the fan attracts by concealment; it produces desire by dissimulating and obscuring the signs of desire. The peeper's fan in *Spectator* 53 unfolds to reveal an erotic scene that mythologically allegorizes the entire flirtatious dynamic it serves: "There lay in the Body of the Piece a *Venus,* under a Purple Canopy . . . half-naked, attended with a Train of *Cupids,* who were busied Fanning her as she slept. Behind her was drawn a Satyr peeping over the silken fence, and threatening to break through it." Of course the allegory casts the peeper behind the fan as Venus behind the silken curtain, as feminine desire sleeping and inactive. But it goes a step further to imply an identity between the young lady's own peeping and the peeping of the satyr. As much as she, like Venus, is curtained off behind her fan, she also, like the satyr, peeps over it. The allegory supports the gentleman's accusation: the young lady produces masculine desire with the same gesture she uses to modestly screen her own. Moreover, the allegory suggests that as *her* product, masculine desire is *her* responsibility. She should own up to it. After all, the link between the lady peeper and the peeping satyr suggests, the sleeping Venus is only an alibi for an active female desire that peeps over the silken fence of female modesty and, indeed, threatens to break through it.

What we can see is that the (male) starer who looks and the (female) peeper, Pict, or coquette who would be looked at are guilty of the same vanity and even narcissism: the object of their desire is the gaze that mirrors their image back to them as the object of desire. And just as (unreformed) male desire takes as its object the woman who spends her days before the mirror, "examining that Face in the Glass, which does such Execution upon all the Male Standers-by," so (unreformed) female desire has eyes only for the man who has eyes only for himself. *Tatler* 5 examines one instance of this "ordinary" course of female desire that focuses its enraptured gaze on "a Fellow, who stares in the Glass all the Time he is with her, and lets her plainly see, she may be his Rival, but never his Mistress." Oblivious in his perfect narcissism, this fellow attracts on the sheer strength of his own indifference. Masochistic, full of a sense of their own essential emptiness, women throw themselves at men who seem to lack nothing and want no one. Addison laments the narcissism he sees as "ordinary" in women: "To be short, the Passion of an ordinary Woman for a Man, is nothing else but Self-love diverted upon another Object; She would have the Lover a Woman in every thing but the Sex" (*S* 128).

But the satire in *Tatler* 5 is leveled not only at the self-defeating perversity of female desire but also at the self-absorbed man of fashion. And I think that the female attraction to the indifferent fop itself follows a further turn in the screw of narcissistic desire; for the lady's attraction to the self-absorbed man may be based on their similarity rather than their differences. Like likes like: opposites aren't the only things that attract. So Narcissa is most smitten with "a gay empty Fellow, who by Strength of a long Intercourse with [her], joined to his natural Endowments, had formed himself into a perfect Resemblance with her" (*S* 392). He and only he can rival Narcissa's mirror for her attention. Identity makes for a susceptibility. Fashionable men, like women, are involved in a pathological identity-mirroring. They have eyes only for the same, and women, mirroring the fops's own tautological desire, have eyes only for them. The elaborately decked-out fops and beaux who may seem to us like flamboyant homosexuals are often the great ladies' men of their time: the lady's man is both a man who likes the ladies and a man like the ladies.[60] He comes under the sway of the feminine in the pursuit of his desire. His passion for the ladies becomes imitation of them: "Your Woman's Men have always a Similitude of the Creature they hope to betray, in their own Conversation" (*S* 156).

Addison and Steele disapprove of the exercise of this desire that seeks identity rather than difference. When human nature is constructed on a paradigm of innate sexual difference, such same-type, if not same-sex, desire looks like a perversion. Women who fancy fancy men are not respecting sexual difference. Assuming a sex in souls, Addison calls for matches made up of complementary opposites that balance woman's natural feminine levity with her husband's masculine gravity: "Men and Women were made as Counterparts to one another. . . . Care and Cheerfulness go Hand in Hand" (*S* 156). Unfortunately, women show a real indifference to "nature" and pursue their attractions to men who are more like them; perhaps they figure that these men will like them more. Coming perilously close to letting the prescribed and ideological nature of this theory of "natural" sexual differences surface, an incredulous Addison remarks on women's native perversity: "But whatever was the Reason that Man and Woman were made with this Variety of Temper, if we observe the Conduct of the fair Sex, we find that they choose rather to associate themselves with a Person who resembles them in that light and volatile Humour which is natural to them, than to such as are qualified to moderate and counterballance it" (*S* 128). Addison knows what women want and he wants to change it. His accusation serves not only to indict female desire as narcissistic but also to brand the objects of that desire as effeminate. Elegant ladies and dressy men share a kind of queerness defined by narcissism, caprice, and instability. Addison and Steele want to straighten out this queerness, to reform desires in a way that restores both men and women to themselves, nature, and control.

As the papers promote their pair of complementary "opposite" male and female ideals, they apply to each of many of the same standards of judgment. Women are flawed by their contamination with the "bad" feminine foibles—love of display, superficiality, affectation, fashion obsession, inconstancy. The cultivation of a positive feminine role, then, involves, in Friedli's words, the curbing of "the excesses of decorative and sexual femininity."[61] Interestingly, so does the formulation of the ideal masculine type. Especially as regards their relationship to fashion and style, Addison's and Steele's domestic bourgeois male and female are cut from the same mold. This in no way compromises their delegation to separate spheres and their reflection of the new sexual difference, which, after all, is what produces them as sexually compatible, complementary opposites. As I see it, what is purged from each sex with the set of "bad" feminine traits is not femininity per se, not, in any case, the brand of femininity being advocated by the papers. Instead, perceived under the new dispensation of difference, this bad femininity is hybrid and impure, neither sufficiently feminine nor solidly masculine. Unnatural, this "bad" femininity serves as the standard against which the new genders are produced. Of course, it is important that this failure to fully comply with strict categories of sexual difference is coded as a feminine lapse; by blaming the feminine the gender hierarchy is maintained even within the paradigm of difference.

MASCULINITY AND THE OUTING OF FASHION

The Description of a Man of Fashion,
spoken by some with a Mixture of Scorn and Ridicule,
by others with great Gravity as a laudable Distinction,
is in every Body's Mouth.

SPECTATOR 151

The constellation of terms that I take up here—*masculinity, effeminacy, fashion,* and *hetero-/homosexuality*—come into their conventional modern relationships to one another through a number of conceptual alignments, all bearing relation to the notion of sexual difference. I refer to the stereotypical opposition in Anglo-American bourgeois culture between, on the one hand, the masculine, (exclusively) heterosexual male who announces his sexual (as well as ethnic and class) allegiances by a principled inattention to matters of fashion and style, and, on the other, to the effeminate (exclusively) homosexual male who announces his sexual, and with this social, deviation from the straight norm by his hyperconsciousness of matters of fashion and style. Put most baldly, the question that guides my thought on this topic is: "Since when was fashion queer?" When, in other words, did being masculine mean disowning any but the most rationalized and conformist interest in the cultivation of personal appearance? And how did this absence of display come to mark the presence of masculinity and power?

To begin this inquiry, I want to sketch in a few broad strokes the frame of fashion history that surrounds this development in the relation of masculinity to fashion. Between the seventeenth and nineteenth centuries there is in British culture an about-face in the semantics of masculine style. Where conspicuous personal display had once marked status and power, it comes to mean something very different: effeminacy, foolishness, homosexuality, vulgarity. By the nineteenth century, the very *absence* of personal display announces the *presence* of power and status — the plain linen, the naked face, the wigless, uncurled, unpowdered head, the low-heeled shoes or boots, the no-nonsense business suit with its equally sober, physically reserved code of behavior. This event, the greatest style shift in the modern period, is called by J. C. Flugel, early psychoanalyst of fashion, the Great Male Renunciation.[62] At times and to degrees that varied from context to context, men gave up the cultivation of personal beauty. In England during the eighteenth century, the relinquishing of the more lavish features of fashion and continued positive influence of rural working and sporting wear on male dress mark the beginning of the male renunciation.[63] Early leaders of this trend, *The Tatler* and *The Spectator* advocate a style of unostentatious dress, advancing the war on foppery by promoting a masculinity disdainful of the superfluities of costume and in revolt against the reign of style. The new male mode is both specifically bourgeois and specifically masculine. It marks the self-assertion of men in the professional and commercial classes against the socially, politically, and sexually corrupt society associated with Restoration and French court culture.

As part of the redefinition of gendered spheres, the conventional association between stylishness and homosexuality begins to emerge gradually through a chain of linkages: fashion with a kind of bad femininity; the sodomite with effeminacy and even transvestism, and so with other things feminine, such as fashion. When, as we see in *The Tatler* and *The Spectator*, love of superficial display and vigorous pursuit of fashion become the signs of an innate female nature, then the man who shares these traits may be categorized not simply as effeminate but as feminine in a more deeply compromising way that suggests he shares with women a certain kind of essentially female psyche and certain inherently female desires.

The remarkably transitional position of the papers in these emerging conventions of masculinity, sexuality, and style makes *The Tatler* and *Spectator* material especially interesting, and especially tricky. The association of male dressiness and same-sex desire is not firmly in place in the early eighteenth century. Such an association becomes possible only after mainstream fashion dictates an abandonment of dressiness — lace, velvet, brocade, makeup, high heels, ribbons — for the majority of men. This has not yet been completed by 1709-11, but is emerging.[64] In relation to what people were actually wearing or even usually aspiring to wear, Addison and Steele are a good deal ahead of their time, and their influence on the history of taste may itself have had considerable influence on fashion, especially on masculine fashion. The papers, in any case, presage principles of style that would become dominant by the middle of the century and clear the ground for truly radical revolutions in costume by the century's end.

I have argued that, in step with the misogyny of their culture, Addison and Steele see as "badly" feminine the whole sphere of fashion-driven society — the world — that they oppose. In line with this, they tend to feminize as weak and inconstant those types of men they want to delegitimize. And these two discourses — of the faulty feminine sphere of the fashionable world and of the rhetorically emasculated and so feminized male character type — work in tandem to condemn any male type perceived as suspiciously modish. *The*

Tatler and *The Spectator* define the sober (heterosexual) bourgeois male by invoking, in order to displace, preexistent male types: the Restoration rake; the rakish, stylish turn-of-the-century beau; the exquisitely civil and extravagantly overdressed fop; and that foppish, foolish, effeminate type quite prevalent in the papers, the "Pretty Fellow." The new ideal masculine character is a domesticated man who, nonetheless, is not a fop; an unequivocally masculine man who, nonetheless, is not a rake; a man with a certain degree of worldly savoir faire who is by no means a beau or a pretty fellow.

Men in fashionable society—the world—are "feminized" not always in the strict sense of displaying overtly feminine traits, but sometimes simply in the sense of succumbing to the mode that rules that world—its concerns with the latest thing, with style, its obsession with the news and gossip. So, in distinction to women of fashion, men of fashion, "the reigning Favorites," are made so not so much by some innate unstable and suspect aspect of their nature as men but quite simply by their privileged role in a social exchange controlled by women (*S* 156). Colonel Brunett in *Tatler* 24 is one such favorite, loved by the women and laughed at, Addison says, by the men. He gets by on fashion alone: "He is admitted in one Place, because he is so in another." Colonel Brunett occupies the social position, then, of "a true Woman's Man, and in the first Degree, *A very Pretty Fellow*" (*T* 24).

Women's ascendancy in matters of style wins them eager male devotees of the mode; and though men may pursue reputations as high stylers, fashion remains a dominantly feminine preserve. In a letter to her friend Amanda in the country, the coquette Lindamira writes of the town and her admirers. She speaks openly of her desire for sway: "I will stick . . . to my old Maxim. To have that Sort of Man, who can have no greater Views than what are in my Power to give him Possession of" (*T* 22). Lindamira's greatest pleasure is being "followed and admired." Of all her admirers Lindamira favors most Beau Frisk, not because he loves her only for herself but because he loves her only for the fashion: "The utmost of my dear Frisk's Ambition is, to be thought a Man of Fashion; and therefore has been so much in Mode, as to resolve upon me, because the whole Town likes me." In Frisk's desire she sees the potential for a greater constancy: "He that judges for himself in Love, will often change his Opinion; but he that follows the Sense of others, must be constant as long as a woman can make Advances" (*T* 22). As long as she leads the style advance, he will follow with unswerving loyalty.

And this following of the "feminine" forces of fashion is the problem with stylish men like Beau Frisk. In *The Tatler* and *Spectator* papers, blind submission to fashion is emphatically the nonsensical, though passionate foible of women and of silly and, in an often complex sense, feminized men. Men in the middle and upper classes were almost inevitably participants in social spheres largely controlled by women and by the standards of display, novelty, and style that Addison and Steele admonish as bad feminine characteristics. It is because women retained interest and investment in social spheres beyond the home that so much ink was spilt in the effort to render them more purely domestic. "We have carryed Womens Characters," writes Steele, "too much into publick Life, and you shall see them now a–Days affect a sort of Fame" (*S* 342). "Fashion ruled the world of the eighteenth century and women ruled fashion," declares the narrator of *The Eighteenth Century Woman*, a video of Diana Vreeland's exhibition at the Metropolitan Museum.[65] There is considerable truth in this statement, enough truth, in any case, that Addison and Steele spend a good deal of time and energy writing against this state of affairs: "I cannot help venturing to disoblige [women] for their service, by telling them, that the utmost of a Woman's Character is contained in Domestick Life" (*S* 342). By advocating the containment of women to the domestic sphere, Addison and Steele are also calling for the removal of feminine forces and values from other spheres where their operation contaminates social relations and threatens social stability.

But, as I have suggested, this feminization of fashion and of the men engaged in it works both to condemn and to pardon. Ultimately, it allows Addison and Steele to criticize certain traits of bad masculinity while leaving the basic sexual hierarchy in place. Steele is eager to attribute the great part of men's capitulation to the mode, whether in clothes or (as in *Tatler* 29) in dueling, to women. This

"Tailleur d'Habits" (Tailor's Shop), from *Encyclopédie, Recuiel de Planches.*

"Perruquier, Barbier" (Wig maker, Barber), from *Encyclopédie, Recuiel de Planches.*

shifts the blame back to women and lets the men pretty much off the hook. So though "such Men *appear* reasonably Slaves to the Fashion," their irrationalities of dress (wearing "a long Duvillier [wig] full of Powder") and of behavior (engaging in duels) are finally traceable to a regrettable, but pardonable, conformity to feminine directives: "Dress and Chivalry have always been encouraged by the Ladies, as the Two principal Branches of Gallantry" (*T* 29, italics reversed; my emphasis). The formulation of "Dress and Gallantry" as feminine preserves the categorical purity of masculinity, if not every individual man, from the contaminations of fashion and foolishness.

In their catalogs of contemporary male characters, Addison and Steele differentiate between various degrees of fashion victimization. In *Tatler* 29 an important distinction is made between the man who "complies with the Dress commonly received" "to avoid being sneer'd at for his Singularity, and from a Desire to appear more agreeable to his Mistress," and those guilty of a more reprehensible complicity. These latter "would do any thing contrary to the Course and Order of Things out of Fondness to be in Fashion" (*S* 478). Such is the smart fellow, "with his Cane tied at his Button, wearing red-heel'd Shoes," recognizable by a "short Trip in his Steps," the "well-fancied Lining of his Coat," a gentleman who really is what "his Taylor, his Hosier, and his Milliner, have conspired to make him" (*T* 28).

Mocked for their affectations, the elaborate smart fellows, the smooth operators, the faddish students in the Temple are flawed by a departure from their masculinity into feminine spheres of fashionable behavior. Yet their masculinity seems to remain essentially intact; it is there waiting for them when they take their leave of the fashion and return to their senses. Masculine submission to fashion is, then, most generally (though as we will soon see with the mollies, not always) motivated by one of two sorts of desire: explicitly heterosexual desire that is compromised by its faulty object, or a desire sublimated away from specific sexuality into a passion for a social distinction based on degradingly trivial, feminine standards. This last case is exemplified by the foppish student and the smart fellow; these men are "vain Things" who, just like women, "regard one another for their Vestments" (*S* 49). In the coffeehouse society of *Spectator* 49, social

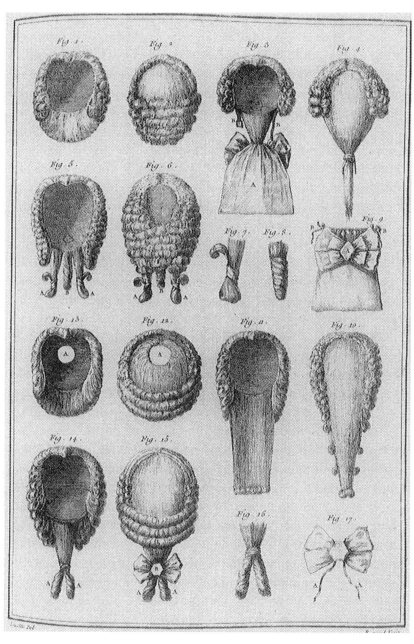

"Perruquier, Barbier, Perruques" (Wigs), from *Encyclopédie, Recuiel de Planches.*

standing among fops is dependent on criteria already specified (in *Tatler* 29, also by Steele) as explicitly feminine: "The Superiority among these proceeds from an Opinion of Gallantry and Fashion." And it is the design of Addison and Steele to modify these patterns of social relations by moderating and rechanneling men's passion for fashion, which is tightly tied up with their desire for women's attention and compliance with feminine social values.

Accordingly, one difficulty Addison and Steele encounter in selling their reformed masculine character to men is that it doesn't go over with the ladies. Before you can get men to adopt it you have to change what women want. The problem with the domesticated mild-mannered man is that women don't want him. Even nice girls, complains a gentleman in *Spectator* 154, don't want a nice man: "I found a sober, modest Man was always looked upon by both sexes as a precise unfashioned Fellow of no Life or Spirit." The gentleman loses all respect when word gets out that he is a virgin. "Why how do you know more than any of us?" the girls exclaim, laughing out loud at him. Their disrespect comes, he knows, "for no other Fault in the World than that they really thought me as innocent as themselves." Only when he begins to live "at large" with a set of rakish men about town, throwing off the hobbles of his "sober Education," does he earn respect: "In due process of Time I was a very pretty Rake among the Men, and a very pretty Fellow among the Women" (S 154).[66]

The tale this gentlemen tells in *Spectator* 154 suggests that women want sexually adventurous, transgressive men who are very different from them, whereas in *Spectators* 128 and 156 women seem to want men that, according to Addison, are too much like them. But in both cases, the "bad" masculine type mirrors faulty female desires and achieves erroneous social distinction and favor among women, while the "good" masculine ideal, bland and chaste, advocated by the papers is passed over. This ideal is less aggressive visually, verbally, and sexually, more domesticated and modest, and so in some sense more feminized than the fashionable types he is meant to displace. It is precisely in order that this good type not seem feminine that the papers produce effeminate types as his foible. They tell us that it is not the new, milder man who is really effeminate but the other types. This effeminacy, as we have seen, may be established simply by men's overinvestment in feminine spheres of activity and by their function as mirrors for flawed female desires. It is also established by the overt transvaluation of gendered characteristics. Traits and conduct that had marked masculine potency and privilege are often disowned as "feminine." In order to delegitimize types they do not approve, the papers change what it means to be a "real man." So they not only maintain the sexual status quo, an advantage previously noted, but also guarantee the pure gender identity of the ideal masculine type.

For example, by renaming it, Steele revalues the sexual adventurism characteristic of the rake and makes it a sign of weakness rather than strength. A letter from one "Melania" complains of the "male Jilts" who conquer the hearts of women they have no intention of marrying (*S* 288). Steele's response is sympathetic and he gives them an even harsher name, "Friblers." To frible is to falter or stammer in speech, or totter in walking. Equating the flirtatious man's "Irresolution of Mind" with an "Impotence of Body," Steele says that coxcombs are cripples, not conquerors (*S* 288).

Exposing the character for what he truly is, the papers promote the ideal of authenticity against affectation and artifice. Affectation may take the form of wholesale identity simulation, a kind of piracy of identity copyright. In male characters the quality of affectation differentiates the "true" type from his base imitator.[67] The real gentleman has his false double in the pretty fellow and the agreeable man his imitator in the fop (*T* 21; *S* 280). Unless exposed for what they truly are, these simulated men "pass" in legitimate society under identities that are not their own.

The only types of exclusively homosexual men identified as such appear as part of this process of sorting out the authentic character from his imitators. This speaks to the close affiliation between personal authenticity and gender legitimacy in the recasting of masculine (as well as feminine) roles taking place in early modern England. So as Steele pursues his distinctions between the true and the "second hand" rake in *Tatler* 27, he makes a brief allusion to homosexuals as those "Persons of the Epicene Gender, who gaze at one another in the Presence of Ladies." These persons are listed along with "All Pretty Fellows" as types that must not be mistaken for rakes. The rake, a character that in the Restoration had been identified by his libertine bisexuality, is distinguished by Steele from those homosexual epicene men.[68] Conceived in opposition to those men of the epicene gender, Steele's rake assumedly is defined as heterosexual: Steele's typology of the rake does not accommodate male sexual object choice, even if that choice is nonexclusive. It is less clear from this paper, taken alone, that the pretty fellows are to be lumped with the epicene gentleman as homosexuals; though they do share with them an identity as counterfeit rakes and lesser men. Yet an editorial note identifies these pretty fellows with those "effeminate fops" that appear in *Tatler* 26 two days before. In *Tatler* 26 the pretty fellows referred to are members of the molly-club subculture then blossoming in London.[69]

But *Tatler* 26 alludes to the identity between the pretty fellow and the molly only in an attempt to dislodge it. News of these mollies calling themselves pretty fellows comes in a letter from a correspondent indignant at what he contends is a misappropriation of the title. Relating this contest over exactly what a pretty fellow is and who can call himself one, his letter dramatizes the state of categorical flux in the gendering and stylization of masculinity typical of the papers at large.

He writes complaining of a coterie of effeminate men who "assume the Name of *Pretty* Fellows": "[They] even get new Names. . . . Some of them I have heard calling to one another, as I have sat at *White's* and *St. James's*, by the names of *Betty, Nelly*, and so forth. You see them accost each other with effeminate Airs: they have their Signs and Tokens like Free-Masons" (*T* 26, italics reversed). That a set of effeminate homosexual men call themselves "Pretty Fellows" seems unexceptional — to us. The writer of this complaint, however, is outraged at what he sees as a gross abuse of an honorable title and so he petitions Bickerstaff to use his authority to "exclude all this Sort of Animals" from the category "Pretty Fellows." Just as, in the next paper, Steele bars "Persons of the Epicene Gender" from the category of rake, so this correspondent calls for the exclusion of homosexuals from the category of pretty fellows, who then would be legitimated as purely masculine, if stylish, characters. And just as Steele aligns the authentic rake in opposition to a set of homosexual fakes, so this aggressively masculine gentleman defines his own right to the title against its appropriation by a set of mollies. We can see here an emerging association among, on the one hand, masculinity, heterosexuality, and authenticity, and, on the other, effeminacy, homosexuality, and counterfeit. But the correspondent to *Tatler* 26 wants to further claim superior fashionability for the first set of positive masculine characteristics.

The correspondent gives his own character as a man about town who has honestly earned the appellation "Pretty Fellow" by pursuing a course of (emphatically heterosexual) libertinism and modish hooliganism. He cites his sexual prowess and rakish machismo as proof of his greater right to the title: "I have not lost my Time since I came to Town. . . . I have compounded Two or Three Rapes; and let out to Hire as many Bastards to Beggars. . . . I have more than once had sufficient Witnesses of my drawing my Sword both in Tavern and Playhouse" (*T* 26). Most remarkably, he maintains his protest against the claim of the mollies to the title "Pretty Fellows" even as he notes their cultivation of all sorts of "unintelligible Prettinesses" (*T* 26).

Clearly there is some contestation over not only what mode of man "Pretty Fellow" refers to but also what in fact "prettiness" is. The letter presents the options as (1) as a positive quality of worldly, masculine modishness or (2) a set of despicable mincing effeminacies. The correspondent is caught in a paradigmatic shift in gender categorization. "Prettiness," in the sense that the correspondent uses, means only a grandly cultivated sense of fashion and personal style. But these qualities have acquired such explicitly feminine connotations that when "prettiness" is attributed to men it may cancel out masculinity and denote effeminate homosexuality. So it is appropriated by the set of mollies.

There is a third reading of "pretty fellow" that, although he refers to it, the correspondent has not fully understood. This is found in

Tatler 21, where Steele defines the pretty fellow in opposition to true gentleman, not as in *Tatler* 27 to the rake. Here in *Tatler* 21 the difference between the gentleman and the pretty fellow lies not in categories of gender but in qualities of authenticity. The pretty fellow is simply an imitation gentleman. So Steele's definition draws on the sense of "pretty" as a trivialization of the more solid, more real qualities of a gentleman. Arguing for his legitimate status as a pretty fellow, the correspondent to *Tatler* 26 is, according to the standards established by Bickerstaff, only arguing for the authenticity of a type that can only be a facsimile. He just doesn't get it. Moreover, though Steele does not explicitly gender the category, the qualities that his pretty fellow epitomizes are part of a constellation of modish traits — superficiality, unstable value, mimicry, lack of autonomy, submission to the mode — that are gendered feminine and associated with excessive modishness in these papers. And it seems that the association between effeminacy and the pretty fellow is well enough established to provide some ground for Bickerstaff's satire against the correspondent. Turning his charges of appropriation against him, Bickerstaff calls his claims to the title pretty fellow a pretension and suggests that he may more prudently call himself instead a "Smart Fellow." There is a hint that everybody except the correspondent knows what a pretty fellow *really* is.

But Addison and Steele share with that gentleman correspondent his concern with the right (re)alignments between trait, character, and name. In a paper that perfectly defines the opposition between the man of sense and the man of fashion, Addison, ironically, asks the fops not to abandon their finery but to leave it on as a mark of their true character in order "to show to what Class they belong. . . . A cane upon the Fifth Button shall from henceforth be the Type of a Dapper; Red-heeled Shoes, and a Hat hung upon one Side of the Head, shall signify a Smart. . . . But . . . Men of real Merit should avoid any Thing particular in their Dress, Gait, or Behavior" (*T* 96). The man of sense is marked by his lack of distinctive traits, by his virtual invisibility, a trait that mirrors Mr. Spectator's own dominant feature. The body of true masculinity is a pure body, free of the stigma of fashion; this absence marks the presence of true value.

Most generally in *The Tatler* and *The Spectator*, modishness in men is reviled as capitulation to, or complicity with, rogue feminine forces at play in worldly arenas where they have no right to be. But they show as well how fashion begins to turn queer and how modishness in men starts to be darkened with those suspicions of gender treachery that persist to this day in Anglo-American bourgeois culture.

FIVE

Fashioning Taste
on the Culture Market

⊲⊳

COMMERCIAL CULTURE AND AESTHETIC TASTE

In the first of his series of lectures on eighteenth-century English literature and society, Leslie Stephen asks, "Are changes in literary fashions enveloped in the same inscrutable mystery as changes in ladies' dresses?"[1] The question alludes to, without completely confirming, two assumptions: first, that the irrational senselessness of fashions in dress, especially of female dress, dooms any critical examination of them to an equally senseless futility; and second, that a clear line divides the distinct spheres of sartorial and literary fashions. But Stephen's question also points to a set of difficulties that beset the exposition of any cultural change, whether in dress, manners, or literary taste — difficulties that may limit, yet do not prohibit, projects of historical inquiry. The problem is that change is overdetermined. We may identify important circuits of agency and influence, but simple origins and clear determination are elusive. This is what makes changes in fashion — literary as well as sartorial — seem so "mysterious" and "inscrutable."

While both the history of fashion and of literature respond to their own internal logics, both are more strongly governed by responses to larger sociocultural movements, and both literature and fashion are in part shaped by the discourses of other sorts of cultural production. Literature may be discussed in the rhetoric of fashion as in these lines of Alexander Pope's *Essay on Criticism*:

> Poets like Painters, thus, unskill'd to trace
> The *naked Nature* and the *living Grace,*
> With *Gold* and *Jewels* cover ev'ry Part,
> And hide with *Ornaments* their *Want of Art.*
> *True Wit* is *Nature* to Advantage drest. (293-97)[2]

Dress may be described by the formal categories of architectural discourse, and vice versa. There is in both the history of dress and the history of literature a dialectical play between internally and externally motivated changes. And, as evidenced in *The Tatler* and *The Spectator*, there is a wide net of transgeneric stylistic influence that spreads through all sorts of cultural productions — clothes, conversation, manners, poetry, opera, horticulture, architecture. The gardening enthusiast who describes his "Plantations" in a letter to *Spectator* 477 relies on a discourse that unites literary and horticultural productions within analogous generic categories: "I think there are as many kinds of Gardening, as of Poetry; Your Makers of Parterres and Flower-Gardens, are Epigrammatists and Sonneteers in this Art. Contrivers of Bowers and Grotto's, Treillages and Cascades, are Romance Writers." His own "Compositions in Gardening," he tells us, "are altogether after the *Pindarick* manner, and run into the beautiful Wildness of Nature, without affecting the nicer Elegancies of Art."[3]

Addison speaks of music, architecture, painting, poetry, and oratory in a single breath; he says that none of these arts should be determined by internally derived rules. His is a strenuously antiformalist aesthetic: "Musick, Architecture, and Painting, as well as Poetry and Oratory, are to deduce their Laws and Rules from the general Sense and Taste of Mankind, and not from the Principles of those Arts themselves; or, in other Words, the Taste is not to conform to the Art, but the Art to the Taste" (*S* 29). Likewise, specialization is distrusted as narrow pedantry, and it has no place in the more broadly cultural criticism pursued by Addison and Steele: "The truth of it is, there is nothing more absurd, than for a Man to set up for a Critick, without a good Insight into all the Parts of Learning" (S 291).

The dominant influence of external social transformations on literary developments leads Stephen to a frank, if deflating, evaluation of literature: "To say the truth, literature seems to me to be a kind of by-product."[4] Historical changes in literature, then, cannot be accounted for with any immanent literary history. Likewise, Georg Simmel emphasizes that changes in fashion are unaccountable from any perspective that looks at fashion in and for itself: "Fashion is merely the product of social demands. . . . This is clearly proved by the fact that very frequently not the slightest reason can be found for the creations of fashion from the standpoint of an objective, aesthetic, or other expediency."[5] So even if we consider *The Tatler* and *The Spectator* as "literary" productions, no literary history (nor, I would add, any history of ideas) can satisfactorily account for their production.[6] And our classification of the papers as "literature" may itself be anachronistic, or, at least, in need of considerable extenuation. Notions of both "literature" and "culture" in the sense of discrete, aesthetically defined arenas are only beginning to emerge at this time. Addison and Steele do not treat literature as a formally, internally determined sphere of cultural production; they do not view it as an art in and for its own sake.[7] Instead, they work cross-generically, but in ways that do begin to define modern cultural categories, like the aesthetic.

As Michael McKeon argues, the division of knowledge from which the discrete aesthetic sphere emerges developed alongside an ongoing production of integrative, what we call interdisciplinary, models of knowledge, and this division was by no means complete in the eighteenth century.[8] Both epistemological impulses — that which divides and specializes categories of knowledge and that which unites and integrates them — are evident in Addison's pioneering formulations of the aesthetic realm. The formation of the aesthetic arena itself involved bringing together of various types of cultural production; these are pulled into alignment and analogy through the formulation of a standard of taste equally applicable to all. The concept of a set of cultural forms all brought together under the rubric "the fine arts" may seem natural to us, but it is a specifically modern phenomenon.[9] Moreover, evidence from this period suggests that the discourse of the aesthetic embraced more than these fine arts — painting, poetry, music, sculpture, architecture — reaching out to encompass more "mundane," ephemeral cultural forms like dressing and horticulture. Nor was it clear that all these arts were truly fine. Addison has his reservations about music and, in his aesthetic hierarchy, sets the performative art of tragic drama above it (*S* 18). Finally, the discourse of the cultural aesthetic developed in relation to other realms of arenas of experience and knowledge.

The transitional position the papers occupy in the institution of the aesthetic has its counterpart in their transitional position in the definition of ideal types of bourgeois subjectivity. And, because the aesthetic and the standard of taste it depends upon are so heavily ethical and subjective, their formulation is intimately tied to that of ideal character types. Because taste is so inextricably involved in character, it serves as well as an ethical criterion for the evaluation not only of aesthetic but also of moral value. In true Platonic fashion, taste has to do not simply with what is beautiful but also with what is good.

The notion of modern aesthetic taste emerged along with the constitution of the modern individual and of the capitalist culture market. Robert Holub links the rise of critical aesthetic thought to the rise of bourgeois interests in eighteenth-century English society. He argues for the close affiliation of the peculiarly subjective critical standards promoted by Addison (for example) to the commercial cultural marketplace:

The artist's product becomes a commodity in an objectified market system which mystifies the relationship between artists and audience, and the artwork is consumed on an individual basis. The effects on criticism in the eighteenth century are drastic. For the presupposition underlying the new aesthetic theories is an ideal reader, an ideal viewer, or an ideal listener, in other words a person who consumes the work of art as an individual and whose responses are assumed valid for all men. Paradoxical as it may sound, the study of individual, subjective experience does not become fully developed until the art*work* becomes an art *object*, that is, until it appears in its commodity form on a free market.[10]

As we have seen in the last chapter, perhaps the most central object of *The Tatler* and *The Spectator* is the creation of ideal human models for their audience's emulation. The critical aesthetic papers may be seen as a strand in this larger ethical fabric. For the ethically ideal individual is an essentially aestheticized individual: he or she displays fineness of character through the exercise of an inborn taste, bearing witness to a personal integrity through the decorous consumption of proper cultural products.

Just as their ideal characters emerge out of critical negotiations with sets of other, discredited, prestigious types, so are these conceptions of critical taste and the cultural aesthetic forged in relation to sets of other, discredited, powerfully active cultural standards — tastes. The sorts of tastes that *The Tatler* and *The Spectator* seek to replace and reform are often manifest in popular, commercial cultural productions: the opera, puppet shows, contortionist shows, and other sorts of popular news- or scandal-oriented periodical papers. Indeed, as *The Tatler* and *The Spectator* distance themselves from these other cultural forms in order to define their own sphere of operation, they go far to articulate the modern realm of *aesthetic* culture: a genteel bourgeois arena for the improvement of human nature, one responsive to criteria outside the standards of status, sensationalism, wealth, and fashionability that mark the commercial ethic of the world.

As always, the relationship bourgeois culture bears to the very commercial tastes, including the taste for fashion, that it seeks to at once supersede and appropriate is vexed by its own invested complicity with commerce, fashion, and the popular. Guided by a widely applicable notion of taste, Addison and Steele treat fashions in "culture" (literature, drama, opera, music, painting) much as they treat fashions in dress — as avenues for sociocultural reform, and there is a clear and conscious correspondence between the kinds of fashions in dress and the kinds of fashions in other cultural productions supported and denounced by Addison and Steele. One way that fashion works is as a purely negative critical category: true cultural value lies outside the province of the merely fashionable. Yet fashion also functions in more positive ways. Advocating their popularized and broadly applicable standard of good taste, the papers produce a kind of good fashion, or at least a fashion for good taste. Addison and Steele want to make their standard of taste popular, indeed the popularizing qualities of simplicity, clarity, and accessibility are built into the very notion of taste they advocate. They want to institute cultural standards that are both fashionable (somewhat prestigious yet still accessible) *and* stable. By submitting fashion to a fairly egalitarian and rational standard of taste Addison and Steele want to fix it.

As popular periodicals, *The Tatler* and *The Spectator* work to extend the breadth of their audience and so the range of their influence; as pedagogical advisors, as they seek to enhance the depth of that audience's understanding of issues previously confined to the conversation of professional scholars and aristocratic elites. The periodical essay form, as Addison discusses in *Spectator* 124, is ideally suited to this popularizing task:

> When Knowledge, instead of being bound up in Books, and kept in Libraries and retirements, is thus obtruded upon the Publick; when it is canvassed in every Assembly, and exposed upon every Table; I cannot forbear reflecting upon that Passage in the *Proverbs, Wisdom cryeth out, she uttereth her Voice in the Streets: She cryeth in the chief Place of Concourse, in the Openings of the Gates.*

Noting the lack of philosophical specialization in Addison's meditations on culture, Stephen sketches the categories that *do* inform the method of these essays: common sense, wit, taste, and a thoroughgoing antipedantry. Further, this commonsensical approach serves as a means of ethical persuasion, winning to Mr. Spectator his wide lay following.

> He fully shares the characteristic belief of the day, that the abstract problems are soluble by common sense, when polished by academic culture and aided by a fine taste. It is a case of *sancta simplicitas*; of the charming, because perfectly unconscious, self-sufficiency with which the Wit, rejecting pedantry as the source of all

evil, thinks himself obviously entitled to lay down the law as theologian, politician, and philosopher. His audience are evidently ready to accept him as an authority, and are flattered by being treated as capable of reason.[11]

Indeed, the papers are famous for the policy of popularization stated by Addison in *Spectator* 10: "I shall be ambitious to have it said of me, that I have brought Philosophy out of Closets and Libraries, Schools, and Colleges, to dwell in Clubs and Assemblies, at Tea-tables, and in Coffee-Houses."

As this suggests, the papers are intimately connected with two institutions whose emergence goes far to define the social geography of eighteenth-century London, the coffeehouse and the domestic realm ("Tea-tables"), both of which are oriented around ideals of sociability and discursive interchange that inform a newly emergent standard of culture institutionalized in a new discursive realm: the bourgeois public sphere.[12] These public papers foster a kind of intimate community among their readers, proffering guidance in matters of domestic, cultural, and social life and providing a forum for readers' responses and suggestions. They are sites of dialectical exchange between the writer and reader, the public and private spheres, the commercial and aesthetic arenas of life.

Taste is an object produced in the rational space of the public sphere, a space which in its openness and cultivation of personal equality mirrors the structures of the market itself. Indeed, Steele speaks of his paper's participation in "the Commerce of Discourse" in *Spectator* 11. In *Tatler* 225, Bickerstaff lays out the blueprint of the public sphere as institutionalized both in popular meeting places like the coffee-house and club and in popular papers like *The Tatler* and *The Spectator*. As central institutions of the bourgeois public sphere, *The Tatler* and *The Spectator* provide not only a discursive venue but also the currency for cultural exchange. Taste is the coin of the cultural realm. Submitting various cultural productions — fashion, opera, ballads, conversation, architecture, landscaping, painting — to an identical aesthetic standard, the papers put into discursive circulation an aesthetic currency — "good taste" — that can purchase all manner of cultural capital. And just as money, in Engels's words, is "the commodity of commodities," so taste operates as the currency of the aesthetic.[13] In taste is distilled the very essence of the aesthetic that determines value on the cultural marketplace; so it passes as the common coin of cultural exchange. In a society largely governed through the formation of hegemonic consensus, taste then — rather than "rules" — provides the site of aesthetic commonality for all cultural products.

Taking on the broadening spectrum of commercial, popular entertainments of their day, the papers advocate a standard of taste as broad, accessible, and popular as the cultural productions they would reform. Ideally obtainable by all rational creatures, the sort of taste advocated in *The Tatler* and *The Spectator* provides a universal tool — as applicable to gardening as to painting as to dress as to literature as to architecture — for sorting through the markets of goods and entertainment. As such, taste contains within itself the features of equivalency — of access and applicability — that mark the economies of exchange within which its objects circulated. And indeed, taste itself becomes a commodity bought and sold through popular texts like *The Tatler* and *The Spectator*.

However, even as aesthetic value is constructed on models of consumption and property that reflect market exchange (as in the papers on the pleasures of the imagination), this is done in order to distinguish between market value and cultural value, between quantitative and arbitrary criteria (such as those that govern fashion) and more substantial criteria — those of "good taste." For the standard of taste advocated here explicitly rejects criteria of wealth and status and so purchases access to a (utopian) aesthetic realm free of the social and economic injustices of the world to which it offers a corrective alternative.[14] The specifically aesthetic anxieties motivating the reformative standards in *The Tatler* and *The Spectator* respond to the conditions imposed by a literary and more generally cultural marketplace: the quantification of value; the reification of human potential; the seemingly endless proliferation of forms generated by what seems an unnatural and promiscuous exchange. These anxieties, of course, are common to the age and appear with epic urgency in, for example,

Pope's *Dunciad*. But while Pope disowns his own participation in cultural commerce in order to maintain legitimacy within a, finally apocalyptic, vision of cultural decline, *The Tatler* and *The Spectator* take a more moderated position. Their vision is less reactionary, more reformative; the threats of commercialization are recognized not as portends of the end of civilization but as motives for cultural improvement.

So while mirroring the market and its economy, the public sphere does so in order to produce a separate arena of identification and exchange, with alternative values that compete with, in order to displace, the conventional values of both the marketplace and the beau monde. Social space should be bought with the currency of good sense, benevolence, and reason, not with status and wealth. In fact, the criteria of wealth and status should be disregarded in all rational conversation:

> Equality is the Life of Conversation. . . . Familiarity in Inferiors is
> Sauciness; in Superiors, Condescension; neither of which are to
> have Being among Companions, the very Word implying that
> they are to be equal. When therefore we have abstracted the
> Company from all Considerations of their Quality or Fortune, it
> will immediately appear, that to make it happy and polite, there
> must nothing be started which shall discover that our Thoughts
> run upon any such Distinctions. (*T* 225)

Terry Eagleton speaks of how the notion of abstract equality found in the concept of natural rights is actualized in this "region of discourse," the bourgeois public sphere: "The truly free market is that of cultural discourse itself, within of course, certain normative regulations; the role of the critics is to administer those norms, in a double refusal of absolutism and anarchy."[15] So while the function of taste in the aesthetic criticism of *The Tatler* and *The Spectator* is popularizing, it also operates to cancel out the "anarchic" qualities of superficiality, display, and mere novelty that seem to accompany popular, commercial culture.

This "double refusal" of dangers from both above and below does not afford the bourgeois public sphere a position outside class and status positions; rather, it becomes the ground on which a new class base is established. As Nancy Fraser points out, while the standard of taste advocated within the public sphere stressed public accessibility, rationality, and the bracketing of status differentials, it is nonetheless itself "deployed as a strategy of distinction."[16] Pierre Bourdieu stresses the constitutive element of *distinction*, of distaste, disgust, and exclusion, in every economy of taste:

> Tastes (i.e. manifested preferences) are the practical affirmation of an inevitable difference. . . . In matters of taste, more than any-where else, all determination is negation; and tastes are perhaps first and foremost distastes, disgust provoked by horror or visceral intolerance ("sick-making") of the taste of others. "De gustibus non est disputandum": not because "tous les gous sont dans la na-ture," but because each taste feels itself to be natural . . . which amounts to rejecting others as unnatural and therefore vicious.[17]

What is curiously paradoxical about the standard of taste advocated in *The Tatler* and *The Spectator* is that it makes it a distinction *not* to make distinctions. The target of Addison and Steele's reform is the sort of style that draws attention to itself, that hyperbolically *distinguishes* itself. Style should efface itself, appearing not as style per se but only as a transparent medium for the communication of character, value, and meaning. Style should disown as unnatural any traces of its own stylization, of its artificiality. Even as it apparently repudiates the arrogance and elitism of distinction, this standard of bourgeois taste, then, perfectly fulfills Bourdieu's logic of distinction which ends in taste's ideological naturalization of itself.

Unleashed from the elitism of the court, refusing the worldly standards of status and wealth, the type of taste promoted within the bourgeois public sphere finds validation on the grounds of nothing less than human nature itself. No longer affirmed by the innate values of status, seeking distance from the purely economic, quantitative standards that bolster newly ascendant class distinctions, the values of the aesthetic realm find their origin and confirmation in inborn, naturalized capacities of the individual. So Addison specifies the conditions for the acquisition of good taste in *Spectator* 409: "It is very dif-

ficult to lay down Rules for the acquirement of such a Taste as that
I am here speaking of. The Faculty must in some degree be born
with us, and it very often happens, that those who have other Qualities in perfection are wholly void of this." So, while fine taste refuses
worldly distinctions and conventional standards of exclusion, it is itself produced through natural, inscrutable processes capable of establishing a sort of native aesthetic aristocracy. Naturally enough, fine
taste comes naturally. That taste, like gender, is constructed as inherent, natural, and essentially integral to the individual allows it, like
gender, to function as a guarantor of cultural-aesthetic identity, just
as gender serves as the ground of personal identity. Because they are
such absolute values both gender and taste serve as gold standards
within, respectively, bourgeois sexual and cultural economies.

The emergence of modern categories of taste, literature, and culture occurs, then, alongside the saturation of commerce and fashion
in everyday London life. The commercialization of literature (with
its attendant commodification of knowledge) and that of entertainment and leisure are two aspects of this history immediately relevant
to the cultural aesthetic realm. J. H. Plumb examines the commercialization of leisure as part of the larger "commercial revolution"
that took place in England around the turn of the century; and Pat
Rogers looks at the relationship between literature and popular entertainments, especially those of the opera and masquerade.[18] In *The
Shows of London*, Richard Altick examines another strand of this rich
and various fabric of public, popular entertainment. He characterizes
the topic of his study as "the broad stream of urban culture which
ran parallel to and sometimes mingled with that of the printed word:
a great variety of public nontheatrical entertainments, here called exhibitions."[19] Exhibitions include the collections in early museums,
such as those discussed in my second chapter, as well as freak shows,
waxworks, and clock-works, and more mobile forms of spectacle
like the raree-show. Advertisements in *The Spectator* describe a number of these performances, such as that of the "famous Posture-Mas-
ter of Europe," who "extends his Body into all deform'd Shapes,"
and "the famous English Artist, who turns his Balls into living Birds;
and takes an empty Bag, which after being turn'd, trod, and stampt

on, produces some Hundreds of Eggs, and at last a living Hen."
These delights were to be witnessed at a tavern, the Duke of Marl-
borough's Head in Fleet Street. At the same venue appeared mechanical works, or "moving-pictures": "a new Invented Machine,
composed of five curious Pictures, with moving Figures, representing the History of the Heathen Gods, which moves as Artificially as
if Living."[20]

Altick points to the wide accessibility of such displays for which
literacy was not a necessary qualification. The shows were open to all
who could pay the (usually low) entrance fee and were popular
among both the literate and the illiterate classes. Jonathan Swift was
a dedicated spectator of the contemporary street theater.[21] And, as
we will see in a number of papers in *The Tatler* and *The Spectator*, exactly what performances belonged in the legitimate theaters and
which belonged on the streets and in the taverns was a matter of
contention. Indeed, the realm of popular entertainment constituted
a competing public arena over which early founders of the bourgeois
public sphere, like Addison and Steele, must assert ascendancy in order to discipline and regulate.[22]

One celebrated debate surrounds the cultural legitimacy of Italian
opera. Addison and Steele contribute a number of papers to this debate, which centers on issues of nationalism, of translation and communicability, of the proper role of spectacle in judicious taste, and,
most significantly, on the relative status of the arts and the problem
of the popular.[23] *The Tatler* and *The Spectator* by no means simply
condemn opera; indeed, they show a good deal of appreciation for
the famous singer Nicolini. Recognized within its limitations, opera
may be admitted to the English stage: "An Opera may be allowed to
be extravagantly lavish in its Decorations, as its only Design is to
gratify the Sense, and keep up an indolent Attention in the Audience" (*S* 5). But it should not dominate that stage. For opera addresses not the reason but the senses; it is a sensationalist mode of
theater. The papers clearly outline an aesthetic hierarchy within
which opera occupies a lower rung than do purely dramatic performances, especially tragedy. Seeing opera as a more popular, in the
sense of "lower," performance mode than legitimate theater, Addi-

son is apprehensive lest its great popularity supplant other stage productions (*S* 18).

In *Spectator* 31 Addison has a daft coffeehouse projector present his plan for an opera that encyclopedically encompasses every form of "low," nondramatic performance theater popular in London at the time.

> [The projector] said, that he had observed the great trouble and Inconvenience which Ladies were at, in travelling up and down to the several Shows that are exhibited in different Quarters of the Town. The dancing Monkies are in one Place; the Puppet Show in another; the Opera in a third; not to mention the Lions, that are almost a whole Day's Journey from the Politer Part of the Town. By this means People of Figure are forced to lose half the Winter after their coming to Town, before they have seen all the strange Sights about it. In order to remedy this great Inconvenience, our Projector drew out of his Pocket the Scheme of an Opera, Entitled, *The Expedition of* Alexander *the Great*; in which he had disposed all the remarkable Shows about Town, among the Scenes and Decorations of his Piece. The Thought, he confest, was not originally his own, but that he had taken the Hint of it from several performances which he had seen upon our Stage: In one of which there was a Rary-Show; in another, a Ladder-dance; and in others a Posture Man, a moving Picture, with many Curiosities of the like nature.

As we can see from this, one problem presented by opera and other "low" forms of entertainment is that they are popular with the "high" classes — with, for example, the "Ladies" who will go to such trouble to attend puppet shows, monkey dances, operas, contortionist and raree-shows, ladder-dancing, and so on. As Addison says in his history of opera on the English stage, what is amazing about opera is that "it is not the Taste of the Rabble, but of Persons of the greatest Politeness, which has establish'd it" (*S* 18).

Peter Stallybrass and Allon White note how bourgeois taste was established as a field of negotiation between higher aristocratic and lower folk forms of cultural production. This negotiation could take positive, conciliatory forms. So we see how *The Tatler* and *The Spectator* want to introduce a notion of taste that is accessible and popular, yet also nobly refined. But of course this negotiation within the cultural hierarchy could also take a more negative form that shows low and high meeting on the same faulty aesthetic ground. We see this in accounts of the opera and other spectacular, nondramatic performance art, such as the contortionist show an appalled Addison witnesses in *Tatler* 108. In either case, the inadequacies of both the higher and lower sociocultural arenas are understood to necessitate the intervention of a middle-brow aesthetic free from the faults of both.

> This refined public sphere occupied the centre. That is to say, it carved out a domain between the realm of kings and the world of alley-ways and taverns, and it did so by forcing together the high and the low as contaminated equivalents, somehow in league with each other and part of a conspiracy of exchange and promiscuity in which the low was ebbing higher to flood the court and the court was sinking into the filthy ways and pastimes of the low.[24]

This bad confluence of low and high is one of Pope's obsessive concerns in his *Dunciad* and *Peri Bathous* and a source of much uneasiness in Addison's papers on opera.

Anxiety about opera certainly fed into an aesthetic critique but was itself fed by general fears about the galloping commercialization of life. The "conspiracy of exchange and promiscuity" between high and low perceived by eighteenth-century cultural critics speaks of the operations of a cultural marketplace. As Pat Rogers points out, it is the blatant and exorbitant commercialism of the opera that disturbs all its critics, regardless of their other complaints.[25] So in the fourth book of his *Dunciad* Pope allegorizes Opera as an unsteady, meretricious slut:

> When lo! a Harlot form soft sliding by,
> With mincing step, small voice and languid eye;
> Foreign her air, her robe's discordant pride
> In patch-work flutt'ring, and her head aside:
> By singing Peers up-held on either hand,

She tripp'd and laugh'd, too pretty much to stand.

. . . .

"O *Cara! Cara!* silence all that train [of Muses]
Joy to Great Chaos! let division reign!" (44-54)[26]

Italian opera, then, at its worst is a feminine, meretricious, perniciously flighty form of theater. Its devotion to (empty) spectacle and reliance on sensual, rather than rational, appeals align it with a specific form of degenerate, faulty feminine taste. As Addison's papers, as well as Pope's *Dunciad*, show, opera is a dangerously seductive, explicitly *fashionable* pastime in the beau monde.

Both the threats and promises posed by the commercialization of culture are inseparable from the production of the modern category of aesthetic culture itself. By distinguishing what should *not* be subject to the "corrupting" forces of commercialization—human values and emotions, social and familial bonds, aesthetic cultural products—aesthetic criticism shows how commercialization generates the very categories that are posited as alternatives to it. *The Tatler* and *The Spectator* papers are social texts that exemplify and criticize the conditions of cultural production in the early eighteenth century. In a society where, fostered by the accelerated generation of commercialization and its standards of fashionability, cultural forms are proliferating at a great rate, the papers advocate an aesthetic standard that seeks to stabilize and regulate these forms by submitting them to normative standards of accessibility, permanence, and clear reference. But, like the public and commercial shows of London, *The Tatler* and *The Spectator* are addressed to a (relatively) broad urban audience; anyone can *buy* them; access is gained not through status and court connections but through a market where culture and prestige are exchangeable for money.

WHAT'S NEWS? "THE TATLER," "THE SPECTATOR," AND THE INFORMATION MARKET

The Tatler and *The Spectator* bear a complex relation to the market in news and the coffeehouse and club societies that grew up in tandem with it. Unraveling some of the strands of this relation between the papers and the news culture of town talk reveals tightly woven connections between the forces of speed, novelty, news, and fashion; it reveals as well the ambivalent stance *The Tatler* and *The Spectator* take in regard to these forces.

Both papers situate themselves in the coffeehouses and so in the nexus of news culture. At the coffeehouses, *The Tatler* and *The Spectator* take their places among a growing stock of periodicals. In these assembly places, all manner of information was disseminated through print and, just as importantly, by word of mouth. Papers like *The Tatler* and *The Spectator* were written to be talked about. The essays addressing literary and aesthetic issues enter into a cultural debate that, far from predominately textual and academic, was highly oral and social, conducted most usually at coffeehouses and taverns.[27] Indeed the coffeehouse was the tribunal of literary judgment; reception there could make or break an author.[28] So the stereotypical theater critic Sir Timothy Tittle, who "puts Men in Vogue, or condemns them to Obscurity," laughs to scorn any author not known at Will's (*T* 165).

The coffeehouse was the site for the consumption of commodities central to Britain's commercial imperialism: coffee and tea, the sugar that always went into both, tobacco, and *news*. In their physiological, as well as commercial, effects all these substances are emblematic of the intensified stimulation of trade and of imperialism in post-Restoration England. And as the portraits of news-hounds like Thomas Quid-nunc and the pathetic gazette-junky of *Tatler* 178 show, news became as addictive a substance to the man as it was to the market. News, moreover, is more central to the consolidation of commerce than any other single commodity: "Almost simultaneously with the origin of stock markets, postal services and the press institutionalized regular contacts and regular communication."[29] At first this delivery of news was conducted privately among merchants, but as trade became more capital intensive it also started to be broadcasted more publicly.[30] Economic events become a matter of public interest. News supplies material for this curiosity — both as information about foreign and domestic events that bear on economic activity and as a forum in which the pursuit of this activity — its nature, its aims, its effects — could itself be debated. Part and parcel of both the "commercial" and the "financial" revolutions, news becomes a stimulant as powerful in the awakening market as were coffee, tea, tobacco, and sugar: "For the traffic in news developed not only in connection with the needs of commerce; the news itself became a commodity."[31]

As clearinghouses of the latest foreign and domestic news, coffeehouses were meeting places for tradesmen, merchants, stock dealers, insurance brokers, and politicians; they functioned as headquarters for any number of entrepreneurial and corporate enterprises.[32] And there were especially chic coffeehouses that functioned as places of fashionable resort, providing Temple students with a stage for the styling crucial to their social prestige. Here young men won status by successfully conforming to the standards of "Gallantry and Fashion" that rule their fraternity (*S* 49). Perhaps the most basic connection between these two aspects of coffeehouse life — the communication of information and the setting of fashions — may be found in the principles of speed and novelty that govern both.

Pursuit of the news serves as a kind of exemplary instance of the forces of acceleration and novelty that were beginning to determine the contours of everyday life. These forces hit earliest and hardest in the printing industry, which was the first and most fully capitalized modern business, and, after 1694, a substantially deregulated one. The production of information soon takes on a role that presages its ever-increasing centrality in modern markets. The picture of information in *The Tatler* and *The Spectator* shows a commodity that seems about to burst through the temporal and spatial limitations of existing technology; hardly does one get a piece of news before it becomes stale, useless. "Our news," writes a correspondent to *Spectator* 251, "should indeed be Published in a very quick time, because it is a Commodity that will not keep cold." News was the most perishable commodity on the market; the high stakes of currency on this early modern information highway were anxiously realized by contemporaries.

News, like fashion, is a growth industry. And the addictive pursuit and relentless retailing of the news is part of fashionable urban life.

To keep up with the latest thing, with the talk of the town—let alone to set the fashion and become the talk of the town—requires speed sufficient to outstrip one's competitors. This accelerated production and distribution of information produced specific types of human character. So Thomas Quid-nunc relates his breathless course through the city's coffeehouses as he rushes to keep up with the news: "A Piece of News loses its Flavour when it hath been an Hour in the Air. . . . I assure you, that I post away from Coffee-house to Coffee-house, and forestall the *Evening-Post* by two-hours" (S 625). On the one hand, this is absurd because it represents a consumer competing with the very commodity he is after. On the other, it is a telling depiction of the sometimes indistinguishable identities of the news commodity and the news consumer. By becoming more current than the *Evening-Post*, running faster down the thoroughfares than the *Daily Courant*, the consumer himself becomes a news-bearing commodity valuable in the commerce of discourse transacted at the coffeehouses. In the publication of himself, the news junky, like the news itself, is put under extreme temporal pressures, becoming (in every destabilizing, ambiguity-generating sense of the term) more mercurial than the *Mercure Galant*. Addicts become their drugs. Consumption is incorporation; in the case of powerful substances, it transforms people in self-alienating ways. In chapter 2 we saw how the old visiting lady, the beau, and the coquette incorporate and in important senses *become* the fashion commodities they so avidly consume. The news junky is another variation on this consumer type. Consumed in excess, the news, like the fashion commodity, takes over the personality of the individual by re-creating that person in its own image.

As a kind of newspaper antidote against the news, *The Tatler* and *The Spectator* would prevent and even cure the evils of addiction to newspapers. Comparing the frenzy brought on by news addiction with Don Quixote's romance-induced distemper, Steele in *Tatler* 178 describes the "Epidemick Ill" of news junkies, such as the unfortunate "political Upholsterer," who frequents the low haunts of "ragged Assemblies" and "Alley-Coffeehouses." Bickerstaff warns his readers: "the News-Papers of this Island are as pernicious to weak

Heads in *England* as ever Book of Chivalry to *Spain*." These "weak Heads" include those, like "the Blanks," "who were not born to have Thoughts of their own, and consequently lay a Weight upon every Thing which they read in Print." News dependency brings on diseases of the imagination; it becomes a malady of the passions manifest in a range of symptoms running from professional lethargy to lunacy:

> The Tautology, the Contradictions, the Doubts, and Wants of Confirmations, are what keep up imaginary Entertainments in empty Heads, and produce Neglect of their own Affairs, Poverty, and Bankruptcy, in many of the Shop-Statesmen; but turn the Imaginations of those of a little higher Orb into Deliriums of Dissatisfaction, which is seen in a continual Fret upon all that touches their Brains, but more particularly upon any Advantage obtained by their Country, where they are considered as Lunaticks, and therefore tolerated in their Ravings. (*T* 178)

Steele's loyalty to his comrades fallen on the killing fields of print culture spurs him to acts of personal charity. He escorts one victim from the coffeehouse to a special ward of Bedlam (a project proposed in *Tatler* 125) and sees that carefully regulated doses of the *Mercure Galant* are administered to ease the addiction without breaking the constitution.

In a more generalized way, Addison's series of essays on the pleasures of the imagination may be understood to perform a similar psychically restorative function (*S* 411–21). Briefly noting that there are pains as well as pleasures of the imagination, Addison cites the lunatic as the most perfect embodiment of the anguished imagination: "There is not a Sight in Nature so mortifying as that of a Distracted Person, when his Imagination is troubled, and his whole Soul disordered and confused. *Babylon* in Ruins is not so melancholly a Spectacle" (*S* 421). Feeding on the unwholesome provender provided by the news market, the lunatic's fancy is disordered. In contrast, the man who cultivates his fancy according to the guidelines offered by Addison's discourse on the pleasures of the imagination bolsters both his psychic and his physical well-being. The pleasures of the imagination are "conducive to Health," writes Addison in *Spectator* 411:

"Delightful Scenes, whether in Nature, Painting, or Poetry, have a kindly Influence on the Body, as well as the Mind, and not only serve to clear and brighten the Imagination, but are able to disperse grief and Melancholy, and to set the Animal Spirits in pleasing and agreeable Motions." The aesthetic realm, with the healthy pleasures it generates from the fancy, then, and the arena of news discourse, with the sordid, fretful deliriums it produces, occupy opposite psychic poles.

Using their papers — in many respects themselves *news*papers — to issue warnings against addiction to newspapers, Addison and Steele exploit the reflexive, self-critical potentials of the early modern periodical. As a commodity "subject to the laws of the same market to whose rise it owed its existence," the newspaper becomes a public forum for conversation about this market.[33] It becomes a self-reflective medium — a commodity that debates the proper regulation of the conditions of its own existence. Thus, in an self-regulating move, *The Spectator* produces its satiric prescription against the abuse of the news by Thomas Quid-nunc and other news-hounds, warning the consumer against the frenzied and addictive pursuit of the talk of the town. Satirizing the news junkies, these papers are also telling their readers not to consume *The Tatler* and *The Spectator* like news. They instruct against their own misappropriation through a mode of consumption that conforms too neatly to the forces of acceleration and novelty. This is one strategy in their construction of the ideal reader.

In the first essay that he writes for *The Tatler*, Addison addresses the difference between this and the more news-oriented papers (*T* 18). *Tatler* 18 begins with Bickerstaff including himself as "an unworthy Member" among "the ingenious Fraternity" of news journalists. But it ends with him dissociating himself from this fraternity. His interests, his field of operation, his material — all differ from those of the common run of news-hounds who, at this time, were mostly chasing after war stories. While their concerns are "Camps, Fortifications, and Fields of Battle," Bickerstaff covers another territory, a land of domestic culture where the "chief Scenes of Action are Coffee-houses, Play-houses, and my own Apartment." Drawing this distinction between his own and the journalistic project even more firmly, Addison commends himself and his readers in *Spectator*

262. He reflects on his paper's popularity, gained despite its refusal to retail the standard items of fashionable information:

> I think my self highly obliged to the Publick for their kind Acceptance of a Paper which visits them every Morning, and has in it none of those *Seasonings* that recommend so many of the Writings which are in vogue among us.
>
> As, on the one Side, my Paper has not in it a Single Word of News, a Reflection in Politicks, nor a Stroke of Party; so, on the other, there are no fashionable Touches of Infidelity, no obscene Ideas, no Satyrs upon Priesthood, Marriage, and the like popular Topicks of Ridicule. (*S* 262)

It is testimony, Addison goes on to say, to the high standards of his audience that they enjoy his paper despite its lack of both political news and personal scandal — two highly popular sensationalist discourses. What his readers get instead is "news" about themselves. Addison claims that the content of his paper bears a closer, more valuable relation to its audience than any newspaper: "Is it not much better to be let into the Knowledge of ones-self, than to hear what passes in *Muscovy* or *Poland?*" (*S* 10).

According to Addison, periodicals had previously been exploited only by scandal mongers, news writers, and party propagandists; he promises to use popular journalism in new ways "more advantageous to Mankind" (*S* 124). Conventional news removes a man from his immediate and personal concerns, transporting him to exotic, foreign scenes rendered all the more fantastic by the ill-informed, speculative nature of the reports made about them. Concerned at this time primarily with the war with France, the news is foreign, alien; it imaginatively — and all the more powerfully for that — divorces a man from the context within which he grounds his identity. The news then has a self-alienating, disorienting effect on its readers. More than information about events they play no immediate part in, happening in countries they will never visit to people they don't know, men (here Addison refers specifically to his male readers) need "to be instructed in Wisdom and Virtue . . . to be made good Fathers, Husbands, and Sons" (*S* 124). Further, readers should have their psychological and ethical needs attended to. Accordingly, *The Spectator* sets out to "clear up their Understandings, animate their Minds with Virtue, dissipate the Sorrows of a heavy Heart, or unbend the Mind from its more severe Employments" (*S* 124).

Filling their papers not with public, political, and military information but with ethical, psychological, social, and domestic material, Addison and Steele engage in a kind of twofold transformation. They initiate a new mode of essay writing that branches off from the newspaper and leads into the popular magazine, making the periodical paper subjective, personal. Yet, they also seek to reform the alienating news discourse with their more subjectively oriented essays, thus entering these spheres of life onto the fashion-driven cultural market of which they are so wary. From one perspective, *The Tatler* and *The Spectator* are turning their pet topics — standards of personal conduct, processes of aesthetic judgment and affective experience, and the formation of taste — into the news. Perhaps an alternative sort of news, but news nonetheless. Their news is about taste and manners, not troop movements. And their attention to psychological, moral, cultural, and social phenomena open these arenas to a kind of public and popular institutionalization related, if not identical, to the trend setting that determines the vagaries of dress and manners. So while the papers seem dedicated to curbing the rampant gallop of fashion and novelty, the ways they do this extend the domain of these forces into areas of life that were before left out of the news market.

THE TALK OF THE TOWN: SETTING THE FASHION FOR PLAIN ENGLISH

For 'tis the Fashion now to be the Town talk;
and you know, one had as good be out of the World,
as out of the Fashion.

LOVE'S LAST SHIFT: OR, THE FOOL IN FASHION *(1721)*[34]

With their essentially therapeutic discourse, *The Tatler* and *The Spectator* aimed first and foremost at the well-being of their audience, whose heads they sought to stock with a more worthwhile cargo of intellectual goods than those carried in the newspapers of the day. Citing those "Blanks" of the town who are at a loss for conversation until they have read all the papers, Addison claims that *The Spectator*, better than any newspaper, can supply them with a good stock of talk, instilling "into them such sound and wholesome Sentiments, as shall have a good Effect on their Conversation for the ensuing twelve Hours" (*S* 10). So, just as they distinguish between their own and other (news)papers, Addison and Steele are eager to differentiate the kind of talk they supply from other popular modes of town talk. They want to refashion the talk of the town, which, if one credits the complaint in *Tatler* 244, has devolved into overwrought gibberish: "In the ordinary Conversation of this Town, there are so many who can, as they call it, talk well, that there is not One in Twenty that talks to be understood." Along with this recurrent refrain of the corruption of conversation comes a critique of those low, venial, sensationalist books, periodicals, and plays that foster the decay of discourse. In response, *The Tatler* and *The Spectator* do not merely criticize the fashionable, sensationalist journalistic discourses of their day but present themselves as corrective alternatives to them. Restocking the minds, they refurbish the conversation of their readers, and so would set off a kind of chain reaction of discursive reform that would catch on by becoming the talk of the town.

The Tatler and *The Spectator* were written to be talked about. Addison and Steele exploit print culture for its effects on oral culture. While readers today approach the papers as literary texts to be written about, in their own day the papers were consumed more as food for discussion. They worked within an everyday social circuit between text and talk that we in the late twentieth century associate with the mass media, especially the visual texts of television, movies, and music videos, though magazines and newspapers still have a place in this circuit. These provide many of the myths, narratives, examples, and information through which people produce and experience their lives. But while *The Tatler* and *The Spectator*, like these contemporary media, presented topics and narratives that fed back into the everyday concerns and conversations of their audiences, they were more localized and more accessible to consumer response than most forums of late-twentieth-century mass media. *The Tatler* and *The Spectator* saturated and were saturated by a community of discourse. They were designed—by constant reference to their public and moral goals, by the heavy inclusion of letters from readers—to break down the barriers between text and social practice, between print and talk.[35]

The proposed reform of town talk also has a metacritical function. Proper criticism depends on taste and judgment; conversation is a pedagogical tool for the development and exercise of both. In *Spectator* 409, Addison names conversation "with Men of a Polite Genius" among the methods for "improving our Natural Taste." Coffeehouse and club society were the sites of critical debate, and the course of conversation there went far to determine the course of cultural trends: "The clubs at which the politicians and authors met each other represented the critical tribunals, when no such things as literary journals existed. It was at these that judgment was passed upon the last new poem or pamphlet, and the writer sought for their good opinion as he now desires a favourable review."[36] By setting the terms and standards for polite conversation, Addison and Steele, with help from Swift, established the language in which sociocultural criticism is conducted.

Reforms of journalism, conversation, theater, literature, and language are all undertaken as corrections of fashionable excess. In *Tatler* 230, Swift parodies fashionable slangy, abbreviated, (and in his view) debauched English; and in *Spectator* 58, Addison refers to the "Fashion of false Wit" that corrupts the taste of the nation. Both Swift's attack on what passes as polite conversation and Addison's on what passes as wit share a distaste for forms of verbal manipulation that call attention to the body of language, to the material word, to the autonomy of the signifier. They see in these a disregard for sense and a cultivation of features of language that have little to do with verbal stability, permanence, reason, and easy communication.

In one of his papers on true, mixed, and false wit, Addison provides a test for diagnosing the presence of puns and so the quality of wit under examination:

The only way therefore to try a Piece of Wit, is to translate it into a different Language: If it bears the Test you may pronounce it true; but if it vanishes in the Experiment you may concluded it to have been a Punn. In short, one may say of a Punn as the Country-man described his Nightingale, that it is *vox & praeterea nihil*, a Sound, and nothing but a Sound. On the contrary, one may represent true Wit by the Description which *Aristinetus* makes of a fine Woman, when she is *dressed* she is Beautiful, when she is *undressed* she is Beautiful: Or, as *Mercerus* has translated it more Emphatically, *Induitur, formosa est: Exitur, ispa forma est.* (*S* 61)

This method allows one to see if there is in a piece of verbal wit a "true" correspondence between ideas, or rather, as with the pun, a mere "Conceit arising from the use of two Words that agree in the Sound, but differ in the Sense" (*S* 61). Such a connection determined merely by sound, by the auditory signifier alone, is reckoned illegitimate, for it operates without reference to the signified, the meaning of the words. Such puns are empty sounds: *vox & praeterea nihil*.

These standards of sound and sense emerge as well in Addison's papers on the Italian opera in England. One problem presented by the production of opera, either in Italian or English, on the English stage is precisely this rupture between sound and sense which may resolve as a pure independence of sound, such as operates in the pun. Londoners, it is assumed, do not understand Italian; so if the performance is given in its native tongue, all sense is lost. But translating the opera into English does not solve the problem since under the pressure of an English rhyme scheme words and music are disjointed, destroying any sensible correspondence between the two. So Addison cites one instance where "the soft Notes that were adapted to [the word] *Pity* in the *Italian*, fell upon the Word *Rage* in the *English*; and the angry Sounds that were tuned to *Rage* in the Original, were made to express *Pity* in the Translation" (*S* 18).

Ultimately, the problem that Addison addresses here is that the audience for Italian opera is enjoying sound without sense and so cultivating an irrational pleasure. Sound itself is not to be trusted. Music, such as the song of the nightingale alluded to in *Spectator* 61, is more likely than not *vox & praeterea nihil*. First, music is, inherently, a somewhat low species of performance on the scale of cultural value Addison would establish: "If the *Italians* have a Genius for Musick above the *English*, the *English* have a Genius for other Performances of a much higher Nature, and capable of giving the Mind a much nobler Entertainment" (*S* 18). Addison specifies dramatic tragedy here as an example of these nobler English performances. Second, and related to its low cultural value, music in itself is senseless; meaning is understood to reside entirely in words. Therefore, music that functions independently of words presents a threat to good sense, to reason. So Addison concludes: "Musick is certainly a very agreeable Entertainment, but if it would take the entire Possession of our Ears, if it would make us incapable of hearing Sense, if it would exclude Arts that have a much greater tendency to the Refinement of humane Nature: I must confess I would allow it no better Quarter than *Plato* has done, who banishes it out of his Commonwealth" (*S* 61). (Addison does not remember here that Plato banished poets as well.)

Sound, then, is identified with the sensual external form of the signifier and, as we see in both the case of Italian opera and of puns, the independent performance of this form cannot signify. In the passage on puns quoted above, we see how sound as the sensuous form of language is compared with the external trappings of a woman's clothes, the ornaments which may in themselves be "a very agreeable Entertainment" but are nothing to the delights offered by stripping that woman/word down to her naked sense. With his first quotation, Addison seems to point to a perfect aestheticized correspondence between the external/internal, the signifier/signified: "when she is *dressed* she is Beautiful, when she is *undressed* she is Beautiful." But in the second "translation" of this tag the position of the terms shifts slightly in favor of the naked body of sense, stripped of its external trappings: "Induitor, formosa est: Exuitur, ipsa forma est" (Dressed she is beautiful; undressed she is beauty itself.)

Addison's final paper on wit relates an allegorical dream vision of the region of false wit where this vestimentary metaphor of language is in full play (*S* 63). Here, the party of puns appear in masquerade: "They were divided into Pairs, every Pair being covered from Head to Foot with the same kind of Dress. . . . By this means an old Man was sometimes mistaken for a Boy, a Woman for a Man, and a Black-a-moor for an *European*." Mediation here bears no correspondence to significance and confounds the differences that constitute recognizable (i.e., "natural") identity. As the allegory in this passage evidences, anxieties about preserving the identifying marks of difference in language are analogous, and related to, anxieties about preserving sociocultural signs that mark gender, age, and race. Moreover, these marks must be recognized as natural, as what is to be seen when the costume is pulled off.

In this conventional trope of verbal wit as the dressed and undressed body, especially the female body, eighteenth-century criticism addresses the relation between the authentic and inauthentic, the artificial and the essential. Most generally in sociocultural criticism, this stripping of the female, as Laura Brown shows, reveals an impulse "to strip away the mystifying 'clothing' of the commodity and to discover the lost human essence that lies beneath." In the context of discussions of wit, like that in *Spectator* 61, the naked female body becomes the ambiguous and problematic ground on which rests essential, naturalized signification. Problematic because true wit, as Pope formulates it in his *Essay on Criticism*, is nature dressed, not undressed, to advantage.

> Poets like Painters, thus, unskill'd to trace
> The *naked Nature* and the *living Grace,*
> With *Gold* and *Jewels* cover ev'ry Part,
> And hide with *Ornaments* their *Want of Art.*
> *True Wit* is *Nature* to Advantage drest. (293-97)

Looking at the role of the female figure in the mediation between history and aesthetic theory, Brown summarizes: "Ornament and nature are in the same ambiguous relation as dress and undress: 'True Wit' arrives to dress nature to advantage at precisely the moment when she is stripped naked in the critique of the unskilled poet."[37] True wit, then, cannot be neatly identified with the purely essential but is always involved in the realm of the externally mediated, ornamental, and artificial. Yet it must veil and mystify that involvement in order to makes its claims on the naked truth. In the context of Brown's discussion, this formulation of wit mirrors the logic of the fetish and its mystifying conflation of the thing and essence, of the commodity and the human. Brown traces some of the anxieties, aesthetic and sexual, that this logical situation evokes in eighteenth-century critics. In Addison's papers on opera and true wit, we see these typical anxieties, expressed in *Spectator* 61 with the typical naked lady trope, centered on the problem of determining the ground of signification, identifying what is essential to language.

Finally, the reading of the stripped female body as beauty itself is as much a masculine fiction as the empty translation of the nightingale's song as *vox & praeterea nihil*. I want to return briefly to the passage at the close of *Spectator* 61:

> In short, one may say of a Punn as the Country-man described his Nightingale, that it is *vox & praeterea nihil*, a Sound, and nothing but a Sound. On the contrary, one may represent true Wit by the Description which *Aristinetus* makes of a fine Woman, when she is *dressed* she is Beautiful, when she is *undressed* she is Beautiful: Or, as *Mercerus* has translated it more Emphatically, *Induitur, formosa est: Exuitur, ispa forma est.*

At the risk of "overreading" this passage, I suggest that it contains, in the paired figures of the nightingale and the naked lady, a sort of semiotic allegorization connecting the silencing of woman's voice, the violation of her body, and the imposition on that body of aesthetic ideals. Addison's allusion here to an obscure tale of a "Country-man's" nightingale simultaneously invokes and represses the narrative of that much more renowned nightingale from Greek legend, Philomela, as well as her song of male violation. The imposition on woman's body of the male critic's aesthetic ideal requires that the body, like Philomela, be silenced, that it have nothing to say for itself. What she has to tell names her violation by the male who would have her bear the weight of *his* meaning, and so the scandal of its imposition, in silence. The naked truth here then lies in the voice of the nightingale whose song, rather than being translated, is dismissed as devoid of all meaning, *vox & praeterea nihil*.

As the conventional dressed/undress metaphor might imply, there
are quite exact stylistic analogies between good and bad modes of
language and good and bad modes of dress and manners. In eighteenth-century stylistic criticism, conceptual analogies between fashions in language and fashions in dress are foregrounded by rhetorical
figures applicable to both. As we have seen, Pope's dress/language
play in his *Essay on Criticism* (commended by Addison in *Spectator*
253) unfurls these conceptual commonplaces: "*True Wit* is *Nature* to
advantage drest"; "Expression is the *Dress of Thought*"; "In *Words*, as
Fashions, the same Rule will hold."[38] Steele's commendation of Lady
Courtly's refined simplicity in *Tatler* 62 depends on the intimately related discourses of language, dress, and women that we have just seen
at work in Addison's and Pope's formulation of wit. In a compliment
more than a little left-handed, Steele commends the conversation of
women for its freedom from the pedantry and self-consciousness that
riddle the discourse of men "who read much." Women talk easily
and engagingly because they are free from the distractions of knowledge. The example Steele cites of this "wonderful Freedom" of expression is a conversation he had with Lady Courtly about (of all
things) dress.

> My Lady *Courtly* . . . was talking the other Day of Dress, and did
> it with so excellent an Air and Gesture, that you would have
> sworn she had learned her Action from our *Demosthenes*. Besides
> which, her Words were particularly well adapted to the Matter she
> talked of, that the Dress was a new Thing to us men. She avoided
> the Terms of Art in it, and described an unaffected Garb and
> Manner in so proper Terms, that she came up to that of *Horace's*
> *Simplex Munditiis*; which, whoever can translate in two Words, has
> as much Eloquence as Lady *Courtly*. (*T* 62)

The anecdote is self-reflexive in the extreme: a lesson about the
proper dress of thought exemplified in a conversation about a properly stylized ("unaffected") dress. Most importantly, the proper style
of language is identical to the proper style of dress and manner advocated in the papers: simple, unadorned, natural, easy, unaffected.
These are the virtues summed up in the tag *simplex munditiis*. The

advocacy of this aesthetic is central to the moral reform pursued by the papers, as it is to the ideology of the bourgeois public sphere itself. As Bickerstaff assures the ladies in *Tatler* 151, "there is nothing touches [men's] Imagination so much as a beautiful Woman in a plain Dress."[39] Lady Courtly's speech performs the virtuous qualities of the "unaffected garb and manner" that she describes (*T* 62).

Perfect simplicity lies at the heart of the good taste applicable to all cultural forms. The tag *simplex munditiis* recurs throughout the papers, though no direct translation is ever offered. Lady Courtly does not even ask for one; she just smiles and compliments Bickerstaff on his scholarship when he tells her "that all she had said with so much good Grace was spoken in Two Words by *Horace*" (*T* 62). In a later *Tatler* paper, a more curious, slightly ridiculous allegorical lady who signs herself "Plain English" writes in to ask about the translation of the tag, which her brother has told her means her own name (*T* 212). Bickerstaff confirms this reading of the phrase and goes on to elaborate the proper standards of style that it entails: "Nothing is to be more carefully consulted than Plainness. In a Lady's Attire this is the single Excellence; for to be what some call fine, is the same Vice in that Case, as to be florid is in Writing or Speaking" (*T* 212). Language, like dress, should be used in the service of something other than itself; it should draw attention away from itself and toward the sense it would communicate. Neither language nor dress should indulge in the "vice" of self-display. The only display language and dress should make is of their own transparency; both should be as unmarked as possible in order to highlight the object served — true character, meaning, good sense. These principles apply to all the arts: even a painting should not be "made for the Eyes only" (*S* 244).

Reflecting the same ideals, often in similarly vestimentary and fashion-critical figures, Swift's essay satirizing language fads is printed as a letter to *Tatler* 230. The letter appeals to Bickerstaff to use his position as censor to reform "our Style." It assumes analogical systems of representation among various forms of media — clothing, literature, architecture — and so applies to them all that same single standard of simple elegance invoked throughout the papers: "that Simplicity which is the best and truest Ornament of most Things in Life, which the politer Ages always aimed at in their Building and Dress, (*Simplex Munditiis*) as well as their Productions of Wit" (*T* 230). In typical eighteenth-century fashion, Swift works with the common-place and blanketing assumption of the analogous operation of dress and language. In his *Proposal for Correcting . . . the English Tongue*, Swift notes the regional variations in abbreviation, or, as he calls it, the "maiming" of the English language. At the current rate of change, Swift predicts, "in a few Years" all these various regional di-alects will "differ from themselves, as Fancy or Fashion shall direct: All which reduced to Writing, would entirely confound Orthogra-phy. (It would be just as wise to shape our Bodies to our Cloathes and not our Cloathes to our Bodyes.)"[40] Just as excessive ornament, slanginess, and preciosity mark the style of bad English, so they mark the style of those who use it. So in his *Tatler* paper, Swift attacks the idiosyncratic, "phonetic" spelling practiced by men of fashion: "A noble Standard for Language! To depend upon the caprice of every Coxcomb, who because Words are the Cloathing of our Thoughts, cuts them out and shapes them as he pleases, and changes them more often than his Dress" (*T* 230). If continued unchecked, this practice would mutilate language and generate a senseless plethora of word forms, all unstable claimants on a single referent. Irregular spelling points up the instability of the signifier, the mutability of the word's mortal body, and exposes the soul of sense to danger.

Spelling, like all matters of language use, is an ideologically charged issue. Irregular spelling, with its willful proliferation of word forms and overtaxing of sense (of the signified), becomes associated with a profligate and irregular life that taxes the patience and peace of decent citizens. Will Honeycomb, aging representative of Re-storation high-life, is guilty of just this sort of orthographic violation. His spelling habits become a defining stroke in the portrait of a ludi-crous social type: the fashion-conscious, gentleman rake. In *Spectator* 105 Honeycomb pulls out a billet-doux to support his reputation as a ladies' man and as a gentleman. Claiming that "he spelt like a Gen-tleman and not like a Scholar," he defends his spelling style and crit-icizes the narrow pedantry that insists on uniform orthography. Will's writing style is of a piece with the reckless, destructive, and ridiculous lifestyle he cultivates. He "fancies he should never have been the Man he is, had he not broke Windows, knocked down Constables, disturbed honest People . . . and beat up a Lewd Woman's Quarters, when he was a young Fellow. . . . [This] Will calls the studying of Mankind, and terms this Knowledge of the Town the Knowledge of the World" (*S* 105). Will privileges the indulgence of his own impulses over the common interests of his neighbors. He will break windows and words if he feels like it; these are expressions of his spirit, the indulgence of which is more than his prerogative; it is even his duty as a gentleman of the town. He stands, so he thinks, above the law — civil and grammatic. He defies punctuation and orthography just as he beats the watch: as a show of his fine mettle. The rakish man of fashion will not be constrained, no matter what the cost to common language or public peace.

As discussed in the previous chapter, Addison and Steele were eager to discredit the masculine ideal represented by rakish beaux like Will Honeycomb and replace it with a less flamboyant, more sober, civic-minded, mild-mannered version of the gentleman, a gentleman, moreover, who could — and would — spell. The imposition of one's idiosyncrasies on others is marked in these papers as ludicrous affectation or insufferable arrogance rather than as high styling. As a medium integral to cultural production, language must not be jeopardized by the idiotic, sometimes violent and transgressive whims of the coxcomb and his fashions.

In order to function as an instrument of communication and historical continuity, language needs to have staying power beyond the brief seasons allotted to the blooms of fashion. Exposing a structural paradox of fashion, Swift points out how the newest things are the first to grow stale. "'Tis manifest," he writes, "that all new affected Modes of Speech, whether borrowed from the Court, the Town, or the Theatre, are the first perishing Parts in any Language" (*T* 230). In a satiric scenario Steele writes for *Tatler* 12, the accelerated production and obsolescence of modish slang is dramatized to show how "a man who has been out of town but one half-year, has lost the LANGUAGE."

Fashions start in the city and fade by degrees as one progresses further and further out into the country. In *Spectator* 129 a lawyer relates his journey out of London toward his home in Cornwall, noting the progressive obsolescence of local dress. And in *Spectator* 119, Addison remarks on the holdover of stiffly formal manners in the countryside long after they had been replaced in London by new modes of "agreeable Negligence." This phenomenon affects language as much as it does dress. In *Tatler* 88, Bickerstaff calculates that a newly minted London word "in its ordinary Circulation" will reach York in about five years. So when Mr. Acorn, the honest country gentleman in *Tatler* 12, visits London, he depends on his city friend to translate the talk of the town for him. Similarly, in *Tatler* 88 a "Friend in the Country" asks Bickerstaff to define a number of city expressions "for the Information of such as live at a Distance from this Town and Court." Likewise, in *Tatler* 21, a gentleman from the country writes in asking Bickerstaff to explain what is meant by the names: gentleman, pretty fellow, toast, coquet, critic, wit, and "all other Appellations of those now in the gayer World." All these terms, such as the word "Biting" that Steele examines in *Tatler* 12 and *Spectator* 504, are part of an urban discourse the modish world uses to talk about itself.

Fashion marks language, as it does dress, to define regional (as well as class, national, and gender) differences. Bickerstaff's programs to translate town talk into plain speech and the recurrent satire on slang and fashionable idioms are both conducted in order to make conversation and literature adhere more closely to an aesthetic of easy communicability. This aesthetic depends on the standard of "Plain English," simple and accessible to all, explicitly commended in *Tatler* 212. Standing on the very threshold of English cultural (as well as economic and political) imperialism, these papers work toward the definition and dispersal of a form of standard English that (ideally) would be comprehensible throughout Britain. After all, the papers are not written for the English alone but for people in all the "Territories of *Great Britain*" (*S* 58). A uniform and universal English idiom is a crucial instrument in the establishment of a national, imperial British culture.

Unfortunately the mounting glories of imperial Britain, Steele complains in *Tatler* 12, are not reflected in a similar elevation of its "Publick Diversions." From the lowness of its conversation and most popular leisure activities, one could not guess at the "present Grandeur" of the nation, its "Advancement in Glory and Power": "Survey this Town, and you'l [*sic*] find, Rakes and Debauchees are your Men of Pleasure; Thoughtless Atheists and Illiterate Drunkards, call themselves Free Thinkers; and Gamesters, Banterers, Biters, Swearers, and Twenty new-born Insects more, are, in their several Species, the modern Men of Wit" (*T* 12). This diatribe against the low forms of pleasure pursued by swarms ("Twenty new-born Insects more") of men about town reveals the close-knit network of ethical, social, and literary-aesthetic issues. Steele's campaigns against gambling and dueling are well known, as are Addison's programs for cultivating true wit, good taste, and the pleasures of the imagination. But the extent to which these projects are mutually informative and subject to the same simultaneously ethical and aesthetic criteria of taste perhaps needs some emphasis. Otherwise, there is a tendency to separate these ventures into discrete categories — the aesthetic, the literary, the ethical, the social — and to miss the extent to which these spheres of life are brought together under a set of shared cultural standards.

Language, again, is the medium for the development and transmission of these standards and so a particular object of their application. One source of Steele's concern in *Tatler* 12 is the degradation of language brought on by a proliferation of slangy idioms, dredged up from the social gutters and cultivated by men of fashion in the coffeehouses, taverns, and in the theaters. *Tatler* 12 plays the same dire theme Swift harps on in *Tatler* 230 — simplicity of language and manners "is utterly lost in the World" and has been replaced by "a Thousand little Inventions" (*T* 12). As the dialect of that swarming species of "insects" who threaten to overrun the public venues of London life, slangy town talk perpetuates social devolution. Those who speak it are only cheap imitations of the better men they have displaced; likewise, their conversation is a bad copy of true wit: "Him whom we allow'd formerly for a certain pleasant Subtilty, and a natural Way of giving you an unexpected Hit, call'd a *Droll*, is now mimick'd by a *Biter*, who is a dull fellow, that tells you a Lye with a grave Face, and laughs at you for knowing him no better than to believe him" (*T* 12). The relatively open social exchange that is one of the founding conditions of the bourgeois public sphere also becomes one object of its regulation. There is a need to patrol, and so define, the borders of the good, decent "middle" arena of society against predations from both "above" and "below." And as mentioned earlier, within the cultural discourse of the bourgeois public sphere, the "low" and "high" often meet in a vicious confluence of exchange: here the world of high fashion adopts the slang of the criminal underworld.

Steele, then, traces this decay in conversation to a kind of trickleup fashion in slang and social behavior, a process encouraged by the same fluid, open coffeehouse society that it threatens to corrupt. In *Spectator* 504, he defines the "Biter" with Swiftian precision: "a Biter is one who thinks you a Fool, because you do not think him a Knave." "Biting" is a specifically fashionable conversational vice, one that has seeped up from the criminal underground into modish society: "The Sharpers [con-artists] about Town very ingeniously understood themselves to be to the undesigning Part of Mankind what Foxes are to Lambs, and therefore used the Word *Biting* to express any Exploit wherein they had over-reach'd any innocent and inadvertent Man of his Purse" (*S* 504). Because social prestige is bought with flash and fashion, these "sharpers" became "the Gallants of the Town, and carry'd it with a fashionable haughty Air." In emulation of these flashy tricksters, "Shallow Fops, who are govern'd by the Eye, and admire every thing that struts in Vogue" have taken up this phrase "biting" and "used it upon all Occasions" (*S* 504). Fashion follows low-life and everyone follows the fashion.

In *Tatler* 12, the slang word *biting* baffles Mr. Acorn, who has been out of town for half a year. Steele uses the word here to show that trendiness in language works against communication and sociability. But *biting* offends in more than its mere slanginess. Part of the con artist's cant, *biting* refers to practices of predatory deception, to the violation of trust and sociability. Its social operation as an opaque, esoteric cant term duplicates the discourse of deception that it names.

The scenario Steele paints in *Tatler* 12 and the genealogy he provides in *Spectator* 504 show up the close associations between fashion, vice, and language abuse established by those who would reform all three. And the practice of fashion, as much as that of biting, may be used to impose on the innocent and unwary.

The biter preys on those, like Acorn in *Tatler* 12, who, out of the loop of the town talk, reveal their ignorance and thus their vulnerability. Acorn walks in on a coffeehouse scene where Pip has just lost a wager to the Count and so has had to give him an IOU (this is being "Vowel'd"):

> *Pip.* Pox on it! don't talk to me, I am Vowel'd by the Count, and cursedly out of Humour.
> *Ac*[orn]. Vowel'd! Prithee, *Trimmer*, What does he mean by that?
> *Trim*[mer]. Have a Care, *Harry*, speak softly; don't show your Ignorance:—If you do, they'l Bite you where-e'er they meet you; they are such cursed Curs,—the present Wits.
> *Ac*[orn]. Bite me! What do you mean? (*T* 12)

Just as Acorn risks being played because of his ignorance of town talk, so, Jack Modish complains, the whole town of Exeter risks being imposed on by people promoting false fashions because of their ignorance of the city styles (*S* 175). And indeed town talk not only constitutes a form of fashion in itself but also often has as its content fashion itself—in dress and manners, as well as in entertainments and cultural events. Just as Acorn looks to his London acquaintance, Mr. Friendly, to protect him from the biters, so Jack Modish appeals to Mr. Spectator for his support of a society in London "for the *Inspection of Modes and Fashions*" (*S* 175).

Ignorance of town talk and town fashion is dangerous; one must know enough to secure oneself against its deceptions. The directors of the institution Jack Modish proposes would be fashion experts enlisted to protect the innocent against fashion fraud. They would act as customs agents of the fashions exported to the countryside and assure that these are "answerable to the Mode at *London*." And in a very real sense, Jack Modish's society for the inspection of fashions is realized in *The Tatler* and *The Spectator* themselves, though they aim not only to *inform* provincial Englishmen about the London fashions but also to *reform* Londoners into proper fashion practices.

Jack Modish's request for accurate information about city styles, like the country gentlemen's requests for accurate definitions of city types and city terms, points to a tension that ripples through the papers. Even as *The Tatler* and *The Spectator* work to erect bulwarks against fashion's flood and to rechannel energy and attention away from standards of fashionability and toward ideals of rationality, the very act of producing, publishing, and distributing information about fashionable vice, folly, and slang inevitably contributes to fashion's further cultural saturation. The remarkable, in some cases unprecedented, currency of the papers suggests that Addison and Steele more than kept up with the trend-setters they so disparage. For example, Richmond Bond's editorial notes to *Tatler* 12 inform us that Steele's reference to "biting" and being "Vowel'd" are the first for which textual citations have been found. Because fashionability feeds on the kind of media saturation and sheer immediacy that papers like *The Tatler* and *The Spectator* foster, we are always left with the question: Do their interventions serve to suppress or rather to stimulate the proliferation of the fashions they denounce?

GOTHIC MUTILATIONS: REPAIRING THE BODY OF STYLE

Just as words like *Vowel'd* and *biting* were associated with vice and even crime, other new, modish styles of speech (and dress and entertainment) were frequently associated with the "barbaric" aesthetic of ancient "Gothick" modes. The use of *gothic* as a term of disparagement calls up its positive counterpart *classical* and all those qualities of ease and simplicity associated with a neoclassical, rationalist aesthetic at odds with the prolific ornament, savage distortions, irregular proportion, the elaborate conceptual and formal artifice — most simply, the irrational excess of the gothic. Appearing almost sixty years before Horace Walpole published his gothic romance *The Castle of Otranto* (1765), which glorifies a sensibility based on the allure of the irrational, mysterious, and exotically barbaric, the usage of the term in these papers confirms basic features of this sensibility, even if assigned a negative connotation.

As it appears in *The Tatler* and *The Spectator*, the gothic violates principles of classical design identified not merely with good taste but with civilization itself. Most importantly, "Gothick" refers to a barbarism associated as much with the emergent forces of fashion as it is with the residual features of a medieval, antiquated style. Equating the acceleration of fashion and novelty with regressive and barbaric culture, gothicism is invoked to deny the progressive nature of the new. This logic is monumentally performed in Pope's *Dunciad,* where the advance of the reign of Dulness in England is represented as an apocalyptic, entropic decline of civilization into the darkness of gothicism, senselessness, sleep, and finally, of chaos itself. The bad aesthetic cultivated by the hack writers and meretricious editors in the *Dunciad* shares features of uncontrollable proliferation, monstrosity, and alienation from nature that marks the gothic aesthetic condemned in *The Tatler* and *The Spectator*. The poet laureate dunce, Cibber, has a "monster-breeding breast"; his production is not a process of creation but deformation: "Round him much Embryo, much Abortion lay." "A Gothic Library" provides material for the pyre he lights as propitiatory sacrifice to his goddess, Dulness (1.105-63). While Addison and Steele are greater optimists than Pope, their vision of what should be purged from culture has much in common with Pope's prophecy of what will annihilate it.

Gothic becomes a key eighteenth-century term in a strain of cultural criticism that stretches well into the twentieth century, one that identifies forms of popular, commercial, and (with industrialization) mass culture with the decline of Western civilization. The term serves as a battle standard in what becomes a fierce contention over the principles and values that are to direct the course of modern culture. Later in the eighteenth century, with the enormous popularity of gothic modes of design and literature, the gothic emerges as a site of psychological, historical, literary, and architectural innovation that challenges enlightenment assumptions and ideals.

"Gothick" is a stylistic term applied in *The Tatler* and *The Spectator* equally to architecture, dress, theater, and language. In *Tatler* 230, Swift performs a rather extended analysis of a conventionally modish letter; he remarks on the "*Gothick* Strain" of the style which threatens a relapse "into Barbarity." Swift speaks of the "barbarous Mutilations of Vowels and Syllables" and the offense these commit against "good Sense." Specifically he is referring to the stylish use of abbreviations ("rep," "phizz," "hipps," "pozz") and elliptical contractions. The exemplary letter begins: "I *cou'd n't* get the Things you sent for all *about Town*—I *thot* to ha' come down my self, and then *I'd h'brot 'um*; but I *ha'n't don't*, and I believe I *can't do't*, that's *Pozz*—." Swift finds these modes of expression monstrous, deformed, even inhuman. Abbreviations of words are figured as brutal, corporeal amputations, a "maiming" analogous to the strategies of the owl who "fattened her Mice after she had bit off their Legs, to prevent them from running away" (*T* 230).

Swift claims here that the gothic style is the rule rather than the exception in fashionable discourse, both written and spoken: "You may gather every Flower in it, with a Thousand more of equal Sweetness, from the Books, Pamphlets, and single Papers, offered us every Day in the Coffee-houses" (*T* 230). In what seems to Swift a scarcity economy of meaning, these sorts of innovations do not simply sit beside other available forms of (sensible) discourse but indeed take their place, standing like tombstones over the language they have slain.

Echoing Swift's complaint in one of the later papers on wit, Addison laments that English authors have an "extremely *Gothick*" taste (*S* 62). In *Spectator* 63, the next paper and the last of the series, gothic taste is architecturally and allegorically embodied in a dream vision (*S* 63). Here at the very heart of the region of false wit, in the midst of a dark and secret grove, stands a temple consecrated to the "God of *Dullness*": "A monstrous Fabrick built after the *Gothick* manner, and covered with innumerable Devices in that barbarous kind of Sculpture" (*S* 63). Here we see the irrational superfluity of ornamentation that is one primary target of Addison's and Steele's reform of taste, and a feature identified with gothic design. The temple here in *Spectator* 63 devoted to the god of dullness has a later counterpart in Pope's description of the realms presided over by the goddess of dullness in his *Dunciad*. Both in the Cave of Poverty and Poetry in the first book, and in the vision of the new inverted world order in the third, Pope's gothic goddess fosters the linguistic degeneration,

generic hybridity, chaotic proliferation, and general perversion of order allegorized more mildly in Addison's dream vision of the realm
of false wit in *Spectator* 63. So Pope's goddess in her cave observes:

> How new-born nonsense first is taught to cry,
> Maggots half-form'd in rhyme exactly meet,
> And learn to crawl upon poetic feet.
> Here one poor word an hundred clenches makes,
> And ductile dulness now meanders takes;
> There motley Images her fancy strike,
> Figures ill pair'd and Similies unlike.
> She sees a Mob of Metaphors advance,
> Pleas'd with the madness of the mazy dance:
> How tragedy and Comedy embrace;
> How farce and Epic get a jumbled race. (1.60–70)

Just as in Pope's nightmare vision, in Addison's region of false wit
figures of speech become animate; the region is peopled by a "Body
of *Acrosticks*," "two or three Files of *Chronograms*," "a Party of *Punns*."
In book 3 of *The Dunciad*, the "new world to Nature's laws unknown" prophetically unfolds. Here, "the forests dance, the rivers
upward rise, / Whales sport in woods, and dolphins in the skies"
(3.241–46). The same illogic of creation controls Addison's region of
false wit. There, the organic and artificial conjoin in surreal hy-
bridization; natural order is suspended:

> Several of the Trees blossomed in Leaf-Gold, some of them pro-
> duced Bone-Lace, and some of them precious Stones. The Foun-
> tains bubbled an Opera Tune, and were filled with Stags, Wild-
> Boars, and Mermaids, that lived among the Waters; at the same
> time that Dolphins and several kinds of Fish played upon the
> Banks, or took their Pastime in the Meadows.

In *The Dunciad,* Pope's vision of cultural descent into gothic dim-
ness is cosmic in scope. In his essays on false wit, Addison's is more
contained, less bitterly pessimistic, and less apocalyptic. Yet both sets
of texts show the contaminations of gothic taste across a broad spectrum of cultural practices. Exploiting the shared stylistic principle

between architecture and dress, a female correspondent to *Spectator* 145 complains of the "Gothick" "architecture" of masculine dress. Men's coats have started to swell out like women's petticoats. The lady is indignant because, on Mr. Spectator's advice, she and all her friends have renounced big hoops only to find men indulging (with impunity) in similar stylistic vices in their own dress: "We find you Men secretly approve our Practice, by imitating our Pirimitical Form" (*S* 145). She implies that men have appropriated this glorious, indeed, monumental sartorial structure for themselves. Incensed at the hypocrisy that reigns in the masculine critique of female dress, she presents her case against the male mode and does so in architectural terms. Women, she says, have decreased the height of their headdresses in order to balance their skirts (which, even without hoops, remain full), but men have made no such harmonizing accommodation to their wide, wired coat skirts: "We make a regular Figure, but I defy your Mathematicks to give Name to the Form you [men] appear in. Your Architecture is mere *Gothick*, and betrays a worse Genius than ours" (*S* 145).

The lady correspondent's complaint addresses what is easily recognizable as a gothic *fashion* in men's coats. Addison's project in his series on true and false wit is no less an argument against *fashions* in gothic taste. Spurred by the recent reemergence of forms of false wit that had "been long exploded out of the Common-wealth of Letters," his purpose is to trace the waxing and waning of "this Fashion of false Wit" through history (*S* 58). As tends to be true whenever these gothic fashions are noted, there is a tension between the status of false wit as an antiquated mode, consigned long ago to the dustbin of history, and as a contemporary fad. In one breath Addison refers to the current craze for puns, acrostics, and so on, and in the next speaks of it as "obsolete" (*S* 58).

The process at work here involves the recycling of forms through the channels of fashion. Fashion's economy depends not only on the apparent logic of novelty and obsolescence but also on stylistic recirculation, and so a kind of preservation of historical forms.[41] Taking the stance of a progressive cultural critic, Addison figures the reemergence of "those antiquated Modes of Wit" as an aesthetic and

intellectual regression. False wit pops up like a return of the culturally repressed. Ideally, Addison's reforms would not only put an end
to these literary mannerisms but would foster a redemptive historical
consciousness in contemporary authors so that they could recognize
false wit for the outmoded nonsense that it is. Addison wants to discredit any claims that these forms of verbal exploitation make to
fashion, for it is specifically as verbal fashions that they get recircu-
lated from the dark past into the enlightened present. But if writers
can be made aware of the historical, as well as the aesthetic, context
of these forms of wit, they can move out of this pattern of cyclical
return to the verbal fashions of the past and march forward into a
brighter era of literary enterprise.

The kind of maiming of language that Swift dwells on in *Tatler*
230 is a dominant feature of one of Addison's first examples of false
wit—the emblem poem in the shape of an altar, a pair of wings, and
so on. The reliance of such poems on pictorial criteria violates decorum by introducing visual references that have no place in literary
productions. These poems are a sort of unnatural hybrid conflation
of two different species of representation: visual and verbal. Addison
notes how the producer of such poems has to be "a kind of Painter,
or at least a Designer" (*S* 58). It is specifically in his capacity as
painter or designer that the emblem writer slaughters language; in
order to fit the verses into his emblematic design, he hacks away at
lines and words, regarding their shape more than their sense. These
Procrustean poets mutilate language and meaning (*S* 58).

Verses in the shape of *things* not only mutilate language and sense
but also produce a peculiarly reified kind of poetry. Here is the poem
as a thing in itself, often a specifically fashionable thing. Since emblem poems are becoming quite fashionable, it is only natural that
they take on the shapes—not of altars, axes, and cupids' wings—but
of fashionable commodities. "I do not question," writes Addison at
the end of *Spectator* 58, "that we shall see the Town filled in very little Time with Poetical Tippets, Handkerchiefs, Snuff-Boxes, and the
like Female Ornaments." The poems would then emblematize their
own status as fashionable, trivial reifications of language.

At its most innocuous, bad taste shows up as ostentation, ridiculous spectacle, and senseless affectation; but at its most dangerous, it threatens nothing less than a crippling distortion of the human body and spirit. The vogue for the mutilation of the body of language in emblem poems has analogies in fashions for mutilations of the human body, and, in turn, these are linked back to forms of false wit (*T* 77). Examining this phenomenon in *Tatler* 77, Steele traces the modish affectations of lameness, venereal infection, short-sightedness, and speech impediments to misguided desires for a reputation for wit and gallantry. In men of weak judgment, aspirations for eminence lead to the affectation of desperate and tasteless distinctions.

In a paper that begins by deploring the invasion of legitimate theater by contortionists, then moves through an argument against the cynicism of fashionable French authors, and ends with an enthusiastic reflection on the evolution of the human spirit through aesthetic cultivation, Addison exposes an unquestioned and profound association between two forms of culture that may seem quite disparate — the performances of contortionists on the popular stage and the literature of fashionably skeptical French authors (*T* 108). As Addison sees it, both the contortionist and the fashionably cynical author represent humanity in ways that degrade it. Intellectual actors, no less than "Bodily" actors, may twist humanity into monstrous forms (*S* 141). The contortionist exploits the body in ways that undermine our sense of a characteristic human *form* and so our sense of a stable and purely human *nature*. These papers reflect negatively on the human fascination with the elasticity of the human form, a fascination indulged in in the eighteenth century not only by watching contortionists but also, for example, by participating in "grinning contests" — popular competitions where contestants contorted their faces for valuable prizes (*S* 173). Addison discusses these contests in *Spectator* 173, closing his description with the same questions he answers positively in *Tatler* 108: are not these contests "Immoral as well as Ridiculous" and those who participate "guilty, in some measure, of an Affront to their Species, in treating after this manner the *Human Face Divine*, and turning that part of us . . . into the Image of a Monkey" (*S* 173)? These texts are all engaged in drawing the limits of the human. To do so they must designate as sub- or inhuman a number of practices undeniably engaged in by human beings. This strategy easily moves from excluding as nonhuman certain kinds of sociocultural practices — grinning contests, contortionist shows, the fashionable affectation of infirmities — to excluding certain classes of people. As Addison's comparison of the grinning contestant to a monkey ominously foreshadows, this logic of defining what is truly human through the relegation of whole sectors of humanity to different species status has its dark apotheosis in modern racism.

Addison opens *Tatler* 108 with an anecdote that takes on the surreal horror of a nightmare. His account resonates with the fluid, shifting images, the uncanny appearances, the baffling incidents that later in the century mark the literary gothic:

> I found the Audience hushed in a very deep Attention, and did not question but some noble Tragedy was just then in its Crisis. . . . While I was in this Suspence, expecting every Moment to see my old Friend Mr. *Betterton* appear in all the majesty of Distress, to my unspeakable Amazement there came up a Monster with a Face between his Feet. . . . It afterwards twisted it self into the Motions and Wreathings of several different Animals, and after great Variety of Shapes and Transformations, went off the Stage in the Figure of a human Creature. (*T* 108)

To Addison, even more shocking than the contortionist's performance is "the admiration, the Applause, the Satisfaction, of the Audience." These reactions put him in fear not merely for the taste but for the souls of his fellow spectators: "There is something disingenuous and immoral in being able to bear such a Sight." As is the case with opera, the class standing of this audience, moreover, is out of sync with the lowness of their taste. One would, Addison says, expect to find some tolerance for such a show among "the Vulgar," but he is astounded to find it among an apparently polite audience (*T* 108).

The polite, fashionable world is fascinated as well by the "modish *French* authors" and their English imitators who provide Addison with his next example of debased cultural producers. Because, as Addison formulates it in *Tatler* 108, "Man is a Creature made up of different Extremes"—the very good and the very bad—"a skillful Artist may draw an excellent Picture of him in either of these Views." But the truly great artists take the sunnier view, and so promote "the natural Grandeur of the Soul" and "feed her with Hopes of Immortality and Perfection." This is culture's purpose, one that is obstructed by the texts of those "modish *French* Authors" who prefer instead to dwell on the meaner side of human nature. Elaborating only the base aspects of humankind, these authors, like the contortionists and the dueling grinners, erase the distinction "between the Species of Men and that of Brutes." A menace to society, they "destroy those Principles which are the Support, Happiness, and Glory, of all publick Societies, as well as private Persons." Culturally regressive, they cancel the advances humankind has made through the refinement of the "design of Dress, Good-breeding, outward Ornaments . . . Architecture, Painting, and Statuary" (*T* 108).

Like the distortions of modish language, the distortions of the contortionists produce a proliferation of forms and so confuse any stable image of the human. These papers on language and popular entertainments show a world inundated with a great flood of cultural stuff: there are more books, more papers, more coffeehouses, more faddish word forms, more shows open to more people in more places, more, that is, than proves easy to take in, digest, and manage. Representing such proliferation as a threat to the progress of culture, *Tatler* 197 deplores the seemingly endless production of pointless texts, taking as its central example a collection of the letters of obscure German writers. Books by writers of little genius but extremely "fertile Imaginations" and "endless Loquacity" inundate the cultural marketplace. As literature becomes commercialized, following the logic of the market, its values become quantified. Producing a glut of mediocrity, such texts achieve a kind of cultural dominance by sheer strength of numbers. Any possibility for taste reform and cultural progress lies in wiping the slate clean of a great chunk of literary history: "It seems therefore a fruitless Labour to attempt the Correction of the Tast of our Contemporaries, except it was in our Power to burn all the senseless Labours of our Ancestors" (*T* 197).

The glut of the literary marketplace, the monstrous, hybrid prolif-

eration of cultural forms, the apparently endless, often senseless production and reproduction of cultural objects — these are all aspects of
the "new gothicism" admonished by *The Tatler* and *The Spectator* and
despaired of by *The Dunciad*. *Tatler* 257 describes the curtain of a
waxwork show that seems an emblem of the monstrous and fascinating proliferation of popular leisure activities in the eighteenth-century. Woven in the "Figure of a monstrous *Hydra* that had several
Heads," the curtain's design is overdetermined. It exemplifies both
the form of popular culture in general and the specific content of
the show it conceals: an extravagant allegorical representation of the
manifold faiths of Great Britain. For as Steele comments, in this nation religions "shoot up and flourish in this Climate more than in
any other" (*T* 257). They shoot forth, that is, like hydra heads. The
appeal of the waxworks show lies precisely in its wondrous variety.
But cashing in on the religious division that had scarred Britain's history with the brand of bloody civil wars, the "entertainment" the
waxwork show offers is shaded with morbidity. So while the viewer
marvels at the technical virtuosity of the display, he does so in hor-
ror-tinged terms similar to those used to describe the verbal and
physical deformations in *Tatler* 210 and 108: "[The viewer] did not
think it possible for [wax] to be *twisted* and *tortured* into so many
skrew'd Faces and wry Features" (*T* 257; emphasis added).

This twisting and torturing of form marks what Addison, Steele,
Pope, and Swift call the "Gothick" taste. The discomfort with what
are not simply unnatural *distortions* but also unnatural *proliferations* of
forms signals an anxiety about the promiscuous generation of signifiers, of images, and about the conditions that foster this twisted proliferation: the lack of stable identity between form and matter, between image and substance, between signifier and signified.

TAKING THE CULTURAL MIDDLE GROUND

The popularity, the explicit fashionability, of gothic styles of language and entertainment make them especially dangerous. Accordingly, it becomes important for *The Tatler* and *The Spectator* to harness
the engines of popularity and fashion to their own reformative ma-
chines. While they do disdain some merely fashionable and mindless

forms of entertainment, the papers do not adopt a simplistically an-
tipopular, elitist stance in regard to either culture or their audience.
The cultural criticism in the papers, as in the bourgeois public sphere
more broadly, is most notable for the middle ground it establishes between the two dominant sensibilities of its time, both historically
somewhat residual: the puritanical and repressive, on the one hand,
and, on the other, the aristocratic and libertine. This middle ground
is created in relation to another set of cultural categories, what we
call today "high" and "low" cultural forms.[42] In fact, although the
discussion so far in this chapter has concentrated on the criticism of
more popular, "lower" forms of culture — opera, conversation, grinning contests, contortionists, waxworks, newspapers — *The Tatler* and
The Spectator are better known in twentieth-century academia for
their treatment of the "higher" cultural ground: Addison's essays on
the pleasures of the imagination, the course of papers on Milton, the
papers on the theater, even those on *Chevy Chase* and *Two Children in
the Woods*, which can be seen as the translation of popular forms of
literature to their "true" home among the English classics.

These categories of "high" and "low" culture are constituted in
dialectical relation to one another; yet, in *The Tatler* and *The Spectator* their constitution is effected through a third or middle cultural
level, which is that of the papers themselves. The papers' treatment
of such "lower" forms of cultural production as opera, contortionist
shows, and journalism takes a stance "above" its object, submitting it
to loftier moral and aesthetic standards. In an analogous and mirroring movement, the treatment of the "high" forms of literary production, such as *Paradise Lost*, takes a position somewhat "below"
their objects and translates them into forms of speech and conceptual
categories recognizable by the "ordinary Reader," whose normative
common sense the papers respect. This mediation, which is sometimes a virtual translation, between registers of discourse and culture
takes place through a middle space constructed as an arena of disinterested critical rationality. This is, of course, the bourgeois public
sphere, a place from which all culture, like all mankind, may be seen
in its true colors. This is not to imply that the critical stance adopted
by either Bickerstaff or Mr. Spectator is one of cold, clinical detach-

ment; early forms of sensibility and sentimentality are much in evidence in the critical precepts advocated in the essays. Typifying the aesthetic discourse of the bourgeois public sphere, the papers define a critical position responsive to standards of both refinement and accessibility, wit *and* morality, neoclassical principles *and* modern sentimentality, formal beauty *and* social value. What this discourse creates is a utopian aesthetic realm where competing cultural values are united. And the ground of this resolution is provided by the newly emergent and increasingly respectable commercial markets in literature and entertainment.

The treatment of literary texts in the cultural criticism of *The Tatler* and *The Spectator* is fully involved in the fashion- and market-generated tensions that I have noted throughout. These tensions play into the establishment of standards of literary taste and so of literary canons. On the one hand, the increasing supply of printed material on the market creates a need for institutions that sort through and classify it. The institution of criticism can be seen, in part, as a response to this need for traffic control on the high roads of cultural commerce. Of course, the critic, while he serves the market, sometimes in ways he does not intend, is often at odds with the forces that drive that market, forces he labels as irrational, superficial, ephemeral, and fashion-oriented. So the critic sets up to sort culture's bounty into categories that seem more immediately motivated, more saturated with meaning, more rational than those of the "fashionable" and the "unfashionable," the "popular" and the "unpopular." As the ground of overcoming, fashion and sheer commercial opportunism form a necessary context for that set of transcendent and universal categories that come to be identified with cultural value.

But, on the other hand, the critic also *wants* and *needs* popularity and fashionability on his side to support his "higher" and more rationally chosen cultural objects. Popularity and fashionability are prestige. That fashionability and popularity, rather than being conferred on objects because of some other "real" virtue, are values in themselves presents a central problem for the critic of modern commercial culture. One way he deals with this is to subordinate fashionability and popularity to other, more "significant" criteria; then he can claim that if the work, or style, or opinion he advocates is fashionable and popular, it is for very good reasons.

So, in *The Tatler* and *The Spectator* criticism is not a matter of handing down judgments from above to a mass audience below. Rather, it works horizontally, not vertically; Addison and Steele reach across to their audience as to their peers. They assume, even as they create, an equity of sensibility, taste, and intellectual cultivation. If at times one gets the sense that Addison does condescend to his audience, this sense is always equivocated by the understanding that both Addison and Steele maintain a principled dedication to equity, accessibility, and communicability. The same ethic of equality that produces the space of public discourse in the coffeehouses and clubs informs the critical stance of the papers. In the interest of popular access, the aesthetic standard advocated by *The Tatler* and *The Spectator* rejects all forms of specialized, esoteric knowledge and language.

Communication is a two-way street: the papers aim at clarity in order that they may most effectively cultivate the taste and comprehension of their readers. So cultivated, the readers in turn are more ready to understand and thus appreciate the papers. Addison is *producing* as much as he is *addressing* his audience: "I shall endeavor to make what I say intelligible to ordinary Capacities; but if my Readers meet with any Paper that in some Parts of it may be a little out of their Reach, I would not have them discouraged, for they may assure themselves the next shall be much clearer" (S 58). Of course, whether the greater clarity of this next paper should be attributed more to improvements in Addison's style or to refinements in the audience's comprehension remains an open question.

Seeking the cultivation of their audience, *The Tatler* and *The Spectator* depend on a rhetoric of improvement. They will lift the merely middling or the merely fashionable reader into an appreciation of the finer things in life. They also assure the "ordinary Reader" that she or he is just as capable of appreciating what is valuable in literature as the "most refined" reader (S 70). These papers operate a switchboard between popular and elite culture, connecting the "ordinary Reader" to a direct line on aesthetic pleasures and literary refinements.

This cultural project is erected on a popular foundation and based to a great extent on qualitative criteria—on sheer numbers. Mr. Spectator counts his success in numbers of copies sold (*S* 555). Interestingly, there seems to be an especially big market for the critical papers, especially for the course of lectures on *Paradise Lost*.[43] This is a market standard of value, and to some degree the papers work according to the same logic as the advertisements that Addison discusses in *Tatler* 224. Like advertisements, the papers themselves are "of great Use to the Vulgar," for both are "Instruments of Ambition." Just as the critical stance of the papers works within a dialectic of "high" and "low," so the advertising page of the paper creates a dialectic between the "great" world of public affairs and the "small" worlds of domestic events and commodity exchange. By reading *The Tatler* and *The Spectator*, the ordinary reader gains access to a "higher" world of aesthetic pleasures and intellectual cultivation previously reserved for a scholarly or aristocratic elite. Through the advertising page a "Man that is by no Means big enough for the *Gazette*" may participate in the great world of affairs right alongside "a Plenipotentiary" or "an Ambassador" (*T* 224). Advertisements often rely on promises of inside information, of getting the real deal, the trade secrets of the world of goods. These appeals of access and privilege are at work as well in the critical papers of *The Tatler* and *The Spectator*, which provide entry into the world of higher learning, more refined sensibilities, and more transcendent pleasures. As Addison notes in *Tatler* 224, people read advertisements to get information about where to go for the things they need. These needs may be physiological, ethical, or spiritual; advertising acts as a kind of guide. And of course, Bickerstaff and Mr. Spectator are most strongly defined by their custodial and advisory functions: they tell their readers where they need to look to find good conversation, poetry, theater, painting, music, opera. As does advertising , the advice given in the critical papers adopts a therapeutic stance: all is done in the interest of the reader/consumer's improved well-being. In their mutual emphasis on self-improvement and the cultivation of status and pleasure, the cultural-critical project of the papers works through the same channels of desire exploited by advertising.[44]

Addison's reading of the advertisements is gently satiric in its application of serious, neoclassical literary criticism to popular, commercial discourse. He refers to the "*Ciceronian* Manner" of a favorite ad for a lavender essence and catalogs the rules of advertising rhetoric (*T* 224). On the one hand, the satire depends on an assumed distinction between the two discourses — commercial and literary. The language of criticism is supposed to appear ridiculous in this application to a "low" commercial object. But on the other hand, this mock-critique of advertising also creates a kind of equivalence between these discourses. For, while this juxtaposition of discourses produces the humor, this humor in no way invalidates the readings of the ads produced by submitting them to a critical practice conventionally reserved for the "higher" productions of literature.

Addison turns to the ads to entertain himself when there is "a Dearth of News" in the rest of the paper (*T* 224). Many of these are personal ads containing narratives that Addison calls "Accounts of News from the little World." Ads are a kind of alternative news in themselves. Revealing "a certain Weakness" for these narratives, Addison explains how his attraction to advertisements stems from something more than sheer boredom. He is deeply touched by the "little Domestick Occurences" reported in the personal ads; indeed he has "frequently been caught with Tears in [his] Eyes over a melancholy Advertisement" (*T* 224). So while his reading of the advertisements for goods and services rests on a kind of rational neoclassical critical program, his perusal of the personal ads is sentimental. It depends on those responses that make up what comes to be known as "sensibility." Based on universal human connections sensed through the physiopsychological response of sympathy, sensibility, at least in theory, can be a democratizing phenomenon and so go hand in glove with the institution of the public sphere. As Steele writes in *Tatler* 225, when considerations of wealth and status drop out of the social picture, "Benevolence must become the Rule of Society, and he that is most obliging must be the most diverting." While, in practice, it was often restricted to the refined lifestyle of the rich, privileged, and hysterical, sensibility contains at least the potential for shared experience across all the divisive cultural lines — class, race, nation, and gender. These values of shared emotional experience are crucial to the standards of aesthetic and cultural value erected by *The Tatler* and *The Spectator* and inform their appreciation of both "high" and "low" forms of literature and entertainment.

The papers on the popular ballads *Two Children in the Wood* and *Chevy Chase* point up this broad appreciation. By submitting the conventionally "low" genre of popular ballad to serious critique, these papers duplicate, though in a more sober register, the strategy of *Tatler* 224 on advertising. And, as in that paper, the discussion of the ballads in *Spectators* 70, 74, and 85, is informed not only by analytical categories of rhetorical criticism but also by the psychological criteria of sensibility. The manner in which these two strands of critical discourse come together to elevate the ballads into a legitimate and, especially in the case of *Chevy Chase*, largely classical literary sphere shows how the ethics of sensibility and sympathy are tied to an aesthetic of natural simplicity and transparent representation.

The link between *Tatler* 224, on advertising, and *Spectator* 85, on *Two Children in the Wood*, is strengthened by the frame as much as by the critical movements of the paper. Like *Tatler* 224, the paper on the ballad begins with the reflections that fill Addison's head as he contemplates lower forms of print culture. And the forms of print he is considering in *Spectator* 85 are, in one sense, much lower than the advertisements he reflects on in *Tatler* 224: he is looking through trash. *Spectator* 85, as much as it is a critical essay on the popular ballad, is an essay on waste paper. It is interesting to compare Addison's basically redemptive reading of the trash with Swift's bleak and apocalyptic meditations on the same theme. While for Swift waste paper emblematizes the entropic decline and futility of human intelligence and industry, for Addison it becomes a site for the recovery of unheralded value, for the discovery of diamonds in the rough. Swift's message warns us that all the fruit of human culture will one day rot in the compost heap of history. In "The Gulf of All Human Possessions" Swift describes the ultimate end of human endeavor as a cesspit: "A Treasure here of learning lurks, / Huge heaps of never-dying works; / Labours of many an ancient sage, / And millions of the present age" (39–42).[45] Addison teaches a quite different moral. Excavating the ballad from a piece of paper used to patch the wall of a friend's country house, Addison shows how textual refuse may be recovered and restored, how we may redeem the past through a reevaluation of what we have (mistakenly) discarded.

Opening the paper with the ethnographic observation, "It is the Custom of the *Mahometans*, if they see any printed or written Paper upon the Ground, to take it up and lay it aside carefully, as not knowing but it may contain some Piece of their *Alcoran*," Addison sets a tone of mock-seriousness that parodically frames the observations and confessions that follow. He admits to participating in the same scrupulous scrutiny of waste paper; he is addicted to print and can't overlook even the doilies under the candle without reading them. Addison's reclamation of literature involves the recycling of texts through two stages of consumption and distribution. First, books are bought and sold as intellectual and cultural commodities; at this stage they are valued for what is printed on their pages. Next, they are recycled as purely material objects; at this stage they are valued solely for the paper they are printed on. Addison picks up the material bodies of the texts and reinstates them to their initial status as intellectual objects. His library includes, on the shelves that hold his "Folios," "two long Band-Boxes . . . lined with deep Erudition and abstruse Literature" (*S* 85).

But what begins as a self-mocking, comic reflection on the material lives of texts turns into a earnest discussion of the literary merits of a scrap found among "several printed Papers" pasted on a wall. Beginning with a comic frame — looking for god, or at least wisdom, in the trash — Addison explicitly marks his shift into earnest criticism: "My Reader will think I am not serious, when I acquaint him that the Piece I am going to speak of was the old Ballad of the *Two Children in the Wood*, which is one of the darling Songs of the common People, and has been the Delight of most *Englishmen* in some Part of their Age" (*S* 85). The assumption that Addison can't be serious would come not only from the comic tone established at the beginning of the essay but also from the conventionally "low" cultural status of the popular ballad as a genre, one which precludes serious critical attention.

While Addison's initial retrieval of "high" forms of learning from their degradation as mere wastepaper maintains a comic juxtaposition between "high" and "low," intellectual and material and creates the play of humor in the first section of the paper, there is no *conventional* contrast between the "low" ballad and its equally humble material incarnation as wastepaper. Where before we had high and low, here we have just low and low, but only for a second. Addison's purpose in this essay is to elevate the ballad, not to the comically inflated pretensions of that "deep Erudition and abstruse Literature" lining the bandbox, but to another category of cultural and aesthetic value. He does not match the "high" and "low" of the first section with a parallel pair; instead he resolves the contrast between the "low" ballad and the "high" critical discourse with which he treats it. The piece of make-do wallpaper on which Addison finds the ballad becomes the parallel, not so much to the puffed-up sheets of stuffy erudition lining the bandbox, as to the "Piece of their *Alcoran*" for which the Muslims always keep a weather eye open (*S* 85).

The ballad earns this place of analogical honor on its merits as a "plain simple Copy of Nature, destitute of the Helps and Ornaments of Art." Plain and unadorned, one might say, like the gospel truth. Its literary "destitution," its utter lack of sophistication and polish recall on the level of style its material destitution as a wallpaper patch. This stylistic candor is matched with an equally frank and immediate emotional content. Like those pieces of news from the "little World" of advertising, the ballad appeals to universal human sympathies that the most refined can enjoy along with the common run of mankind: "There is even a despicable Simplicity in the Verse; and yet, because the Sentiments appear genuine and unaffected, they are able to move the Mind of the most polite Reader with Inward Meltings of Humanity and Compassion" (*S* 85).

However, even as he commends the ballad for its simplicity and emotional immediacy, Addison still apologizes for its low style. In fact, because it shows "such an abject Phrase and Poorness of Expression, that the quoting any part of it would look like a Design of turning it into Ridicule," he cites no verses from the ballad. Instead, in order "to shew the Genius of the Author [of the ballad] amidst all his Simplicity," Addison substitutes a quotation from Horace's third ode for one from *Two Children in the Wood*. After all, the passage in question relies on "just the same kind of Fiction" that Horace uses there (*S* 85). This substitution serves rhetorically as a kind of translation of the (unquoted) passage of the English poem into the (quoted) Latin of the Horatian ode. *Two Children in the Wood* takes its place in the classically ordered canon of legitimate literature.

What these English ballads share with classical literature is an inherent simplicity, a freedom from that gothicism Addison campaigns against. The wide popularity and comprehensibility of both types of literature depends on this simplicity:

> *Homer, Virgil,* or *Milton,* so far as the language of their Poems is understood, will please a Reader of plain common Sense . . . [and] an ordinary Song or Ballad that is the Delight of the common People, cannot fail to please all such Readers as are not unqualified for the Entertainment by their Affectation or Ignorance; and the Reason is plain, because the same Paintings of Nature which recommend it to the most ordinary Reader, will appear beautiful to the most refined. (*S* 70)

In contrast, the "Gothick Manner of Writing" pleases "only such as have formed to themselves a wrong artificial Taste upon little fanciful Authors and Writers of Epigram" (*S* 70). What Addison formulates in these passages is a logic that allows the popularity and simplicity of the common English ballads, qualities that may (wrongfully) delegate them to low generic status, to serve as common ground with the conventionally "high" canon of classical literature. What by virtue of its "essential and inherent Perfection of Simplicity of Thought" is truly classical is also truly popular, and vice versa (*S* 70). Appropriately, the epigram that Addison chooses for *Spectator* 70 on *Chevy Chase* cites a "high" classical source validating the "low" and popular: *Interdum vulgus rectum videt*; sometimes the public sees straight (Horace, *Epistles* 2.1.63).

The translation in *Spectator* 70 works in two directions. On the one hand the comparison of passages from the ballad with those from Virgil lifts the English poem into the neoclassical critical context and the literary canon. But the second movement is directed not toward validation of literary merit via classical sources but toward the stabilization of semantic clarity and ethical value via modern colloquial English. In two places Addison translates *Chevy Chase* into a more contemporary idiom. He clarifies an ethical point—that the Earl's "Sentiments and Actions are every Way suitable to an hero"— by paraphrasing:

> One of us two, says he, must dye: I am an Earl as well as your self, so that you can have no Pretence for refusing the Combat: However, says he, 'tis Pity, and indeed would be a Sin, that so many innocent Men should perish for our Sakes; rather let you and I end our Quarrel in single Fight. (*S* 70)

He then goes on to quote three stanzas from the ballad that say, of course, the same thing but in archaic language. Similarly, Addison glosses the idiom of the poem: "*Merry Men*, in the Language of those Times," he explains, "is no more than a chearful Word for Companions and Fellow-Soldiers" (*S* 70). His repetition is deliberate and pedagogical. Addison is *teaching* the ballad, as he will teach *Paradise Lost*.

Addison's translation of *Chevy Chase* accommodates it to the contemporary contexts of his readers. One of these contexts is a set of literary-cultural assumptions about genre hierarchies—popular ballads are low, and classical odes, high literary forms. Addison reformulates the terms of this hierarchy by introducing an axis of similarity on which the popular English ballad may be aligned with classical poetry by virtue of a shared clarity and simplicity. The other dominant context is ethical: the formal clarity and simplicity that makes these works universally comprehensible is part and parcel with their ethical content, which is also of enduring, universal relevance. The obstacles that Addison must remove in order to unveil the true value of the simple English ballads seem to be twofold: on the one hand, there is that mistaken elitism that disregards a work because it is popular and simple; on the other hand, there are those difficulties of poetic and archaic language that may obscure the sense of the ballad. One wonders if Addison conceived of a kind of double audience— a set of the literary elite and a set of unliterary folks unversed in poetic language. A more interesting possibility, however, is that both these characters were understood to reside in the same person, who, while having internalized the orthodox bias of literary culture, had not mastered its conventions—a literary snob.

A parallel set of negotiations takes place in the papers on Milton's *Paradise Lost*; here I refer not only to Addison's course of lectures on the poem but also to Steele's papers—especially *Tatler* 217, where he translates Adam and Eve's postlapsarian quarrel into modern "Domestick Stile." And while Addison's methodical course through the epic in his months of Saturdays is in many ways a very different project from Steele's frequent but more improvisational citations, both share strategies with Addison's papers on the ballads.[46] Most generally, both mediate between the divine heroic poem and the more mundane contexts of their readers. And the mediation both in *Tatler* 217 and in Addison's series calls attention to the difficulties of Milton's grand style. Steele's treatment does this by directly translating the speeches of Adam and Eve into conversational prose. So Steele has Adam complain, quite colloquially: "Madam, If my Advice had been of any Authority with you when that strange Desire of Gadding possessed you this Morning, we had still been happy" (*T* 217). Addison conducts his translation more discursively, commenting on the strengths and weaknesses of Milton's language, which, while usually sublime, could lapse into pedantry, latinism, and obscurity.

Steele's domestication of Milton's Adam and Eve shows the popularizing impulse that runs through all the literary critical papers. Addison's treatment of Milton exploits the popular and periodical format of the papers; this allows him to maintain a continuous stream of exposition while pacing the papers in a way that may have improved their reception. The essays on Milton come only every Saturday, leaving adequate time for their digestion and perhaps for a little brushing up on *Paradise Lost* between papers. Relatively heavy material is thus made less taxing for a general audience. The papers form a kind of correspondence course on *Paradise Lost*; several treat the general qualities of the poem's action, genre, structure, and language, but most are relatively straightforward expositions, with ample quotation, of the events of the poem and their significance. As in the case of *Chevy Chase*, Addison applies the standards of classical epic to the modern English poem in order to institutionalize that poem in the canon.

While the dominate direction of Addison's translation of Milton is from "higher" to "lower," there are aspects of his treatment that work in the other direction. Just as the reputation of the ballads suffer because they are written in the nonclassical, "pedestrian" English language, so may the beauties in Milton somewhat obscured by the relatively low status of English as a literary language. For while Milton is "a perfect Master in all these Arts of working on the Imagination," his "Divine . . . Poem in *English*, is like a stately palace built of Brick, where one may see Architecture in as great a Perfection as in one of Marble, tho' the Materials be of a coarser Nature" (*S* 417). To truly appreciate the beauties in *Paradise Lost*, we must look to where all true beauty resides, not on the surface but beyond it to the ideal formal structure. This delegation of real value to a realm beyond superficial ornamentation is just one more example of the aesthetic ideals we have seen at work throughout.

What may be most remarkable about Steele's and Addison's treatment of Milton, especially Addison's essays on *Paradise Lost,* is its popular success. Addison remarks at the end of the series on "the uncommon Demands which my Bookseller tells me has been made for these particular Discourses" and sites this popular success as the great reward of his efforts (*S* 369). And in his life of Addison, Johnson remarks that these essays made Milton "an universal favorite, with whom readers of every class think it necessary to be pleased."[47] As a universal favorite with readers of every class, *Paradise Lost*, then, perfectly embodies the successful institution of the cultural ideals of the bourgeois public sphere. This success, accordingly, was not achieved through learned, specialized discourse but through that universally communicative discourse of the rational public sphere, which, it might seem, can translate everything into its own terms. Quite simply, the papers set a fashion for Milton. As Theophilus Cibber notes in his *Lives of the Poets* (1753), "it had become unfashionable not to have read" *Paradise Lost* since the publication of Addison's papers explicating the poem.[48] But Addison's popularization of the poem was not achieved single-handedly. As Lillian Bloom points out, by the end of the seventeenth century *Paradise Lost* had been awarded high marks by critics of note; and, more importantly, it had just been issued in an affordable, pocket-book sized, duodecimo edition (1711) by Addison's friend, the publisher Jacob Tonson.[49] The canonization of *Paradise Lost* within the specifically bourgeois, middle-brow canon of English literature depends equally on its commercial and conceptual availability. Only by working in tandem with the commercial literary market does Addison set the fashion for Milton's divine poem.

The Tatler and *The Spectator* undertake the cultivation of a broad and popular appreciation of Milton and other native English poets, a familiarity with the principles of aesthetic and ethical criticism, and through these, the cultivation of a revised standard of taste. They furnish the minds of their readers with the equipment necessary for participation in a cultural realm that is becoming more commercial, more various, and more accessible. Removing taste from domination by arbitrary standards of novelty and the senseless play of false wit, they set a fashion for values that, in themselves, lie outside the arena of fashionability. Yet, and this is crucial, in order to effect any substantial change of taste, those values must be successfully retailed through commercial distribution on the market of public opinion. And so, what derives its value from its origin outside the fashion market can only realize that value on the market.

Explicitly hostile to exclusivity, specialization, and pedantry in any form, the critical papers in *The Tatler* and *The Spectator* validate a public, nonacademic audience. As much as Addison advocates aesthetic values that ultimately derive from outside the realm of mundane existence, he commits himself to the *use* of the aesthetic in the everyday life of the average bourgeois man and woman. In the papers on *Paradise Lost*, Addison makes available to the common reader not only the beauties of "plain, simple and unadorned" verse but also the grandeur of the sublime (*S* 303). The pursuits of such pleasures are not merely rewarding in themselves but pay off in palpable emotional and physical benefits. They awaken the mental faculties "from Sloth and Idleness, without putting them upon any Labour or Difficulty" and "have a kindly Influence on the Body, as well as the Mind, and not only serve to clear and brighten the Imagination, but are able to dispel Grief and Melancholy, and set the Animal Spirits in pleasing and agreeable Motions" (*S* 411). Further, even as it depends on the discourses of property ownership and imperial domination, Addison's plan for the cultivation of the imagination uses these discourses to formulate different kinds of "ownership" and "domination" not subject to the constraints of wealth (or poverty) and power (or powerlessness). Indeed, as he says, these arenas of pleasure should be accessible to the most disenfranchised and bereft: "a Man in a Dungeon is capable of entertaining himself with Scenes and Landskips more beautiful than any that can be found in the whole Compass of Nature" (*S* 411). The realm of the interiorized imagination may later become a kind of dungeon of its own, imprisoning the aesthete in his solipsistic fantasies, but here, subject to the popularizing and social directives of these fashionable periodical papers, aesthetic taste and imagination are liberating and inclusive.

At least, that is the aim of their formulation in these papers. But I hope that I have shown some of the structures of distinction, prescription, and exclusion that underlie the very formulation of these promises, which, after all, can only be fulfilled through an internalized adoption of quite particular, class-based ideological regulations. These regulations follow the modern paradoxes of a bourgeois, hegemonic social order whose most formidable strengths lie not in outright censorship but in widespread consensus garnered through the free assent of each individual; not in coercive and repressive prohibition but in the deep subjective identification of each person with sociocultural norms that become integral to his or her very psyche; not in the performance of power and authority as imperious display but in the fashioning of each strand of the fabric of everyday life through the management of taste, style, and manners.

Notes

PREFACE

1. Kennedy Fraser, "The Fashionable Mind," in *The Fashionable Mind: Reflections on Fashion, 1970–1981* (New York: Alfred A. Knopf, 1981), 146.

2. Joanne Finkelstein, *The Fashioned Self* (Philadelphia: Temple Univ. Press, 1991), 5.

3. In their critique of Neil McKendrick's adoption, in his study of eighteenth-century fashion, of a Veblenesque trickle-down model of consumption as social emulation, Ben Fine and Ellen Leopold garner a good deal of counter evidence in their "Consumerism and the Industrial Revolution," *Social History* 15, no. 2 (1990): 151–79. Practically, there was not any simple unidirectional force of fashion at work, and ideologically the very concept of fashion was undergoing examination, refutation, and in many instances redirection. The fashions of the eighteenth-century gentleman increasingly draw on elements of rural labor and sport, and urban trade costume. The adoption by the urban middle and then upper class of the frock coat, worn traditionally by the rural working man, is a dominant example of trickle-up fashion trends. Although the practical, comfortable frock coat does not begin to appear as an urban fashion until the 1730s, there is already strong sentiment toward the simplification and rationalization of fashion in the *Tatler* and *Spectator* papers twenty years earlier. See, for example, C. Cunnington and Phillis Cunnington, *Handbook of English Costume in the Eighteenth Century* (Boston: Plays, Inc., 1972), 16–19; and Anne Buck, *Dress in Eighteenth-Century England* (New York: Holmes & Meier, 1979), esp. 52–58.

4. Michael Warner, "The Mass Public and the Mass Subject," in *The Phantom Public Sphere*, ed. Bruce Robbins for the Social Text Collective, Cultural Politics Series, vol. 5 (Minneapolis: Univ. of Minnesota Press, 1993), 241.

5. Georg Simmel, "Fashion," *International Quarterly* 10 (1904); rpt. *The American Journal of Sociology* 62 (1957): 544.

6. Jean Baudrillard, *For a Critique of the Political Economy of the Sign*, trans. Charles Levin (St. Louis, Mo.: Telos Press, 1981), 79.

7. Grant McCracken, *Culture and Consumption: New Approaches to the Symbolic Character of Consumer Goods and Activities* (Bloomington: Indiana Univ. Press, 1988), 81.

8. Roland Barthes, *The Fashion System* (1967), trans. Matthew Ward and Richard Howard (New York: Hill & Wang, 1983); Jane Gaines, "Introduction: Fabricating the Female Body," in *Fabrications: Costume and the Female Body*, ed. Jane Gaines and Charlotte Herzog (New York: Routledge, 1990), 13.

9. Interestingly, Addison's metaphor of old plate explicitly calls up McCracken's argument that by the eighteenth century patina value had been utterly replaced by the value of fashion. This value shift is fully evident in Addison's metaphor. There is no suggestion that these voguish papers will gain in value due to the patina of the past that they will acquire. Nor do the "timeless" papers rely on such fetishization of the past for their future popularity, but rather on their embodiment of eternal human values and concerns that shine forever bright with the glow of Truth.

INTRODUCTION: CULTURAL CRITICISM AND THE TATLER AND SPECTATOR PAPERS

1. *The Tatler*, ed. with an introduction and notes, Donald F. Bond, 3 vols. (Oxford: Clarendon Press, Oxford Univ. Press, 1987). References are made parenthetically in the text to *T* followed by the number of the paper. *The Spectator*, ed. with an introduction and notes, Donald F. Bond, 5 vols. (Oxford: Clarendon Press, Oxford Univ. Press, 1965). References are made parenthetically in the text to *S* followed by the number of the paper.

2. Mary Douglas and Baron Isherwood, *The World of Goods: Towards an Anthropology of Consumption* (New York: Basic Books, 1979), 68.

3. This may account for the differences between my approach to fashion and that of ethnographers who employ fashion as a transcultural, and to some extent then, transhistorical category in an effort to decide, among other things, whether fashion is a phenomenon limited to Western capitalist countries. See, for example, Jennifer Craik, *The Face of Fashion: Cultural Studies in Fashion* (London: Routledge, 1994). While doubtless many cultures have dress codes determined to some extent by what we call fashionable change, the meaning of these changes, the meaning indeed of change itself, is not something that can be read cross-culturally.

4. The development of the fashion system and its attendant consumer culture, with its fetishized modes of representation and reified social relations, has been so amply documented for the nineteenth century as to suggest that these phenom-

ena have their origins in that century. See Rosalind H. Williams, *Dream Worlds: Mass Consumption in Late-Nineteenth-Century France* (Berkeley: Univ. of California Press, 1982), 65–66. Rachel Bowlby makes similar claims for the "innovations" in nineteenth-century consumer culture in *Just Looking: Consumer Culture in Dreiser, Gissing, and Zola* (New York: Methuen, 1985), 1–11. See also, for example, Bowlby, "Modes of Modern Shopping: Mallarmé at the *Bon Marché*," in *The Ideology of Conduct: Essays on Literature and the History of Sexuality*, ed. Nancy Armstrong and Leonard Tennenhouse (New York: Methuen, 1987), 185–205; Walter Benjamin, "One-Way Street" and "Paris, Capital of the Nineteenth Century," in *Reflections*, trans. Edmund Jephcott, ed. Peter Demetz (New York: Schocken Books, 1986), 61–94, 146–62; Susan Buck-Morss, *The Dialectics of Seeing: Walter Benjamin and the Arcades Project* (Cambridge, Mass.: MIT Press, 1991); and Emily Apter, *Feminizing the Fetish: Psychoanalysis and Narrative Obsession in Turn-of-the-Century France* (Ithaca: Cornell Univ. Press, 1991).

5. Karl Marx, *Capital*, vol. 1, trans. Ben Fowkes (London: Penguin/ New Left Review, 1976), 250–51.

6. Anne Hollander, *Sex and Suits* (New York: Alfred A. Knopf, 1994), 16. Roland Barthes, *The Fashion System* (1967), trans. Matthew Ward and Richard Howard (New York: Hill & Wang, 1983).

7. *Colley Cibber: Three Sentimental Comedies* ("Love's Last Shift, Or, The Fool in Fashion"; "The Careless Husband"; "The Lady's Last Stake: Or, The Wife's Resentment"), ed. Maureen Sullivan (New Haven: Yale Univ. Press, 1973). Citation is 2.1.363–65.

8. Peter Uwe Hohendahl, *The Institution of Criticism* (Ithaca: Cornell Univ. Press, 1982), 50.

9. Kennedy Fraser, "The Fashionable Mind," in *The Fashionable Mind: Reflections on Fashion, 1970–1981* (New York: Alfred A. Knopf, 1981), 146.

10. Simmel, "Fashion," 548.

11. Fernand Braudel, *The Structures of Everyday Life: The Limits of the Possible*, vol. 1 of *Civilization and Capitalism, 15th–18th Century*, trans. Siân Reynolds (New York: Perennial Library/Harper & Row, 1985), 328.

12. Grant McCracken, *Culture and Consumption: New Approaches to the Symbolic Character of Consumer Goods and Activities* (Bloomington: Indiana Univ. Press, 1988). McCracken points out that "in contradistinction to virtually all ethnographic precedent," people in the "hot," industrial commercial societies of the West "live in a world that is not only culturally constituted but also historically constituted." Such societies "willingly accept, indeed encourage the radical changes that follow from deliberate human efforts and the effect of anonymous forces. . . . Indeed it does not exaggerate to say that hot societies demand this change and depend on it to drive certain economic, social, and cultural sectors of the Western world" (80–81).

13. Arjun Appadurai, "Introduction: Commodities and the Politics of Value," *The Social Life of Things: Commodities in Cultural Perspective* (Cambridge: Cambridge Univ. Press, 1986), 38.

14. McCracken, *Culture and Consumption*, 19; and see chap. 2, "'Ever Dearer in Our Thoughts': Patina and the Representation of Status before and after the Eighteenth Century" (31-43).

15. Neil McKendrick, "Introduction: The Birth of a Consumer Society," in Neil McKendrick, John Brewer, and J. H. Plumb, *The Birth of a Consumer Society: The Commercialization of Eighteenth-Century England* (Bloomington: Indiana Univ. Press, 1982), 1.

16. Braudel, *The Structures of Everyday Life*, 316.

17. Chandra Mukerji, *From Graven Images: Patterns of Modern Materialism* (New York: Columbia Univ. Press, 1983), 8-9. Mukerji is using Marshall Sahlins's definition of a materialistic culture as one in which material interests are autonomously valued rather than given value in reference to other social ends they serve (8).

18. Ibid., 9.

19. McCracken, *Culture and Consumption*,40-41. Michael McKeon outlines this early modern transition from status to class in *The Origins of the English Novel, 1600–1740* (Baltimore: Johns Hopkins Univ. Press, 1987), 162-75: "It is precisely during this period that the traditional, qualitative criteria of honorific status were being definitively infiltrated by the quantitative criteria of socioeconomic class. . . . Class criteria gradually 'replace' status criteria: which is to say not that the regard for status is obliterated but that it is subsumed under and accommodated to the more dominant and insistent regard for financial income and occupational identity" (162-63).

20. McKendrick, *The Birth of a Consumer Society,* 52.

21. Braudel, *The Structures of Everyday Life,* 333.

22. Kathryn Shevelow makes this point: "Too many literary histories, serving the distinction between 'literary' and 'sub-literary' forms, have allowed the significance of the periodical to pale by comparison with that of the novel or other genres." *Women and Print Culture: The Construction of Femininity in the Early Periodical* (London: Routledge, 1989), 195.

23. Samuel Johnson, "Addison," in *Lives of the Poets*, 2 vols. (London: Oxford Univ. Press, 1959), . 1:446.

24. Brean McCrea makes part of this point in his *Addison and Steele Are Dead: The English Department, Its Canon, and the Professionalization of Literary Criticism* (Newark: Univ. of Delaware Press): "Those texts [Addison's and Steele's] cannot sustain the sophisticated formal analysis that academic critics must practice" (117). But what McCrea does not see is that these texts *can* sustain analysis, but only if what he understands as their unequivocal "simple moral and social agenda" is probed. This can only be done by looking into the construction of those very categorical standards of simplicity, transparency, and common sense that McCrea uncritically accepts at their eighteenth-century valuation as natural and self-apparent.

25. Jürgen Habermas, *The Structural Transformation of the Public Sphere: An Inquiry into a Category of Bourgeois Society*, trans. Thomas Burger with Frederick Lawrence (Cambridge, Mass.: MIT Press, 1991).

26. Perhaps the most renowned sociological study of taste is Pierre Bourdieu's

Distinction: A Social Critique of the Judgement of Taste, trans. Richard Nice (Cambridge, Mass.: Harvard Univ. Press, 1984), which provides an extensively documented account of taste formation in twentieth-century France. Bourdieu emphasizes the centrality of exclusion — of *distinction* — to the affirmation of taste: "Taste (i.e. manifested preferences) are the practical affirmation of an inevitable difference. . . . In matters of taste, more than anywhere else, all determination is negation" (56). Wherever taste, then, is a dominant standard of value (and where is it not?) there will be a considerable degree of negation and exclusion. The curious paradox of the specific standard of bourgeois taste promoted by *The Tatler* and *The Spectator* is that it advances a fairly inclusive and nonelitist standard of taste; yet this of course necessitates the exclusion of other "more exclusive" modes of taste. What is important here is that exclusivity becomes a negative value, one which can be leveled at those who need to be excluded. Fraser points out this irony in reference to Habermas's bourgeois public sphere: "There is a remarkable irony here, one that Habermas's account of the rise of the public sphere fails to fully appreciate. A discourse of publicity touting public accessibility, rationality, and the suspension of status hierarchies is itself deployed as a strategy of distinction" (6).

27. Hohendahl, *The Institution of Criticism,* 52.

28. Terry Eagleton, *The Function of Criticism from "The Spectator" to Post-Structuralism* (London: Verso, 1984), 18.

29. Revisionist critical debates point out how Habermas's account fails to sufficiently explore the operations of power in this sphere. See, for example, Bruce Robbins, Introduction, in *The Phantom Public Sphere,* ed. Bruce Robbins for the Social Text Collective, Cultural Politics Series, vol. 5 (Minneapolis: Univ. of Minnesota Press, 1993), xx.

30. Michael Warner, *The Letters of the Republic: Publication and the Public Sphere in Eighteenth-Century America* (Cambridge, Mass.: Harvard Univ. Press, 1990), 46.

31. Nancy Fraser, "Rethinking the Public Sphere: A Contribution to the Critique of Actually Existing Democracy," in *The Phantom Public Sphere,* 10–11.

32. Ibid., 6.

33. Ibid., 10–11.

34. Hohendahl, *The Institution of Criticism,* 49.

35. Eagleton, *Function of Criticism,* 10.

36. See Fraser, "Rethinking the Public Sphere": "The official bourgeois public sphere is the institutional vehicle for a major historical transformation in the nature of political domination. This is the shift from a repressive mode of domination to a hegemonic one, from rule based primarily on acquiescence to superior force to a rule based primarily on consent supplemented with some measure of repression" (8); and Terry Eagleton, *Ideology of the Aesthetic* (Oxford: Basil Blackwell, 1990), 19–23.

37. Eagleton, *Ideology of the Aesthetic,* 20. See also Peter Stallybrass and Allon White, "The Grotesque Body and the Smithfield Muse: Authorship in the Eighteenth Century," in their *The Politics and Poetics of Transgression* (Ithaca: Cornell Univ. Press, 1986), 80–124. They point out that in the operation of bourgeois

hegemony "manners, regulations of the body, thus become the site of a profound interconnection of ideology and subjectivity, a zone of transcoding at once astonishingly trivial and microscopically important" (89-90).

38. See Appadurai, *The Social Life of Things,* 31-32. Also Michael McKeon, "Historicizing Patriarchy: The Emergence of Gender Difference in England, 1660-1760," *Eighteenth-Century Studies* 28 (1995): "By the early eighteenth century, a double revolution was under way. The demise of status-based sumptuary laws signalled the challenge to status by class criteria, whose more fluid conception of social difference spurned the crudity of legally stipulated physical signs. However, the impulse to enforce difference by dress did not disappear in the modern world. Sumptuary laws were replaced by less formal means of social regulation, by polemic rather than legislation" (305).

39. Ibid., 32.

40. Simmel, "Fashion," 556.

41. Geoff Eley, "Nations, Publics, and Political Cultures: Placing Habermas in the Nineteenth Century," in *Habermas and the Public Sphere,* ed. Craig Calhoun (Cambridge, Mass.: MIT Press, 1992), 291.

42. Michael Warner, "The Mass Public and the Mass Subject," in *The Phantom Public Sphere,* 240; Timothy Breen, "The Meaning of Things: Interpreting the Consumer Economy in the Eighteenth Century," in *Consumption and the World of Goods,* ed. John Brewer and Roy Porter (London: Routledge, 1993), 256-57.

43. Habermas, *The Structural Transformation of the Public Sphere,* 16.

44. Ibid., 74.

45. Eley, "Nations, Publics, and Political Cultures: Placing Habermas in the Nineteenth Century," 291. See also Habermas, *The Structural Transformation of the Public Sphere,* 1-56.

46. See Eagleton, *Ideology of the Aesthetic,* esp. 8-9 and 64, on the analogous autonomy of the aesthetic and human subject.

47. Theodor Adorno, "Cultural Criticism and Society," in *Prisms,* trans. Samuel and Sherry Weber (London: Neville Spearman, 1967), 19. While I do not subscribe to his apocalyptic view of contemporary consumer culture ("in the open-air prison which the world is becoming . . . . absolute reification, which presupposed intellectual progress as one of its elements, is now preparing to absorb the mind entirely"[34]), I think Adorno effectively isolates some of the tensions faced by the critic of capitalist culture.

48. Ibid., 22.

49. Joyce Oldham Appleby, *Economic Thought and Ideology in Seventeenth-Century England* (Princeton: Princeton Univ. Press, 1978), 16.

50. Ibid., 242.

51. "Dozens of publications declared the goal of favorable balances outmoded, argued for free trade as a sure way to prosperity, and dismissed the idea that gold and silver had any peculiar value. Yet political decisions made between 1696 and 1713 turned England toward a different course of economic development, and the moribund balance-of-trade theory was called into service as a defense. This check to the expression of liberal economic thought at the end of the seventeenth century

has not been thoroughly explored, and the intellectual responses to capitalism remain tangled in the ideological origins of classical economic theory" (ibid., 248).

52. Here Addison informs his readers of his intention "to enter into the Passions of Mankind, and to correct those depraved Sentiments that give Birth to all those little Extravagancies which appear in their outward Dress and Behaviour" (*S* 16).

CHAPTER ONE: FASHION, THE FETISH, AND THE RISE OF CREDIT

1. Joyce Oldham Appleby, *Economic Thought and Ideology in Seventeenth-Century England* (Princeton: Princeton Univ. Press, 1978), 164–65.

2. P.G.M. Dickson, *The Financial Revolution in England: A Study in the Development of Public Credit, 1688–1756* (London: Macmillan; New York: St. Martin's Press, 1967).

3. Christopher Hill, *The Century of Revolution: 1603–1714*, vol. 5 of *A History of England*, ed. Christopher Brooke and Denis Mack Smith (London: Nelson, 1961), 212.

4. Joan Thirsk, *Economic Policy and Projects: The Development of a Consumer Society in Early Modern England* (Oxford: Clarendon Press, 1978), 9.

5. Neil McKendrick, "Introduction: The Birth of a Consumer Society," in Neil McKendrick, John Brewer, and J. H. Plumb, *The Birth of a Consumer Society: The Commercialization of Eighteenth-Century England* (Bloomington: Indiana Univ. Press, 1982), 1–33. For a wide-ranging anthology of work on consumption in the early modern period, see the recent *Consumption and the World of Goods*, ed. John Brewer and Roy Porter (London: Routledge, 1993).

6. For a discussion of what's at stake in this difference of emphasis see R. J. Holton, *The Transition from Feudalism to Capitalism* (New York: St. Martin's Press, 1985), 11–24, 64–102.

7. Working from the statistics gathered by Gregory King and Arthur Young, Keith Tribe postulates that "while 'manufacturing' grew rapidly between the later seventeenth and the later eighteenth centuries, it did no more than keep roughly in step with the growth in agriculture and commerce. Not until the end of the Napoleonic Wars did the role of agriculture begin to decline in the national economy." *Genealogies of Capitalism* (Atlantic Highlands, N.J.: Humanities Press, 1981), 43.

8. Karl Marx, *Capital*, vol. 1, trans. Ben Fowkes (London: Penguin/New Left Review, 1976), pt. 8, "So-Called Primitive Accumulation," 874–940. For a discussion of Marx's account of early agrarian capitalism and subsequent historical work that has grown out of it, see Holton, *The Transition from Feudalism to Capitalism*, 64–103. Tribe works through Marx's theory of primitive accumulation in some detail in "The Structure of Agrarian Capitalism—The English 'Classic Model,'" 35–100. He takes issue with Marx's identification of the rural wage laborer with the industrial proletariat (36–37, 68–69).

9. Holton, *The Transition from Feudalism to Capitalism*, 12–13. The insight into capitalism's generation of the very category of "the economic" is Perry Anderson's: "Precapitalist modes of production like feudalism . . . cannot be conceptu-

alized by reference to such 'economic' criteria, since the 'economic' (i.e., material production) is so closely interwoven with the rest of social life, such as law, politics, and culture. . . . Anderson's explanation of the rise of capitalism, therefore, involves analysis of the development of purely 'economic' relations of surplus extraction characteristic of that particular mode of production. As such it refuses to take 'the economic base' for granted as a generic feature of all modes of production" (Holton, 92). Throughout the seventeenth and eighteenth centuries there is residual resistance to the institutionalization of this autonomous economic sphere, such as that documented by E. P. Thompson in his account of the "moral economy" of the eighteenth-century crowd, which refused to take lying down the complete demoralization and desocialization of food production and distribution. "The Moral Economy of the English Crowd in the Eighteenth Century," *Past and Present* 50 (1971), reprinted in *Customs in Common* (New York: New Press, 1991), 185–258 (page references are to reprint edition). For a more general discussion of the resistance to capitalization that results from a lack of faith in its economic categories, see Michael Taussig, *The Devil and Commodity Fetishism in South America* (Chapel Hill: Univ. of North Carolina Press, 1980), 18–22.

10. On the modern categorization of knowledge see Michael McKeon, "The Origins of Interdisciplinary Studies," *Eighteenth-Century Studies* 28 (1994): 17–28.

11. C. B. Macpherson, *The Political Theory of Possessive Individualism: Hobbes to Locke* (Oxford: Oxford Univ. Press, 1962), 53–61.

12. Lawrence Stone, *The Crisis of the Aristocracy, 1558–1641* (Oxford: Clarendon Press, 1965), 36–38, 164–66.

13. Michael McKeon, *The Origins of the English Novel, 1600–1740* (Baltimore: Johns Hopkins Univ. Press, 1987), 167. And Hill puts it neatly in his early study, *The English Revolution: An Essay* (London: Lawrence & Wishart, 1955): "In feudal England land has passed by inheritance from father to son, cultivated all the time in traditional ways for the consumption of one family; it had changed hands comparatively rarely. But now, the law adapting itself to the economic needs of society, land was beginning to become a commodity bought and sold in a competitive market" (15).

14. Hill, *Century of Revolution*, 11–13; Appleby, *Economic Thought and Ideology*, 31–32.

15. Whether or not these seventeenth- and early-eighteenth-century innovations added up to something we can call an "agricultural revolution" is a matter of some debate. Eric Kettridge stakes the claim in *The Agricultural Revolution* (London: George Allen & Unwin, 1967). For a quick sketch of the debate see Joan Thirsk, *England's Agricultural Regions and Agrarian History, 1500–1750*, Studies in Economic and Social History (London: Macmillan/Economic History Society, 1987), 56–61.

16. Hill, *The English Revolution*, 17; Appleby, *Economic Thought and Ideology*, 32, 57–59.

17. "The land transfers must have had the effect of disrupting traditional relationships between landlord and tenant, of replacing them by purely monetary relations." Hill, *Century of Revolution*, 125.

18. Appleby, *Economic Thought and Ideology,* 59.

19. Ibid., 28, 101.

20. Thompson, "The Moral Economy," 185–200.

21. Hill, *Century of Revolution,* 126–28, 176.

22. E. P. Thompson, "Patrician Society, Plebeian Culture," *Journal of Social History* 7, no. 4 (1974): 382.

23. Macpherson, *The Political Theory of Possessive Individualism,* 48. See Appleby, who also cites this passage in her discussion of the central position that the alienation of land and labor has in the establishment of "market momentum" (*Economic Thought and Ideology,* 15).

24. Macpherson discusses Locke's emphasis on this notion of man's "*Property* in his own *Person*" and so his property in his own labor (*Second Treatise on Government,* section 27): "The more emphatically labour is asserted to be a property, the more it is understood to be alienable. For property in the bourgeois sense is not only a right to enjoy or use; it is a right to dispose of, to exchange, to alienate" (214–15). As Habermas puts it, "Locke's basic formulation of 'the preservation of property' quite naturally and in the same breath subsumed life, liberty, and estate under the title of 'possessions'; so easy was it at that time to identify political emancipation with 'human' emancipation — to use a distinction drawn by the young Marx" (56).

25. Elizabeth Wilson, *Adorned in Dreams: Fashion and Modernity* (Berkeley: Univ. of California Press, 1985), 13.

26. Nicholas Barbon, *A Discourse of Trade* (1690), *A Reprint of Economic Tracts,* ed. J. Hollander (Baltimore: Johns Hopkins Univ. Press, 1903), 32–33.

27. Bernard Mandeville, "The Grumbling Hive," *The Fable of the Bees,* ed. Phillip Harth (London: Penguin, 1970), 61–76.

28. See Daniel Defoe, *An Essay upon Projects* (London, 1697); *The Villainy of Stock-Jobbers Detected, And the Causes of the Late Run upon the Bankers Discovered and Considered* (London, 1701). For Defoe's recognition of the indispensability of credit in trade and his advice on how to get, maintain, grant, and manipulate it, see *The Complete English Tradesman* (1726; Gloucester: Alan Sutton, 1987). Defoe's allegorization of Lady Credit appears in his *A Review of the State of the British Nation,* ed. Arthur Wellesley Secord, Facsimile Text Society (New York: Columbia Univ. Press, 1938), 22 vols.; see vol. 3, no. 5; vol. 6, nos. 32 and 33; vol. 8, no. 134. While in *The Spectator* and in Defoe's essays there is considerable attention paid to the origins and progress of credit, thirty or so years later David Hume engages in apocalyptic speculation on the final days of credit in "Of Public Credit," *Essays Moral, Political, and Literary* (1741, 1742; London: Oxford Univ. Press, 1963), 355–71. In this essay Hume echoes the earlier arguments of Jonathan Swift, who polemicizes against credit, stock-jobbers, and Whigs in *The Conduct of the Allies* (1711), *Political Tracts 1711–1713,* vol. 6, *Prose Works of Jonathan Swift,* ed. Herbert Davies (Princeton: Princeton Univ. Press; London: Basil Blackwell & Mott, 1951), 1–66.

29. William Pietz, "Fetishism and Materialism: The Limits of Theory in Marx," in *Fetishism as Cultural Discourse,* ed. Emily Apter and William Pietz, 149.

Pietz cites Karl Marx, *Theories of Surplus Value*, pt. 3, trans. Jack Cohen and S. W. Ryazanskaya (Moscow: Progress, 1971), 494, 498.

30. See Dickson, chaps. 1–3, and Fernand Braudel, *The Wheels of Commerce*, vol. 2 of *Civilization and Capitalism*, trans. Siân Reynolds (New York: Harper & Row, 1982), 390–95.

31. J.G.A. Pocock, *Virtue, Commerce, and History: Essays on Political Thought and History, Chiefly in the Eighteenth Century* (Cambridge: Cambridge Univ. Press, 1985), esp. "The Mobility of Property and the Rise of Eighteenth-century Sociology," 103–23.

32. Ibid., 110.

33. Ibid., 112–14. For Defoe's allegorization of Lady Credit see his *Review*, vol. 3, no.5; vol. 6, nos. 32 and 33; vol. 8, no. 134.

34. Anne Buck, *Dress in Eighteenth-Century England* (New York: Holmes & Meier, 1979), 189.

35. Ibid., 190.

36. Appleby, *Economic Thought and Ideology*, 168–69.

37. Mukerji, *From Graven Images: Patterns of Modern Materialism,* 166–209.

38. Laura Brown, *Ends of Empire: Women and Ideology in Early-Eighteenth-Century English Literature* (Ithaca: Cornell Univ. Press, 1993), 116; Brown's discussion of this *Tatler* passage is also on page 116; and see her *Alexander Pope*, Rereading Literature Series, ed. Terry Eagleton (Oxford: Basil Blackwell, 1985).

39. For a discussion of woman as the figure through which imperial history is mediated in aesthetic theory, see Brown, "Capitalizing on Women," in *Ends of Empire*: "In eighteenth-century aesthetic writing, history is mediated most consistently through the category of gender; in particular . . . the figure of woman is the discursive means to the connection of imperialism and aesthetic theory" (104).

40. Hill, *Reformation*, 123–43.

41. Ibid., 184.

42. C.G.A. Clay, *Economic Expansion and Social Change: England 1500–1700*, vol.2, *Industry, Trade, and Government* (Cambridge: Cambridge Univ. Press, 1984), 163–64.

43. Hill, *Reformation*, 123.

44. Ibid., 129.

45. Ibid., 123–34; 184–86.

46. Hill, *Century of Revolution*, 262–63: "The strength of the clothing industry, which had destroyed the Irish cloth industry in 1699, was demonstrated again the next year [in 1700/01], when Parliament excluded eastern printed calicoes and silks from the English market" (263).

47. Of course, there probably is no such thing as "free trade," which, like "free speech," is one of the myths of capitalist liberalism. Interestingly, Hill (*Century of Revolution*) sees in these events a liberalization of commerce, and Appleby sees a further regulation.

48. Appleby, *Economic Thought and Ideology,* 162.

49. Ibid., 169.

50. Ibid., 169.

51. Mukerji, *From Graven Images,* 168–209.

52. McCracken, *Culture and Consumption,* 20.

53. "In sum, more and more social behavior was becoming consumption, and more and more of the individual was subsumed in the role of the consumer" (ibid., 20).

54. Brown, *Alexander Pope,* 44–45.

55. Emily Apter provides an overview of theoretical work on the fetish, "Fetishism in Theory: Marx, Freud, Baudrillard," in *Feminizing the Fetish: Psychoanalysis and Narrative Obsession in Turn-of-the-Century France* (Ithaca: Cornell Univ. Press, 1991), 1–14. For a discussion of commodity fetishism per se, see Taussig, *The Devil and Commodity Fetishism in South America,* 3–38. William Pietz provides a history of the word and of the evolution of the concept of fetishization in a series of articles: "The Problem of the Fetish, I" *Res* 9 (1985): 5–17; "The Problem of the Fetish, II" *Res* 13 (1987): 23–45; "The Problem of the Fetish, IIIa" *Res* 16 (1988): 105–23. Pietz shows how the fetish "as an idea and a problem, and as a novel object" is not proper to any discrete society but originated in the cultural and material exchange between Europeans and Africans on the West African coast during the sixteenth and seventeenth centuries. Likewise, the concept of fetish is not really proper to any discrete discipline; "promiscuous" and "indiscriminate," the word has been nonetheless indispensable to sociology, psychoanalysis, and marxian critical theory ("Fetish I," 5).

56. Although the abstract noun "fetishism" was not coined until 1757 by *philosophe* Charles de Brosses, discourse about fetish worship was well established in proto-ethnographic travel narratives by the turn of the eighteenth century; especially well known was that of the Dutch merchant Willem Bosman, which appeared in 1703 and in an English edition in 1705 (Pietz, "Fetish, IIIa").

57. For the fashionable woman as a modern "Pict" see *Spectator* 41.

58. Pietz, "Fetish, II," 23.

59. Pietz, "Fetish, II," 42, 45; "Fetish, IIIa," 106.

60. Pietz, "Fetishism and Materialism."

61. C. John Sommerville, *The Secularization of Early Modern England: From Religious Culture to Religious Faith* (New York: Oxford Univ. Press, 1992), 186.

62. Sommerville emphasizes the difference between secularization—as a process of differentiation of various spheres of life from the sacred—and decline in religious belief (ibid., 4–5). He traces the secularization of time and space in his study (18–43), and locates one watershed for these developments in Henry VIII's dissolution of the monasteries (12–14).

63. Pietz, "Fetishism and Materialism," 130. Pietz is citing Marx, *Capital: A Critique of Political Economy,* vol. 3, trans. David Fernbach (New York: Random House, 1981), 969.

64. Luce Irigaray, "Women on the Market," in *This Sex Which Is Not One,* trans. Catherine Porter with Carolyn Burke (Ithaca: Cornell Univ. Press, 1985), 183.

65. Marx, *Capital,* 1:165.

66. Pietz, "Fetish IIIa," 109.

67. Hal Foster presents a related thesis in "The Art of Fetishism," in *Fetishism*

as Cultural Discourse, where he argues that "commodity fetishism partly replaced religious fetishism, or at least compensated for its partial loss" (255).

68. Twentieth-century cultural critic Mike Featherstone notes how in consumer culture "traditional values and mores gave way as more and more aspects of life were brought under the influence of the expanding market with its propaganda for commodities" and that "a further effect of the progressive expansion of the market is to discredit traditional norms and unhinge long held meanings which were firmly grounded in social relationships and cultural objects," "The Body in Consumer Culture," *Theory, Culture, and Society* 1, no. 2 (1982): 19. These are exactly the processes that elicited anxiety in early modern social thinkers.

69. Rosalind H. Williams, *Dream Worlds: Mass Consumption in Late Nineteenth-Century France* (Berkeley: Univ. of California Press, 1982), 65-66. Rachel Bowlby makes similar claims for the "innovations" in nineteenth-century consumer culture in *Just Looking: Consumer Culture in Dreiser, Gissing, and Zola* (New York: Methuen, 1985), 1-11. See also, for example, Bowlby, "Modes of Modern Shopping: Mallarmé at the *Bon Marche*," in *The Ideology of Conduct: Essays on Literature and the History of Sexuality*, ed. Nancy Armstrong and Leonard Tennenhouse (New York: Methuen, 1987), 185-205; Walter Benjamin, "One-Way Street" and "Paris, Capital of the Nineteenth Century," in *Reflections*, trans. Edmund Jephcott, ed. Peter Demetz (New York: Schocken Books, 1986), 61-94, 146-62; Susan Buck-Morss, *The Dialectics of Seeing: Walter Benjamin and the Arcades Project* (Cambridge, Mass.: MIT Press, 1991); and Apter, *Feminizing the Fetish*.

70. Of course, the nineteenth-century shift to a truly mass-produced culture brought about by the industrial revolution did change the face of culture and the practices of fashion. The sheer quantity of new things, their cheapness, and so the sheer numbers of people who participated in fashion and consumption generated qualitative differences between the culture of the industrial age and its antecedent. Yet I do not think that the link between commodity and fantasy, between the fabulous and the commercial, and the concomitant investment of consumer desires in world of goods are themselves dependent on the broader distribution of consumer goods afforded by the industrial revolution.

CHAPTER TWO: IN THE VERY SPHINX OF FASHION:
THE FANTASTIC FASHION COMMODITY

1. Hoh-Cheung and Lorna H. Mui, *Shops and Shopkeeping in Eighteenth-Century England* (Kingston: McGill-Queen's Univ. Press; London: Routledge, 1989), 13.

2. John Cleland, *Memoirs of a Woman of Pleasure* (1749), ed. Peter Sabor (New York: Oxford Univ. Press, 1985), 6.

3. See, for example, Jonathan Swift's satire on the kind of empirical experimentation fostered by the Royal Society in his account of the Laputian Academy in *Gulliver's Travels*, pt. 3, chap. 5.

4. Alexander Pope, *The Dunciad*, in *Poetry and Prose of Alexander Pope*, ed. Aubrey Williams (Boston: Houghton Mifflin, 1969), 295-378. Karl Marx, *Capital*, trans. Ben Fowkes (London: Penguin/ New Left Books, 1976), 165. Of course, Pope's standard of religious value remains positive where Marx's is ironic.

5. See, for example, *Spectator* 1 and 15. A discussion of the beau and coquette follows in this chapter.

6. Michael G. Ketcham, *Transparent Designs: Reading, Performance, and Form in the "Spectator" Papers* (Athens: Univ. of Georgia Press, 1985), 2.

7. In his first essay on the pleasures of the imagination, Addison comments explicitly on the interchangeability of the terms *fancy* and *imagination*: " By the Pleasures of the Imagination or Fancy (which I shall use promiscuously) I here mean such as arise from visible Objects" (*S* 411).

8. Fraser, "Rethinking the Public Sphere," 16.

9. The lesson here is that their fondness for fashion opens women up to all manner of manipulation. Fostered and exploited by her family, Mrs. Margery's narcissism short-circuits the circulation of heterosexual desire and mirrors, finally, not so much her own desires but those of a family devoted to the cultivation of itself at the cost of any ties to others.

10. For a more complete discussion of these gender issues see chapter 4.

11. See *Tatler* 88 and 153 for the description of the men who are so punished. The term *squib*, literally a small roman-candle, applies both to an impertinent would-be wit and his lampoons. A satiric pamphlet, *The Character of a Coffee-House, with the Symptoms of a Town-Wit* (London, 1673), describes the wit as squib: "He is a kind of *Squib* on a Rope, a *meteor* composed of Self-conceit and noise, that by *blazing and crackling* engages the wonder of the ignorant, till on a sudden he vanishes and leaves a *stench*, if not *infection* behind him" (4).

12. See also *Tatler* 62.

13. Edward Ward, *The London Spy* (4th ed., 1709), ed. Paul Hyland (East Lansing, Mich.: Colleagues Press, 1993), section 3, p. 62.

14. Sigmund Freud, "Fetishism" (1927), *The Standard Edition of the Complete Psychological Works of Sigmund Freud*, trans. James Strachey with Anna Freud, Alix Strachey, and Alan Tyson, vol. 21 (London: Hogarth Press, 1961), 149–57.

15. August 13, 1741; cited in Bond's note to *Tatler* 143, vol. 2, p. 316.

16. Daniel Defoe, *The Complete English Tradesman* (1726), (Gloucester: Alan Sutton, 1987), 184.

17. Defoe, "Of Fine Shops, and Fine Shows," *Complete English Tradesman*, 180.

18. Ibid., 184–85.

19. Ibid., 81–92.

20. Ibid., 86.

21. For the sociocultural function of the masquerade in eighteenth-century England see Terry Castle, *Masquerade and Civilization: The Carnivalesque in Eighteenth-Century English Culture and Fiction* (Stanford: Stanford Univ. Press, 1986). For the sexual connotations of the eighteenth-century theater and its actors see Kristina Straub, *Sexual Suspects: Eighteenth-Century Players and Sexual Ideology* (Princeton: Princeton Univ. Press, 1992). Beth Kowaleski-Wallace discusses the sexual status of castrati opera singers in "Shunning the Bearded Kiss: Castrati and the Definition of Female Sexuality," *Prose Studies* 15 (1992): 153–70.

22. My citations are from the original paper. There is a paperback edition of *The Female Tatler*, ed. Fidelis Morgan (London: J. M. Dent/Everyman's, 1992).

23. So Bickerstaff sees the opera as a corruption of the legitimate theater where instead of exercising their understanding the audience is "given up to the shallow Satisfaction of the Eyes and Ears only" (*T* 4). I discuss *The Tatler*'s and *The Spectator*'s criticism of the opera in chapter 5.

24. Randolph Trumbach, "The Birth of the Queen, " *Hidden from History: Reclaiming the Gay and Lesbian Past*, ed. Martin Bauml Duberman, Martha Vicinus, and George Chauncey (New York: Penguin/New American Library, 1989), 134. I discuss the male homosexual type and his relation to fashion in chapter 4.

25. Straub, *Sexual Suspects*, 19. Empirical science, with its strict subject/object dichotomy establishing the spectator in the powerfully dominant position of the one who knows, is one important agent of this shift. Another is the ideology of hegemonic rule, which worked not as absolutism has through spectacular display of power but through increasingly veiled and dispersed, almost invisible micronetworks of influence.

26. Sir John Midriff [pseud.], *Observations on the Spleens and Vapours: Containing Remarkable CASES of Persons of Both Sexes, and all Ranks, from the aspiring DIRECTOR to the humble BUBBLER, who have been miserably afflicted with those melancholy Disorders since the Fall of SOUTH-SEA, and other publick Stocks; with the proper Method taken to the new and uncommon Circumstances of each Case* (London, 1721). Sir Midriff's recording of these cases, although satirical, nonetheless reflects the mass hysteria attendant on the market crash of 1720.

27. Ibid., 4-7.

28. Karl Marx, *Capital*, vol. 1, trans. Ben Fowkes, Penguin Classics (London: Pelican/New Left Review, 1976), 163.

29. See John Mullan, *Sentiment and Sociability: The Language of Feeling in the Eighteenth Century* (Oxford: Clarendon Press, 1988), esp. introduction (1-18) and chap. 5, "Hypochondria and Hysteria: Sensibility and the Physicians" (201-40). Bernard Mandeville wrote a treatise on hysteria and hypochondria in which he traces the aetiology of these diseases to the disruption and even more the inadequacy of the internal spirits: *A Treatise of the Hypochondriack and Hysterick Passions, Vulgarly call'd the Hypo in Men and Vapours in Women* (London, 1711). Hypochondria is the male version of hysteria. Hysteria was called both spleen and vapors; hypochondria also went by the name of spleen. Both were above all *nervous* disorders that played havoc with the passions and the imagination. The symptoms of hysteria—mood swings, fantastic imaginings, investment in improbable desires, the rising and falling of fainting spells—mimicked the movements of the contemporary stock market and were commonly linked to it, as in Midriff's "case studies."

30. An "A.B." had also written to *Tatler* 84 and 145. In his edition of *The Tatler*, Aitken suggests in a note to *Tatler* 84 that this A. B. may be Alexander Bayne, "an advocate then living in London, and afterwards Professor of Scots Law at Edinburgh." *The Tatler*, ed. George Aitken (London: Duckworth & Co., 1898), 4 vols. In his edition, Bond notes the information Aitken gives for this A. B. in *The Tatler*. But Bond gives no identification of A. B. for this *Spectator* paper. The use of the first two letters of the alphabet as pseudonymous initials was commonplace and so may have here no intended referent.

31. Grant McCracken, *Culture and Consumption: New Approaches to the Symbolic Character of Consumer Goods and Activities* (Bloomington: Indiana Univ. Press, 1988), 21.

32. Ibid., 20.

33. Mary Douglas and Baron Isherwood, *The World of Goods: Towards an Anthropology of Consumption* (New York: Basic Books, 1979), 59, 65.

34. Ibid., 68.

35. The plan for the fashion museum here is presented as a project and A. B. as a "projector"—one who comes up with schemes for social, cultural, or financial improvement. What we would call an entrepreneur or promoter, the "projector" was a prominent eighteenth-century social type. But unlike *entrepreneur, projector* carried a negative connotation; the eighteenth-century projector was the victim of suspicion and satire. He was distrusted as a shady dealer, a kind of con artist spinning webs to catch the gullible investor: early stockbrokers and venture capitalists were two species of projectors. The projector could also be ridiculed as a kind of visionary idiot, an erector of fantastic schemes, like A.B.'s project for this sphinx-shaped fashion repository. Perhaps the best known, and certainly one of the most sinister satires on the projector, is Jonathan Swift's "A Modest Proposal."

36. Richard Sennett makes this point in *The Fall of Public Man: On the Social Psychology of Capitalism* (New York: Vintage/Random House, 1976), 45–88.

37. Ibid., 67–68.

38. The sphinx of fashion may serve as well as an emblem of the hybrid nature of everyday life: familiar and mysterious, mundane and exotic, petty and profound. See Henri Lefebvre, *Critique of Everyday Life* (1947), vol. 1, trans. John Moore (London: Verso, 1991): "The simplest event—a woman buying a pound of sugar, for example—must be analysed. . . . The humble events of everyday life [have] two sides: a little, individual, chance event—and at the same time an infinitely complex social event, richer than the many 'essences' it contains within itself. . . . It remains for us to explain why the infinite complexity of these events is hidden, and to discover why—and this too is part of their reality—they appear to be so humble" (57).

39. Anne Buck points out that the average Englishman had an astounding casual knowledge of textiles. He could spot French fabrics from a distance and sometimes jeered the men wearing them. See *Dress in Eighteenth-Century England* (New York: Holmes & Meier, 1979), 34.

40. Ibid., 33–55.

41. This is a formalized style that wants to pass as not a style, not artificial. Addison acknowledges this: "In a word, Good Breeding shows it self most, where to an ordinary Eye it appears least" (*S* 119).

42. Rosalind H. Williams, *Dream Worlds: Mass Consumption in Late Nineteenth-Century France* (Berkeley: Univ. of California Press, 1982), 28.

43. Defoe, *The Complete Tradesman*, 184.

44. Worn in Elizabethan times, the farthingale is the great-grandmother of the hoop. A furbelow is a ruffled trim.

45. Mui, *Shops and Shopkeeping in Eighteenth-Century England*, 65.

46. Amy Boesky discusses the sociocultural functions of the categorization schemes of early modern museums in "'Outlandish-Fruits': Commissioning Nature for the Museum of Man," *ELH* 58 (1991): 305-30. She points out that in the sixteenth century there arises "a new interest in things as *things*, an interest in preservation, in publicly displaying naturalia or exotica, in seeing such booty as part of the national and cultural domain. . . . The act of *consuming*—hunting down the object, bartering for it, bringing it home—imitated the original 'capture' which gave the object value" (312).

47. Michael Hunter, "The Cabinet Institutionalized: The Royal Society's 'Repository' and Its Background," in *The Origins of Museums: The Cabinet of Curiosities in Sixteenth- and Seventeenth-Century Europe*, ed. Oliver Impey and Arthur MacGregor (Oxford: Clarendon Press, 1985), 161. Nehemiah Grew gives a list of the sponsors in an appendix to his *Musaeum Regalis Societatis, or, a Catalogue & Description of the Natural and Artificial Rarities Belonging to the Royal Society and Preserved at Gresham College* (London, 1681).

48. Hunter,"The Cabinet Institutionalized," 159-68. Nehemiah Grew cataloged the collection in *Musaeum Regalis Societatis*.

49. J. A. Bennett, "Wren's Last Building?" *Notes and Records of the Royal Society of London* 27 (1972-73): 107-18.

50. Here Addison echoes the hopes for British trade expressed in literature, for example, by John Denham's *Coopers Hill* (1642, 1655, 1668) and Alexander Pope's *Windsor Forest* (1713). In a reading that has much to say about *Spectator* 69 as well, Laura Brown explicates the rhetoric of commodity fetishism and, in particular, the effect it has on the identity of England in these poems. *Alexander Pope*, Rereading Literature Series, ed. Terry Eagleton (Oxford: Basil Blackwell, 1985), 28-45.

51. See Anne Buck on the spectrum of style strung between the imported/fashionable and the domestic/dowdy: "At one extreme, in the clothes of the fashionable woman, the fabrics were almost entirely imported; other groups wore a decreasing proportion of imported fabrics, until in the lower ranks of the common people clothing was entirely home-produced" (186).

52. Impey and MacGregor, *The Origin of Museums*, 2.

53. Boesky cites this universalizing impulse as one that characterizes the early modern museum and one that results in categorical schema that have recently been misinterpreted as random: "Rather than 'things on holiday' [i.e., free from the disciplinary logic of categorization], however, these materials were highly organized in an attempt to recreate the 'all' of Nature, to make, in Donne's terms, 'one little roome, an every where'" ("'Outlandish Fruits,'" 310).

54. Thomas Sprat, *The History of the Royal Society* (1667), ed. Jackson I. Cope and Harold Whitmore Jones (St. Louis: Washington Univ. Studies, 1958), 251. In the preface to his catalog of the collection, Nehemiah Grew names the aim of the repository: "to facilitate and Improve Knowledge."

55. Hunter, "The Cabinet Institutionalized," 164.

56. Douglas Crimp, "On the Museum's Ruins," in *The Anti-Aesthetic: Essays on Postmodern Culture*, ed. Hal Foster (Port Townsend, Wash.: Bay Press, 1983), 45.

57. Crimp touches on a related tension in his analysis of the excessive, disorderly, heterogenous body of materials that museums seek to order and control: "The history of museology is a history of all the various attempts to deny the heterogeneity of the museum, to reduce it to a homogeneous system or series" (49).

58. Robert Altick, *The Shows of London* (Cambridge, Mass.: Harvard Univ. Press/Belknap, 1978), 1–21.

59. This phenomenon is not limited to postmodern style. In the eighteenth century, the appearance of the hooped skirt is often identified as a stylistic repetition of the farthingale; while the hoop, in turn, reemerges in the middle of the nineteenth century as the crinoline.

CHAPTER THREE: LADY CREDIT AND THE STRANGE CASE OF
THE HOOP-PETTICOAT

1. See, for example, *Modes et Revolutions, 1780–1804* (Paris: Musée de la Mode et du Costume, 1989), 26–27.

2. Edward Maeder, *Hollywood and History: Costume Design in Film* (Los Angeles: Los Angeles County Museum, 1987), 17.

3. Of course, I refer here to the image of the up-market eighteenth century. There is also a popular image of the rougher, earthier eighteenth century of mobs and filthy London streets, of gin molls and highwaymen. Both stereotypes are marked by excess, by extremes of high and low. The popular historical imagination probably concentrates on these extremes because they are vividly removed from the gray mundanity of the present. After all, one main function of the past (as well as the future), like that of the geographically exotic, is to serve as a space for fantasy.

4. *A Collection of Voyages round the World performed by Royal Authority. Containing a complete Historical Account of Captain Cook's First, Second, Third and Last Voyages*, 5 vols. (London, 1790), 5:1552.

5. Ibid.

6. See Nigel Arch and Joanna Marschuer, *Splendour at Court: Dressing for Royal Occasions since 1700* (London: Unwin Hyman, 1987), 39.

7. Francois Boucher, *20,000 Years of Fashion: The History of Costume and Personal Adornment*, expanded edition with a chapter by Yvonne Deslandres (New York: Harry Abrams, 1987), 273. Boucher takes no final stand on the origin of the hoop (295–96). Some historians claim it as a specifically English fashion. Diana de Marly places the introduction of the English hoop in the context of the ongoing fashion war between France and England: "As the Press commented on hoops in January 1709, they must have come out in 1708. . . . Despite the hostilities, hoops *à la Britannique* crossed the Channel and appeared at Versailles. The Duc de Saint Simon was astounded. . . . Louis XIV was even more horrified—British hoops at court, when Britannia was leading the Grand Alliance against him!" *Costume and Civilization: Louis XIV and Versailles* (New York: Holmes & Meier, 1987), 111.

8. *Fashion: A Poem* (London, 1733), 6.

9. *The Hoop-Petticoat. An Heroi-comical Poem; in four Cantos. Address'd to the Ladies of Great-Britain* (London, 1748), 27.

10. Ibid., 29-30.

11. Ibid., 78.

12. *Hoop-Petticoat* (1736), 6.

13. Rhead G. Woolliscroft, *Chats on Costume* (London: T. Fisher Unwin, 1906), 160.

14. J. C. Flugel, *The Psychology of Clothes*, International Psycho-Analytical Library, no. 18 (London: Hogarth Press/Institute of Psycho-Analysis, 1930), 47.

15. Michael Warner, "The Mass Public and the Mass Subject," in *The Phantom Public Sphere*, 240. And see Timothy Breen, "The Meaning of Things: Interpreting the Consumer Economy in the Eighteenth Century," in *Consumption and the World of Goods*, ed. John Brewer and Roy Porter (London: Routledge, 1993), 256-57.

16. Peter Stallybrass and Allon White, "The Grotesque Body and the Smithfield Muse: Authorship in the Eighteenth Century," in their *The Politics and Poetics of Transgression* (Ithaca: Cornell Univ. Press, 1986), 80-124.

17. Kathryn Shevelow, *Women and Print Culture: The Construction of Femininity in the Early Periodical* (London: Routledge, 1989), 23-24.

18. Ibid., 1.

19. See *The Female Tatler*, ed. Fidelis Morgan (London: J. M. Dent/Everyman, 1992). Walter Graham identifies Baker as the author, in *The Beginnings of English Literary Periodicals: A Study of Periodical Literature, 1665–1715* (New York: Oxford Univ. Press, 1926), 74. According to Graham, Baker's was the most successful of the many *Tatler* spin-offs. Fidelis Morgan suggests that Baker wrote the paper in a partnership with Delarivier Manley (viii).

20. Shevelow, *Women and Print Culture*, 23-24.

21. Graham discusses the evolution of the *Tatler* and *Spectator* and finally the *Guardian* in his *Beginnings of English Literary Periodicals*, 61-84, and in *English Literary Periodicals* (New York: Thomas Nelson & Sons, 1930), 65-84. In the latter he describes all the imitators of the *Tatler* and *Spectator* before 1750 (85-118). Graham locates the evolution of the literary essay in the development of *Tatler's* multipurpose format into the *Spectator's* single theme design.

22. Shevelow, *Women and Print Culture*, 24.

23. "It seems that eighteenth-century women needed a good deal of educating into their 'inborn,' 'natural,' feminine qualities": Jane Spencer, *The Rise of the Woman Novelist, from Aphra Behn to Jane Austen* (Oxford: Basil Blackwell, 1986), 15.

24. In a note to the paper, Bond tells us that the letter is written by John Hughes, who contributed to both the *Tatler* and the *Spectator*. For Hughes's involvement see Bond's introduction, *The Spectator*, 1: lvi-lvii; and Graham, *Beginnings of English Literary Periodicals*, 68, 81.

25. de Marly, *Costume and Civilization*, 110-11, 122.

26. John Essex, *The Young Ladies Conduct: or, Rules for Education, under several heads; with instructions upon dress, both before and after marriage, and advice to young ladies* (London, 1722), xvii. This book reflects the earlier *Tatler* and *Spectator* in much of its ideology and even some of its phrasing. For example, Essex writes: "Hence, LADIES, while you only consider the Drapery of the Species, and neglect

the Ornaments of the Mind," echoing *Spectator* 15: "In short, they [women] consider only the Drapery of the Species, and never cast away a Thought on those Ornaments of the Mind" (Essex, 96). Essex never cites *The Spectator*, whether this quotation is conscious or not is unclear. Either way, the echo attests to the pervasive influence of the papers.

27. Lawrence Stone, *The Family, Sex, and Marriage in England ,1500–1800* (New York: Harper & Row, 1979).

28. Nancy Armstrong and Leonard Tennenhouse, "The Literature of Conduct, the Conduct of Literature, and the Politics of Desire: An Introduction," in *The Ideology of Conduct* (New York: Methuen, 1987), 12. See Armstrong's essay, "The Rise of the Domestic Woman," in the same volume (96-141).

29. As I note in the previous chapter, Addison and Steele are themselves deeply invested in these "feminine" qualities and forces—fashion, conceit, fancy, variousness—which are crucial to the psychology of their reform, the persuasive appeal of their papers, and the popular success of their project.

30. As I say in my first chapter, the growth of the fashion market produces its own need for a censor in the form of an arbiter of elegance who legislates taste. See Arjun Appadurai, who discusses how the expansion of trade and the development of modern systems of consumption and production determined by fashion depend on limitations imposed by the taste-makers of society. This arbitration of taste functions much as sumptuary legislation and taboo and is "no less effective in limiting social mobility, marking social rank and discrimination, and placing consumers in a game whose ever-shifting rules are determined by 'taste makers' and their affiliated experts." "Introduction: Commodities and the Politics of Value," *The Social Life of Things: Commodities in Cultural Perspective*, ed. Arjun Appadurai (Cambridge: Cambridge Univ. Press, 1986), 32. Chandra Mukerji sketches the career of sumptuary legislation in Europe, pointing out its overall inefficacy and relatively early demise in England by the seventeenth century, in *From Graven Images: Patterns of Modern Materialism* (New York: Columbia Univ. Press, 1983), 179-82.

31. Alexander Pope, *The Rape of the Lock* (1714), *Pope: Poetical Works*, ed. Herbert Davis (London: Oxford Univ. Press, 1966), 86-109.

32. The effects of this miserable gentleman are cataloged in *Tatler* 113 in an eloquent litany of goods that speaks volumes about fashionable life in London in 1709. It speaks as well of the character of the beau whose excessive stock of the totems of contemporary fashionable life— "a Dozen Pair of Red-heeled Shoes," "Four Pounds of scented Snuff," "Six clean Packs of Cards"—damns him as a dissolute beau, as does his all-too apparent poverty. In contrast with his abundant stock of shoes, snuff, and playing cards, his store of ready cash is meager: "a *Bath* Shilling, a crooked Sixpence." Of course, he is in debt; his apartment is littered with tailors' bills.

33. There is a whole body of literature, some of it pornographic, that uses specific fashions like the hoop and crinoline as focal points for the facetious expression of sexual aggression against women. Modes associated with female sexual autonomy provoked particular attack. In such jokes, lampoons, and satires, the assault

on fashion is paired with sexual aggression in order, as the author of *Whipping-Tom: or, a Rod for a Proud Lady* (1722) puts it, "to touch the Fair Sex to the Quick." Cited by Peter Wagner in *Eros Revived: Erotica of the Enlightenment in England and America* (London: Secker & Warburg, 1988), 158. Wagner discusses sexually charged satires against the hoop at some length (157-58). The project of reform through penetration of a person's very inner-being is here presented in a brutally satiric, sexual, and threatening form. Addison's and Steele's reforms work through a much gentler, mental and affective penetration.

34. In *Tatler* 144 Steele censures this unequal distribution of public space, which, he argues, is for use, not sale. With their elaborate, expensive equipages, the rich try to buy up more space than they have a title to; this breaches justice.

35. James Laver, *Taste and Fashion from the French Revolution until Today* (New York: Dodd, Mead & Company, 1938), 61.

36. Ovid, *Remedia Amoris*, trans. J. H. Mozley, *The Art of Love and Other Poems*, vol. 2 of *Ovid in Six Volumes*, Loeb Classical Library (London: William Heinemann; Cambridge: Harvard Univ. Press, 1969), 178-233. Epigraph is line 344.

37. Defoe allegorizes the character and biography of Lady Credit at length in his *Review of the State of the British Nation*, ed. Arthur Wellesley Secord, Facsimile Text Society (New York: Columbia Univ. Press, 1938), 22 vols. Subsequent citations to the *Review* are made in the text by volume and page number. For Lady Credit see 3:5, 6:32, 6:33, 7:134, papers that run from 1706 to 1711. See also Defoe's *Essay upon the Public Credit* (London, 1710). He explores the issues of credit-financed projects (speculations, ventures) in *An Essay upon Projects* (London, 1710); subsequent citations are made in the text. For a bibliographical note on the figure of Lady Credit see Paula R. Backscheider, "Defoe's Lady Credit," *Huntington Library Quarterly* 44 (1981): 89-100.

38. P.G.M. Dickson, *The Financial Revolution in England: A Study in the Development of Public Credit* (London: Macmillan; New York: St. Martin's Press, 1967), esp. chaps. 1-6.

39. For the intense dependency on private credit see John Brewer, "Commercialization and Politics," in *The Birth of a Consumer Society: The Commercialization of Eighteenth Century England*, Neil McKendrick, John Brewer, and J. H. Plumb (Bloomington: Indiana Univ. Press, 1982), 199-216. Fernand Braudel follows Defoe's account of the saturation of debt/credit in the commercial networks of the day and emphasizes that "this was a kind of credit inherent in the commercial system, generated by it — an internal form of credit *which was interest-free*." The *Wheels of Commerce, Civilization and Capitalism, 15th–18th Centuries*, vol. 2, trans. Siân Reynolds (New York: Harper & Row, 1982), 385.

40. *Jonathan Swift: The Complete Poems*, ed. Pat Rogers (New York: Penguin, 1983), 207-14.

41. Pocock argues that from Defoe to Addison the figure of Lady Credit shifts from an allegory of *Fortuna* to one of Virtue: *The Machiavellian Moment: Florentine Political Thought and the Atlantic Republican Tradition* (Princeton: Princeton Univ. Press, 1975), 452-56. In his "Mobility of Property" essay, Pocock does discuss at length the hysteria of eighteenth-century economic man in its connection to the

feminine Credit. Perhaps he assumes though he never makes explicit Credit's own hysteria. Rather than looking at how the early-eighteenth-century pictures of Credit draw on the contemporary medical profile of the hysteric, Pocock here, as in *Machiavellian Moment*, emphasizes her genealogy from conventional allegories of Fortune and Luxury (*Virtue, Commerce, and History*, 113-14). Backscheider notes the decline in the health of Addison's Lady Credit and recognizes her as a "vaporish" woman (95-96). But Backscheider, like Pocock, emphasizes the traditional allegorical character of the figure, and makes no reference to the popular, contemporary case histories of hysteria from which I think the representation of Credit also drew.

42. Bernard Mandeville, *A Treatise of the Hypochondriack and Hysterick Passions Vulgarly call'd the Hypo in Men and Vapours in Women* (London, 1711).

43. A commonplace: see Mandeville's assumptions (ibid., 165-66).

44. These are the symptoms listed by Mandeville's "patient" Philatheca (196). As Mandeville explains in his preface, Philatheca is an exemplary composite of many actual female patients.

45. John Mullan, *Sentiment and Sensibility: The Language of Feeling in the Eighteenth Century* (Oxford: Clarendon Press, 1988), 16.

46. Sir John Midriff [pseud.], *Observations on the Spleens and Vapours: Containing Remarkable CASES of Persons . . . who have been afflicted with those melancholy Disorders since the Fall of SOUTH-SEA, and other Publick Stocks* (London, 1721). As this parody suggests, even before Dr. Cheyne's famous work on hysteria and hypochondria in the 1730s, there is an established literature of actual case studies, including cases of hysterics, such as John Hall's *Select Observations on English Bodies of Eminent Persons in Desperate Diseases*, trans. James Cook (London, 1679).

47. Midriff, *Observations on the Spleens and Vapours*, 3.

48. Alexander Pope, "Epistle II, to a Lady," *Pope: Poetical Works*, ed. Herbert Davis (London: Oxford Univ. Press, 1966), 291-99. Citation is line 2.

49. For another example of exactly this construction of female nature, see Pope's "Epistle to a Lady."

50. Here I am emphasizing the disturbing potentials of Credit, as perceived by her contemporaries in the eighteenth century. I have noted Addison's and Defoe's ambivalent view of Credit and so should point out the more positive potential Credit had as well. After all, public adventurism and enterprise supported and stabilized domestic prosperity and institutions. This apparently irresolvable doubleness of promise and threat contributes in large part to contemporary fascination with credit.

51. I think this "correspondent" is a persona created by Addison to provide support for his own antihoop policies. Addison admits that he gives himself considerable editorial latitude even when printing actual letters, taking the liberty "to change the Language or Thought into my own way of speaking and thinking" (*S* 271). Even if this ever was a genuine letter, it has been so perfectly adapted to Addison's own style, argument, and ideology that only an empty distinction could be made between it and something entirely from Addison's own hand. As Michael Ketcham points out, the letters in the *Spectator*, although they ostensibly represent

an exchange of diverse opinions, "are mirrors of *The Spectator* that reflect its ideas and its vocabulary as transposed into other hands. . . . The published *Spectator* may be seen as an actual dialectic of opinions. . . . or it may be seen as a fabrication, where all responses to *The Spectator* are *The Spectator*." *Transparent Designs: Reading, Performance, and Form in the "Spectator" Papers* (Athens, Ga.: Univ. of Georgia Press, 1985), 132.

52. While in the *Spectator* and in Defoe's essays there is considerable attention paid to the origins and progress of credit, thirty some years later David Hume engages in apocalyptic speculation on the final days of credit in "Of Public Credit," in *Essays Moral, Political, and Literary* (1741, 1742; London: Oxford Univ. Press, 1963), 355–71. Drawing, deeply if not explicitly, on the traditional characterization of credit as a very unsteady lady, Hume's account of the credit apocalypse, though certainly a worst-case scenario, is a kind of logical conclusion to earlier narrative allegories of credit as a hazardous, feminine force of instability. Indulging in what may be called wishful, if grim, thinking and in a kind of speculation that mirrors the operations generated by credit herself, Hume forecasts two alternatives for the death of credit. In this essay Hume echoes the earlier arguments of Jonathan Swift, who polemicizes against credit, stock-jobbers, and Whigs in *The Conduct of the Allies* (1711), *Political Tracts, 1711–1713*, vol. 6, *Prose Works of Jonathan Swift*, ed. Herbert Davies (Princeton: Princeton Univ. Press; London: Basil Blackwell & Mott, 1951), 1–66.

53. For the conflict between fashion and reason see also *Spectator* 27, where a reader writes of the contest "between Reason and Fashion" in his "Own Mind" and asks for advice on how to "live in the World, and out of it, at the same time," a discipline that Mr. Spectator claims to have mastered. The way of the world is the way of fashion and conflicts with the dictates of reason that require retirement, or at least detachment, from the world.

54. At the conclusion of the same paper, Addison advises women to give more thought to what goes into rather than what goes onto their heads. This injunction to pay more attention to weighty matters seems at odds with his dismissal of the hoods as serious political statements. Basically, Addison trivializes the fashion practices of women and then rebukes them for being so frivolous.

55. Alexander Pope, *The Rape of the Lock* (1714), *Poetical Works*, 86–109.

56. Boucher, 273. See also the entries for "Farthingale" and "Panier" in Doreen Yarwood, *The Encyclopedia of World Costume* (New York: Charles Scribner's Sons, 1978). On the subsequent incarnation of the hoop in the steel-framed crinoline, see James Laver, "Rise and Fall of the Crinoline," 59–71; and Alison Gernsheim, "The Rise and Fall of the Crinoline," *Fashion and Reality* (London: Faber & Faber, 1963), 25–59.

57. In *Spectator* 478, a project for just such a repository of fashion is offered, and although the hoop itself is not mentioned there, the farthingale is. See chapter 2, where I discuss this museum of fashion at length.

58. Pocock, *Virtue*, 44.

59. See *Spectator* 69 for Addison's panegyric on trade. The passions that are inseparable from the interests of men are unabashedly affirmed as Addison gushes

over the spectacle of the Royal Exchange. Of course the sunny view of this paper assumes a quite unreal, Edenic state of trade balance—a harmonious system benefiting all. Here Addison echoes the utopian views of British trade expressed in literature by, for example, John Denham's *Coopers Hill* (1642, 1655, 1668) and Alexander Pope's *Windsor Forest* (1713). *Spectator* 69 contrasts with a paper Addison had written only a few weeks earlier where he registers deep apprehensions about what trade might admit to English shores, advocating even peacetime embargoes against the importation of "French Fopperies" *(S 45)*. This earlier paper insists that feminine fashions must be restricted and controlled by legislation that limits the provision of their materials. Focusing specifically on feminine access to the market of French fashion, this paper treats trade as an occasion of anxiety rather than celebration.

60. Laura Brown discusses this passage in her "Capitalizing on Women: Dress, Aesthetics, and Alexander Pope," chap. 4 in *Ends of Empire: Women and Ideology in Early-Eighteenth-Century English Literature* (Ithaca: Cornell Univ. Press, 1993), where she relates it to the discourse of imperialism: "Of course, the collaboration represented here is only a rationalized version of imperialist expansionism. In the discourse of early-eighteenth-century mercantile capitalism this is the most common trope of all, by which the agency of the acquisitive subject and the urgency of accumulation are concealed and deflected through the fantasy of a universal collaboration in the dressing of the female body" (116). I discuss this trope in my first chapter.

61. In his satiric poems, such as "A Lady's Dressing Room," Swift aggressively redirects the same logic of desire against his sentimental male protagonists.

CHAPTER FOUR: FASHION PLATES: SUBJECTIVITY, STYLE, AND GENDER

1. Samuel Johnson, *Life of Addison*, in *Lives of the English Poets*, with an introduction by Arthur Waugh, 2 vols. (London: Oxford Univ. Press, 1959), 1:407.

2. C. S. Lewis, "Addison," in *Essays on the Eighteenth Century Presented to David Nichol Smith* (London: Oxford Clarendon Press, 1945), 7.

3. Johnson, *Life of Addison*, 448.

4. See Michael McKeon, "Historicizing Patriarchy: The Emergence of Gender Difference in England, 1660-1760," *Eighteenth-Century Studies* 28 (1995): 295-322.

5. See Thomas Laqueur, *Making Sex: Body and Gender from the Greeks to Freud* (Cambridge, Mass.: Harvard Univ. Press, 1990), esp. chap. 5, "Discovery of the Sexes," 149-92. Laqueur notes that while the "one-flesh" hierarchical model of male and female was not absolutely supplanted in the eighteenth century, "it met a powerful alternative: a biology of incommensurability in which the relationship between men and women was not inherently one of equality or inequality but rather of difference that required interpretation. Sex, in other words, replaced what we might call gender as a primary foundational category" (154). The model of sex as incommensurable difference pervades the *Tatler* and the *Spectator* papers. In *Tatler* 172, Steele writes: "I am sure I do not mean it an Injury to Women,

when I say there is a Sort of Sex in Souls"; and Addison, less positively, alludes to such an assumption in *Spectator* 128: "Whether, as some have imagined, there may not be a kind of Sex in the very Soul, I shall not pretend to determine." However, Addison does not hesitate to situate innate differences in women's *nature* if not their very soul: "Women in their Nature are much more gay and joyous than Men" (*S* 128). Of course, Addison and Steele are here referring not to biological sex per se, but to two sorts of abstractions of it as "soul" or "nature."

6. Of course this is not to say that male and female dress were indistinguishable, but that they shared many of the same elements and reflected similar principles of ornamentation, structure, and even body type. Thus the lace, ribbons, brocade, and so on of baroque dress in the seventeenth century showed up in the dress of both sexes. During the eighteenth century men's and women's dress begins to diverge, and by the nineteenth century each followed its own path. We can see this in contemporary mainstream fashion where men's fashions follow a slower, more conservative course than do women's fashions. Attempts by more avant-garde designers to bring masculine and feminine fashion into some relationship to one another have had only limited success.

7. See Randolph Trumbach, "The Birth of the Queen: Sodomy and the Emergence of Gender Equality in Modern Culture, 1660-1750," in *Hidden from History: Reclaiming the Gay and Lesbian Past*, ed. Martin Bauml Duberman, Martha Vicinus, and George Chauncey (Markham, Ontario: New American Library/ Penguin, 1989), 129-40. Here Trumbach distinguishes between the Restoration and eighteenth-century male character types of rake, fop, and beau and traces their respective development in relation to same-sex desire. Trumbach, building on the earlier work of Mary McIntosh, locates a major shift in the definition of masculine gender identity at the turn of the eighteenth century. See McIntosh, "The Homosexual Role," *Social Problems* 16 (1968): 182-92. Part of this shift, and a sign of its occurrence, is the change in the structure of male homosexual relations in urban Europe around 1700. Trumbach emphasizes the emergence at this time of a masculine gender identity defined by *exclusively* same-sex object choice (130). Like Laqueur (whose work his precedes), Trumbach links these shifts in masculine sexual identity to a fundamental rethinking of sexual distinction no longer as a hierarchy but as difference.

8. I deal with this paradox at more length later in this chapter, especially as it relates to the more general stance the papers take vis à vis representation.

9. Pierre Bourdieu's *Distinction: A Social Critique of the Judgement of Taste*, trans. Richard Nice (Cambridge, Mass.: Harvard Univ. Press, 1984). Bourdieu emphasizes the centrality of exclusion — of distinction — to the affirmation of taste: "Taste (i.e. manifested preferences) are the practical affirmation of an inevitable difference. . . . In matters of taste, more than anywhere else, all determination is negation" (56). Wherever taste, then, is a dominant standard of value (and where is it not?) there will be a considerable degree of negation and exclusion. Nancy Fraser points out this irony in reference to Habermas's bourgeois public sphere: "There is a remarkable irony here, one that Habermas's account of the rise of the public sphere fails to fully appreciate. A discourse of publicity touting public ac-

cessibility, rationality, and the suspension of status hierarchies is itself deployed as a strategy of distinction." "Rethinking the Public Sphere: A Contribution to the Critique of Actually Existing Democracy," in *The Phantom Public Sphere*, 6.

10. J. W. Smeed, *The Theophrastan "Character": The History of a Literary Genre* (Oxford: Clarendon Press, 1985), 38.

11. See *Tatler* 96, where dress marks "Class," not in the sense of socioeconomic standing but in terms of the spectrum of fashionable male character types: "A Cane upon the Fifth Button shall henceforth be the Type of a dapper; Red-Heeled Shoes, and a Hat hung upon one Side of the Head, shall signify a Smart; a good Periwig made into a Twist, with a brisk Cock, shall speak a Mettled Fellow; and an upper Lip covered with Snuff, denotes a Coffee-house Statesman."

12. Smeed, *The Theophrastan "Character,"* 71.

13. Ibid., 71–73.

14. Impressed by the vibrancy of these characters and the dynamism of the narratives that surround them, twentieth-century academic writer Donald Kay claims the *Spectator* as the originator of the short story. See *Short Fiction in "The Spectator,"* Studies in the Humanities, no. 8: Literature (University, Ala.: Univ. of Alabama Press, 1975). While I have no interest in this particular revision of literary history, I have profited from the author's exhaustive analytic catalog of the various "character types" in the *Spectator* (24–51).

15. Johnson, *Life of Addison*, 407, 408.

16. Michael Warner, "The Mass Public and the Mass Subject," in *The Phantom Public Sphere*, 239–40. And see Warner, *The Letters of the Republic: Publication and the Public Sphere in Eighteenth-Century America* (Cambridge, Mass.: Harvard Univ. Press, 1990), 11–13, 34–49, 62–66.

17. "There are three very Material Points which I have not spoken to in this Paper, and which, for several Reasons, I must keep to my self, at least for some Time: I mean, an Account of my Name, my Age, and my Lodgings. . . . I cannot yet come to a resolution of communicating them to the Publick. They would indeed draw me out of that Obscurity which I have enjoy'd for many Years, and expose me in publick Places to several Salutes and Civilities, which have always been very disagreeable to me" (*S* 1).

18. See Jean Braudillard, *For a Critique of the Political Economy of the Sign*, trans. Charles Levin (St. Louis, Mo.: Telos Press, 1981), 79.

19. In fact, this drive to do/be something simply because everyone else is, this drive toward conformist emulation, is one of the most maligned aspects of fashion, in these papers and generally. Yet this urge to belong can also be a powerful source of positive socialization and community. *The Tatler* and *The Spectator* advocate a set of social types distinguished by their commitment to the preservation of their unique, inalienable individuality. But they are not advocating anarchy; they pursue that paradoxical dream of the Enlightenment—a community of autonomous individuals.

20. Michael Ketcham, *Transparent Designs: Reading, Performance, and Form in the "Spectator" Papers* (Athens, Ga.: Univ. of Georgia Press, 1985), 177.

21. Ibid., 2.

22. See McKeon, "Gender Difference": "Sexual difference was not invented in the early modern period; it ceased then to be embedded in the other registers of social situation and became relatively autonomized through association with biological condition. So in this respect, the modern co-emergence of sexuality and class depended on a corollary *separation* of the sexual from the social" (304).

23. Ibid., 301.

24. Laqueur, *Making* Sex, 149.

25. Ibid., 152.

26. This is not to give to sexual difference a prior causality in relation to these other conceptual divisions. The emergence of sexual difference works as an integral and operative part of the redrawing of social geography during the late seventeenth and early eighteenth centuries. As Laqueur says, it was used to "support or deny" claims in a whole range of contexts (152).

27. Kathryn Shevelow, *Women and Print Culture: The Constitution of Femininity in the Early Periodical* (London: Routledge, 1989), 10. For her discussion of *The Tatler's* and *The Spectator's* relationship to their female audience, see chap. 4 (93–145).

28. Ibid., 3.

29. Laqueur, *Making Sex,* 149.

30. As Laqueur says, "the cultural work that had in the one-flesh model been done by gender devolved now onto sex," and "difference that had been expressed with reference to gender now came to be expressed with reference to sex, to biology" (151, 152–53).

31. See McKeon, "Gender Difference," esp. 304–5.

32. Lynne Friedli, "'Passing Women'—A Study of Gender Boundaries in the Eighteenth Century," in *Sexual Underworlds of the Enlightenment*, ed. G. S. Rousseau and Roy Porter (Chapel Hill: Univ. of North Carolina Press, 1988), 234–60.

33. Kathryn Norberg, "The Libertine Whore: Prostitution in French Pornography from Margot to Juliette," in *The Invention of Pornography: Obscenity and the Origins of Modernity, 1500–1800*, ed. Lynn Hunt (New York: Zone Books, 1993), 228. Norberg contrasts the libertine whore with "the virtuous courtesan," that sometimes virginal victim forced into prostitution. She includes Cleland's Fanny Hill among her libertine types. She notes the residual cultural strata occupied by these libertine women, who "at a time when sexual difference was becoming an established idea" seem "curiously out-of-date" (240).

34. Ibid., 240.

35. Trumbach, "Erotic Fantasy and Male Libertinism in Enlightenment England," in *The Invention of Pornography*, 257.

36. Trumbach, "The Birth of the Queen," 137. The same argument appears in "Erotic Fantasy" (255–56); and see Trumbach, "London's Sodomites: Homosexual Behavior and Western Culture in the Eighteenth Century," *Journal of Social History* 11 (1977): 1–33.

37. Trumbach, "Erotic Fantasy," 256.

38. Elizabeth Wilson, "Fashion and the Postmodern Body," in *Chic Thrills: A Fashion Reader*, ed. Juliet Ash and Elizabeth Wilson (Berkeley: Univ. of California Press, 1993), 6.

39. Laqueur comments on the centrality of women to the shift in social relations: "As the natural body itself became the gold standard of social discourse, the bodies of women — the perennial other — thus became the battleground for redefining the ancient, intimate, fundamental social relation: that of woman to man" (150).

40. Ellen Pollak, *The Poetics of Sexual Myth: Gender and Ideology in the Verse of Swift and Pope* (Chicago: Univ. of Chicago Press, 1985), 42.

41. Ibid., 41–42. As Friedli puts it: "In precisely the period when women's opportunities for gainful employment were undergoing erosion, an image of femininity involving qualities incompatible with competing on the market-place gained currency" ("Passing Women," 237).

42. Jane Spencer, *The Rise of the Woman Novelist, from Aphra Behn to Jane Austen* (Oxford: Basil Blackwell, 1986), 15.

43. Commenting on *Spectator* 342, Pollak spells out its concise definition of female identity: "A woman has positive value to the extent that she submerges her identity in the identities of those to whom she is related, in whose houses she lives, and for whom (Steele is specific here as if to establish the natural basis of his terms) she has been born" (62).

44. In *Spectator* 15, the ideal wife Aurelia is contrasted with the gadabout Fulvia, and in *Spectator* 302 the virtues of the modest Emilia are drawn out in lengthy contrast to the vanity of Honoria. A woman both beautiful and virtuous, Emilia embodies a kind of transcendent harmony of these traits, one that cancels out, apparently, the "over-weaning self-sufficient" arrogance of beauty, while rendering virtue not only more attractive but even, somehow, more virtuous: "As therefore Virtue makes a beautiful Woman appear more beautiful, so Beauty makes a virtuous Woman really more virtuous." Emilia expresses the unaffected, "natural" style of manners advocated, for example, in *Spectator* 119. Her style looks like no style at all; her charms are ethereal, almost invisible and all the more potent for their veiled subtlety. Honoria's beauty is compromised by the self-conscious, outright, assertive use she makes of it. "Wholly bent upon Conquest and arbitrary Power," she uses her beauty to get the specifically sexual power she craves.

45. Swift satirizes this sort of stylized, "affected," gestural language as the indispensable auxiliary to "polite conversation": "There is hardly a polite Sentence in the following Dialogues, which doth not absolutely require some peculiar graceful Motion in the Eyes, or Nose, or Mouth, or Forehead, or Chin; or suitable Toss of the Head, with certain Offices assigned to each hand; and in Ladies, the whole exercise of the Fan, fitted in the Energy of every Word they deliver: By no Means omitting the various Turns and Cadencies of the Voice, the twistings, and Movements, and different Postures of the Body; the several Kinds and Gradations of Laughter, which the Ladies must daily practice by the Looking-Glass." *A Complete Collection of Genteel and Ingenious Conversation According to the Most Polite Mode and Method Now Used at Court, and in the Best Companies of England*, in *A Proposal for Correcting the English Tongue, Polite Conversation, etc.*, vol. 4 of *The Prose Works of Jonathan Swift*, ed. Herbert Davis (Oxford: Basil Blackwell, 1957), 112.

46. "The stock deviants," notes Pollak, "generated by the myth of passive

womanhood are typically women who endeavor to become subjects of desire within an ideological context that objectifies female sexuality as property" (*The Poetics of Sexual Myth*, 65).

47. Ibid., 35–39. Pollak is here discussing the institution of pin money, which "demonstrates by its very existence that the wife is a consumer rather than a producer both of goods and of money itself" (37).

48. In a letter to the Ugly Club, the Spectator presents two potential new members "of more undoubted Qualifications" than himself: "an old Beau and a modern Pict" (S 48).

49. This anecdote seems to be historical. In his monograph *The "Spectator's" Essays Relating to the West Indies* (Demerara, 1885), Nicholas Darnell Davis writes: "The original of this essay is to be found in one of the letters written by a Captain Walduck, a resident for fourteen years in Barbados, and addressed to Mr. James Petiver." Petiver was an apothecary to the Charter House and a member of the Royal Society. Davis thinks that Steele "himself an old Charter House boy, would no doubt be acquainted with the *Apothecary*" and that Petiver, knowing of Steele's interests in Barbados, would have told Steele of this story related to him by Captain Walduck (10–11). Steele's first wife was a Barbadian heiress. For Steele's involvement in Barbados see James Alsop, "Richard Steele and Barbados: Further Evidence," *Eighteenth-Century Life* 6, no.1 (1981): 21–28.

50. Edward Ward, *The London Spy* (4th ed., 1709), ed. Paul Hyland (East Lansing, Mich.: Colleagues Press), 279.

51. Stereotypically, the Creole was a degenerate character, marked in exotic and seductive but usually unwholesome ways by immersion in the tropics and the decadent plantocratic society of the West Indian colonies. See Wylie Sypher, "The West-Indian as a 'Character' in the Eighteenth Century," *Studies in Philology* 36 (1939): 503–20.

52. J. B. Moreton, *West India: Customs and Manners* (London: J. Parsons, W. Richardson, H. Gardner, J. Walter, 1793), 105.

53. Ibid., 105.

54. Of course, I have been making the point throughout that the kind of bourgeois identity advocated by the papers itself aims at the stripping away of conventional, distinguishing particularities, like class and status. And while, from a critical perspective, this may itself appear as a kind of homogenization of difference, it was represented and understood as a *return* from "false" distinctions to true values and one's true character, understood as individual, inimitable, and irreducible.

55. The Spectator's advocacy of the aestheticized visual consumption that attends the pleasures of the imagination and his condemnation of other kinds of visually derived pleasures speak of a concern to discriminate between proper and improper visual practices. And while I think they operate within the same specular economy of reification and appropriation that also sustains the workings of the sexual gaze and its desires, the (chaste) pleasures of the visual imagination are presented as a kind of alternative and fully legitimate realm of pleasure (S 411).

56. Pollak, *The Poetics of Sexual Myth*, 16.

57. I discuss the modes of power characteristic of the hegemonic governance of the public sphere in the introduction. An Enlightenment phenomenon theorized by Michel Foucault and applied to the epistemology of eighteenth-century fiction by John Bender, the exercise of power through invisible surveillance is part of a general shift from older aristocratic forms of display to more diffuse operations of power that depend on their voluntary internalization by the individual. Michel Foucault, *Discipline and Punish: The Birth of the Prison*, trans. Alan Sheridan (New York: Vintage/Random House, 1979); John Bender, *Imagining the Penitentiary: Fiction and the Architecture of Mind in Eighteenth-Century England* (Chicago: Univ. of Chicago Press, 1987). See also Nancy Fraser, "Rethinking the Public Sphere: A Contribution to the Critique of Actually Existing Democracy," in *The Phantom Public Sphere*: "The official bourgeois public sphere is the institutional vehicle for a major historical transformation in the nature of political domination. This is the shift from a repressive mode of domination to a hegemonic one, from rule based primarily on acquiescence to superior force to a rule based primarily on consent supplemented with some measure of repression" (8); and Geoff Eley, "Nations, Publics, and Political Cultures: Placing Habermas in the Nineteenth Century," in *Habermas and the Public Sphere*, ed. Craig Calhoun (Cambridge, Mass.: MIT Press, 1992), 322–23. The notion of hegemony is Antonio Gramsci's; see *Selections from the Prison Notebooks of Antonio Gramsci*, ed. and trans. Quintin Hoate and Geoffrey Nowell Smith (New York: International Publishers, 1971). "Hegemony" is explicated by Raymond Williams, *Marxism and Literature* (Oxford: Oxford Univ. Press, 1977), 108–14. See also Terry Eagleton, *The Ideology of the Aesthetic* (Oxford: Basil Blackwell, 1990), 19–23.

58. The female Starer, the Peeper is in fact identified as a Pict—and so as one of an atavistic and alien race—in Steele's response to the gentleman's complaint in *Spectator* 53: "*This Peeper using both Fan and Eyes to be consider'd as a* Pict, *and proceed accordingly.*" Nancy Armstrong discusses how the institution of the bourgeois domestic woman served as a refusal and critique of aristocratic forms of display. See *Desire and Domestic Fiction: A Political History of the Novel* (New York: Oxford Univ. Press, 1987), 73–79. "The production of female subjectivity entails the dismantling of the aristocratic body" (77).

59. Swift, *Polite Conversation*, 112.

60. In "The Birth of the Queen," Trumbach traces the transition of the fop from 1660 to 1750, noting the shifts in evaluations of his domestic orientation and effeminacy: "In the three generations between 1660 and 1790, public attitudes toward the fop changed dramatically by generation. Between 1160 and 1690, restoration drama firmly rejected the fop in favor of the rake. After 1690, however, the rake himself fell to the power of romantic marriage on the stage, and the fop's domesticated interests came to be more highly valued. But between 1720 and 1750, the fop's effeminacy came under a new kind of criticism. . . . After 1720 the fop's effeminacy, in real life and on the stage, came to be identified with the effeminacy of the then emerging role of the exclusive adult sodomite—known in the ordinary language of his day as a *molly*, and later as a *queen*" (133–34). Susan Staves notes that in Restoration drama, "though fops are in various ways effeminate they

are rarely presented as homosexual, in "A Few Kind Words for the Fop," *Studies in English Literature* 22 (1982): 414. However, Staves fails to notice how the emerging effeminate homosexual type intersected with the typology of the fop, seeing instead the fop as a precursor type to the new sentimentalized domestic male (420). As Trumbach says, "Staves does not fully see the significance of her own evidence" ("Birth of the Queen," 134). Furthermore, I question Staves's assertion that fops are "asexuals" (414). Trumbach (in what is presented as agreement with Staves but does not take into account her arguments for the fop's "feminine" "lack of strong sexual appetite") asserts that "fops, while effeminate in manner from their contemporaries' point of view, were also presumed to be sexually interested in women" (Staves, 415; Trumbach, "Birth of the Queen," 133). What we see in *The Tatler* and *The Spectator* is a condemnation of the fop's fanciness, narcissism, and effeminacy and a direct alignment of these with female identity. The fop shares these qualities with the beau, a role that emerged in the 1680s and that "mediated between the fop and the rake and . . . made it possible for foppish effeminacy by the end of the 1690s to be associated with sodomy." For the invariably overdressed beau took on some of "the splash of the old-style Rake. And part of that splash was sex with boys" (Trumbach, "Birth of the Queen," 135). I am particularly concerned here with the connection between extravagance of manner and dress and suspicions of sodomy that emerges around the fop and beau in the decades surrounding the turn of the century. *The Tatler* and *The Spectator* contain additional types of suspiciously effeminate men that Trumbach does not discuss, most importantly the "Pretty Fellow" whom I look at below. One thing all these types have in common is their modishness, their preoccupation with fashion. And what neither Trumbach nor Staves takes into their accounts is that fashion itself must be branded feminine in order for their investment in it to condemn fops, beaux, and pretty fellows.

61. Friedli, "Passing Women," 236.

62. J. C. Flugel, *The Psychology of Clothes*, International Psycho-Analytical Library, no. 18 (London: Hogarth Press/Institute of Psychoanalysis, 1950), 110–13. Noticing the shift after it had already been completed and consolidated by the political and cultural revolutions in France and England by the end of the eighteenth century, Flugel dates the advent of this renunciation, I think, too late, especially for England. His model seems to be France. Flugel's overall reading of the event applies in any case, if according to different chronologies: "Man abandoned his claim to be considered beautiful. He henceforth aimed at being only useful"; "It is, indeed, safe to say that, in sartorial matters, modern man has a far sterner and more rigid conscience than has modern woman. . . . Modern man's clothing abounds in features which symbolize his devotion to the principles of duty, of renunciation, and of self-control" (111, 113). Masculine WASP-wear is by no means blank, free of crucial signs of power: "The whole relatively 'fixed' system of his clothing is, in fact, an outward and visible sign of the strictness of his adherence to the social code (though at the same time, through its phallic attributes, it symbolizes the most fundamental features of his sexual nature)" (113).

63. See Elizabeth Wilson, "Fashion and the Postmodern Body," 26–30, and

Anne Buck, *Dress in Eighteenth-Century England* (New York: Holmes & Meier, 1979), 31–32, 55–59.

64. For example in *Spectator* 326, a country squire complains of the plague of deer stealers and fops that have invaded his park. The latter are after his daughter and ride by under his windows "as sprucely dressed as if [they] were going to a Ball." Here fops present a clearly heterosexual menace.

65. *The Eighteenth Century Woman*, produced and directed by Suzanne Bauman and Jim Burroughs, ABC Video Enterprises and the Metropolitan Museum of Art, 1982.

66. Women's attraction to outlaws, to "bad" transgressive men has much to do with their own oppression and fantasies of liberation. Women see in the outlaw, in the libertine, in the rake men who dare to balk the system that oppresses them. They may construct around these romantic MacHeath and Heathcliffe figures all sorts of rescue fantasies. The sober, modest, domesticated man, on the other hand, lends himself to no such satisfying visions; he looks not like a liberator but like another victim, one all the more despicable for throwing away the privileges of liberty allowed to his sex.

67. The deep association between, on the one hand, foppish style and dissimulation, and, on the other, plain dress and truth is allegorically embodied in the two figures Alethes and Verisimilis in *Tatler* 48. They are observed during a walk Bickerstaff takes with his "Guardian Angel" Pacolet (see *Tatler* 13 and 15). Alethes, the character of truth, "seem'd to have a natural Confidence, mix'd with an ingenuous Freedom in his gesture, his Dress very plain, but very graceful and becoming. Verisimilis, in contrast, images forth his own nature as false simulation by the extravagant spectacle he makes of himself: "This Person was much taller than his Companion, and added to the Height the Advantage of a Feather in his Hat, and Heels to his Shoes so monstrously high, that he had three of four times fall'n down, had he not been supported by his Friend." Simulation is foppishness; every man in the Exchange recognizes and distrusts it as such: "The One was laugh'd at as a Fop . . . and a great Enemy to Trade."

68. For the sexuality of the libertine rake, see Trumbach, "The Birth of the Queen" (130–33); for an overview of the literature of the type, see Harold Weber, *The Restoration Rake-Hero: Transformations in Sexual Understanding in Seventeenth-Century England* (Madison: Univ. of Wisconsin Press, 1986).

69. For the emergence of the molly club see Alan Bray, *Homosexuality in Renaissance England* (London: Gay Men's Press, 1982), 81–114. For contemporary accounts (Bray cites many as well) see Jonathan Wild, *An Answer to a Late Insolent Libel, entituled, A Discovery of the Conduct of Receivers and Thief-Takers . . .* (London, 1718), reprinted as appendix 2 in Frederick J. Lyons, *Jonathan Wild: Prince of Robbers* (London: Michael Joseph, 1936), 278–81; and Edward Ward, "The Mollies Club," *The History of the London Clubs. Or, the Citizens' Pastime* (London, 1709), 28–29.

CHAPTER FIVE: FASHIONING TASTE ON THE CULTURE MARKET

1. Leslie Stephen, *English Literature and Society in the Eighteenth Century* (New York: G. P. Putnam's Sons; London: Duckworth and Co., 1904), 18.

2. Alexander Pope, *An Essay on Criticism*, in *Poetry and Prose of Alexander Pope*, ed. Aubrey Williams (Boston: Houghton Mifflin, 1969), 37–57.

3. Addison echoes this analogy in *Spectator* 583, a meditation on the personal delights and public benefits of gardening: gardening "has something in it like Creation. For this Reason the Pleasure of one who plants is something like that of a Poet."

4. Stephen, *English Literature and Society*, 22.

5. Georg Simmel, "Fashion," *International Quarterly* 10 (1904); rpt. *American Journal of Sociology* 62 (1957): 544.

6. See Carole Fabricant, "The Aesthetics and Politics of Landscape in the Eighteenth Century," in *Studies in Eighteenth-Century British Art and Aesthetics*, ed. Ralph Cohen (Berkeley: Univ. of California Press, 1985): "The growth of interest in aesthetic issues during the eighteenth century was clearly related to contemporary developments in philosophical thought and scientific ideas — in Lockean epistemology and the rise of empiricism, in associationist theories and the emphasis on subjective mental responses, in Newtonian optics and the resulting preoccupation with matters of light and color, along with new interest in the act of perception itself. These developments fit easily into a history of ideas framework — indeed, rather *too* easily, considering the abundance of abstractions they have produced. Too often ignored in (would-be) explanations of the rise of aesthetics in the eighteenth century are its links to contemporary social and economic, in the broadest sense political, realities: for example, to the changed and changing shape of English society in the years following the Glorious Revolution" (52–53).

7. Terry Eagleton makes this point about the literary criticism in the *Tatler* and *Spectator* and emphasizes the interdependence among the various forms of cultural production and criticism: "Criticism here is not yet 'literary' but 'cultural': the examination of literary texts is one relatively marginal moment of a broader enterprise which explores attitudes to servants and the rules of gallantry, the status of women and familial affections, the purity of the English language, the character of conjugal love, the psychology of the sentiments and the laws of the toilet." *The Function of Criticism from "The Spectator" to Post-Structuralism* (London: Verso, 1984), 18. See also Eagleton, *The Ideology of the Aesthetic* (Oxford: Basil Blackwell, 1990), 1–69; here, concentrating largely on the discourse of aestheticized sensibility, Eagleton traces the emergence of the category of the aesthetic in British discourse.

8. See Michael McKeon, "The Origins of Interdisciplinary Studies," *Eighteenth-Century Studies* 28 (1994): 17–28. McKeon rejects the conventional association of the eighteenth century with "an absolute commitment to the sort of disciplinary and epistemological division that it bequeathed to modernity." He argues that "the naturalization of modern categories was achieved only when their experimental and contingent constitution in the early modern period was sufficiently distanced as a historical phenomenon to be detachable from the categories 'themselves.' This was not an eighteenth-, but a nineteenth- and twentieth-century achievement" (18).

9. See, for example, M. H. Abrams. "From Addison to Kant: Modern Aes-

thetics and the Exemplary Art," in *Studies in Eighteenth-Century British Art and Aesthetics*, ed. Ralph Cohen (Berkeley: Univ. of California Press, 1985), 16-48: "In the course of the eighteenth century, however, the various arts (especially poetry, painting, sculpture, music and architecture), so patently diverse in their media and modes, in the skills they require, and in the occasion and social function of individual works, came to be systematized as 'the fine arts,' or simply as 'art.' They were treated for the first time, that is, as a single class of products, sharing an essential feature that made them sui generis" (16).

10. Robert C. Holub, "The Rise of Aesthetics in the Eighteenth Century," *Comparative Literature Studies* 15 (1978): 280.

11. Stephen, *English Literature and Society,* 73.

12. See Stallybrass and White for a discussion of the reconfiguration of social space that takes place in the eighteenth century in order to accommodate the priorities of the bourgeois public sphere. The coffeehouse was the central site of the public sphere: "It is no exaggeration to say that the development of the bourgeois public sphere was consonant with the growth of the coffee-house. . . . This specific combination of 'democratic' accessibility with a cleansed discursive environment, a new realignment of the male public body and status, was the basis of the coffee-house's importance" (*Politics and Poetics of Transgression,* 95). For more discussion of the of the bourgeois public sphere see my introduction.

13. Friedrich Engels, *The Origin of the Family, Private Property, and the State* (1884) (London: Penguin, 1986), 204.

14. Michael McKeon's comments have been integral to my thinking on this dialectical relation between the aesthetic realm and the realm of exchange.

15. Eagleton, *Function of Criticism,* 15. As Peter Hohendahl points out, this ideal public sphere was never fully realized in social reality and "by the end of the eighteenth century the assumption that the literary public consisted of a homogeneous circle of informed laymen was being exposed as a fiction." "Literary Criticism and the Public Sphere," *The Institution of Criticism* (Ithaca: Cornell Univ. Press, 1982), 53.

16. Nancy Fraser, "Rethinking the Public Sphere: A Contribution to the Critique of Actually Existing Democracy," in *The Phantom Public Sphere*, ed. Bruce Robbins for the Social Text Collective, Cultural Politics Series, vol. 5 (Minneapolis: Univ. of Minnesota Press, 1993), 6.

17. Pierre Bourdieu, *Distinction: A Social Critique of the Judgement of Taste*, trans. by Richard Nice (Cambridge, Mass.: Harvard Univ. Press, 1984), 56

18. J. H. Plumb, "The Commercialization of Leisure, " in Neil McKendrick, John Brewer, and J. H. Plumb, *The Birth of a Consumer Society: The Commercialization of Eighteenth-Century England* (Bloomington: Indiana Univ. Press, 1982), 265-85; Pat Rogers, *Literature and Popular Culture in Eighteenth-Century England* (Sussex: Harvester Press; Totowa, N.J.: Barnes & Noble, 1985).

19. Richard D. Altick, *The Shows of London* (Cambridge, Mass.: Belknap/Harvard Univ. Press, 1978), 1.

20. Lawrence Lewis, *The Advertisements of "The Spectator"* (Boston: Houghton Mifflin, 1909), 260, 258.

21. Rogers, *Literature and Popular Culture in Eighteenth-Century England,* 1-2.

22. Peter Stallybrass and Allon White, "The Grotesque Body and the Smithfield Muse: Authorship in the Eighteenth Century," in their *The Politics and Poetics of Transgression* (Ithaca: Cornell Univ. Press, 1986), 80-124. See Geoff Eley, "Nations, Publics, and Political Cultures: Placing Habermas in the Nineteenth Century," in *Habermas and the Public Sphere*, ed. Craig Calhoun (Cambridge, Mass.: MIT Press, 1992), 306, 320-21.

23. See *The Spectator* 5, 13, 14, 18, 22, 31.

24. Stallybrass and White, *The Politics and Poetics of Transgression*,109.

25. Rogers, *Literature and Popular Culture in Eighteenth-Century England*, 47-49. Commercialism brings with it two new cultural institutions: publicity and the "star system" of celebrities, both intimately connected through the advertisements and puffs in the periodical press. Much of the popular entertainment of the day was produced by entrepreneurs who shared with financial and political speculators their suspicious status as "projectors." So in *Spectator* 31 Addison relates the plan for an opera motivated by a projector's desire to bring together into one place all the various shows of London — the dancing monkeys, the puppet shows, the lions, and so forth. This would save people the trouble of traveling from one end of town to the other in order to take in all the sights.

26. *The Dunciad*, in *Poetry and Prose of Alexander Pope*, 295-378.

27. On the values of commonality and public access that informed eighteenth-century criticism in the bourgeois public sphere, see Hohendahl, *The Institution of Criticism*, 44-61. Hohendahl refers to Habermas, who, somewhat idealistically, posits the eighteenth-century bourgeois public sphere as a (now lost) arena of rational debate. Terry Eagleton discusses these ideals (*The Function of Criticism*, 9-27). On the coffeehouse as the paradigmatic institution of the public sphere, see Stallybrass and White, *The Politics and Poetics of Transgression*. For a descriptive, historical account of coffeehouse society, see Aytoun Ellis, *The Penny Universities: A History of the Coffee-Houses* (London: Secker & Warburg, 1956).

28. "The clubs at which the politicians and authors met each other represented the critical tribunals, when no such things as literary journals existed. It was at these that judgment was passed upon the last new poem or pamphlet, and the writer sought for their good opinion as he now desires a favourable review" (Stephen, *English Literature and Society in the Eighteenth Century*, 43). "Literary criticism as a professional activity in the modern sense began in the coffee-houses" (Stallybrass and White, *The Politics and Poetics of Transgression*, 99).

29. Jürgen Habermas, *The Structural Transformation of the Public Sphere: An Inquiry into a Category of Bourgeois Society* (1979), trans. Thomas Berger and Frederick Lawrence (Cambridge, Mass.: MIT Press, 1989), 16.

30. Ibid., 19.

31. Ibid., 21.

32. T. S. Ashton, *An Economic History of England: The 18th Century* (New York: Barnes & Noble, 1955), 133-35. Stallybrass and White note how "coffee-houses had a habit of metamorphosing into professional or business institutions" (*The Politics and Poetics of Transgression*,99). And see Ellis, *The Penny Universities*, 107-28.

33. Habermas, *The Structural Transformation of the Public Sphere*, 19.

34. *Colley Cibber: Three Sentimental Comedies. "Love's Last Shift, Or, The Fool in Fashion"; "The Careless Husband"; "The Lady's Last Stake: Or, The Wife's Resentment,"* ed. Maureen Sullivan (New Haven: Yale Univ. Press, 1973). Citation is 2.1.363–65.

35. Michael Ketcham discusses *The Spectator's* relationship with its audience throughout his study; for the use of letters in the papers see *Transparent Designs: Reading, Performance, and Form in the Spectator Papers* (Athens: Univ. of Georgia Press, 1985), 125–32. In the last decade or so, more local venues of cultural discussion like the fanzine and the electronic forums (bulletin boards, discussion groups, MOOs, and MUDs) have proliferated, and these share some of the participatory, interactive functions of *The Tatler* and *The Spectator.* These late-twentieth-century alternative arenas of information exchange and debate meet a need for communities of discourse, a need that the extremely homogenized, impersonal, and totalizing dominant media can no longer meet.

36. Stephen, *English Literature and Society,* 43.

37. Laura Brown, "Capitalizing on Women: Dress, Aesthetics, and Alexander Pope," chap. 4 in *Ends of Empire: Women and Ideology in Early-Eighteenth-Century English Literature* (Ithaca: Cornell Univ. Press, 1993), 109. Earlier in this discussion Brown lays the problem out in these terms: "Though not a part of 'Nature,' 'True Wit' seems to have an indispensable role in representation. But at the same time the couplet ["*True Wit* is *Nature* to advantage drest / What oft was *Thought,* but ne'er so well *Exprest*"] implies a subordination or trivialization of language as merely an elegant form of 'expression,' which stands in contrast to a more essential, originary 'Nature' located either in the classical models, in human reason as it imitates the divine, or in a general universal order" (106).

38. Alexander Pope, "An Essay on Criticism," in *Poetry and Prose of Alexander Pope,* 37–57. Citations are lines 296, 317, and 333.

39. According to the ongoing criticism of women's love of gaudy finery, this is not a style that women come to naturally. Instead, they must, as Bickerstaff says in this essay "take [his] Word for it, (and as they dress to please Men, they ought to consult [men's] Fancy rather than their own in this Particular)" (*T* 151). That women, indeed, do not always dress to please men is a point that comes up in my third and fourth chapters.

40. Jonathan Swift, *A Proposal for Correcting, Improving, and Ascertaining the English Tongue,* in *Jonathan Swift: A Proposal for Correcting the English Tongue, Polite Conversation, etc,* ed. Herbert Davis and Louis Landa, vol. 4 of *Prose Works of Jonathan Swift,* 13 vols. (Oxford: Basil Blackwell, 1957), 11.

41. See the discussion of the repository of fashion in chapter 2.

42. Stallybrass and White discuss this sociocultural negotiation: the "refined public sphere occupied the centre. . . . It carved out a domain between the realm of kings and the world of alley-ways and taverns, and it did so by forcing together the high and the low as contaminated equivalents" (*Politics and Poetics of Transgression,* 109).

43. See *Spectators* 58, 369, 548.

44. Something of the same mutuality of commerce and culture appears in

strategies of the twentieth-century Book-of-the-Month Club and the *Reader's Digest*, both of which sell their readers a specifically middle-class type of "cultural improvement." See Janice Radway, "The Scandal of the Middlebrow: The Book-of-the-Month Club, Class Fracture, and Cultural Authority," *South Atlantic Quarterly* 89 (1990): 703–36. It is with such cultural institutions that I think *The Tatler* and *The Spectator* are most nearly allied. Of course, the relative intellectual status of eighteenth-century popular journalism differs from that of its twentieth-century counterparts. This status was higher in the eighteenth century because the academy had not, as it seems to have in the twentieth century, granted itself a monopoly on all "legitimate" critical thought.

45. *Jonathan Swift: The Complete Poems*, ed. Pat Rogers (New York: Penguin, 1983), 306–8. See also, for example, the "Dedication to His Royal Highness Prince Posterity" in *A Tale of a Tub*. This theme plays throughout Swift's texts and is central as well in Pope's *Dunciad*.

46. Addison's papers on *Paradise Lost* run every Saturday through nos. 267–369.

47. Samuel Johnson, " Addison," in *The Lives of the Poets*, 2 vols. (London: Oxford Univ. Press, 1959), 1:447.

48. Theophilus Cibber, *Lives of the Poets* (London, 1753), 280; quoted by Lillian Bloom, "Addison's Popular Aesthetic: The Rhetoric of the *Paradise Lost* Papers," in *The Author in His Work: Essays on a Problem in Criticism*, ed. Louis L. Martz and Aubrey Williams (New Haven: Yale Univ. Press, 1978), 267.

49. Bloom, "Addison's Popular Aesthetic," 266.

Index

Index

Index

Printing industry, 219
Projector, 57, 86, 88
Prude, 174
Public sphere, x-xi, xiii, xv, 7-10, 64, 148-49, 151-52, 155, 185, 209-13, 250, 253
Pun, 226-27

Rake, 158, 168, 192, 197, 199, 234, 236
Raree-show, 213
Reason, 62, 133; and nature, 133-43
Repository (of curiosities), 54-55, 59, 68, 83-84, 96-99
Representation, 159
Richardson, Samuel: *Clarissa*, 129-30; *Pamela*, 73-74
Rogers, Pat, 213
Royal African Company, 97
Royal Society, 56, 92, 95, 97, 99, 132

Satire, 133-34
Secularization, 51-52, 149
Sennett, Richard, 90
Sentiment and sensibility, 120; and hysteria, 129-30; and public sphere, 253
Sexual difference: and authenticity, 166; and bourgeoise subject, 146; and gender, 164-69; and narcissism, 188; and popular periodical, 165. *See also* Gender difference
Shearer, Norma, 105, 106
Shevelow, Kathryn, 114-15, 165
Shops and shopping, 54, 55-103 *passim*
Sight, 58-59
Simmel, Georg, xiv, 11, 22, 205
Slang, 235, 237-39
Smart fellow, 195, 201
Smeed, J. W., 149
South Sea Project, 127-28
Spectacle/spectator, 58, 77-79, 84; and gender, 71-72, 79; and narcissism, 184-86
Spelling. *See* Orthography
Spencer, Jane, 170
Sphinx, 91-92, 99-100, 113
Spleen, 81-83. *See also* Vapors and Hysteria
Sprat, Thomas, 99
Stallybrass, Peter and Allon White, 215-16
Stephen, Leslie, 1, 203, 205, 208

Stone, Lawrence, 34
Straub, Kristina, 79
Street theater, 214
Subjectivity: and authenticity, 158-64; bourgeois, 144-46; and interiority, 150, 158. *See also* Individualism
Swift, Jonathan: "The Gulf of All Human Possessions," 254; poems on women, 175; *Proposal for Correcting . . . the English Tongue*, 233, 241; and street theater, 214; *Tatler*, 230, 232-33, 236; "Upon the South Sea Project," 127-28

Tahiti, 107-9
Taste, 4, 6, 18, 20, 22, 75, 94, 148; and the aesthetic, 204-8, 210, 211, 224; bourgeois, ix, 215-16; and fashion, 207-8; gothic, 240-41; and news, 224; and popular culture, 210; and the public sphere, 209-12; and standards of English, 234-38
The Tatler and *The Spectator*: and audience, 251, 261; and conduct books, 144; and cultural criticism, 1-2; and direction of women, 112-43, *passim*; history of, 1-2; and literary canon, 15-17, 249-50; and news and newspapers, 220-24; paternalism of, 120; and the popular, 209-10, 248-50; as production of bourgeois culture, 46-47, 249-62; as project of sociocultural reform, 20-22, 122, 144-45, 150, 207-9; and reform of conversation, 224-26; and reform of language, 224-48; satiric tone of, 120, 133-34; standard of taste advocated in, 210; style advocated in, 148; and surveillance, 155-56, 178, 185
Theater, 76-79, 214, 245
Thirsk, Joan, 31-33
Thompson, E. P., 35
Town Talk, 224-26, 235
Treaty of Utrecht, 141
Trumbach, Randolph, 78, 167-68
Two Children in the Wood, 254-58

Universal language, 99

Vapors, 81-83, 113. *See also* Hysteria
Versailles, 95
Virtuoso, 57, 58, 69

Ingram Content Group UK Ltd.
Milton Keynes UK
UKHW012100240323
419131UK00001B/30